French Influence in Russian Society

Stepan Muravyov

Contents

Translation and transliteration

Unless otherwise noted, all translations from Russian to English are my own. Because of the linguistic bent of this dissertation, the etymology, usage, and translation of individual Russian words is an inevitably prominent feature within the text of each chapter, especially the lexical analysis in chapter two. It is not always possible, however, to give an accurate one-word English translation of every Russian term. Conveying the meaning of such words sometimes requires explanation or the substitution of an English approximation. To make this distinction clear, exact translations of Russian words are placed inside inverted commas while explanations and approximations are not. Both types of translation are illustrated, for example, in the discussion of nineteenth-century entertainment terms in chapter two which refers to the words '...*kabare* ('cabaret') and *taper* (a restaurant performer who sings and dances)...' In other cases, a precise English equivalent exists, but because the English translation has multiple meanings is provided within a longer explanation using inverted commas. For example, chapter two's discussion of architectural terminology refers to '...a *rel'ef* (as in a sculptural 'relief' that adorns the outside of a building)...' For the sake of consistency, inverted commas are always used for exact translation, even when the parenthetical translation contains only a single word. As a general rule, parentheses are used for English translations of individual Russian words within a sentence, but square brackets are used when transliteration of the Russian original is provided within an English translation, or for supplied words that aid in smoother translation but are not strictly part of the original.

Throughout the dissertation, transliteration of Cyrillic characters follows the Library of Congress system of romanization for Russian. For the sake of clarity, however, diacritical marks other than the soft sign (ligature ties, final hard signs, breves, and so forth) have been omitted. The words юбилейная and немецкий, for example, are rendered *iubileinaia* and *nemetskii* rather than *i͡ubile͡ina͡ia* and *nemet͡skiĭ*. Also, many of the primary sources used in this dissertation were published or handwritten well before the 1918 orthographic reform which made the Russian characters Ѣ, I, Ѳ, and Ѵ obsolete. For words containing one of these characters, the equivalent modern character is substituted and the word is transliterated accordingly. Therefore, the words Вѣстникъ, Ѳеатр, and Мiръ are rendered *Vestnik*, *Featr*, and *Mir*. Apart from these obsolete letters and diacritical marks, however, archaic spelling, conjugations, and declensions are preserved when encountered in a primary source: '*bol'shago*' instead of '*bol'shogo*' and so forth. This is an important distinction, especially when referencing the original titles of certain imperial Russian publications such as *Moskovskoi zhurnal* or *Sanktpeterburgskiia vedomosti*, since some Russian catalogues and reference books modernize the spelling as '*Moskovskii*' and '*Sanktpeterburgskie*', respectively.

For rendering of proper nouns, the aforementioned system of transliteration is generally followed, except when anglicized spelling has become standard practice for a particularly well-known historical figure. This exception applies primarily to the forenames of Russian rulers—Peter, Catherine, Alexander, and Nicholas in place of Petr, Ekaterina, Aleksandr, and Nikolai—but also to a few literary figures such as Aleksandr Herzen about whom much has been written in English, but who is almost never referred to as 'Gertsen' (his Russian surname). Another exception is Russian authors (émigrés and others) who have published their work in English. In such cases, their names are provided as published.

Dates

All Russian dates prior to 1918 conformed to the old Julian calendar which was, during the nineteenth century, twelve days behind the Gregorian calendar used in the West. (The difference was eleven days in the eighteenth century, thirteen days in the twentieth century.) In this dissertation, dates are generally given based on the country in which the events occurred. For diary entries written by Russian soldiers abroad, however, it is impossible to know whether the diarist allowed for this discrepancy. Likewise, when Russian newspapers and journals reprinted news dispatches from abroad, it is unclear whether the Russian editors adjusted the dates to their own Julian calendar or printed the Gregorian date, which was stamped on the European newspaper from which they copied the article. In both cases, dates are simply given as supplied by the primary sources themselves. For events of historical significance for both France and Russia, and when the exact date is known, the Gregorian date is given in parentheses after the Julian date which Russians would have recorded. For example, Napoleon entered Moscow on 2 (14) September 1812, and Russian troops entered Paris on 18 (30) March 1814.

INTRODUCTION

Russian culture has always been shaped in meaningful ways by foreign stimuli. While the same could certainly be said of other countries,[1] one historian has suggested that 'no other culture in the course of its development absorbed and assimilated as many different foreign influences as Russia did.' Indeed, Fedor Dostoevskii, attributing this tendency to Russia's Eurasian location and her special place in world history, is quoted as having romantically predicted Russia's unique role in unifying all of mankind by integrating cultural patterns from many different nations.[2]

A more common 'outsider' interpretation, however, is that Russia's significant borrowing from other cultures has been for the sake of her own advancement or modernization, and this has largely meant westernization. Rapid change has necessitated the bloc-importation of foreign elements as means of progress. In his classic treatise on Russian culture, James Billington concluded that 'repeatedly, Russians have sought to acquire the end products of other civilizations without the intervening process of slow growth and inner understanding.'[3] Even the Russian scholar A. F. Zamaleev, who writes with a distinct nationalistic tone, has admitted significant foreign influence. According to Zamaleev, the study of Russian culture may be divided into three ideological-historical periods: Byzantine Russia, characterized by holiness; Europeanized Russia, characterized by enlightenment through knowledge; and, finally, the pursuit of Communism, characterized by equality for all.[4] Zamaleev asserted that, in each of these periods, Russian culture indeed borrowed from other cultures and assimilated chosen aspects, but then took these to a new level. Russian

---

[1] For a general treatment of this issue, see Adda Bozeman 'Civilizations Under Stress: Reflections on Cultural Borrowing and Survival', *Virginia Quarterly Review* 51 (1975) <www.vqronline.org/issues/51/1/winter-1975> [accessed 19 February 2015]

[2] B. B. Bogoslovsky, 'The Genius of the Russian Language', *The Russian Review*, 4 (1944), 18 – 29 (pp. 28 – 29).

[3] James H. Billington, *The Icon and the Axe: an Interpretive History of Russian Culture* (New York: Knopf, 1970), p. 595.

[4] A. F. Zamaleev, *Istoriia russkoi kul'tury* (St. Petersburg: Sankt-Peterburgskii gosudarstvennyi universitet, 2005).

icon painters produced works unparalleled in Byzantium; Dostoevskii and Tolstoi, though partially the products of European literary influence, went on to achieve their own superlative fame; the Russian revolution was even grander than its French inspiration had been, and so forth. As this brief survey illustrates, explanations and characterizations of Russia's cultural emulation of the West vary, but the fact of this propensity is undisputed.

The case of French cultural influence, however, is far more than simply an additional ingredient in the generic trend of European stimulus during the second of Zamaleev's three periods. While, initially, French import was indeed a component of Russia's overall westward march towards modernization, by the end of the eighteenth century, the Franco-Russian cultural bond was uniquely important. The work of S. A. Simonova and I. V. Satina on the cultural interaction of Russia and France has found that the impact of this connection has been both mutual and deep. They argue for the full assimilation of French elements into the Russian culture, versus the creation of 'cultural enclaves' as, for example, in the American experience of cultural integration.[5] The historical contour of Russia's cultural development as described by Soviet dissident philosopher G. S. Pomerants is similar to that of Zamaleev, though referring more directly to French influence and suggesting a less flattering characterization of the Soviet period. In one of his later essays, Pomerants suggested that Russian culture has always been at its best when borrowing from other traditions. He wrote of his love for the Byzantine 'language' to be read in the brushstrokes of icon painters like Andrei Rublev, but confessed himself more fluent in the French-influenced language of the literary geniuses of the nineteenth century, because it is essentially the Russian language as we know it today. He then referred to a 'new Muscovy' period (the Soviet era) in which Russian culture echoed sixteenth- and seventeenth-century Muscovy by turning

---

[5] S. A. Simonova and I. V. Satina, *Rossiia i Frantsiia: opyt kul'turnogo vzaimodeistviia* (Voronezh: Voronezhskii gosudarstvennyi universitet, 2005), p. 113.

inward and was the worse for it.[6] The substantial nature of French influence is demonstrated by its surviving this second Muscovy. All of these authors have depicted the uniqueness and permanence of French influences upon Russian culture. These were not fads that 'came and went', but rather shaping influences that came and stayed and are part of what Russian culture is, not just what it was.

The Franco-Russian bond is still palpable in the twenty-first century. M. B. Piotrovskii, director of Russia's State Hermitage Museum since 1992, has suggested that 'France and Russia are connected by a wonderfully complex history of political and cultural relations.'[7] In 2010, the then Russian president, D. A. Medvedev, commented that Russia and France are two countries joined together by 'political, cultural, and just plain human ties.'[8] One of Russia's leading educational publishers has produced a short anthology of French-language texts, currently in its sixth reprinting, of medium difficulty as a supplemental resource for Russian school children and university students who are studying French as a foreign language. In the Russian-language preface, the editor, a professor at Moscow State University, in addition to thanking her University colleagues, a linguistic attaché of the French embassy, and a faculty member at Moscow's lycée français de Moscou Alexandre Dumas for their help in compiling the texts, made the following statement: 'The image of France and the French style of life has always been perceived by Russians with particular fondness [*simpatiia*].'[9] The willingness of an accomplished scholar, writing for a reputable publisher, to make such a broad generalization—speaking for all 'Russians' and how they have 'always' felt— without so much as a footnote or any specific historical reference is testimony to the fact that such an assertion is considered common knowledge among Russians.

---

[6] G. S. Pomerants, 'Frantsuzskii sled v russkoi kul'ture', *Obrazy mira* <http://www.niworld.ru/Statei/pomerants/Franz_sled.htm> [accessed 20 February 2015]
[7] Natal'ia Zolotova, *Parizh—Sankt-Peterburg 1800 – 1830: kogda Rossiia govorila po-frantsuzski* (Moscow: Interros, 2003), p. 13.
[8] Cited in *Rossiia-Frantsiia: na perekrestke kul'tur*, ed. by A. A. Kornienok (Piatigorskii: PGLU, 2010), p. 6.
[9] T. Iu. Zagriazkina, *Frantsiia segodniia* (Moscow: KDU, 2014), pp. 3 – 4.

In her preface, the aforementioned editor admits that Russian perceptions of France, while positive, are often reduced to certain iconic images: Parisian landmarks, cuisine, fashion, and so forth.[10] This became obvious in an interview conducted in 2011 in honour of Bastille Day on a morning television program in St. Petersburg. The two Russian presenters were speaking with Elisabeth Barsacq, then a diplomat with the French consulate in St. Petersburg. The interview began with compliments from the presenters for the French people as 'guardians of fashion' whose cuisine 'is the best in the whole world.' They then asked whether the diplomat had visited any of the French restaurants in St. Peterburg and whether she liked them. Madame Barsacq immediately pivoted to industry and wanted to talk about the new electric power plant recently opened in Russia with French help. People 'are always talking about French culture and French cuisine,' she said, 'and this is very good. Of course, we love this very much, but we also have very good engineers. We also have good products for industry.' Undeterred, one of the presenters said, 'Fine, Elisabeth, but if we try to taste an electric "monobloc" we could lose our teeth. All the same, have you visited any French restaurants here in St. Petersburg?' Then, a pre-recorded segment was shown where Russian passersby were stopped and asked 'why they love France.' Predictably, food, champagne, certain landmarks, and France's 'great culture and beauty' were given as answers. Later in the interview, when asked about tourism in France, the diplomat returned to the topic of French technological innovation and the high-speed trains which run between the cities. The Russian interviewers listened politely and then asked if she would be so kind as to say something in French for the viewers at home.[11]

Russia's connection with France is a connection to its culture. A stroll through the two historic capitals confirms this, if one knows where to look. St. Petersburg still

---

[10] Ibid.

[11] 'Za chto russkie liubiat Frantsiiu?', *Odnazhdy utrom*, Telekanal 100 TV, 14 July 2011 <http://www.tv100.ru/video/view/Za-chto-russkie-ljubjat-Franciju-54760/> [accessed 4 September 2015]

bears the influence of French architecture, and Moscow contains clues as well: a bronze

bust of Victor Hugo in Hermitage park, the French-sounding names of Russian perfume

companies *L'etual'* and *Brokard* in store windows, and the popular café *Zhan-Zhak*,

obviously named for Jean-Jacques Rousseau, just to name a few examples.

The greatest tangible evidence of this deep-rooted connection is the wealth of

borrowed French words currently present in the Russian language. A one-volume

Russian dictionary published in 2007—intended, by its brevity, to reflect the Russian

lexicon actually in use—includes as many as 1,883 words of French origin.[12] This fact

in itself is a meaningful commentary on the extent of French influence in the Russian

language. A full quarter of all the words gathered by V. Iu. Nikitina in her Russian

dictionary of foreign words are of French origin (2,016 words). This is significantly

larger than the number of German loanwords (1,556) and virtually dwarfs the English

contribution (618 words). Like other European languages, Russian owes a great debt to

Greek and Latin which contributed 1,557 and 1,322 words respectively, but even

compared to these ancient languages, French is historically the single greatest

contributor of existing loanwords in the Russian language.[13]

The purpose of the present study is to explore the historical origins of this

significant level of influence. The current body of scholarship on the history of Russia

only obliquely deals with this issue. General histories of Russian culture, such as the

aforementioned works of Zameleev and Billington, or the more recent work of Orlando

Figes,[14] focus primarily on the upper nobility when referencing French culture. The

French inspiration behind Catherine II's court and the popularity of the French language

as a mark of class distinction are often cited. However, though the fact of this

popularity in late eighteenth-century Russia has become a matter of common

---

[12] S. A. Kuznetsov and others, eds, *Sovremennyi tolkovyi slovar' russkogo iazyka* (St. Petersburg: Norint, 2007).

[13] V. Iu. Nikitina, *Bol'shoi slovar' inostrannykh slov* (Moscow: Dom Slavianskoi Knigi, 2012).

[14] Orlando Figes, *Natasha's Dance: a Cultural History of Russia* (London: Penguin, 2002).

knowledge, the very 'first large-scale, multidisciplinary history of the French language in Russia' was only completed as recently as 2014 and stops short of exploring the broader cultural implications. Rather, the study primarily focused on uses of the French language in imperial Russia, examples of French references in Russian literature, and bilingualism among the Russian nobility.[15]

As the historical overview in chapter one will show, some recent studies deal with French influence in particular areas of Russian culture (literature, for example) or within narrow chronological windows (the Petrine epoch, the influence of French philosophes on Catherine's governing philosophy, and so forth.) Likewise, the events through which Russia and France as countries have interacted—war with Napoleon, French capital investment in late eighteenth-century Russia, and two world wars, to name a few—are well documented, and the fact of French influence upon Russian culture, as indicated by the aforementioned statements from Russian educators, politicians, and television presenters, is intuitively obvious to Russians. However, despite generalizations such as these, a comprehensive study of the historical origins of French influence upon Russian culture has yet to be written.

Stated simply, this dissertation explores the following question: 'How and when did French influence make its permanent impact upon Russian culture, and what kind of influence?' Borrowed words in the Russian language are the tell-tale signs which suggest answers to the 'what' of French influence. Following the chronological patterns of their appearance in various Russian dictionaries gives an estimate of 'when,' and the study of primary source material from the resultant period will shed light on 'how.'

Ever since the very concept of 'culture' emerged in the nineteenth century as an object of scholarly inquiry, its importance to multiple disciplines has continued to grow

---

[15] This collaborative study project on 'The History of the French Language in Russia' was conducted from 2011 – 2014 at the University of Bristol. <http://www.bristol.ac.uk/arts/research/french-in-russia/> [accessed 4 February 2015]

but the task of defining the term has always been a challenge.[16] The historian Peter

Burke has admitted that culture 'is an imprecise term, with many rival definitions.'[17]

The narrow goals of early anthropologists, who began using the term extensively in

their behavioural studies of tribal peoples, or in hypotheses about our prehistoric

ancestors, have complicated the matter. The vocabulary that emerged from their early

study of culture seems awkwardly utilitarian once anthropology began to also include

the study of more advanced societies. How does one, for example, explore early

modern or modern European culture and all of its creative innovations in the arts and

sciences using the stale constructs of Bronisław Malinowski, who insisted that culture is

ultimately little more than the way that man, as an animal, copes with the dangers of his

surroundings and provides for the basic needs of his own organism?[18] Such categories

are obviously ill-suited to a discussion of perceptions of beauty or nuances of social

interaction that go beyond rudimentary survival. Andrew Sartori's historical overview

of the culture-concept is helpful on this point by referring, among other dichotomies, to

the various 'anthropological' versus 'humanistic' definitions of culture.[19]

Despite Sartori's best efforts to surmise a global coherence in the 'resonance' of

the concept, the fact remains that 'culture' has meant and continues to mean many

different things to many different people. Some of the key features common to many

definitions of culture provided by historians, anthropologists, and other social scientists

include patterns of behaviour, religious beliefs, social institutions, and shared

understandings of the meanings of various symbols, including language.[20]

Anthropologist Clifford Geertz has written extensively on the subject and argued that,

---

[16] Andrew Sartori, 'The Resonance of "Culture": Framing a Problem in Global Concept-History', *Comparative Studies in Society and History,* 47 (2005), 676 – 699.
[17] Peter Burke, *Popular Culture in Early Modern Europe* (New York: Harper, 1978), p. xi.
[18] Bronisław Malinowski, *A Scientific Theory of Culture* (Chapel Hill: The University of North Carolina Press, 1944).
[19] Sartori, 'Resonance of "Culture"', 687.
[20] Richard Handler, 'Cultural Theory in History Today', *The American Historical Review,* 107 (2002), 1512 – 1520.

while making universally definitive statements about culture is always precarious, genuinely scientific analysis requires that terms be clearly defined. His own definition suggests that culture 'denotes an historically transmitted pattern of meanings embodied in symbols, a system of inherited conceptions expressed in symbolic forms by means of which men communicate, perpetuate, and develop their knowledge about and attitudes toward life.'[21]

In addition to these general cultural issues, the present study is concerned with another very specific dimension: the growing sense of national identity in Russia beginning in the eighteenth century and the way in which shared values, customs, beliefs, and behaviours were a part of this growing self-awareness.[22] In other words, the present thesis is not a study of culture (or cultures) within Russia, but rather a study about 'Russian culture.' For the purposes of this dissertation, then, 'Russian culture' may be defined as the values, customs, attitudes, behavioural patterns and shared understandings of meaning which are characteristic to Russian people. Russian culture is the way Russian people think, live, and interact with others. This will include topics as rudimentary as Russian houses, clothing, food, and drink, as well as more abstract considerations such as morality and religious belief. Various forms of social interaction, artistic and literary expression, and even the collective pursuit of knowledge are also considered relevant.

The present study will identify specific areas of French influence upon Russian culture through the examination of the loanwords currently in use and then trace these influences back to their historical origins. Given the precarious nature of something as potentially subjective as the study of 'culture'—plagued with vagueness, not because the word means so little, but because it has meant so much—the examination of

---

[21] Clifford Geertz, *The Interpretation of Cultures* (New York: Basic Books, 1973), p. 89.
[22] Hans Rogger, *National Consciousness in Eighteenth-Century Russia* (Cambridge, MA: Harvard University Press, 1969).

borrowed words is intended to provide a measure of historical objectivity to the study of French influence on Russian cultural identity. Loanwords can be counted, grouped by category, and observed chronologically and are, therefore, invaluable to the historian as empirical handles. Following an historical overview of French influence in Russia as gleaned from extant secondary literature (chapter one of this study), the core of this dissertation is an analysis of Russian dictionaries from the eighteenth to the twenty-first century.

The rationale for using dictionaries as primary sources in a historical study of culture is connected to two assumptions: that language is basic to culture and that loanwords are significant, indicating at least some level of interaction between the culture that is borrowing words and the 'donor' culture from which they are borrowed. That language is basic to culture is an assertion that is intentionally broad. According to Karen Risager, various linguists have asserted that 'language and culture are inseparable'; 'language and culture are intimately linked'; or even 'language is culture and culture is language.'[23] Writing much earlier, Ismael Silva-Fuenzalida cited similar definitions: 'language is the bearer of culture,' 'language is the vehicle of culture,' and the like.[24] Risager takes issue with over-simplified identification of language and culture, and emphasizes that the relationship between the two is quite complex.[25] To say, however, that the connection is complex or under-studied (as Risager insists) does not negate the simple fact that there is a connection. While an in-depth study of the nature and limits of the link between culture and language is beyond the scope of this

---

[23] Karen Risager, *Language and Culture: Global Flows and Local Complexity* (Clevedon: Multilingual Matters, 2006), p. 1.
[24] Ismael Silva-Fuenzalida, "Ethnolinguistics and the Study of Culture", *American Anthropologist,* 51 (1949), 446.
[25] Risager, *Language and Culture.*

thesis,[26] the widely accepted notion that there is a significant link will be a point of departure for the present study.

The notion that language is fundamentally important to culture is illustrated, for example, in Silva-Fuenzalida's description of the necessarily linguistic nature of joining a foreign culture:

> As each culture has its own way of looking at things and at people and its own way of dealing with them, the enculturation of an individual to a foreign body of customs will only be possible as he learns to speak and understand the foreign language and to respond with new selection and emphasis to the world around him—a selection and emphasis presented to him by this new culture.[27]

The American anthropologist Franz Boas, a pioneer in anthropological linguistics,[28] described the relationship between language and culture as follows in in his 1938 *General Anthropology*: 'Language is a reflection of the state of culture and follows in its development the demands of culture. In another way, however, language exerts an influence upon culture. Words and phrases are symbols of cultural attitudes and have the same kind of emotional appeal that is characteristic of other symbols.'[29] In recent years, cultural historians, linguists, and anthropologists have studied language and culture and offered a range of views which demonstrate the complexity of the relationship between the two. Rare, however, are any published opinions that deny a necessary relationship in principle.[30] Relating this specifically to Russia, Iurii Lotman and Boris Uspenskii in their respective studies of Russia's cultural history both trace a distinct parallel between the development of the Russian language and behaviours

---

[26] Risager's introductory chapter in *Language and Culture* provides an excellent overview of recent scholarship on the subject, pp. 1 – 18.

[27] Silva-Fuenzalida, 'Ethnolinguistics', 446.

[28] Because his study of language did not fit neatly into the existing academic disciplines of his day, Boas's early articles on language appeared either in anthropological publications or German philological journals. See Stanley Newman's comments in his short biography of Boas' pupil, Edward Sapir, a ground-breaking linguist in his own right. Stanley Newman, 'Edward Sapir (1884 – 1939)', *International Journal of American Linguistics,* 50 (1984), 355.

[29] Franz Boas, ed., *General Anthropology* (Boston: D.C. Heath and Co, 1938), p. 142.

[30] Risager, *Language and Culture,* pp. 1 – 18.

associated with culture and society.[31] Likewise, Boris Gasparov explored the

importance of language to Russia's self-awareness in terms of nationality. Though

citing conflicting schools of thought on the interplay of language and national identity

in Russia, the importance of language to Russia's national identity is confirmed.[32]

Regarding the significance of loanwords specifically, Edward Sapir, a student of

Boas and innovator in the field of ethnolinguistics,[33] suggested a direct correlation

between one culture's influence upon another and the appearance of borrowed words.

According to Sapir, 'The careful study of such loanwords constitutes an interesting

commentary on the history of culture. One can almost estimate the role which various

peoples have played in the development and spread of cultural ideas by taking note of

the extent to which their vocabularies have filtered into those of other peoples.'[34] This

is precisely how lexical analysis is meant to aid the present study of French influence

upon Russian culture. By studying the body of borrowed words broadly, various areas

of influence in different chronological periods have been observed and weighed in

comparison to one another. General thematic trends related to types of words and time

of borrowing are more important to this study than any technical details related to the

linguistic process itself. For example, tracing the mechanics of lexical borrowing and

determining why certain words are imported rather than forming new words in the

receptor language is a relatively new topic in the field of linguistics and is well beyond

the scope of this dissertation.[35] Rather, the appearance of French terms in Russian at

---

[31] See Boris Gasparov's introduction to Iu. M. Lotman and others, eds, *The Semiotics of Russian Cultural history: Translated from the Russian* (Ithaca: Cornell University Press, 1985), p. 21.

[32] Boris Gasparov, 'Identity in Language', in *National Identity in Russian Culture: An Introduction*, ed. by Simon Franklin and Emma Widdis (Cambridge: Cambridge University Press, 2004), p. 132.

[33] Stanley Newman, 'Edward Sapir (1884–1939), 355 – 357.

[34] Edward Sapir, *Language: An Introduction to the Study of Speech* (New York: Harcourt, Brace, 1921) (Chapter 9, para. 2 of 14) <http://www.bartleby.com/186/> [accessed 26 August 2013]

[35] Loanwords as a general study are explored in Martin Haspelmath and Uri Tadmor, *Loanwords in the World's Languages: A Comparative Handbook* (New York: De Gruyter Mouton, 2009) In particular, see Haspelmath's discussion of the complexity of this linguistic issue in chapter 2, "Lexical borrowing: concepts and issues," pp. 35 – 54.

various times and around certain topics have been examined to provide, in Sapir's words, a cultural 'commentary' and to give an 'estimation' of influence that is more precise and analytically grounded than the broad passing references to France's cultural influence upon Russia that have been most common in previous historical studies.

The aim of the lexical analysis in chapter two is to identify the most important chronological period and topical areas of French influence. Based on the results of this analysis, the chapter argues that patterns of French lexical import point to the primacy of the late eighteenth and early nineteenth century where cultural impact is concerned. With this established, the remainder of the dissertation explores other primary source material from the newly-identified target period for a narrower, more in-depth narrative study of some of the people, events, and trends which left such an enduring French mark upon Russia.

The next two chapters are narrower in focus, examining archival documents related to French immigration to Russia during the period and memoir recollections of Russian military officers in France in 1814 respectively. Having already determined the time and types of influence through dictionary analysis, these two chapters explore a key means of influence: people abroad. References to French governesses, tutors, merchants and domestic servants encountered in archival documents and periodical publications suggest the importance of French people living within Russia's boundaries where cultural influence is concerned. Likewise, the cultural experiences of Russian officers and soldiers inside of France are described in the autobiographical recollections that they left behind.

The impact of immigrants upon their destination cultures is a topic that is being studied with increasing interest. Culture has always been a relevant factor in the study

---

<http://www.academia.edu/3453003/Lexical_borowing_Concept_and_issues> [accessed 26 August, 2013]

of migration but has, until recently, 'lurked beneath the surface' of other inquiries.[36] In the early twentieth century, ground-breaking anthropologist Franz Boas responded to the academic needs of his time by debunking myths that certain races were inherently predisposed to be more or less 'primitive' or 'civilized' by citing empirical evidence that physical traits, language and culture were not permanent anthropological features but could be altered over time by the movement of people into new environments and by their intermingling with other ethnic groups.[37] Claude Lévi-Strauss carried this discipline to a new level, creating the field of 'structural anthropology', whereby observable human behaviour (that is, 'culture') is categorized by the broader 'unconscious forms' or 'structures' to which they belong.[38] While the geographical movement of people was not his primary focus, Lévi-Strauss did give consideration to 'the invasion of a population by an immigrant group' and the 'fusion between two neighbouring groups' as part of his broader theoretical study.[39] These innovations occurred at a time when the study of anthropology in general was evolving and becoming more interested in the 'so-called civilized societies' rather than merely examining smaller exotic tribes, as had been more characteristic of the Boas generation.[40] E. E. Evans-Pritchard, renowned for his contributions to the young field of social anthropology in the 1950s, made important distinctions within the discipline of anthropology itself, giving focused attention to human cultures and societies and defining ethnology as the task of classifying people on social or cultural bases and then 'to explain their distribution at the present time, or in past times, by the movement and mixture of peoples and the diffusion of cultures.'[41]

---

[36] Gil S. Epstein and Ira N. Gang, eds, *Migration and Culture* (Bingley: Emerald Group Publishing, 2010), p. 1.

[37] Franz Boas, *The Mind of Primitive Man* (New York: Macmillan, 1911).

[38] Claude Lévi-Strauss, *Structural Anthropology* (New York: Basic Books, 1963).

[39] Ibid., p. 11.

[40] Ibid., p. 347.

[41] E. E. Evans-Pritchard, *Social Anthropology* (Glencoe, Illinois: the Free Press, 1954), p. 4.

From the late twentieth century forward, globalization has prompted scholars to focus even more intently on human migration and its observed and potential impacts upon societies. This growing research interest has become a new field of interdisciplinary study in its own right. In 1990, one anthropologist reported a 'veritable boom in immigration research' during the previous fifteen years, citing numerous studies by sociologists, anthropologists, and historians.[42] Much of this and subsequent sociological work has focused on the economic ramifications of immigration or made arguments in favour of various government legislation related to current immigration policy.[43] Insofar as it touches upon culture, the focus was primarily on the immigrants themselves and dealt with issues of their 'integration' or 'assimilation' into the host culture.[44]

More recently, however, the work of sociologist Stephen Castles and political scientist Mark Miller has lamented this one-sided approach. Their work, which has become prominent in 'migration studies,' argues that the cultural aspect of this field of study should explore 'the ways in which migration brings about change in both sending and receiving societies.'[45] Concurring with this assessment, anthropologist Leo Chavez has produced an analysis of American migration which focuses on 'multidirectional' cultural change, including discussions of cultural 'bleeding, fusion, syncretization, hybridization and creolization,' which he found to be more productive than 'the more unidirectional flow of changes presented by models of assimilation, which are often inadequate to capture the complex process of cultural change.' As an example of this more holistic approach, Chavez sights the many aspects of American cowboy culture which are clearly of Mexican origin and likewise notes permanent features of Tex-Mex

---

[42] Silvia Pedraza-Bailey, 'Immigration Research: A Conceptual Map', *Social Science History,* 14 (1990), 43.

[43] For an example of this approach, see Douglas S. Massey and others, 'Theories of International Migration: A Review and Appraisal', *Population and Development Review,* 19 (1993), 431 – 466.

[44] The bibliographic references in Epstein and Gang, *Migration and Culture* are an excellent overview of this tendency.

[45] Stephen Castles and Mark J. Miller, *The Age of Migration: International Population Movements in the Modern World* (Basingstoke: Palgrave Macmillan, 2009), p. 20.

folk music which can be traced to the influence of German immigrants who brought their accordions and lively polkas to Texas in the nineteenth century.[46] German scholar Wolfgang Schmale has explored the impact that migration has had on European history and culture, but confesses that there is not yet a sub-discipline dedicated to what he refers to as the 'transcultural history of Europe.'[47] Schmale has reviewed the important developments in related research over the last thirty years, beginning with French historians Michel Espagne and Michael Werner, whose innovative notion of 'cultural transfer' was developed in the 1980s,[48] and the more recent work of Peter Burke dealing with 'cultural exchange.'[49] All of these recent scholars argue for the significant cultural impact that accompanies the movement of people across national borders.

The present study applies this notion of immigration as a significant cultural phenomenon for both sending and receiving countries by exploring French immigration to Russia during the period of inquiry. To gain a better understanding of when, how, and why Frenchmen and French women arrived in Russia, what they did for a living, and how they interacted with their Russian surroundings, government documents—laws, official correspondences, and especially immigration case files—have been studied from the period.

Likewise, the timing of the war with Napoleon within the period most indicative of French cultural influence (as per the lexical study) suggests a correlation between the war and cultural trends. To explore this, military memoirs from the period have been examined. Following the failed French invasion of Russia, the foreign campaign of the Russian Army took an unprecedented number of Russian men into the heart of Europe.

---

[46] Leo R. Chavez, 'Culture Change and Cultural Reproduction: Lessons from Research on Transnational Migration', in *Globalization and Change in Fifteen Cultures: Born in One World and Living in Another,* ed. by Janice Stockard and George Spindler (Belmont, CA: Thomson-Wadsworth, 2006), p. 297.

[47] Wolfgang Schmale, *A Transcultural History of Europe* (Mainz: Inst. f. Europ. Geschichte, 2010) <http://www.ieg-ego.eu/schmalew-2010a-en> [accessed 13 February 2015]

[48] See, for example, Michel Espagne and Michael Werner, eds., *Transferts: les relations interculturelles dans l'espace franco-allemand (XVIIIe et XIXe siècle)* (Paris: Éditions recherche sur les civilisations, 1988).

[49] See, for example, Peter Burke, *Cultural Hybridity* (Cambridge: Polity Press, 2009).

Of particular interest to the present study is the time they spent inside France, hence chapter four's focus on Russian military memoirs of 1814. In addition to providing very specific descriptions of cultural interaction, these memoirs shed light on language use as expressed in a literary genre very different from the newspapers and journals studied later in the dissertation.

The use of military and other memoirs as historical sources is a practice that actually predates the modern discipline of historiography itself.[50] Prior to the source-based historical approach championed by Leopold Von Ranke (1795 – 1886), memoir literature was one of principal resources by which scholars understood the past. The modern emphasis on more 'factual' primary sources such as archival documents undermined the singular importance of memoirs.[51] The inherent subjectivism of first-person narratives written for posterity has often been cited as a drawback. Likewise, in the case of retrospective memoirs, factual accuracy is only as good as the memory of the one writing, and embellishment and omission cannot be ruled out, due to institutional loyalties (especially in the case of military memoirs written by high-ranking officers), awareness of potential censorship, and the benefit of hindsight. For reasons such as these, modern historians have tended to treat memoirs as enriching but empirically inferior sources.[52] As late as the 1980s, John Keep expressed this sentiment, arguing that Russian military memoirs 'should be treated only as an auxiliary source to flesh out the dry bones of official histories and legislative compendia.'[53]

---

[50] Gabriel Motzkin, 'Memoirs, Memory, and Historial Experience', *Science in Context,* 7 (1994), 103 – 119.

[51] See discussions of the Rankean revolution as it relates to memoirs in John Tosh, *The Pursuit of History* (Harlow: Pearson, 2006), pp. 63 – 65 and in Jennifer Jensen Wallach, *Closer to the Truth Than Any Fact: Memoir, Memory, and Jim Crow* (Athens, Ga.: University of Georgia Press, 2010), pp. 5 – 6.

[52] Yuval Noah Harari, 'Military Memoirs: a Historical Overview of the Genre from the Middle Ages to the Late Modern Era', *War in History,* 14 (2007), 289 – 309.

[53] John Keep, 'From the Pistol to the Pen: the Military Memoir as a Source on the Social History of Pre-Reform Russia', *Cahiers du monde russe et soviétique,* 21 (1980), 296.

In recent years, however, memoirs and other autobiographical literature have attracted renewed interest, a trend one scholar has ascribed to 'the widespread engagement with history in the contemporary world', arguing for the 'historical seriousness' of memoirs as historical tools, especially to social historians.[54] Historians are still aware of the issues inherent to these sources: first-person subjectivism, the problem of memory, benefit of hindsight in the case of memoirs published after the events they describe, reluctance of officers to speak out against official policy, and the like. Rather than discrediting autobiographical literature, however, these actually add to their value. Jennifer Wallach's recent examination of literary memoirs from the Jim Crow era of the American south argues for a more complex and nuanced treatment of this type of literature as a historical source. The emotions, subjectivity, and felt experiences of those who lived through certain events are not chaff to be sifted through in order to get at the 'real history,' but are, rather, an important part of that history.[55] According to Wallach, the discerning historian should 'embrace the subjectivity' of such sources and 'attempt to connect empathetically with past historical agents and cultivate an emotional understanding of different historical eras.'[56] Regarding military memoirs specifically, one historian has recently argued that they are invaluable for the study of military culture, which is 'among the most important variables in the study of warfare.'[57]

In the case of Russia in the early nineteenth century, the importance of military memoirs extends well beyond 'military culture.' A. G. Tartakovskii has written extensively about the deep cultural importance of Russian memoir literature, especially that of the 1812 era. According to Tartakovskii, the war with Napoleon was a defining moment and the recorded memories of these events have been formative to Russian

---

[54] Paula S. Fass, 'The Memoir Problem', *Reviews in American History*, 34 (2006), 107 – 108.
[55] Wallach, *Closer to the Truth.*
[56] Ibid., p. 9.
[57] Harari, 'Military Memoirs', 307.

literature, the discipline of historiography in Russia, and, more broadly, in the development of Russia's national consciousness.[58] The foreign campaign into France is an important though often overlooked piece of the narrative provided by this crucial Russian literary genre.

These two historical developments—French emigration to Russia in the late eighteenth and early nineteenth century and the presence of Russian soldiers in France following 1812—are of particular relevance to the present study, as the literature review, lexical analysis, discussion of archival material and study of military memoirs will show. For a more holistic overview of French cultural influences during the period in which these key events occurred, chapter five explores examples of Russian periodical literature from the period 1788 – 1825 (beginning just before the French Revolution and through to the end of Alexander I's reign.) In addition to providing the immediate historical context of the aforementioned events, this sampling of contemporary periodical publications also explores more steady cultural influences such as that of French-language printed material upon literate Russians, something mentioned in each chapter as primary sources make anecdotal reference to French books, journals and newspapers. Several Russian literary journals and a St. Petersburg newspaper are sampled for occurrences of the cultural elements discovered in the lexical analysis, reaction to the historical events of chapters three and four, and general reference to French cultural influence in Russian society.

While agreeing that 'historians have always taken what a society writes, publishes, and reads as a guide to its culture', Robert Darnton has warned that this approach is not without its problems.[59] His objection to much of the work of 'intellectual history'—which seeks to reconstruct the thoughts and ideas of a period by

---

[58] A. G. Tartakovskii, *Russkaia memuaristika i istoricheskoe soznanie XIX veka* (Moscow: Arkheograficheskii tsentr, 1997).

[59] Robert Darnton, 'Reading, Writing, and Publishing in Eighteenth-Century France: A Case Study in the Sociology of Literature', *Daedalus*, 100 (1971), 214.

analyzing its literature—is that relatively few literary examples are typically explored,

raising the issue of whether or not the work selected for analysis is truly representative

of the period in terms of what was being written and what was being read at the time.

Further, Darnton argues that the processes beyond the work of the author himself

(namely publication and distribution) are too often ignored as factors.[60] As his case

study of the printing and distribution in eighteenth-century France of Diderot's

Encyclopédie illustrates in painstaking detail, the mechanism of introducing books to

the public included many intermediary participants other than the author and the reader,

each with his own set of interests: government censors, printers, distributors, and local

booksellers to name a few.[61] In her general treatment of the various 'features of print

culture' as it emerged in the western world—including the importance of

standardization and wider dissemination of ideas made possible by printed versus

handwritten communication—Elizabeth Eisenstein has also raised the issue of literacy

in a given language and has challenged frequent generalizations about the 'spread' of an

idea based on the fact that printed examples of it can be found.[62]

These two issues: readership and the apparatus of a work's production and

distribution must be considered before studying Russia's periodical literature for signs

of French cultural influence. Gary Marker has studied the development of Russia's

early printing industry and, rather than considering publishing at the end of the

eighteenth century as a neutral medium or mere tool in Russia's progression towards

modernization, Marker has argued for the significant cultural impact made by the

features of the industry itself: technology, popular demand, political power, intellectual

and religious elites, printers, publishers and booksellers. According to his analysis,

---

[60] Ibid.

[61] Robert Darnton, *The Business of Enlightenment: a Publishing History of the Encyclopédie, 1775 – 1800* (Cambridge, MA: Belknap, 1979).

[62] Elizabeth Eisenstein, *The Printing Revolution in Early Modern Europe* (Cambridge: Cambridge University Press, 2012), pp. 46 – 101.

Russian government control of literature that was not innately political in nature was generally less strict at this time. For non-political writers, this meant a measure of creative freedom, but also introduced the dynamics of free-market influences. As scholars, the educated writers felt responsible for the advancement of Russian society through the civilizing influences that quality literature could provide. As such, these 'literati' were often frustrated when Russian consumers of literature, and with them the publishers whose business it was to please them, preferred popular-level serial novels to the more serious work that the writers wished to produce. In Marker's final analysis, through these tensions, the Russian printing and publishing industry had essentially created a class of intellectuals who found themselves somewhat isolated from the reading public.[63]

Regarding literary journals specifically, Marker's investigation of circulation information suggests that their readership was indeed narrow at the time. Nevertheless, despite their limited reach, the journals were an important institution for developing a scholarly social class. The relative isolation of these writers as a group would eventually lead to the emergence of the Russian intelligentsia of the 1840s.[64] William Mills Todd III's comments on the early nineteenth century have similarly suggested the lasting importance of the Russian 'thick' journals, despite the difficulties related to their immediate circulation. Though their cost made them too expensive for most readers, their creation had begun the process of writing for the public, the experiments of a young journalistic tradition. Furthermore, they were a forum where 'Russia's most talented writers' could openly discuss the issues of the day related to Russian society

---

[63] Gary Marker, *Publishing, Printing, and the Origins of the Intellectual Life in Russia, 1700 – 1800* (Princeton: Princeton University Press, 1985).
[64] Gark Marker, 'The Creation of Journals and the Profession of Letters in the Eighteenth Century', in *Literary Journals in Imperial Russia,* ed. by Deborah Martinsen (Cambridge: Cambridge University Press, 1997), pp. 11 – 33.

and culture.[65] Therefore, despite their limited readership, a study edited by Deborah

Martinsen has suggested that 'Russian literary "thick" journals have served as the

principal means by which Russia has discovered, defined and shaped itself.'[66] Citing

the theoretical observations of generations of literary scholars, one of the authors of this

anthology asserted that assigning such cultural importance to these journals 'has long

been a truism.'[67]

Furthermore, the specific aims of the present study make the aforementioned

problems of distribution and readership less irrelevant. Russian literary journals have

been chosen for the study of French cultural impact in Russia, not primarily because of

any influence they might have had upon their contemporary readers, but because of the

clues they provide as to external influences upon Russian culture. For example,

whether or not Russian readers were persuaded by (or, indeed, even read) arguments

against blindly following French fashion, the repeated presence of articles on this topic

suggests that such a tendency existed in Russia. Also, the aforementioned importance

of these journals to the overall development of Russia's literary tradition (low

readership notwithstanding) is significant to this thesis since the layout, subject matter,

and even titles of the journals themselves obviously emulate French examples. Finally,

opinions expressed in the journals about events abroad or characterizations of French

culture provide at least a narrow glimpse into the attitudes of the authors and editors of

these journals. Compared with one another, and in the context of other primary sources

studied, these clues contribute to a broader sketch of how educated Russians were

interacting with and being influenced by French culture.

---

[65] William Mills Todd III, 'Periodicals in Literary Life of the Early Nineteenth Century', in *Literary Journals in Imperial Russia,* ed. by Deborah Martinsen (Cambridge: Cambridge University Press, 1997), pp. 37 – 63, (p. 60).

[66] Deborah Martinsen, ed., *Literary Journals in Imperial Russia* (Cambridge: Cambridge University Press, 1997), p. i.

[67] Robert Maguire, 'Introduction', in *Literary Journals in Imperial Russia,* ed. by Deborah Martinsen (Cambridge: Cambridge University Press, 1997), p. 1.

The purpose of including a Russian newspaper in this study is somewhat different than the use of journals. Whereas the journals have been read for the impressions about French influence that can be discerned in their intellectual expression, the Russian newspaper has been studied for facts. Classified advertisements provide details about French items for sale in stores or by private owners. Announcements offering or seeking the services of French domestic servants suggest the presence of and demand for immigrant employees. News coverage of events in France provides information about Russia's political climate relative to France. Details, data, and the occasional anecdotal account provide a more narrative account of how French influence was occurring as a compliment to the impressionistic rendering provided by the journals.

Because of the close temporal proximity of their publication to the events recorded, and the fact that they are usually so readily available, newspapers are commonly used by historians as primary sources. Their use, however, has its own set of challenges. The expediency with which a bi-weekly publication must produce news can lead to factual errors, as can the subjectivity of eyewitness accounts. Likewise the biases of newspaper writers and editors and the effects of government censorship have to be considered before any facts can be taken at face value. As one scholar has suggested, the historian must approach any newspaper as a source 'with all his critical instincts on full alert.'[68] Obviously, however, this has not prevented a number of historians from basing significant analytical studies on the use of newspapers. Peter Fritzsche's description of Berlin in 1900 and Bob Harris's exploration of the Scottish reaction to the French Revolution are examples of this.[69]

---

[68] Joseph Baumgartner, 'Newspapers as Historical Sources', *Philippine Quarterly of Culture and Society*, 9 (1981), 258.

[69] Peter Fritzsche, *Reading Berlin 1900* (Cambridge, MA: Harvard University Press, 1996), and Bob Harris, 'Scotland's Newspapers, the French Revolution and Domestic Radicalism (c. 1789 – 1794), *The Scottish Historical Review*, 84 (2005), 38 – 62.

As with the literary journals, the classic cautions related to using newspapers as primary sources are of less concern to the present study. The accuracy of specific details related to French influences—employment opportunities, goods and services advertised, the sale of certain books—are not nearly as important as the prevalence of such advertisements. Concerning the problem of objectivity, any bias on the part of the paper's writers and editors when reporting political events, far from being a detriment, is an important part of the historical narrative. Since *Sanktpeterburgskiia vedomosti* was overseen by the state, nothing like independent journalism is expected of it. Because of this fact, the paper is useful as a 'thermometer' for gauging the Russian government's political feelings at any given point regarding events in France. Alongside the study of literary journals, the study of a single newspaper for the period 1788 – 1825 provides a general overview of French cultural influence during the period.

Scattered throughout the Russian language, and hiding in plain sight on the pages of Russian dictionaries, the words of French origin which have become permanent additions have a story to tell, but only when considered together as a lexical whole. Like so many bees, they 'swarm' in groups around certain temporal periods and topical themes as if to say 'take a closer look here.' They draw attention to the time during which they debuted (the epochs of Peter I, Catherine II, Pushkin, Dostoevskii, the Revolutionary period, the mid-twentieth century and beyond), but also, by their individual type, suggest specific topics of inquiry: literary and performing arts, sartorial and culinary fashion, government administration, science and technology, to name a few. Of course these general impressions are just that, faint echoes from the past, calling for special examination of the late eighteenth and early nineteenth century for French influence around specific cultural themes. This closer examination of the period (through the study of archival records, military memoirs, and periodical literature) provides the narrative context for the appearance of these words at this time.

These borrowed French words come to life as they are featured in storylines of how French influences swept into Russian culture and changed it forever. These stories tell of how Catherine the Great opened the gates of her empire to French adventurers, swindlers, and vagabonds whose fluency in their own native tongue allowed them to be received in the finest Russia homes as honoured cultural mentors. Later, this hospitality was extended to more reputable French émigrés, who fled the terror of the guillotine and settled among the Russians, flooding Russia with French fashion, cuisine, the French language, fine merchandize, and real living examples of what proper salon culture should look like. Their stories are many: A French teacher, moving from city to city within Russia in search of work; a party of middle-class French tradesmen laughing over drinks in a Moscow tavern; multitudes of French men, women, and children of various craft, mercantile, and domestic service professions huddled in line at the local Russian church to publicly swear allegiance to the French crown, have their names recorded and thereby avoid deportation from cities across Russia. Later still, there are stories of young Russian soldiers marching across Europe towards Paris, living in French homes, dining in French restaurants, visiting French theatres, museums, libraries and churches, talking and dancing with French ladies, taking French wives, buying French books, and finding themselves immersed in the culture that their French governesses, tutors and schoolmasters had told them stories about as children. Russia and Russians would never be the same. In the wake of the French Revolution and subsequent Napoleonic Wars France and Russia collided, and the imprint left upon the Russian culture would be permanent.

CHAPTER ONE

HISTORIOGRAPHY OF FRENCH INFLUENCE UPON RUSSIAN CULTURE

Despite the generally accepted notion that French traces exist in Russian culture, there has yet to be written a comprehensive history of French influence on Russian culture. In Russian, historical studies focused on French influence have only begun to appear in the twenty-first century. A trend of scholarship in Russian universities over the last fifteen years has produced numerous conferences on the 'experience of cultural partnership', 'the matter of cultural diffusion', and the historical 'cultural ties' between Russia and France.[1] Several Russian doctoral dissertations have likewise appeared which provide period-specific analyses of French cultural influence: during the reign of Peter the Great, among the Russian nobility in the early nineteenth century, in revolutionary and Soviet Russia, and so forth.[2] This burst of scholarship has come alongside a special diplomatic program which named 2010 the 'Year of France' in Russia.[3]

Generally speaking, western study of this and other cultural topics has largely focused on specific periods of Russian history, often concentrating on the Russian (or Soviet) government and the lives of key individuals, a historiographical tendency some

---

[1] S. A. Simonova, and I. V. Satina, *Rossiia i Frantsiia: opyt kul'turnogo vzaimodeistviia* (Voronezh: Voronezhskii gosudarstvennyi universitet, 2005); L. I. Lipskaia, ed., *Frantsiia – Rossiia: problem kul'turnykh diffuzii*, (Tiumen': Tipografiia 'Pechatnik', 2008); B. P. Borisov, 'Ironiia rossiisko-frantsuzskikh istoricheskikh sviazei', in B. P. Borisov and I. V. Kochubeia, eds, *ACA International Scientific Conferences Series,* Volume V: *Rossiia—Frantsiia: dialog kul'tur: Mezhdunarodnaia nauchnaia konferentsiia* (Krasnodar: Krasnodar State University, 2010), pp. 4 – 6; M. G. Il'iushina, ed., *Frantsuzskaia kul'tura v russkoi provintsii (vologodskii krai): materialy chtenii* (Vologda: Vologodskaia oblastnaia universal'naia nauchnaia biblioteka im. I.V. Babushkina, 2000); A. A. Kornienok, ed., *Rossiia-Frantsiia: na perekrestke kul'tur,* (Piatigorskii: PGLU, 2010).

[2] I. V. Ivanskaia, 'Frantsuzskaia kul'turna v Rossii epokhi Petra I' (unpublished doctoral dissertation, Saint Petersburg State University, 2007); T. A. Shanskaia, 'Vospriiatie frantsuzskoi kul'tury russkim dvorianstvom (pervaia chetvert' XIX veka)' (unpublished doctoral dissertation, Kazan State University, 2001); N. O. Shiralieva, 'Kul'turnye sviazi Frantsii i Rossii v XX veke' (unpublished doctoral dissertation, Moscow, 2004);

[3] 'God Rossii vo Frantsii i Frantsii v Rossii', *Ria novisti,* 14 December 2015 <http://ria.ru/trend/Russia_France_year_25012010/> [accessed 30 June 2015]

scholars have attributed to the so-called 'statist school' of Russian historiography, which émigré scholars passed on to their pupils, the first generation of western historians of Russia.[4] Consequently, reference to French influences by historians of Russian culture such as James Billington and W. Bruce Lincoln have highlighted topics like the empress Elizabeth Petrovna's fondness for French luxury items, Catherine II's correspondences with philosophes and written attitudes towards the French enlightenment, specific works of art commissioned by the Russian state, and so forth.[5] Other historians, notably Orlando Figes and Hans Rogger, have cited Russian literary references such as fictional examples of Francophile Russians in the works of Pushkin and Tolstoi or the mocking of such tendencies in the plays of Denis Fonvizin or eighteenth-century literary journals.[6]

As the historiographical overview which follows will demonstrate, scattered references to French cultural influence abound in such general histories of imperial Russia and Russian culture, biographies, and period studies. They are especially prominent in the more recent thematic histories of Russian culture, which increased access to Russian archives has made possible since 1991. Christine Ruane, for example, uncovered considerable borrowing from French periodicals in her study of the Russian fashion press and garment-making industry.[7] Likewise, Dmitry Shvidkovsky's history of Russian architecture has much to say about French contributions as does P. V.

---

[4] Allan Wildman, 'The Future of Russian History', *The Russian Review,* 60 (2001), 10; David Saunders, 'The Political Ideas of Russian Historians', *The Historical Journal,* 27 (1984), 757 – 771; Taras Kuzio, 'Historiography and National Identity among the Eastern Slavs: Toward a New Framework', *National Identities,* 3 (2001), 109 – 132; Paul Bushkovitch, *Peter the Great* (Lanham: Rowman and Littlefield, 2001), p. 5.

[5] James H. Billington, *The Icon and the Axe: An Interpretive History of Russian Culture* (New York: Knopf, 1970), pp. 210 – 268; W. Bruce Lincoln, *Between Heaven and Hell: The Story of a Thousand Years of Artistic Life in Russia* (New York: Viking, 1998), pp. 69 – 125.

[6] Orlando Figes, *Natasha's Dance: a Cultural History of Russia* (London: Penguin, 2002), pp. 36 – 68, 94 – 118.; Hans Rogger, *National Consciousness in Eighteenth-Century Russia* (Cambridge, Mass.: Harvard University Press, 1969), pp. 45 – 84.

[7] Christine Ruane, *The Empire's New Clothes: A History of the Russian Fashion Industry, 1700–1917* (New Haven: Yale University Press, 2009)

Romanov's history of Russian cuisine.[8] As these recent examples and earlier histories

all demonstrate, however, historians have typically found French influence whilst

looking for something else, a fact which emphasizes the prevalence of French influence

but also its neglect as the direct object of scholarly inquiry.

The present study of Russian culture is more intentional in this regard and

follows the French strain itself, not merely as a means of providing descriptive detail of

a target period but for its own sake and for the insights it provides about Russian culture

more broadly. Namely, this thesis studies evidence of permanent cultural transfer—

identified via thematic groups of French loanwords in the Russian language—and

argues that certain characteristic aspects of the current Russian culture can be

historically traced to Imperial Russia's significant interaction with French people,

French goods, and French books. If there is a key period in the study (and there will be)

it is only because the French echo says so, and that period's great men and key events

will serve as mere descriptors towards a better understanding of Russia's current

cultural fabric. To further borrow Pomerants's analogy of Russian culture as a fabric

(discussed in the introduction), this thesis explores when and how French threads were

interwoven. The present chapter serves as a first step towards framing the context of

this cultural process: an overview of previous scholarship on French influence by

historical period and a review of the most relevant recent topical studies.

Prior to the reign of Peter the Great

Historians have first noted French influence in Russia before the reign of Peter the

Great, though the influence they have cited for this period has been limited. There is

some evidence in unpublished sources of a possible Russian envoy to France as early as

---

[8] Dmitry Shvidkovsky, *Russian Architecture and the West* (New Haven: Yale University Press, 2007); P. V. Romanov, *Zastolnaia istoriia gosudarstva rossiiskogo* (Saint Petersburg: Kristall, 2000).

the 1580s.[9] Likewise, Russian historians cite anecdotal mention of French soldiers in the Swedish army who may have been among prisoners of war exiled to Siberia in the period 1593 – 1645.[10] As Muscovy began trading more actively with the West in the sixteenth and seventeenth centuries, Russians had more opportunity to interact with foreign merchants. French imports included fabric for clothing, writing paper, spices, wines and vinegar, but most of this came through intermediaries like the Dutch or English who traded directly with Russia and made many shipments. Though there had been multiple efforts from 1587 onward, no direct trade treaty would be reached between Russia and France until 1787. In his dissertation on commercial relations between France and Russia in the eighteenth century, Frank Fox chronicled two centuries of failed attempts and false starts which preceded the ratification of this Franco-Russian treaty. Though both countries desired to establish trade relations, Fox ascribes the difficulty in reaching an agreement to French ignorance about Russian realities and the disharmony in both countries between state and commerce.[11]

The classic work of Russian historian Sergei Platonov, representative of the broad statist approach to history, explored Russia's modernization and contact with Europe during the Muscovite period in more detail.[12] Platonov characterized this period as a return to contact with the West after two centuries of relative isolation under Mongol overlords. One French historian, a contemporary of Platonov, likewise described this period as constituting a 'recovery of the European traditions of primitive Russia'.[13] During the reign of Tsar Ivan the Terrible (1547 – 1584), Russia interacted

---

[9] Alexandra Kalmykow, 'A Sixteenth-Century Russian Envoy to France', *Slavic Review,* 23 (1964), 701–705.

[10] A.P. Iarkov, 'Liudi i obrazy Frantsii v zapadnoi sibiri v XVIII – XIX vv.', in *Frantsiia – Rossiia: problem kul'turnykh diffuzii,* ed. by L.I. Lipskaia (Tiumen': Tipografiia 'Pechatnik', 2008), p. 46.

[11] Frank Fox, 'French – Russian Commercial Relations in the Eighteenth Century and the French – Russian Commercial Treaty of 1787' (unpublished doctoral dissertation, University of Delaware, 1966).

[12] S.F. Platonov, *Moscow and the West,* trans. by Joseph L. Wieczynski (Hattiesburg: Academic International, 1972).

[13] Emile Haumant, *La culture Francaise en Russie (1700–1900)* (Paris: Librairie Hachette et Cie, 1913), p. 2 <https://archive.org/details/laculturefrana00haumuoft> [accessed 26 January 2014]

with Europe via commerce. Russians from various levels of Muscovite society near

trade routes had dealings with so-called 'Germans' and 'Frenchmen', though the actual

nationalities of these merchants is uncertain.[14] Boris Godunov (chief advisor 1584 –

1598, reigned 1598 – 1605) also allowed a foreign presence in Russia, and extant

memoir material from visiting foreigners speaks of Godunov's good treatment of them.

Boris also sent several young noblemen abroad to study foreign languages, including six

to France.[15] Conversely, there are a few accounts of students from France and England

studying Russian in Moscow at the turn of the seventeenth century, and Boris's

immediate successor had a number of foreigners in his court and military, including

several Frenchmen.[16]

In his study of foreign travel diaries during this period, Marshall Poe has argued

that European visitors were prone to exaggerate the tyranny of the Muscovite state

because certain 'filters' through which their observations passed.[17] These include the

limited view of Russian society allowed to foreign visitors (they were sequestered in

special communities), the fact that these travel writers often borrowed material directly

from earlier written sources, and the 'mental baggage' of the writers themselves, who

describe Muscovite Russia in terms of their own Western political categories. Poe's

approach, though covering roughly the same period as that of Platonov, provides a more

nuanced and complex cultural analysis, rather than merely focusing on the state and its

policies. According to Poe, early in the seventeenth century, the attitude toward having

foreigners in important positions took a negative turn at least partly for reasons dealing

with religious affiliation. One military commander had been ordered 'to hire military

men who are good and true, but not to hire Frenchmen or others of the Papist faith.'[18]

---

[14] Platonov, *Moscow and the West*, p. 27.
[15] Ibid., 31 – 32.
[16] Ibid., 33.
[17] Marshall Poe, *A People Born to Slavery: Russia in Early Modern European Ethnography, 1476–1748* (Ithaca: Cornell University Press, 2000).
[18] Ibid., 58.

This conflict with Catholicism seems to have subsided somewhat under the reign of the first Romanov, Mikhail Fedorovich (1613 – 1645).[19]

During the reign of Aleksei Mikhailovich (1645 – 1676), certain luxury goods from Western Europe were already popular among the elite.[20] The Tsar himself wished to receive from abroad 'a carriage, like the one in which the kings of Spain and France and Caesar go about, experts who make birds sing in the trees, people who play trumpets and experts in making comedy.'[21] It was also during Aleksei's reign that the various foreign specialists living in Moscow were isolated in the city's so called 'German settlement' [*Nemetskaia sloboda*].[22] It was in this foreign-inhabited suburb that the young Peter Alekseevich (who would become Peter the Great) would supplement his education, meet European soldiers, and gain a lifelong fascination with the West.[23]

The era of Peter the Great

Historians have viewed Peter's eagerness to learn from the West as a factor that continued well into his adult years and drove the forward-thinking approach of his reign. Documents from the early 1690s record him ordering European clothing to be made for him and participants in his mock military exercises. He had foreign goods such as mathematical instruments, clocks, and German wine shipped to him.[24] His intellectual curiosity is particularly evident from accounts of the so-called Grand Embassy of 1697 – 1698 in which the Tsar himself travelled incognito with a Russian delegation through Warsaw, Vienna, Venice, Amsterdam, and London. Though the

---

[19] Ibid., 38.

[20] S.G. Pushkarev, 'Russia and the West: Ideological and Personal Contacts before 1917', *The Russian Review*, 24 (1965), 142.

[21] Platonov, *Russia and the West*, p. 112.

[22] Hans Rogger, *National Consciousness in Eighteenth-Century Russia* (Cambridge, Mass.: Harvard University Press, 1969), p. 13.

[23] Lindsay Hughes, *Russia in the Age of Peter the Great* (New Haven and London: Yale University Press, 1998), p. 4.

[24] Ibid., 15.

primary purpose of the journey was diplomatic as Peter hoped to form alliances in his struggle against the Turks, Peter and his entourage took the time to learn shipbuilding from the English and Dutch while abroad and absorbed as much knowledge as possible. This trip marked a turning point for Peter and the Russian state, as he 'returned to Russia determined to remould his country along Western lines.' For obvious diplomatic reasons, France was excluded from this trip. The French were allied with the Turks at the time and at odds with Austria, Holland, and England.[25] Such considerations would continue to impede direct Franco-Russian relations throughout Peter's reign. For example, a direct commercial agreement with France was stalled in the early eighteenth century at least partially because of Peter's reluctance to damage relations with the English and Dutch who would have been cut out as trade intermediaries.[26]

While Peter's orientation was westward, it was not primarily French. 'In so far as Peter I and his immediate successors preferred any single foreign country as a source of intellectual stimulus for their people, they tended to choose Germany.'[27] Historians have, however, detected signs of Peter's interest in French culture. An early point of contact occurred in 1705 when the Russian ambassador to Holland crossed the border into northern France.[28] In 1714 a French envoy was sent to St. Petersburg in search of supplies for their navy and in the following year Russia's first consular mission was sent to France to recruit skilled craftsmen.[29] Peter himself visited Paris in 1717, hoping to establish diplomatic relations strong enough to minimize interference in the Northern War by the alliance of France, Britain and the Dutch Republic.[30] Politically, this voyage proved unsuccessful, but was an opportunity for direct exposure to French

---

[25] Robert K. Massie, *Peter the Great: His Life and World* (New York: History Book Club, 1999), 155–157.
[26] Fox, 'French – Russian Commercial Relations', p. 18.
[27] M.S. Anderson, 'Some British Influences on Russian Intellectual Life and Society in the Eighteenth Century', *The Slavonic and East European Review*, 39 (1960), 148.
[28] L.A. Letaeva, 'Frantsuzskaia kniga v kul'turnom prostranstve Rossii serediny vtoroi poloviny XVIII veka', in *Frantsiia – Rossiia: problem kul'turnykh diffuzii*, ed. by L.I. Lipskaia (Tiumen': Tipografiia 'Pechatnik', 2008), pp. 28–25 (p. 29).
[29] Fox, 'French – Russian Commercial Relations', pp. 23–25.
[30] Hughes, *Russia in the Age of Peter the Great*, p. 53.

culture. Inspired by what he had seen, Peter returned to Russia and issued an Act on

Assemblies in 1718 to encourage Russian nobility to host social gatherings outside the

court after the European (that is, French) fashion.[31] Further, it appears that Peter had

not been altogether negligent of French culture even before his 1717 visit. According to

the memoirs of the Duc de Saint-Simon, while in Paris, the Tsar 'understood French

well and, I think, could have spoken it if he had wished, but as a matter of pride he

always had an interpreter. Latin and many other languages he spoke very well.'[32]

More importantly, groundwork was laid during Peter's reign for the adoption of

French cultural elements later on. Key among these developments was the birth of the

Russian publishing industry. The 1708 orthography reform introduced a new version of

the Russian alphabet, the so called Civil Script, which was more conducive to typeset

printing. Peter immediately began commissioning books to be printed in the new

typeface, which opened the way to foreign influence as translations were commissioned.

An early example is the publication in 1708 of a Russian letter-writing manual,

translated from German. Letter-writing manuals were popular throughout Europe. In

France, they were mostly for courtiers and other ranking nobility, as a guide to proper

communication among refined individuals. Peter's choice of this book for translation

and publication speaks to the type of European behaviour that he hoped to instil in the

nobility of his day.[33] The publication in Russia of collections of international treaties

during Peter's era would also mean access to Western ideas on foreign diplomacy and

political science.[34] Growth in publication and bookselling would necessarily mean a

deeper interaction with the French language, since the world's literature was being

translated into French at this time.

---

[31] Ibid., 267.

[32] Henri Troyat, *Peter the Great* (New York: Dutton, 1987), p. 183.

[33] Lina Bernstein, 'The First Published Russian Letter-Writing Manual: Priklady, kako pishutsia komplementy raznye. . .' *The Slavic and East European Journal*, 46 (2002), 98–99.

[34] W.E. Butler, 'Treaty Collections in Eighteenth-Century Russia: Encounters with European Experience', in *Russia and the West in the Eighteenth Century*, ed. by A.G. Cross (Newtonville, Mass.: Oriental Research Partners, 1983), pp. 249–255.

Another advance during this period that was important to the adoption of French culture was Peter's encouragement of foreign travel. His own Grand Embassy and later diplomatic trip to France were ground-breaking for a Russian sovereign. Likewise, those traveling with the Tsar's entourage or on other sanctioned trips were shaped by their exposure to European civilization while abroad. Historians have highlighted several individuals who were influenced in this way. According to Max Okenfuss, Count Petr Tolstoi (1697 – 1722) was impacted at a deep philosophical level by his travels to Western Europe, particularly in his reconciling of religious faith and academic study.[35] While his travels did not secularize him per se, his interaction with Western European culture did teach him that tolerance and science were not incompatible with his Christian faith, a radical notion for a culture just emerging from the conservative era of Old Muscovy. Prince Boris Kurakin, another Russian impacted by foreign travel, spent many years abroad in service to the Russian state, and his writings from the 1720s forward are full of French loanwords.[36] These are just a few examples of the early adoption of French culture and ideals that was fostered by foreign travel during this period. Russian journeys abroad and foreign immigration to Russia, traditions essentially begun by imperial example and decree, would be continual means of French cultural import in the century following Peter the Great.

In her dissertation on French culture in Russia during Peter I's reign, I.V. Ivanskaia has found that the French elements that were present during this period were primarily those that met the pragmatic and technical needs of Peter's reforms.[37] Historians have tended to highlight French influence related to the navy and architecture

---

[35] Max J. Okenfuss, 'The Cultural Transformation of Peter Tolstoi', in *Russia and the West in the Eighteenth Century,* ed. by A.G. Cross (Newtonville, Mass.: Oriental Research Partners, 1983), pp. 228–237.

[36] Gesine Argent, 'Noble sociability in French: romances in Princess Natalia Kurakina's album', The University of Bristol's French Language in Russia Project, 2013 <https://frinru.ilrt.bris.ac.uk/texts> [accessed 24 June 2015]

[37] I.V. Ivanskaia, 'Frantsuzskaia kul'tura v Rossii epokhi Petra I' (unpublished doctoral dissertation, Saint Petersburg State University, 2007).

or the imposition of French etiquette for the superficial development of a distinct ruling class in Russia. This was a part of Peter's overall program to effect Russia's modernization through the imposition of Western elements in a way that was arguably artificial in nature. Writing more generally of all European stimuli inherent in Peter's reforms, Lindsay Hughes characterizes the situation as follows:

> Reforming the army, the taxation system, and the Church, creating new administrative institutions, and building a new capital were simple and straightforward in comparison with transforming people... Even some of his admirers doubt whether his reforms went much more than skin deep... We are dealing here with an attempt at cultural engineering rarely attempted in so short a space of time or on such a scale.[38]

Observations such as this suggest that French cultural influences during this period were largely superficial and hardly the origins of permanent cultural transfer with which the present study is concerned.

Further, according to Marc Raeff, there was an inevitable time-lag in Russia's reception of Western ideas, forms of government, society, and culture.[39] Much of what was imported during Peter's reign was from an earlier period—via the translation of outdated books, or inviting artisans and specialists who were past their prime and not representative of the latest fashions or technology—and the new structures that Peter introduced were often mismatched to Muscovite society. These discrepancies would be a source of tension until the nineteenth century.

Nonetheless, Paul Bushkovitch's more recent study views westernization as the most enduring accomplishment of Peter the Great, tempering previous mythical depictions of the lone reformer with more information about Peter's interaction with the Russian aristocracy and its cooperation in the process of change.[40] Also, Bushkovitch underscores the fact that the westernization of this period applied mainly to the Russian

---

[38] Hughes, *Russia in the Age of Peter the Great,* p. 203.

[39] Marc Raeff, 'Seventeenth-Century Europe in Eighteenth-Century Russia?', *Slavic Review* 41 (1982), 611–619.

[40] Paul Bushkovitch, *Peter the Great* (Lanham: Rowman and Littlefield, 2001)

elite. Nevertheless, European cultural influence had been introduced and succeeding

generations would build on this abrupt beginning. In the words of one historian, 'the

days of the German Suburb were behind him, and the period of French influence was on

the way. Its progress was delayed by an interlude of German predominance between

1725 and 1741, but it had made a beginning.'[41]

The more recent histories of Russia up to the eighteenth century—for example

that of Marshall Poe on Muscovy and Lindsey Hughes and James Cracraft for the

Petrine era—have moved away from the old statist approach toward a historiography

that offers a broader view of Russian culture. Poe introduces readers to the often

invisible peasantry. Hughes and Cracraft explore changes to Russian society at large

rather than merely focusing on the towering figure of Peter the Great.[42] Still, much that

is written about these periods, including cultural history, revolves around the Russian

state and its key figures. A notable exception to this is some recent Russian scholarship

related to the eighteenth-century publishing industry and book trade. Examination of

the contents of private libraries and trade documents from the period have yielded new

insights into Russian culture during this period, including French influence via imported

and translated literature.[43] The findings of these recent studies will be covered briefly in

---

[41] Leonide Ignatieff, 'French Émigrés in Russia, 1789 – 1825: The Interaction of Cultures in Time of Stress' (unpublished doctoral dissertation, University of Michigan, 1963), p. 8.

[42] Lindsay Hughes, *Russia in the Age of Peter the Great* (New Haven: Yale University Press, 1998); James Cracraft, *The Petrine Revolution in Russian Culture* (Cambridge, MA: Harvard University Press, 2004).

[43] N. A. Kopanev, 'Frantsuzskaia kniga i russkaia kul'tura v seredine XVIII veka' (unpublished doctoral dissertation, Leningrad State University, 1990); I. E. Barenbaum, *Frantsuzskaia perevodnaia kniga v Rossii v XVIII veke* (Moscow: Nauka, 2006); E. V. Borshch, 'K voprosu o frantsuzskom proiskhozhdenii russkikh knizhnykh vin'etok XVIII v.', in L. I. Lipskaia, ed., *Frantsiia – Rossiia: problem kul'turnykh diffuzii* (Tiumen': Tipografiia 'Pechatnik', 2008), pp. 36 – 40; L. A. Letaeva, 'Frantsuzskaia kniga v kul'turnom prostranstve Rossii serediny vtoroi poloviny XVIII veka', in L. I. Lipskaia, ed., *Frantsiia – Rossiia: problem kul'turnykh diffuzii*, (Tiumen': Tipografiia 'Pechatnik', 2008), pp. 28 – 35; Sergey V. Korolev, 'French Books with Catherine II's Coat of Arms from the Former Hermitage Library', *Cahiers du Monde russe*, 47 (2006), 659 – 666; L. A. Marikhbein, 'Istoriia chastnykh kollektsii frantsuzskoi knigi v Rossii XVIII – XIX vekov i ikh rol' v razvitii russko-frantsuzskikh kul'turnykh sviazei' (unpublished doctoral dissertation, Russian State Social University, 2008).

the discussion of Catherine II's reign, below, and more fully in the context of Russia's literary interaction with French influences in chapter five.

The reigns of Anna and Elizabeth

While historians have noted some small gains in French influence under Anna Ivanovna (r. 1730 – 1740), scholarship on this period suggests that German influence was more indicative of her court via the contribution of the German advisors who attended the empress.[44] In addition to the imperial court, the Academy of Sciences and Cadet Corps served to continue, along Germanic lines, the westernization begun by Peter. This did not mean, however, that French cultural elements were absent. On the contrary, French language, wines, literature and performing arts were a part of court life. The empress Anna invited craftsmen, artists, and a dance instructor from France to 'make her existence more comfortable and amusing.'[45] According to one historian, 'French civilization was propagated by the German rulers of Russia in the time of Anna.' This is 'not surprising since all of Germany at that time was under the sway of French culture.'[46]

Elizabeth's ascension in 1741 marked a turning point as her reign would be characterized by more direct and ongoing attention to French culture.[47] In the words of one historian, 'not only did the reign [of Elizabeth] open the door to French influence which brought ideas of order, logic and consistency into the Russian intellectual world; it also witnessed the growth of anti-Prussian feeling...'[48] The background and personality of this daughter of Peter the Great fostered an atmosphere conducive to

---

[44] Alexander Lipski, 'Some Aspects of Russia's Westernization during the Reign of Anna Ioannovna, 1730 – 1740', *American Slavic and East European Review* 18 (1959), 1–11.

[45] Philip Longworth, *The Three Empresses: Catherine I, Anne and Elizabeth of Russia* (London: Constable, 1972), p. 119.

[46] Ibid., 10.

[47] Letaeva, 'Frantsuzskaia kniga v kul'turnom prostranstve Rossii', p. 29.

[48] John P. Le Donne, 'Catherine's Governors and Governors-General. 1763 – 1796', *Cahiers du Monde russe et soviétique* 20 (1979), 15.

French influence at court. She had received a French education, had at one time been considered as a possible bride for Louis XV, had a passion for French fashion and would purchase large quantities of dresses and interior design items from France during her tenure.[49] Such was her extravagance that on one occasion a French milliner was forced to refuse her further credit.[50] Other members of the Russian nobility such as Mikhail Vorontsov and Ivan Shuvalov shared Elizabeth's love for French luxury items and furnished their mansions with imported furniture, tapestries, and other decorative items.[51]

Mikhail Lomonosov considered Elizabeth's reign as the 'dawn of a golden age' for Russia where cultural and intellectual developments were concerned, and with good reason. Under Elizabeth, Moscow University was founded, as was the Academy of Art in St. Petersburg. Books, journals, and magazines were actively published on the presses Peter had established, and French specialists in sculpture and portrait-painting were invited to work in Russia. The imperial court's relationship with Voltaire—a relationship to be taken up later by Catherine II—included his induction into the Russian Academy of Sciences, and his authorship of a history of Russia during the time of Peter the Great.[52] During her reign (1741 – 1761), French literature and the lightness of French thought became increasingly popular among the upper classes of Russians, a trend that would continue throughout the eighteenth century.[53] As one Russian writer has summarized the century, 'the development which characterized the time of the reigns of Elizabeth and Catherine II was the general attainment of French culture.'[54]

Russian writers' translation of and interaction with French literature was also important to the development of Russia's young literary tradition. The importance of

---

[49] Ignatieff, 'French Émigrés in Russia, 1789 – 1825', pp. 10–12.
[50] Nicholas V. Riasanovsky, *A History of Russia* (New York: Oxford University Press, 1963), p. 274.
[51] Tamara Talbot Rice, *Elizabeth, Empress of Russia* (London: Weidenfeld and Nicolson, 1970), pp. 153 – 154.
[52] Ibid., pp. 153 – 188.
[53] Letaeva, 'Frantsuzskaia kniga v kul'turnom prostranstve Rossii', p. 29.
[54] Ibid., 34.

French classicism to the development of the Russian language and literature in the eighteenth century has been affirmed by historical linguists.[55] As Russian literature experienced its own period of classicism, Russia's pattern seems to follow that of France. Just as there was tension between 'ancients' and 'moderns' in the literature of seventeenth-century France, so there was a similar struggle in Russian literature of the eighteenth century. In the Russian embodiment of classicism, Vasilii Trediakovskii would occupy the 'ancient' literary position, Mikhail Lomonosov the 'middle', and Aleksandr Sumarokov the 'modern.'[56] Iurii Lotman has characterized Russian emulation of French literature during this period as what he calls 'transplantation.' Earlier studies of Russian emulation of French classicist literature in the mid-eighteenth century espouse the more negative view that the resultant literature was not truly Russian. Lotman, however, suggests a more meaningful influence. His notion of transplantation is that 'entire cultural realms' and not merely individual literary works were assimilated. For example, Lotman sees in Trediakovskii's translation of Tallemant's *Voyage a l'ile d'amour* 'an attempt to introduce into Russia the entire salon culture of Paris.'[57] Likewise, Aleksandr Sumarokov's translation and classicistic copying of Voltaire were merely entry points to a deeper kind of emulation. Ultimately, he 'adopted particular Voltairean functions as a model for creating a uniquely Russian literature... his emulation of Voltaire is detectable in his biting polemical style, choice of genres, aesthetic concerns, and in his self-prescribed dual role as Russia's first real

---

[55] G. O. Vinokur, *Russkii iazyk: istoricheskii ocherk* (Moscow: URSS, 2010), pp. 121 – 135; A. P. Vlasto, *A Linguistic History of Russia to the End of the Eighteenth Century* (Oxford: Clarendon, 1988), pp. 138, 377 – 378; V. M. Zhivov, *Iazyk i kul'tura v Rossii XVIII veka* (Moscow: Shkola iazyka russkoi kul'tury, 1996), p. 163.

[56] Karen Rosenberg, 'Images of National Greatness in the St. Petersburg and Moscow *vedomosti*', in *Russia and the West in the Eighteenth Century,* ed. by A.G. Cross (Newtonville, Mass.: Oriental Research Partners, 1983), pp. 238–248.

[57] Cited in Amanda Ewington, 'A Voltaire for Russia? Alexander Petrovich Sumarokov's Journey from Poet-Critic to Russian Philosophe' (unpublished doctoral dissertation, University of Chicago, 2001), pp. 44–45.

poet and philosophe.'[58] French stimulus is apparent in other literary genres as well.

Mikhail Khersakov was among a number of writers who directly followed Diderot's

example in their introduction of sentimentalist drama to Russia in the 1770s.[59] The

poetry of Nikolai Karamzin (1766 – 1826) also shows signs of French influence. As the

events of the French revolution led him to be more conservative in his ideas, he looked

to the French *ancien régime* for inspiration, and even his use of rhyme and meter were

affected.[60]

In her 2001 dissertation, Amanda Ewington explored the education of Aleksandr

Sumarokov and how his interaction with the philosophic essays and other writings of

Voltaire was particularly influential in his literary development. From the Cadet Corps

library and the Academy book store, Ewington reports that Sumarokov and his peers

had access to some of Voltaire's works, and this access would be greater in years to

come. 'By the 1750s Voltaire's works are so widely available in St. Petersburg, both in

the original and in translation, that Sumarokov and his contemporaries have access to all

of his published works, and often within months of their publication in Europe.'[61]

Sumarokov's education and literary career is a case study in the rise of French influence

in Russia, not only as it relates to the importance of French literature in his personal

development but also as a commentary on how French books became increasingly

available in Russia during his lifetime.

The aforementioned scholarly interest over the last couple of decades in books

published in eighteenth-century Russia—especially French books, Russian translations

of French books, and French translations of other foreign titles—has generated new

scholarly discussion about Russia's reception of European 'enlightened thought' during

---

[58] Ibid., p. 2.

[59] Michael Green, 'Diderot and Kheraskov: Sentimentalism in its Classicist Stage', in *Russia and the West in the Eighteenth Century,* ed. by A.G. Cross (Newtonville, Mass.: Oriental Research Partners, 1983), pp. 206–213.

[60] Anthony Cross, 'Problems of Form and Literary Influence in the Poetry of Karamzin', *Slavic Review,* 27 (1968), 39–48.

[61] Ewington, 'A Voltaire for Russia?', p. 147.

this period. Recent studies have found that developments along the geographical peripheries of the Enlightenment can be just as insightful as those which came out of France and Germany itself.[62] Rather than resulting from direct Franco-Russian interacting, it is more likely that the spread of French-language material in Russia flowed from a general cultural and intellectual movement occurring throughout Europe. During this so called Age of Enlightenment, 'the seeds of French culture were planted all over Europe and reached as far as Russia.'[63] Based on examination of various Russian texts, however, it does not appear that Russian writers of the eighteenth century were conscious of being part of a 'Russian Enlightenment' as a separate movement.[64] Nevertheless, historians have demonstrated that the cultural atmosphere of continental Europe was making an impact upon Russia.[65] Sergey Tyulenev asserts that 'In the 1730s, the golden age of French influence set in. French books flooded Russia. The transferred fields were literature, aesthetics, and ethics… the French aesthetic definitely dominated the literary scene. Later, during Catherine's reign, French philosophy, especially that of the Enlightenment, came to shape Russian minds.'[66]

Enlightenment and Gallomania under Catherine II

The impact of the literature and ideas of the French Enlightenment on Catherine II herself has been studied with considerable interest. The vast body of substantive primary material that is available—the political and philosophical writings of the

---

[62] Richard Butterwick, Simon Davies, and Gabriel Sanchez Espinosa, eds, *Peripheries of the Enlightenment* (Oxford: Voltaire Foundation, 2008).

[63] Marek Mosakowski, 'Image of Russia in Eighteenth-Century French Literature' (unpublished doctoral dissertation, The City University of New York, 1997), 1.

[64] Simon Dixon, '"Prosveshchenie": Enlightenment in Eighteenth-Century Russia', in *Peripheries of the Enlightenment,* ed. by Richard Butterwish, Simon Davies, and Gabriel Sanchez Espinoza (Oxford: Voltaire Foundation, 2008), pp. 229–249.

[65] See the analysis of the 'enlightened' mindset perceptible in 260 plays written by various Russian playwrights during this period, in Elise Kimerling Wirtschafter, *The Play of Ideas in Russian Enlightenment Theatre* (DeKalb: Northern Illinois University Press, 2003).

[66] Sergey Tyulenev, 'The Role of Translation in the Westernization of Russia in the Eighteenth Century' (unpublished doctoral thesis, University of Ottawa, 2009), p. 193.

empress as well as her personal diaries and correspondences—has facilitated significant academic debate as to the nature of Catherine the Great's relationship with the French philosophes and the extent to which her rule was actually influenced by their ideals. Inna Gorbatov's book on the subject concluded that Catherine was personally 'enlightened' in her thinking on government and was fascinated by the philosophes, but her domestic policy was ultimately determined by a desire to stay in power and she could be quite tyrannical.[67] Gorbatov saw a duality in Catherine: externally enlightened but domestically a tyrant. She used her relationship with the philosophes to bolster her image abroad more than actually being influenced by them. Marc Raeff likewise concluded that the philosophes were not so directly influential.[68]

Isabel de Madariaga, on the other hand, has fiercely defended Catherine II against the criticism that she 'failed to implement' the ideas of the French philosophes.[69] She made the argument that the philosophes themselves were in disagreement on a variety of issues (serfdom, for example) and it is thus unfair to categorically say that Catherine did not heed their advice. She also points out that Catherine was inclined towards Voltaire's idea of religious tolerance within her empire, though making allowances for the fact that such reforms were difficult to institute in actual practice. Still, de Madariaga asserted that 'throughout [Catherine II's] reign her influence was thrown into the scales in favour of toleration whenever practicable' and cited Voltaire's direct influence.[70] Simon Dixon has also argued for the sincerity of the empress's enlightened intentions and, like Madariaga, suggested the difficulty of implementation. Though she 'lionized' Voltaire, upon taking the throne and becoming acquainted with actual governance, she quickly realized that it would be difficult to 'reduce Voltaire's

---

[67]Inna Gorbatov, *Catherine the Great and the French Philosophers of the Enlightenment: Montesquieu, Voltaire, Rousseau, Diderot and Grimm* (Bethesda: Academica Press, 2006).

[68] Marc Raeff, 'The Enlightenment in Russia and Russian Thought in the Enlightenment', in *The Eighteenth Century in Russia,* ed. by J. G. Garrard (Oxford: Clarendon, 1973), pp. 25–47.

[69] Isabel de Madariaga, 'Catherine and the *Philosophes*', in *Russia and the West in the Eighteenth Century,* ed. by A.G. Cross (Newtonville, Mass.: Oriental Research Partners, 1983), pp. 30–52.

[70] Ibid., 34.

sparkling shafts of wisdom to a practical program of reform.'[71] Ultimately the debate over the sincerity of Catherine's motivations remains unresolved, a fact illustrated by the diverging opinions of Dixon and Gorbatov who continue a decades-long debate in their recent studies.

It is difficult to make a generalized statement about Catherine and the philosophes as she had very different relationships with each of them. Her attitude towards Voltaire was one of deference. She had learned political science by reading Voltaire's works as a young lady. Upon ascending the Russian throne, she began corresponding with Voltaire and continued to do so for fifteen years until his death in 1778. As a part of their relationship, Voltaire even acted informally in Europe as something of a 'goodwill ambassador' on behalf of Catherine's court.[72] Jean-Jacques Rousseau, on the other hand, was no friend of Catherine. He never flattered her or dedicated any works to her honour (as other French writers had done) and even criticized her openly. In turn, Catherine basically rejected Rousseau, and it is difficult to even say that they had a relationship at all.[73] Catherine's relationship with Denis Diderot seems to have been a pragmatic one. According to Gorbatov, Catherine's patronage of Diderot was a means to improve public relations in Europe, much needed after the way she had attained the throne. In 1762, she offered to print Diderot's *Encyclopédie* which had been banned in France. She also helped him out of some financial difficulty by purchasing his entire library and allowing him full access to it thereafter. An interesting study of the French language books in Catherine's imperial library notes a number of nicely-bound editions by lesser-known French authors.[74] It would appear that many aspiring French scholars desired similar patronage, going so far

---

[71] Simon Dixon, *Catherine the Great* (London: Profile Books, 2010), p. 153.

[72] Gorbatov, *Catherine the Great and the French Philosophers of the Enlightenment,* pp. 70–72.

[73] Ibid., 136.

[74] Sergey V. Korolev, 'French Books with Catherine II's Coat of Arms from the Former Hermitage Library', *Cahiers du Monde russe,* 47 (2006), 659–666.

as to have editions of their work embossed with Catherine's royal seal. They presented these special edition prints to the empress, presumably hoping to achieve something like Diderot's enviable position.

Diderot was not only a recipient of favour, however. As a show of gratitude, he assisted Catherine in Europe, helping to arrange her purchase of a number of French works of art. He even entered contract as her personal agent, performing various logistical tasks in Europe and serving as an advocate for her reputation.[75] Finally, as an elderly man he accepted her invitation to visit the imperial court in St. Petersburg in 1773. Arthur Wilson has depicted this trip as stimulating but ultimately unhappy for Diderot. It soon became apparent that his visit was largely for show, another effort by Catherine to make political appearances. While at court, Diderot did have meaningful daily meetings with the empress and he hoped, through their discussions, to influence her toward liberal reforms in the enlightened tradition. In the end it seems that Catherine was amused but not seriously moved.[76]

Of all the philosophes of the French Enlightenment, Charles de Montesquieu had arguably the most tangible influence on Catherine II's reign via the direct influence of his writings on her legal codex. Gorbatov called Catherine's overhaul of Russia's legal system 'the greatest work of her lifetime.'[77] From 1765 to 1767, Catherine personally worked for three hours each day on a new legal codex. The *Nakaz* of Catherine II was basically a compilation of material from various European legal documents already in existence. 250 of the 526 articles in the *Nakaz* are direct translations of material from Montesquieu's *L'Esprit des Lois*.[78] In the end, Gorbatov was sceptical of Catherine's 'enlightened' motivations and concluded that Catherine 'abandoned the principles of

---

[75] Ibid., 152–161.

[76] Arthur Wilson, 'Diderot in Russia, 1773 – 1774' in *The Eighteenth Century in Russia,* ed. by J. G. Garrard (Oxford: Clarendon, 1973), pp. 166–197.

[77] Ibid., 27.

[78] Ibid., 27–28.

Montesquieu' in her actual administration, and that reforms that were introduced by Catherine were based on other principles.[79] Dixon has argued that she never intended her treatise to be a law code, but rather a statement of the kind of principles by which she wished to govern.[80] Paul Dukes was less sceptical of Catherine's motives, arguing that she was genuinely intrigued by the notions of freedom, property rights, and rule of law discussed in Montesquieu's work. Further, both Catherine and the founding fathers of the United States adapted these principles to their own context rather than applying them exactly as written, which Dukes has argued is not an aberration but entirely in line with Montesquieu's original intent.[81]

Nonetheless, the *Nakaz* project is an example of significant interaction with French legal philosophy and the French written word. W. Gareth Jones has approached this episode from a different perspective and suggested that Catherine's *Nakaz* was heavily influenced by Montesquieu in its literary style, whatever one might think about its content or Catherine's implementation of it.[82] Jones made the argument that literature and official documents were, stylistically, not so very different at that time and were meant to be read aloud. In the absence of anything like a French salon for literary interaction, Catherine intended to read her *Nakaz* aloud at her Legislative Commission. She wrote it with public reading in mind and, showing the stylistic influence of *L'Esprit des Lois*, her work had wit and literary genius.

While this survey of French authors and books in eighteenth-century Russia describes a gradual growth in the availability of and interest in French material, it is important not to see the eighteenth century as monolithic in this regard. Rather, the type of French books being purchased throughout the 1700s indicates that there were distinct

---

[79] Ibid., 54.
[80] Dixon, *Catherine the Great,* pp. 156 – 157.
[81] Paul Dukes, *World Order in History: Russia and the West* (New York: Routledge, 1996), pp. 21 – 33.
[82] W. Gareth Jones, 'The Spirit of the "Nakaz": Catherine II's Literary Debt to Montesquieu', *The Slavonic and East European Review,* 76 (1998) 658–671.

periods of Russian interest in French language and culture within the century. In her

recent dissertation, Russian scholar L. A. Marikhbein studied private collections of

French books in eighteenth and nineteenth century Russia.[83] Her topical analysis of

these collections suggests that the choice of books purchased by Russians in the early

eighteenth century reflects the owner's need to learn French as a professional

requirement, presumably an indication of Peter I's modernizing reforms and progressive

notion of civil service. Later in the century, however, French additions to personal

libraries were of a different character. Mid-eighteenth-century private collections show

that lower nobility and even merchants were striving to learn the French language for

social advancement, a reflection of the popularity of French culture and its growing

value as a status symbol. These developments suggest the tendency for cultural trends

to follow official policies and also the fact that France was becoming increasingly

distinct from other European countries in its level of cultural influence.

The combined work of historians has demonstrated that, by the late eighteenth

century, French customs and fashions had become quite popular among the Russian

nobility. Catherine II's court at St. Petersburg was in many ways similar to Versailles

and French literature, fashion, and language became marks of refinement and necessary

tools for social advancement.[84] This led to a certain excess that would come to be

known pejoratively as 'gallomania.' Gallomania has been defined as the 'blind worship

of all things French and use of "salon" jargon in certain circles of high society

[*svetskikh krugov*].'[85] The artificial nature of this cultural mimicking is evidenced by

the contempt with which it is treated in Russian literature. According to D. J. Welsh,

---

[83] L.A. Marikhbein, 'Istoriia chastnykh kollektsii frantsuzskoi knigi v Rossii XVIII – XIX vekov i ikh rol' v razvinii russko-frantsuzskikh kul'turnykh sviazei' (unpublished doctoral dissertation, Russian State Social University, 2008).

[84] S.G. Pushkarev, 'Russia and the West: Ideological and Personal Contacts before 1917', *The Russian Review*, 24 (1965), 138–164 (p. 143).

[85] L.A. Letaeva, 'Frantsuzskaia kniga v kul'turnom prostranstve Rossii serediny vtoroi poloviny XVIII veka', in *Frantsiia – Rossiia: problem kul'turnykh diffuzii*, ed. by L.I. Lipskaia (Tiumen': Tipografiia 'Pechatnik', 2008), p. 28.

gallomania was a favourite target in Russia's eighteenth-century satirical drama.

'Hardly a comedy between 1765 and the 1820s does not contain satirical references to

it.'[86] Viktoria Ivleva has focused specifically on Russian literary references to French-

inspired clothing in Russia. Her study of the writings of Antiokh Kantemir, Ivan

Elagin, Aleksandr Sumarokov, Vladimir Lukin, Denis Fonvizin, Nikolai Novikov, and

others reveals a common thread of satirical reference to the Russian 'fop' or 'coquette'

whose clothing and manner were laughably emulative of French fashions. According to

Ivleva, literary barbs such as these speak to a cultural dichotomy and search for national

identity. Russian thinkers were reacting to foreign incursion and sought cultural

independence and some definition of what it meant to be truly Russian.[87] Hans Rogger

has noted the 'directness' and even 'crudeness with which [Novikov] lashed out against

Gallomania.'[88]

French fashion

In addition to the political, philosophical, and literary borrowings surveyed above,

historians have also noted that French sartorial influence, particularly prominent in

nineteenth-century Russia, began in the eighteenth century. According to Joan DeJean,

French domination of fashion across Europe can be traced directly to the reign of Louis

XIV (1643 – 1715) whose cultural policy, extravagant court, and innovative patronage

basically created the luxury fashion industry and permanently established France as the

world leader in *haute couture*.[89] In Russia, emulation of French trends in clothing

would come later. Of early importance was Peter the Great's 1700 dress reform by

---

[86] D.J. Welsh, 'Satirical Themes in Eighteenth-Century Russian Comedies', *The Slavonic and East European Review*, 42 (1964), 403–414.

[87] Viktoria V. Ivleva, 'Fashion and Sartorial Discourse in Eighteenth-Century Russian Literature and Culture' (unplublished doctoral dissertation, University of Wisconsin-Madison, 2009).

[88] Rogger, *National Consciousness in Eighteenth-Century Russia*, p. 71.

[89] Joan E. DeJean, *The Essence of Style: How the French Invented High Fashion, Fine Food, Chic Cafés, Style, Sophistication, and Glamour* (New York: Free Press, 2005).

which the upper classes were required to wear European-style clothing.[90] While this decree impacted only a narrow segment of the Russian population, it set an important precedent. Even many of Russia's fine clothing firms of the nineteenth century would be established by foreign families who had arrived in Russia during Peter's era.[91] By the end of Peter's reign, Western fashions were worn, not only by the nobility, but also by some manufacturers and merchants.[92] Though French fashions were leading in Western Europe in the eighteenth century, the reforming Tsar himself preferred the Dutch and German clothing styles, which were generally simpler and made from cheaper fabric.[93]

Uniquely French influence began in earnest during the reign of Elizabeth (1741 – 1761) who spent extravagant sums of money on clothing, preferring French styles.[94] As these types of clothing became more popular, tailors and dressmakers arrived from abroad to set up shops. Likewise, the Russian textile industry was propelled forward by the demand for the appropriate fabrics for such styles, which were previously unavailable in Russia and expensive to import.[95]

French fashion continued to grow in popularity in the period leading up to and following the French Revolution, despite some of the reactionary measures of Catherine II and her successor, Paul I. In a clever move, Catherine ordered lower-level police officials to wear French-looking uniforms in public, complete with lorgnettes, and they were instructed to greet pedestrians in French while on patrol. This of course made it less chic for upper-class Russians to wear French fashions in public. Paul was even firmer in his opposition, actually forbidding members of the nobility to wear certain

---

[90] Raisa Kirsanova, 'Early Noble Dress in Russia', in Joanne Eicher, Djurdja Bartlett and Pamela Smith (eds.), *Berg Encyclopedia of World Dress and Fashion* (New York: Berg Publishers, 2010), vol. IX, p. 335.
[91] L. V. Efimova and T. S. Aleshina, *Russian Elegance: Country and City Fashion from the 15th to the Early 20th Century* (London: Vivays, 2011.), p. 98.
[92] Ibid., 104.
[93] Ibid., 101.
[94] Kirsanova, 'Early Noble Dress in Russia', p. 336.
[95] Christine Ruane, *The Empire's New Clothes: A History of the Russian Fashion Industry, 1700–1917* (New Haven: Yale University Press, 2009), p. 23.

European styles. This does not seem, however, to have lessened their preference for those styles. One historian comments that on 'the day that Paul died (23 March 1801), the streets of Moscow and Saint Petersburg were filled with men and women dressed in the trendiest Parisian outfits.'[96] Likewise, following Napoleon's 1812 invasion, there was a brief refusal by noblewomen to wear French dresses. Instead, they wore Russian sarafans or other such folk costumes, adapted of course to be form-fitting after the fashion of the European-cut garments to which they were accustomed. They were not, after all, actually peasants. Far from constituting a rejection of Parisian fashion except as a symbolic gesture, these garments were actually referred to commonly as 'Frenchized sarafans', though Nicholas I's imperial decree of 1834 patriotically called them the 'Russian dress.'[97]

Though protective tariffs made imported clothing very expensive in the wake of the Napoleonic wars,[98] consumer interest in them survived and French styles would once again reign in Russia in subsequent years. The marketing of these garments and styles through a growing fashion press was an important factor. The first Russian-language fashion magazine, with news about the latest styles in Russia and abroad, appeared in Moscow in 1791. Others would soon follow and the Russian fashion press became an important part of the industry in the nineteenth century. Christine Ruane has identified two distinctive periods in the history of the Russian fashion press. In the first period (1830 – 1870) the Russian fashion press was characterized by a sense of inferiority to Western Europe and a need to compete for readership with the journals coming out of Paris, as well as proving to the readership that Russian fashion had much to offer in its own right. Most of these early publications adopted the tactic of reporting

---

[96] Raisa Kirsanova, 'Russia: Urban Dress up to the End of the Nineteenth Century' in Joanne Eicher, Djurdja Bartlett, and Pamela Smith (eds.), *Berg Encyclopedia of World Dress and Fashion* (New York: Berg, 2010), vol. IX, p. 339.

[97] Ibid., 340–341.

[98] Ruane, *The Empire's New Clothes*, p. 70.

the latest styles and cultural events in both Paris and Petersburg (something French journals did not do) and interpreting for the Russian reader the appropriate ways to filter European trends for suitable self-presentation within the unique context of Russia's urban scene. The second period of this new marketing industry (1870 – 1917) did not show the same defensive posture as before (presumably having obtained sufficient Russian-language readership by this time) and simply reported the latest fashion news out of Paris. Common to both these periods is the fact that the fashion press in Russia, as elsewhere in Europe, was driven by French fashions and even the images and content were borrowed from French publications.[99]

Aleksandr Vasil'ev, in an extended commentary on a collection of Russian photographs from 1850 – 2000, provides a history of Russian fashion in this period. French influence dominates throughout the late imperial period, especially for ladies. It is worth pointing out that, in the nineteenth and early twentieth century, women's fashions emulated Paris while men's fashion looked to London.[100] French hairdressers as well as Russian salons with French names operated in Moscow and even the provinces by the 1850s.[101] In addition to providing commentary on the photos and the various influences apparent in the styles of each decade, Vasil'ev presents numerous examples of stylish salons owned or at least inspired by the French in the second half of the nineteenth century, such as *a la ville de Lyon*, which was situated on Miasnitskaia Street in the 1860s. It was owned by 'a Moscow merchant of the first guild, the French subject Jules Picard [*Zhiul Pikar*]. The shop sold fabric, shawls, mantillas and real French ready-made [*gotovye*] dresses.'[102] The examples given by Vasil'ev are anecdotal in nature, but suggest ongoing influence. The world-famous fashion house opened by Louis Vuitton in Paris in 1854 began supplying the Russian imperial court shortly after

---

[99] Ruane, *The Empire's New Clothes,* pp. 87–112.
[100] Aleksandr Vasil'ev, *Russkaia moda: 150 let v fotografiiakh* (Moskva: Slovo/Slovo, 2007), p. 47.
[101] Ibid., 15.
[102] Ibid., 76.

being established, as did the perfume company founded by Henri Brocard in 1861. In

1869 *a Ralle i Ko,* a major perfume company, was established in Moscow by the

Frenchman Friedrich Dufoix. French influence within Russia was further strengthened

in the 1890s by the onset of a trend known as the 'third rococo style' and by the

participation of Russian perfume and design companies in exhibitions in Paris, which

would continue into the early twentieth century.[103]

Due to the industrialization of the textile industry and urbanization in Russia in

the later nineteenth century, historians have noted that fashionable clothing became

increasingly affordable. As a result, Russian people outside the elite class were joining

the ranks of those dressed after the European style at the turn of the twentieth century.[104]

Likewise, peasants who were moving into the cities in search of work following the

1861 emancipation of the serfs exchanged their peasant garments for clothes more

appropriate for an urban environment as their means would allow.[105]

Following the advent of communism in Russia, French influence on fashion

trends would be less pronounced but never disappear completely. Djurdja Bartlett has

led extensive research on Soviet fashion.[106] She refers to a 'utopian' period of clothing

policy in the years immediately after 1917 during which there was tension between

policies of the New Economic Plan, which promoted fashion, and the Bolsheviks who

opposed the very notion of fashion. In the 1930s, fashion was officially permitted in the

Soviet Union by Stalin's administration and would be monitored by the government, but

foreign influence could not be completely removed.[107] Socialist fashion congresses,

initiated in the 1950s, were a controlled environment in which Western fashions—

including those out of France—could be 'safely' introduced to the Soviet public at the

---

[103] Ibid., 121, 433–434.

[104] Elizabeth Durst, 'Russian Fashionable Dress at the Turn of the Twentieth Century' in *Berg Encyclopedia of World Dress and Fashion* (New York: Berg, 2010), vol. IX, p. 349.

[105] Kirsanova, 'Russia: Urban Dress', p. 342.

[106] Djurdja Bartlett, *Fashion East: The Spectre That Haunted Socialism* (Cambridge, Mass: MIT Press, 2010), x.

[107] Bartlett, *Fashion East*, p. 1.

discretion of the State.[108] Though fascination with and longing for western fashionable clothes would continue throughout the Soviet period, opportunities were scarce for the same level of import that had existed before the revolution.

Collectively, these studies of Russian fashion are indicative of a recent tendency to study Russian culture topically, rather than strictly within the confines of a given period. To some degree this reflects increased access to Russian primary sources such as eighteenth- and nineteenth-century fashion journals and trade documents, but the trend is more than a mere matter of sources. The philosophy of historians of Russia seems to be shifting away from the old Hegelian focus on the state and its iconic leaders as the centrepiece of history, which of course has lent itself to 'neater' periods of study: Muscovy, Petrine Russian, Catherinian Russia, and so forth.[109] This newer trend in topical studies—the clothing industry, the book trade, philosophical interaction with Western thought, the interaction of various social strata, and so forth—is enriching the study of Russian history by providing a closer look at Russian culture through something other than a strictly political lens.[110] The present inquiry into French cultural influences—a topical study—joins this trend.

The cultural impact of immigration

Another important means of French influence in Russia that has received some attention from historians is the arrival of emigrants from France who brought their culture with them. In her study of foreigners living in St. Petersburg before the Russian Revolution, A. N. Chesnokova indicated that French specialists had been invited to St. Petersburg since the time of Peter the Great and that migration from France to Russia continued up

---

[108] Bartlett, *Fashion East,* p. 158.

[109] Joseph L. Black, 'The "State School" Interpretation of Russian History: A Re-Appraisal of its Genetic Origins', *Jahrbücher für Geschichte Osteuropas*, 4 (1973), 509 – 530; Anatole Mazour, 'Modern Russian Historiography', *The Journal of Modern History*, 9 (1937), 169 – 202.

[110] Allan Wildman, 'The Future of Russian History', *The Russian Review,* 1 (2001), 9 – 12.

to the twentieth century, though much less from the mid-nineteenth century forward.[111]

A number of established French families were important to Russian society for generations and could trace their heritage back to Peter's program of inviting these specialists. They were engineers, architects, artists, sculptors, dancers, actors, and teachers to name a few of the professions represented. Marc Raeff has written somewhat disparagingly of these early recruits, suggesting that these technicians and artisans 'brought with them the knowledge and intellectual concerns of the middle of the seventeenth century, rather than those of the beginning of the eighteenth.'[112] Nevertheless, their influence in Russia was noteworthy. In Petersburg alone, technical institutes, the Academy of Arts, the Ballet Academy and Drama Theatre all owe a singular debt to French immigrant expertise.

Though Peter had been intentional about inviting foreigners for specific state-sponsored projects, French presence in Russia was relatively small before the reign of Elizabeth, during which historians have identified an increase. The greatest French presence in Russia was during and just after the reign of Catherine the Great.[113] Roger Bartlett noted that under Catherine II tens of thousands of foreigners entered Russia.[114] The empress actively recruited foreign emigrants as part of her land development program and hoped for the positive infusion of culture and technology as a result. According to Bartlett, this settlement was largely German, but also included French migration. One noteworthy example was Catherine's special invitation of the French sculptor Etienne Maurice Falconet, creator of the famous bronze statue of Peter the

---

[111] A.N. Chesnokova, *Inostrantsy i ikh potomki v Peterburge: nemtsy, frantsuzy, britantsy: 1703 – 1917: istoriko-kraevedcheskie ocherki* (St. Petersburg: Satis, 2003).

[112] Raeff, 'Seventeenth-Century Europe in Eighteenth-Century Russia?', 614.

[113] Dimitri Sergius Von Mohrenschildt, *Russia in the Intellectual Life of Eighteenth-Century France* (New York: Octagon Books, 1972).

[114] Roger Bartlett, *Human Capital: the settlement of foreigners in Russia 1762 – 1804* (Cambridge: Cambridge University Press, 1979).

Great on horseback, still one of the famous landmarks of St. Petersburg. Diderot himself assisted Catherine in acquiring Falconet's services for the project.[115]

Marek Mosakowski's review of French memoirs and other contemporary French literature noted an increased interest in Russia beginning in the 1750s and 1760s.[116] According to Mosakowski, 'The assimilation of French culture in Russia was accelerated by a massive wave of French travellers, numerous *maîtres de français,* merchants, traders, or simple *aventuriers* who settled down in St. Petersburg and Moscow during that time and attempted to make their fortune in the promising East.'[117] Another recent study has noted that the Moscow and St. Petersburg French diaspora were distinctly different. Whereas in Moscow the most common French settlers were traders, merchants, or other business entrepreneurs, in St. Petersburg French colonists tended to work as domestic servants and educators.[118]

Written in 1963, when Soviet authorities and official histories minimized foreign influence in Russian history, Ignatieff's dissertation, which relied heavily upon French diplomatic memoirs and anecdotal references in Russian literature, focused on French émigrés in Russia as a result of the French Revolution.[119] From these sources, he identified several key areas where French émigrés had the most impact: the military, administration, the arts, education, and political ideology. One Russian historian quotes the Decembrist A.E. Rozen as identifying three groups among these émigrés:

> The French Revolution expelled to us thousands of immigrants. Among them were highly educated people from the upper classes, many smart abbots, and all

---

[115] Ilse Bischoff, 'Etienne Maurice Falconet—Sculptor of the Statue of Peter the Great', *The Russian Review,* 24 (1965), 369–386.

[116] Marek Mosakowski, 'Image of Russia in Eighteenth-Century French Literature' (unpublished doctoral dissertation, The City University of New York, 1997).

[117] Ibid., 173.

[118] A.V. Kornienko, 'Frantsuzskaia koloniia v Moskve: ot proshlogo k nastoiashchemu', in *Frantsuzskii iazyk i kul'tura Frantsii v Rossii XXI veka: Materialy XV mezhdunarodnoi nauchno-prakticheskoi konferentsii Shkoly-seminara im. L.M. Skrelinoi,* ed. by Z.I. Kirnoze and others (Nizhny Novgorod: Nizhegorodskii gosudarstvennyi lingvisticheskii universitet im. N.A. Dobroliubova, 2011), pp. 270–273 (p. 271).

[119] Leonide Ignatieff, 'French Émigrés in Russia, 1789 – 1825: The Interaction of Cultures in Time of Stress' (unpublished doctoral dissertation, University of Michigan, 1963).

kinds of teachers. The first of these had influence on the upper circle of our society in education and the finer points of living (*tonkosti v obshchezhitii*); the second in religion and… family affairs; and the last [group], together with the abbots took the place of educators and, having escaped revolution themselves, sowed the first seeds of revolution in the young Russian nobility.[120]

Scholars have also noted references in Russian literature to French tutors and governesses in noble homes. In both autobiographical material and fictional literature, disrespectful reference to French tutors is a common theme for a number of Russian authors including Aleksandr Pushkin, Mikhail Lermontov, and Aleksandr Herzen.[121] The comical, bumbling foreigner is a familiar stock character. One literary expert notes the remarkable similarity, for example, between Pushkin's fictional tutor in *Eugene Onegin* and the one described by Aleksandr Radishchev's in *Journey from St. Petersburg to Moscow*.[122] In her recent dissertation, Ulrike Lentz compared historical sources such as memoirs related to foreign tutors and governesses with their treatment in Russian literature.[123] Though they were actually quite complex individuals who were important to the upbringing of noble Russian children, European tutors and governesses are portrayed in Russian literature as marginal and one-dimensional characters. Pushkin's depiction of a foreign employee in his poem *Count Nulin* is indicative of this kind of treatment. Count Nulin's French valet, Picard, is referenced only peripherally, dressing the count, wishing him well as he goes out, bringing him a cigar in the evening, and so forth. He is an auxiliary figure whose presence merely contributes to the description of the frivolous pomp of the Count, who talks about the latest fashions and how he misses Paris.[124] Lentz concluded that European educators and servants fulfilled

---

[120] V.S. Parsamov, *Dekabristy i Frantsiia* (Moscow: Rossiiskii Gosudarstvennyi Gumanitarnyi Universitet, 2010), p. 10.

[121] Leonid Ignatieff, 'French Émigrés in Russia after the French Revolution. French Tutors', *Canadian Slavonic Papers*, 8 (1966), 125–131.

[122] Roderick Page Thaler, 'The French Tutor in Radishchev and Pushkin', *The Russian Review*, 3 (1954), 210–212.

[123] Ulrike Lentz, 'The Representation of Western European Governesses and Tutors on the Russian Country Estate in Historical Documents and Literary Texts' (unpublished doctoral thesis, University of Surrey, 2008).

[124] Alexander Pushkin, *Count Nulin*, trans. by Anthony D. Briggs, *Slavic Review*, 26 (1967), 286–294.

a literary role as a type and qualifier, but also a societal role as Russia dealt with its own crisis of national identity. These identity issues, according to Lentz, were related to feelings of cultural inferiority, and the European 'other' was used as a foil in one's own search for Russianness.

The possibility cannot be ignored, however, that French tutors had gained a negative reputation before the French Revolution because so many of them were really quite poor. It has already been noted that many French wanderers of lower professional quality were to be found in Russia in the last half of the eighteenth century. Because of the high demand for French tutors in Russian society, it is not inconceivable that a number of Frenchmen would pass for language teachers who would be perfectly unqualified for such a position in their native country. D. J. Welsh has suggested that it is this very phenomenon, all too common in the last half of the eighteenth century, which is portrayed in satirical comedies of the day. A foreign teacher who is unqualified and dishonest produces a silly Russian pupil who is enthralled with all things French without really having an education to show for it.[125]

After the French Revolution, Ignatieff and Lentz both affirmed that there was a marked improvement in the quality of French language instruction provided by the educated refugees who had fled France. Stereotypes from earlier generations remained, and émigrés working as tutors 'experienced the combined effects of humiliation, abasement, nostalgia, and otherness.'[126] These stereotypes, however, were no longer generally accurate. 'Even the worst of the teachers and tutors found in Russia at the end of the eighteenth and beginning of the nineteenth centuries were better than the earlier type of French instructor who was well symbolized by Pushkin's Monsieur Beaupré.'[127] The literary analyses of Welsh, Ignatieff, and Lentz all allude to an important set of

---

[125] Welsh, 'Satirical Themes in Eighteenth-Century Russian Comedies', 411–414.

[126] Andre Liebich, '"Maitres a l'epee, Maitres a danser, Maitres a penser": Founding French National Consciousness in Russian Exile', *Canadian Slavonic Papers*, 49 (2007), 27–47 (p. 39.)

[127] Ignatieff, 'French Émigrés in Russia after the French Revolution. French Tutors', 130.

considerations toward an historical understanding of Franco-Russian cultural transfer: the disparity between the calibre of French tutors and other cultural mentors available in Russia before and after the French Revolution and lingering Russian stereotypes about French immigrants. This disparity will be explored systematically and in greater empirical detail in the present study through examination of more fact-based primary sources including archival records and employment advertisements.

A final aspect of this incoming wave of French influence that historians have highlighted as a result of the French Revolution was the influx of French property. Works of fine art, furniture, and French books were purchased by Catherine II and other noble Russian families. These were items that had been transported out of France by fleeing nobility, who sought to rescue their personal property from destruction and ended up selling many items from their personal collections in Russia.[128]

The high level of French-language proficiency among the Russian upper classes in the late eighteenth and early nineteenth century is illustrated by the written materials which they left behind. Kelly Herold's study of Russian French-language memoirs and autobiographical novels indicates that this short-lived genre flourished in the years 1770 – 1830.[129] From her study of the French vocabulary, syntax, and style of these works, Herold concluded that the Russians who wrote them appear to have been heavily influenced by French memoirs they had read. In turn, this brief French-language memoir tradition would influence later Russian-language political memoirs like those written by Mikhail Glinka and Aleksandr Herzen.

At this point, it becomes necessary to articulate an obvious fact that has silently underscored the entire discussion thus far: most if not all of these French influences essentially impacted only the upper social classes of the Russian population. The

---

[128] Ibid., 166.

[129] Kelly Herold, 'Russian Autobiographical Literature in French: Recovering a Memoiristic Tradition (1770 – 1830)' (unpublished doctoral dissertation, University of California, Los Angeles, 1998).

cultural gap between common Russians and the noble elite was stark at this time.

Peter's reforms—for all practical purposes the beginning of westernization in Russia—

had essentially only changed the lives of the nobility. Elizabeth's French extravagance

and Catherine's copy of Versailles were hidden behind walls of the imperial court,

utterly inaccessible to the masses of commoners. As the voice of the Russian peasant is

often inaudible to history, it is easy to forget that much of the discussion of Russian

culture—including French influence upon it—really depicts a narrow segment of the

population. There are rare glimpses into the world of the peasants, and these strengthen

the argument that theirs was a very different world, culturally. For example, the French

author Jacques-Henri-Bernardin de Saint-Pierre, while traveling in Russia, took note of

people in various societal classes and was 'astounded', as Mosakowski summarizes, by

'the passivity of the Russians and their unconditional obedience to their despotic rulers.

Saint-Pierre deplored the lack of individuality of these people and their fatalistic

perception of the world, so different from the Western spirit of freedom.'[130] By

contrast, French visitors to Russia in the last half of the eighteenth century would have

observed that the 'Russian upper classes were almost as French in spirit as native

Parisians' and indicated as much in their memoirs.[131] Herold observed that use of the

French language served as a sort of 'caste language' to set apart the very small Russian

aristocracy from the general population, beginning in the 1760s and 70s.[132] Isabel de

Madariaga cautioned, however, against the typical exaggeration that there was,

throughout the reign of Catherine II, a 'total cultural incomprehension' between the

---

[130] Mosakowski, 'Image of Russia in Eighteenth-Century French Literature', p. 190. Here, Marshall Poe's aforementioned warning about the subjectivity of foreign visitors should be considered. For a more complete view of the Russian peasantry, see David Moon, *The Russian Peasantry, 1600–1930: The World the Peasants Made* (London: Longman, 1999).

[131] Mosakowski, 'Image of Russia in Eighteenth-Century French Literature', p. 173.

[132] Herold, 'Russian Autobiographical Literature in French', p. 5, n6.

classes. Still, she admitted that western influence contributed to a 'cultural gulf which now began to separate the Russian nobles from their peasantry.'[133]

The Russian nobility have been the primary focus of the historiography of French cultural influence in Russia. This emphasis has remained consistent over four decades of study related to French immigration to Russia and continues in the University of Bristol's recent project on the French language in Russia.[134] In one sense, this is natural since the elite of society were more likely to retain the services of foreign teachers and servants. This is also a question of sources, however, as it was a particular stratum of society that left behind the memoirs and other literature analyzed in these studies. The study of French immigration in chapter three of this dissertation broadens this discussion to include more detail about the immigrants themselves and their wider interaction with Russian society, drawing from police records and other government documents.

The era of 1812

Naturally, much of the scholarship on Russian interaction with Napoleonic France has focused more on battles than cultural influence.[135] There is, however, a growing literature on the cultural impact of the war and especially Russia's collective memory of the same in subsequent generations. In Russian, the essays of A. G. Tartakovskii—

---

[133] Isabel de Madariaga, *Russia in the Age of Catherine the Great* (New Haven and London: Yale University Press, 1981), p. 557.

[134] <http://www.bristol.ac.uk/arts/research/french-in-russia/> [accessed 2 July 2015]

[135] Chief among them are Dominic Lieven, *Russia Against Napoleon: The Battle for Europe, 1807 to 1814* (London: Allen Lane, 2009); Adam Zamoyski, *Moscow 1812: Napoleon's Fatal March* (London: HarperCollins, 2004); and Armand de Caulaincourt, *With Napoleon in Russia* (Mineola: Dover Publications, 2005); Also, in honor of the bicentennial of the war with Napoleon, an excellent two-volume encyclopedia of the Russian army's foreign campaigns—a topic that has previously received much less attention than the 1812 invasion of Moscow—has been published: V. M. Bezotosnyi and others, eds, *Zagranichnye pokhody rossiiskoi armii, 1813 – 1815 gody: entsiklopediia* (Moscow: Rosspen, 2011).

Russia's leading historian of memoir literature from the period—are noteworthy.[136]

Tartakovskii has explored the importance of the genre in the development of Russian

literature and national consciousness, rather than simply 'mining' the memoirs for

information about the war. Among western historians, Marc Raeff has written on the

broader implications of 1812 for Russian society.[137] According to Raeff, there is a

sense in which the war with Napoleon in the early nineteenth century began to bridge

the aforementioned gap between the classes. Nobleman and commoner alike were

caught up in the swell of patriotic fervour in Russia, and among the new civic

sensitivities to be inspired in some highborn Russian officers during the war was their

'discovery' of the noble peasant alongside whom they fought.

A wealth of recent studies examining nineteenth-century Russian literature and

visual art have argued that the legacy of 1812 continued to impact Russian culture long

after the events themselves. During the reign of Nicholas I, for example, the

aforementioned appreciation of the peasantry was expressed in the idea of *narodnost'*,

and artistic portrayal of the 1812 campaign highlighted the sacrificial contribution of the

common man.[138] This episode in the history of Russia's interaction with France is

significant, not only because a common French enemy brought the nobility and

peasantry temporarily closer together, but because of the more direct exposure to the

West provided to Russia's lower classes.

In 2003, an exhibition of early nineteenth century art was opened under the joint

patronage of the presidents of France and the Russian Federation in honour of St.

Petersburg's three hundredth anniversary. This particular exhibition showcased the

---

[136] The following titles were all written or edited by A. G. Tartakovskii: *1812 god* (Moscow: Sovetskaia Rossiia, 1990); *1812 god v vospominaniiakh sovremennikov* (Moscow: Nauka, 1995); *Russkaia memuaristika i istoricheskoe soznanie XIX veka* (Moscow: Arkheograficheskii tsentr, 1997).

[137] Marc Raeff, 'At the Origins of a Russian National Consciousness: Eighteenth-Century Roots and Napoleonic Wars', *The History Teacher*, 25 (1991), 7–18 (pp. 12–13.)

[138] Andrew Michael Nedd, 'Defending Russia: Russian History and Pictorial Narratives of the "Patriotic War," 1812 – 1912' (unpublished doctoral dissertation, University of Southern California, 2005), pp. 136–137.

longstanding cultural connection between Russia and France and argued that 'the war with Napoleon was the main event of Russian history of the nineteenth century.'[139] The ironic effect of this historical episode upon Russia in the many generations since 1812 is that 'as the cult of Napoleon was strengthened, the traditional love for French culture increased immensely.'[140] In her study of Russian literary culture, Molly Wesling asserted that Napoleon Bonaparte is ever-present in Russia's self-awareness as an iconic image.[141] In the immediate era of the invasion he personified evil itself. In later romantic treatment he was associated with democracy and liberation. According to one scholar, nineteenth-century Russian literature vacillated between visions of Napoleon as either a Great Man or a tyrant.[142]

Whereas earlier interest in all things French was basically restricted to upper class, the 1812 invasion demanded the attention of an entire nation and feelings were stirred at different levels of society. Michael Pesenson's analysis of political journals, sermons, poems, and Old Believer tracts reveals that apocalyptic discourse of the day at the popular level portrayed Napoleon as the antichrist.[143] According to Pesenson, 'Russians increasingly came to believe that they were charged with ridding Europe of the "Gallic Beast" and ushering in a new age of peace and prosperity' which many, including the Tsar, believed 'would precipitate the Second Coming of Christ.'[144] This is just one example of how scholars have seen in the struggle against Napoleon an important symbol in Russia's emerging national consciousness.

Apart from the mystique surrounding the person of Napoleon, recent studies have also discussed the direct cultural interactions with France facilitated by the war

---

[139] Natal'ia Zolotova, *Parizh—Sankt-Peterburg 1800 – 1830: kogda Rossiia govorila po-frantsuzski*, (Moscow: Interros, 2003), p. 13.
[140] Ibid.
[141] Molly W. Wesling, *Napoleon in Russian Cultural Mythology* (New York: P. Lang, 2001).
[142] R. A. Peace, 'The Napoleonic Theme in Russian Literature', in *The Impact of the French Revolution on European Consciousness*, ed. by H.T. Mason and W. Doyle (Gloucester: Alan Sutton, 1989), pp. 47–63.
[143] Michael A. Pesenson, 'Napoleon Bonaparte and Apocalyptic Discourse in Early Nineteenth-Century Russia', *The Russian Review*, 65 (2006), 373–392.
[144] Ibid., 392.

and the implications of this interaction for Russia's development. Yitzhak Tarasulo's

dissertation argued that Napoleon's invasion shook the very social structure of Russia

by threatening the institution of serfdom.[145] Russian nobles were worried that Napoleon

would free the Russian serfs and incite them against the Tsar. Tarasulo studied peasant

uprisings against their landlords in Belorussia, Smolensk, and the Moscow region

during this period of instability associated with the French invasion, and concluded that

such uprisings were indeed more prevalent where French occupation lasted longer.

Tarasulo also explored peasant attacks on French soldiers inside of Russia, ultimately

challenging the notion of this being a 'people's war' in which commoners

spontaneously rallied to the national cause. Of course Napoleon did not emancipate the

serfs, nor is there evidence that incidents of uprising were much more than the

consequence of a general state of instability. Nevertheless, these studies speak to some

interaction between common Russians and Napoleon's army, some of whom would

have been French. Finally, the invasion was another indirect source of foreign

immigration. There is some evidence from private letters that some French prisoners of

war found employment in Russian homes.[146]

Napoleon's invasion of Russia sparked a movement of patriotism and national

pride in Russia, which was accompanied by a general anti-French sentiment in society.

According to Molly Wesling, because of their traditional love of French officers,

novels, and clothing, Russian noblewomen were actually regarded for a time as 'a threat

to national security.'[147] Many Russian noblewomen exchanged their French dresses for

garments reminiscent of Russian folk costumes,[148] there was a very temporary wane in

---

[145] Yitzhak Tarasulo, 'The Napoleonic Invasion of 1812 and the Political and Social Crisis in Russia' (unpublished doctoral dissertation, Yale University, 1983).

[146] Wesling, *Napoleon in Russian Cultural Mythology*, p. 2.

[147] Ibid., p. 11.

[148] Raisa Kirsanova, 'Russia: Urban Dress up to the End of the Nineteenth Century', in Joanne Eicher, Djurdja Bartlett, and Pamela Smith (eds.), *Berg Encyclopedia of World Dress and Fashion* (New York: Berg, 2010), vol. IX, pp. 340–341.

the popularity of studying the French language,[149] St. Petersburg's French theatre troupe was disbanded by imperial order,[150] and the theme of 'Fatherland' appeared in the writings of Russian nobles and national propaganda inspired by German romanticism and in some cases actually written by Germans.[151] Count Fedor Rostopchin, Moscow's governor during the invasion, was particularly vehement in his hatred of Francophilia.[152] His anti-French propaganda broadsheets [*afishi*] are legendary, and there is even record of one incident where he presided over a brutal mob action, the lethal mauling of a Russian man with pro-French leanings.[153]

Because of the war's importance both politically and as an iconic epoch in Russia's discovery of her national identity, other cultural factors of the 1812 period have received less attention. French cultural influence is largely ignored in most scholarship apart from the acknowledgement of the *previous generation's* importation of French culture, the remnants of which was temporarily demonized by official propaganda. The absence of a discussion of *new* cultural importation in so vast a body of scholarship on this period represents a significant historiographical gap. The cultural analysis of military memoirs in chapter four of this dissertation contributes to filling this gap.

The making of the Decembrists

Historians have not, however, deduced from this that French cultural influence was at an end in Russia. A study of Russian memoirs during 1807 – 1814 reveals that even during this period, attitudes towards the French and their culture was not unanimously

---

¹⁴⁹ Lentz, 'The Representation of Western European Governesses and Tutors on the Russian Country Estate', p. 23.
¹⁵⁰ Ignatieff, 'French Émigrés in Russia, 1789 – 1825: The Interaction of Cultures in Time of Stress', p. 174.
¹⁵¹ Tarasulo, 'The Napoleonic Invasion of 1812 and the Political and Social Crisis in Russia', p. 98.
¹⁵² Liebich, '"Maitres a l'epee, Maitres a danser, Maitres a penser": Founding French National Consciousness in Russian Exile', 31.
¹⁵³ Wesling, *Napoleon in Russian Cultural Mythology*, p.17.

negative and there was a clear distinction between military opposition and cultural appreciation which ultimately continued.[154] Further, the dip in popularity of learning the French language was only temporary and foreign tutors would continue to be *en vogue* in Russia into the twentieth century, only to be curbed by the events and aftermath of 1917.[155] French influence had not disappeared. In fact, in some ways it became more profound. John Keep has partially credited the Russian war with Napoleon with helping to advance the notion of moderate reforms inside of Russia.[156] Russian officers brought revolutionary ideas back with them from France, their moral sensitivities had been awakened, and the idea of civic duty—at least partly inspired by their interaction with French society—was an important part of the patriotic spirit. Some of the key Decembrist leaders who would cry out for constitutional government in Russia in 1825 had been officers in France between 1814 and 1818.[157] According to John Keep, ideas of revolutionary reform *a la Français* came to Russia through the army itself, indirectly and in a delayed fashion.[158] The large military build-up in reaction to the French Revolution created an army that was burdensome for the Russian economy, and there was growing dissent under Alexander I because of some service conditions within the army. Russian officers encountered western democratic ideas while in France and these contributed to a cry for reform that resonated in a special way from the army. The war with Napoleon had involved millions of Russian civilians, patriotism was on the rise as were the moral sensitivities of officers, and the western models encountered by them in Europe were often used to rationalize these feelings.

---

[154] Marie-Christiane Torrance, 'Some Russian Attitudes to France in the Period of the Napoleonic Wars as Revealed by Russian Memoirs', *Proceedings of the Royal Irish Academy. Section C: Archeology, Celtic Studies, History, Linguistics, Literature,* 86C (1986), 289–303.

[155] Lentz, 'The Representation of Western European Governesses and Tutors on the Russian Country Estate', p. 23.

[156] John Keep, 'The Russian Army's Response to the French Revolution', *Jahrbücher für Geschichte Osteuropas,* 28 (1980), 500–523.

[157] W. Bruce Lincoln, 'A Re-examination of Some Historical Stereotypes: An Analysis of the Career Patterns and Backgrounds of the Decembrists', *Jahrbücher für Geschichte Osteuropas,* 3 (1976), 357 – 368; Janet M. Hartley, *Alexander I* (London: Longman, 1994), p. 205.

[158] John Keep, 'The Russian Army's Response to the French Revolution', 500 – 523.

In contrast to more generalized studies of the Decembrists and their European influences such as those by Anatole Mazour,[159] M. V. Nechika,[160] Patrick O'Meara and others,[161] V. S. Parsamov's recent work has traced the influence of specific French writers, philosophers and publicists on the thought and actions of the Decembrists Turgenev, Pestel', Murav'ev, Lunin, Orlov, Bariatinskii, and Davydov.[162] Parsamov affirms that the Decembrists had come into contact with enlightened ideas because of their first-hand impressions of 'civilized' France as officers in the Napoleonic war. R. A. Peace also mentioned the effect of direct exposure to western political ideals upon those Russians stationed in Europe. Comparing these events to the previous generation's cultural developments, he asserted that 'direct contact with the West had grafted radical, social and political ideas on to the Russian soul more effectively than the foreign empress Catherine had been able to do in the previous century, and when these officers came back to Russia, they formed debating societies and secret revolutionary groups, starting a movement which led to the Decembrist uprising of 1825.'[163]

The memoirs of Russian officers during this campaign reveal generally positive impressions, and some were sorry to leave when it was time to return home. Many of the young Russian soldiers who returned home in 1814 had been affected by their time abroad, some bringing French wives home with them.[164] Among the impressions

---

[159] Anatole G. Mazour, *The First Russian Revolution, 1825: The Decembrist Movement, Its Origins, Development, and Significance* (Stanford: Stanford University Press, 1964).

[160] M. V. Nechkina, *Dekabristy* (Moscow: Nauka, 1983).

[161] Patrick O'Meara, *The Decembrist Pavel Pestel* (New York: Palgrave Macmillan, 2003); G. R. V. Barratt, *Voices in Exile: The Decembrist Memoirs* (Montreal: McGill-Queen's University Press, 1974); S. N. Chernov, *Pavel Pestel': Izbrannye stat'i po istorii dekabrizma* (St. Petersburg: Liki Rossii, 2004).

[162] V.S. Parsamov, *Dekabristy i Frantsiia* (Moscow: Rossiiskii Gosudarstvennyi Gumanitarnyi Universitet, 2010).

[163] R. A. Peace, 'The Napoleonic Theme in Russian Literature', in *The Impact of the French Revolution on European Consciousness,* ed. by H. T. Mason and W. Doyle (Gloucester: Alan Sutton, 1989), pp. 48–49.

[164] Regarding this formative influence upon the Decembrists, see M. V. Nechkina, *Dekabristy* (Moscow: Nauka, 1983), pp. 18 – 20; and Patrick O'Meara, *The Decembrist Pavel Pestel* (New York: Palgrave Macmillan, 2003), pp. 18 – 19; G. R. V. Barratt, *Voices in Exile: The Decembrist Memoirs* (Montreal: McGill-Queen's University Press, 1974), pp. 142 – 150; and a very focused recent study, V. S. Parsamov, *Dekabristy i Frantsiia* (Moscow: *Rossiiskii gosudarstvennyi gumanitarnyi universitet*, 2010).

gleaned by Marie-Christiane Torrance from her study of these memoirs were observations about the prosperity of French merchants and artisans, the fact that a good portion of the middle class was literate, and administrative and organizational systems that were superior to the ones they had back home.[165] As the time of their departure drew closer, many Russian soldiers deserted the army, presumably hoping for a better life in France. Others who did return home with the victorious Russian army had been changed by their time in France. One memoir reports that they were now 'reading foreign newspapers and games of chess had replaced, amongst the younger soldiers, the drinking bouts and games of cards of previous years.'[166] It was not just officers and regular troops who were affected by direct contact with French culture. One historian writes that even the common masses of Russian militia [*opolchenie*] 'had an adequate look at foreigners.' These 'returned to their homes, in which they recounted what they had seen in Europe.'[167]

T. A. Shanskaia has studied the reception among Russian nobility of French culture during the reign of Alexander I (1801 – 1825) and concluded that attitudes varied.[168] Significant contradictions can be found, even within writings of individual Russian authors, which speaks to a culture that was conflicted during this period. In the eighteenth century, the nobility strove to obtain French culture and join Europe. The Russian nobility of the early nineteenth century had achieved this and were steeped in French culture but now faced a crisis of self-identification as Russians, especially in light of the events of the French Revolution and 1812 invasion. This generation of noble Russians had been immersed in French culture from childhood, grew up in homes

---

[165] Marie-Christiane Torrance, 'Some Russian Attitudes to France in the Period of the Napoleonic Wars as Revealed by Russian Memoirs', *Proceedings of the Royal Irish Academy. Section C: Archeology, Celtic Studies, History, Linguistics, Literature,* 86C (1986), 289–303.

[166] Ibid., 300–302.

[167] Raymond T. McNally, 'The Origins of Russophobia in France: 1812 – 1830', *Slavic and East European Review,* 17 (1958), 173–189 (p. 180.)

[168] T.A. Shanskaia, 'Vospriiatie frantsuzskoi kul'tury russkim dvorianstvom (pervaia chetvert' XIX veka)' (unpublished doctoral dissertation, Kazan State University, 2001).

where they were surrounding by French décor, spoke the French language fluently, had been reared by French governesses and cherished French books. The ideals, refined tastes, and elegant manners of 'Old France' were ingrained in them. The clash with 'New France' that they found themselves in spawned an emotional crisis for self-identity. The simple question of how to feel about France was quite complicated as cultural sensitivities and political realities were suddenly at odds. Shanskaia concluded that the official ideology of the Russian state vis-à-vis France was ultimately ineffective, having indirect influence upon societal opinion at best. Maya Gubina, who has studied the memoirs of those Russians who remained in Moscow during the 1812 invasion, summarized this conflict as aristocratic Russians' struggle with both the external and internal 'other.'[169] Despite their patriotic pride and hard feelings against the French, they could not escape the fact that they themselves were saturated with the culture of the invader. In short, 1812 was 'forcing the Russians to ask themselves searching questions about their own identity.'[170]

This corporate introspection about what it truly meant to be Russian would be seen for generations to come. Art historian Andrew Nedd's recent dissertation analyzed Russian artistic representation of the 'Patriotic War' of 1812 in the century immediately following Napoleon's invasion.[171] According to Nedd, the various portraits and military prints that he examined visually chart the course of Russia's evolving self-identity. Throughout this process, Napoleon and France are the foil against which Russian society pushes in search of 'Russianness.' Over the course of the century the core ideas of this identity would shift from an idealization of Tsar and Orthodoxy to the eventual focus on the people [*narod*] as the common unifier. Alexander Martin has suggested

---

[169] Maya Gubina, 'The Year 1812: The Discovery of What Kind of Other?', in *Other Voices: Three Centuries of Cultural Dialogue between Russia and Western Europe,* ed. by Graham Roberts (Newcastle upon Tyne: Cambridge Scholars, 2011), pp. 178–188.

[170] Ibid., 186.

[171] Andrew Michael Nedd, 'Defending Russia: Russian History and Pictorial Narratives of the "Patriotic War," 1812 – 1912' (unpublished doctoral dissertation, University of Southern California, 2005).

that 1812 had a two-sided effect on Russian society. While acknowledging the validity of the opinion that 1812 had a liberalizing effect—temporarily bringing well-born officers and common soldiers closer together, inspiring the democratic notions of future Decembrists, the founding of a Bible Society, and so forth—Martin also argued for an 'illiberal' legacy of the events of 1812: heightened xenophobia in Russian society, militarism, and a felt need for a strong central government to protect Russia from external threats.[172]

The 'long' nineteenth century

Historians have likewise noted the European contribution to the rise of the Russian intelligentsia in the 1830s and 1840s. Following the failed Decembrist uprising, it was clear that outright dissident action was not a viable option for freethinkers in Nicholas I's Russia. A rapidly developing printing and publishing industry, however, resulted in many new literary journals during this period which provided an outlet for educated Russians to express social, philosophical, and even political opinions, particularly those related to the question of Russia's national identity.[173] According to Gary Hamburg, 'the most crucial immediate stimulus for rethinking the Russian question' was the *Lettres philosophiques* of Petr Chaadaev, the first of which was published in 1836. [174] Chaadaev's shocking essay, originally written in French and suggesting that Russia was backward, barbaric, and had not yet taken her place among the civilized nations of the world, caused an immediate reaction and is widely regarded among historians as an important catalyst for Russian philosophical discourse.[175] The author himself was

---

[172] Alexander Martin, 'Russia and the Legacy of 1812', in *The Cambridge History of Russia*, ed. By Dominic Lieven, 3 vols (Cambridge: Cambridge University Press, 2006), II, pp. 145 – 162.
[173] David Saunders, *Russia in the Age of Reaction and Reform, 1801 – 1881* (London: Longman, 1992), pp. 148 – 172.
[174] Gary M. Hamburg, 'Russian Political Thought', in *The Cambridge History of Russia*, ed. By Dominic Lieven, 3 vols (Cambridge: Cambridge University Press, 2006), II, p. 126
[175] Robin Aizlewood, 'Revisiting Russian Identity in Russian Thought: From Chaadaev to the Early Twentieth Century', *The Slavonic and East European Review*, 78 (2000), 20 – 43.

pronounced insane by the state, but other young intellectuals began actively publishing their own views about Russia's history, place in the world, and best hopes for future development. Two opposing streams of thought emerged, proponents of which came to be known as Westernizers and Slavophiles respectively.[176] The Westernizers, such as Aleksandr Herzen, Vissarion Belinskii and Mikhail Bakunin wished to see Russia join the community of European nations and hoped for 'western' improvements in Russia such as democratic reforms and technological advancement. Slavophiles, on the other hand, such as Aleksei Khomiakov, Konstantin Aksakov, and Ivan Kireevskii wished to protect Russia from western corruption, and valued tradition, the wholesomeness of the Russian peasant, and the strength of their Eastern Orthodox faith.

The philosophical underpinnings of this polemical exchange were not, however, as directly connected to France as the cultural emulation of previous generations had been. Even the traditional nomenclature used to describe the movement bespeaks a more general European orientation in the nineteenth century. In the eighteenth century, fashionable nobles were afflicted with 'gallomania', but the nineteenth-century intellectuals philosophically opposite the Slavophiles are referred to more generically as 'Westernizers.' In fact, the greatest direct foreign philosophical influence upon both sides of the Westernizer-Slavophile debate was not French but German, especially the work of Georg Wilhelm Friedrich Hegel and his historiographical notion of the great destiny of 'historical' versus 'unhistorical' nations.[177] Herzen, for example— considered the father of Russian socialism—was proficient in both German and French

---

[176] Sergey Horujy, 'Slavophiles, Westernizers, and the Birth of Russian Philosophical Humanism', in *A History of Russian Philosophy, 1830 – 1930: Faith, Reason, and the Defense of Human Dignity*, ed. by G. M. Hamburg and Randall A. Poole (Cambridge: Cambridge University Press, 2010), pp. 27 – 51.

[177] Ana Siljak, 'Between East and West: Hegel and the Origins of the Russian Dilemma', *Journal of the History of Ideas*, 62 (2001), 335 – 358; Russell Bova, ed., *Russia and Western Civilization: Cultural and Historical Encounters* (New York: Routledge, 2015), pp. 32 – 51; Nicholas Riasanovsky, *Russian Identities: A Historical Survey* (Oxford: Oxford University Press, 2005), pp. 151 – 161.

and his university education was philosophically steeped in German idealism.[178] While there were French influences upon Herzen—some exposure to the writings of French socialists just after university, meeting Louis Blanc and other French socialists after emigrating to Europe in 1847, and being an eyewitness to the 1848 revolution in Paris— these experiences contributed as much disappointment as they did inspiration to Herzen's process of formulating truly Russian applications of socialist thought.[179] Nevertheless, the earlier 'French notions' of enlightenment, progress and democracy were important preliminary concepts to the debate about the place of Russia's identity between East and West, though it was argued largely within Hegelian categories.[180]

Nevertheless, when the Russian intelligentsia began developing its various ideas of what was best for Russian society in the mid-nineteenth century, some of these groups did look again to France for inspiration. Though by no means pervasive at this time, there was a strain of Russian social thought that would be directly affected by French socialism. In her study of the Petrashevtsy, a literary circle of political thinkers in St. Petersburg, J. H. Seddon marked the particular influence of French thought on this group.[181] The Petrashevtsy read everything written by French socialists of the 1840s. Their so called 'collective libraries' provided members with access to ideas that were considered radical at the time, in particular those found in the writings of Charles Fourier and Henri de Saint-Simon. Particularly affected by the ideas of Fourier, the Petrashevskii Circle digested French socialist thought and then adapted it to something applicable to Russia. The philosophical influence of these authors can be seen in Petrashevskii's *Pocket Dictionary of Foreign Words* (1845 – 1846) which was

---

[178] Martin Malia, *Alexander Herzen and the Birth of Russian Socialism* (New York: Grosset and Dunlap, 1971).

[179] Edward Acton, *Alexander Herzen and the Role of the Intellectual Revolutionary* (Cambridge: Cambridge University Press, 1979).

[180] Elise Kimerling Wirtschafter, 'The Groups Between: Raznochintsy Intelligentsia, Professionals', in *The Cambridge History of Russia*, ed. by Dominic Lieven, 3 vols (Cambridge: Cambridge University Press, 2006), II, pp. 245 – 263.

[181] J. H. Seddon, *The Petrashevtsy: a Study of the Russian Revolutionaries of 1848* (Dover, NH: Manchester University Press, 1985), pp. 46–74.

condemned as 'subversive' because of the political sentiments in some of the definition articles.[182] According to Seddon, by 1849, they had 'come a long way towards forming a Russian socialism adapted to Russian needs.'[183] These were the first Russians to give serious thoughtful treatment to socialism. Seddon concluded that the Petrashevtsy were more important than many have realized and that there were more of them than previously thought.[184] Their pragmatic conception of Russian socialism, roughly based on the French model, marks an important chapter in Russia's political history, though there has been relatively little scholarly interest in this generation of revolutionaries.

As these developments continued, the relationship between Russian political ideology and Western Europe would be a complicated one. According to Ezequiel Adamovsky, some nineteenth century French liberals were mistakenly talking about an emerging communism in Russia long before there was any noticeable socialist movement there. Prominent French thinkers such as Alexis de Tocqueville, Gustave de Beaumont, Jules Michelet, Henri Martin, and Saint-René Taillandier all imagined tsarist Russia as communist in the last half of the nineteenth century. Once such political ideas did in fact take hold later in Russia, however, their connection with European movements was negligible. George Nicoll has studied the relationship of the international socialist movement—particularly the Second International, established in Paris in 1889—and the Russian radicalism of the late nineteenth and early twentieth century.[185] According to Nicoll, Russian participation in the Second International was not significant. Russia would eventually follow its own path and later establish different unions under around Russian control. In a sense, Russia's revolutionary philosophers were loath to admit the foreign origin of their political ideology. In his

---

[182] F. M. Bartholomew, 'V.N. Maykov and the Karmannyy slovar' inostrannykh slov', *The Slavonic and East European Review*, 62 (1984), 85–97.

[183] Seddon, *The Petrashevtsy: a Study of the Russian Revolutionaries of 1848*, p. 74.

[184] J. H. Seddon, 'The Petrashevtsy: a Reappraisal', *Slavic Review*, 43 (1984), 434–452.

[185] George Nicoll, 'Russian Participation in the Second International' (unpublished doctoral dissertation, Boston University, 1961).

famous *History of Russian Social Thought,* Marxist theorist Georgii Plekhanov (1856 –
1918)—while acknowledging Western influence—goes to great lengths to prove truly
Russian roots of Soviet ideology.[186] Plekhanov argued that Soviet ideology predates
Western influences, and he reached all the way back to the reforms of Peter the Great
and the educated advisors in Peter's 'Learned Guard' to explain the origin of Russian
social thought. However, for all his Russification of Soviet political theory he cannot
resist looking to the West—especially France—as the standard for comparison, often
evoking images of the French Revolution in his arguments.

The French Revolution was being discussed by Russian thinkers of all political
and philosophical stripes in the period leading up to the Russian revolution. Dmitry
Shlapentokh, in his book on the subject, traced how different Russian intellectual groups
in the late nineteenth century viewed the French Revolution.[187] Conservatives saw the
French Revolution as an evil to be avoided. Liberals saw something positive in the
example of the revolution, and looked to this example as a cause for reform inside of
Russia. Russia's radicals looked to the French Revolution as the cultural root for a
literal political revolution which must come to pass in Russia. The conclusions and
ideologies of these three groups were all very different, but they were united by the fact
that they studied the French Revolution for perspective on Russia's future. In another
of his works, Shlapentokh remarks on how this intellectual tendency continued as
events escalated inside of Russia.[188] Drawing a parallel between Russia and
revolutionary France was widespread in the Russian Revolutionary period. As
intellectuals followed the unfolding of Russia's revolution, the rise of a 'Russian
Napoleon' was fully expected. (Would it be Aleksander Kerenskii, Lavr Kornilov, or

---

[186] G.V. Plekhanov, *History of Russian Social Thought,* trans. by Boris M. Bekkar and others (New York:
Fertig, 1967).

[187] Dmitry Shlapentokh, *The French Revolution in Russian Intellectual Life: 1865 – 1905* (Westport, CT:
Praeger, 1996).

[188] Dmitry Shlapentokh, *The Counter-Revolution in Revolution: Images of Thermidor and Napoleon at the
Time of Russian Revolution and Civil War* (New York: St. Martin's Press, 1999).

someone else?) The 'Russian Napoleon', of course, never appeared, but Shlapentokh has argued that the alternative histories of 'what might have been' are important for understanding the period.[189]

Not only political philosophers, but the revolutionary actors themselves were drawing these parallels before, during, and after the events of 1917.[190] According to George Jackson, Lenin looked to the French Revolution for philosophical inspiration and even tactical instruction, including his arguments in favour of using terror and the need for a strong centralized state.[191] Lenin often referred to events and key figures from revolutionary France in his speeches and written works. He asked his party to become 'the Jacobins of the Russian Revolution,' and in his 1902 treatise, *What is to be Done*, referred to the Bolsheviks as the 'Montagne' and the opposing party (later to be known as Mensheviks) as the 'Gironde.' Contrary to Marx, Lenin advocated the use of terror, and cited that of the French Revolution as a model.[192] In 1918, a couple of streets in St. Petersburg were renamed in honour of French revolutionary heroes, and statues of the French revolutionaries Georges Danton and Maximilien Robespierre were erected in Moscow.[193] In the early years of the new Soviet state, Lenin often referred to his political opponents as 'Bonapartists' and Trotskii is reported to have compared Lenin to Robespierre on at least one occasion.[194] Russia's theorists and practitioners of revolutionary communism believed that Karl Marx had discovered a 'science of history and revolution' which had its own 'laws' that could be applied universally. As participants in the continuation of a movement that was supposedly sweeping the world,

---

[189] Dmitry Shlapentokh, *The French Revolution and the Russian Anti-Democratic Tradition: a Case of False Consciousness* (New Brunswick: Transaction, 1997).

[190] John Keep, 'The Tyranny of Paris over Petrograd', *Soviet Studies*, 20 (1968), 22 – 35.

[191] George Jackson, 'The Influence of the French Revolution on Lenin's Conception of the Russian Revolution', in *The French Revolution of 1789 and Its Impact*, ed. by Gail M. Schwab and John R. Jeanneney (Westport: Greenwood Press, 1995), pp. 273 – 284.

[192] Ibid., 276 – 278.

[193] Gabriel Schoenfeld, 'Uses of the Past: Bolshevism and the French Revolutionary Tradition', in *The French Revolution of 1789 and Its Impact*, ed. by Gail M. Schwab and John R. Jeanneney (Westport: Greenwood Press, 1995), pp. 285 – 303.

[194] Ibid., 294.

Russian communists looked to the history of France as a way of 'gauging Russia's progress.'[195] Though the French Revolution was a major topic of discussion in late nineteenth- and early twentieth-century Russia, by the 1920s, Russian thinkers were looking to other historical images as parallels to make sense of Russia's destiny.[196]

As these studies suggest, historians have described the French Revolution as having a double impact upon Russia: its immediate impact came in the form of French émigrés who brought French culture with them, the direct interaction of Russian soldiers with French culture and ideas during the 1812 war, and the search for a Russian national identity that was in many ways spawned by the patriotic reaction to French culture in the 1812 era. The French Revolution then returned for a second round of influence during the rise of intellectual discourse in Russia in the nineteenth century. The spectre of late eighteenth-century France cast its shadow across various competing brands of political philosophy, and the contradictory voices which debated about Russia's future all used terminology from the French Revolution to state their case. Identification with events in France would continue at least into the 1920s.

Nineteenth-century foreign policy

As most historical studies of Franco-Russian relations have been diplomatic rather than cultural, it is worth mentioning diplomatic relations as a backdrop to the relatively few studies written specifically about cultural influence during this century. Barbara Jelavich has described Russian diplomacy in general during the period 1814 – 1914 as an effort to maintain the boundaries and prestige achieved by Russia at its 1815 peak as a continental power. Though citing a steady slackening in strength, Jelavich concludes that nineteenth-century Russian diplomacy was largely successful in this regard, not

---

[195] Ibid., p. 288.

[196] Dmitry Shlapentokh, *The French Revolution and the Russian Anti-Democratic Tradition: a Case of False Consciousness* (New Brunswick: Transaction, 1997).

only maintaining its western boundaries, but actually making territorial gains in Asia and the Far East.[197] Patricia Kennedy Grimsted likewise described a peak in Russian influence and prestige abroad during the reign of Alexander I, a level of influence that would be unparalleled for Russia until World War II.[198] In the decades following Alexander's triumph over Napoleon and the Russian delegation's participation in the Congress of Vienna which re-drew national borders and established the balance of European power for the foreseeable future, Russia would find herself sometimes allied with, sometimes opposed to France in various political conflicts.

The foreign policy of Nicholas I (r. 1825 – 1855) was characterized by conservatism and support for the 'legitimate' monarchs of Christian Europe. As such, he despised as a usurper Louis-Philippe who had assumed the throne of France after the Bourbon king Charles X was deposed in the July Revolution of 1830. Nicholas begrudgingly recognized Louis-Philippe as ruler months after other European leaders had already done so and maintained an anti-French attitude throughout his reign.[199] The Tsar's posture seems to have reduced at least some aspects of French influence in Russian society. When gathering research about cholera during the epidemic of the 1830s and 1840s, for example, the Russian government communicated with universities all over Europe except those of France. Likewise, when foreign railroad specialists were first invited to Russia during this period, Frenchmen were intentionally excluded.[200] According to Nicholas Riasanovsky, one of Russia's objectives in agreeing to the 1841 treaty barring foreign warships from the Turkish Straits which connect the Mediterranean and Black Seas—a strategic loss for Russia—was to

---

[197] Barbara Jelavich, *A Century of Russian Foreign Policy, 1814 – 1914* (Philadelphia: J. B. Lippincott Company, 1964).

[198] Patricia Kennedy Grimsted, *The Foreign Ministers of Alexander I: Political Attitudes and the Conduct of Russian Diplomacy, 1801 – 1825* (Berkeley: University of California Press, 1969), p. 3.

[199] Nicholas Riasanovsky, *Nicholas I and Official Nationality in Russia, 1825 – 1855* (Berkeley: University of California Press, 1959), pp. 241 – 260.

[200] Ibid., p. 255, n32.

'promote antagonism between Great Britain and France.'[201] Despite his hatred of Louis-Philippe, however, Nicholas opposed on matter of principle the 1848 revolt that overthrew him as well as condemning (and in some cases deploying Russian troops to quell) other popular uprisings across Europe during the same year.[202]

The Crimean War has been another popular area of historical study during this period. Despite Nicholas I's initially successful strategy of driving a diplomatic wedge between Great Britain and France in near eastern politics, when war finally erupted between Russian and Ottoman forces in 1853, British and French troops fought on the same side against Russia.[203] According to Orlando Figes, traditional reference to this conflict as the Crimean War is something of a geographical misnomer, as fighting between the Russian and Ottoman empires began in areas now part of Romania, later spread to the Caucasus and Crimea, and some of the grievances which led to the war included disputes as far away as Palestine.[204] According to Figes, whose history of the war particularly emphasizes the religious aspects of the conflict, French Catholics were concerned over an increase in the Russian Orthodox Church's influence at sacred sites in the Holy Land. Heated debates over this issue among Russian, French, and Ottoman officials are even cited among the issues leading to the Crimean war.[205] This complicated war, fought in multiple theatres in1853 – 1856 claimed the lives of hundreds of thousands of soldiers, the majority of whom were either Russian or French.[206] The outcome of the war—the final year of which Alexander II inherited from his late father—was a defeated and humiliated Russian empire.

David MacKenzie has described the need during Alexander II's early reign to construct a new foreign policy that would provide a respite during which to rebuild the

---

[201] Ibid., p. 245.

[202] Ibid., p. 236.

[203] Trevor Royle, *Crimea: The Great Crimean War, 1854 – 1856* (London: Abacus, 1999).

[204] Orlando Figes, *Crimea: The Last Crusade* (London: Penguin, 2010), pp. xx – xxi.

[205] David M. Goldfrank, *The Origins of the Crimean War* (New York: Routledge, 1994); Figes, *Crimea*, pp. 5 – 9.

[206] Figes, *Crimea*, p. xix.

Russian army and reestablish Russian prestige in Europe.[207] For this, Alexander was in need of an ally and he found one in Napoleon III of France. The informal entente with France from 1856 to 1863 marked a new period in Russian foreign relations, as it meant a departure from Nicholas I's categorical aversion to alliance with a liberal republic and steadfast support for the legitimate monarchs of Europe. During this period, Russia and France supported—either directly or tacitly by remaining neutral—a number of revolutionary movements in Central and Eastern Europe.[208] Russia sought to reassert its influence in the Balkans and repay Austria who was thought to have betrayed Russia by remaining neutral during the Crimean War after Russia had assisted Austria in suppressing revolution in Hungary in 1848.[209]

International alliances would take on new levels of significance later in the century, when the unification of Germany in 1871 recalibrated the balance of powers on the continent of Europe. George Kennan's study of relations between Russia and France in the period 1875 – 1890 traces the military, diplomatic, and economic developments which ultimately led to an official military alliance.[210] According to Kennan, the 1894 Franco-Russian alliance 'was without question one of the major components out of which the fateful situation of 1914 was constructed, and of particular importance as a factor' causing World War I.[211] This alliance and the Austro-German alliance which had formed in 1879 essentially became the two nuclei around which other European powers would gather to form the two opposing sides of the Great War.[212] The agreement stipulated that France and Russia would intervene militarily in the event that Germany or its proxy attacked either of them. Recent studies of World

---

[207] David MacKenzie, 'Russia's Balkan Policies Under Alexander II, 1855 – 1881', in *Imperial Russian Foreign Policy*, ed. by Hugh Ragsdale (Cambridge: Cambridge University Press, 1993), pp. 219 – 246.
[208] Jelavich, *A Century of Russian Foreign Policy*, pp. 133 – 136.
[209] MacKenzie, 'Russia's Balkan Policies', pp. 222 – 223.
[210] George F. Kennan, *The Decline of Bismarck's European Order* (Princeton: Princeton University Press, 1979).
[211] Ibid., p. 6.
[212] William Leonard Langer, *The Franco-Russian Alliance, 1890 – 1894* (Cambridge, MA: Harvard University Press, 1929).

War I have emphasized that Russia's role in the lead-up to the First World War was much greater than typically recognized by western histories, and also a key factor in Russia's own spiral towards revolution.[213]

Dietrich Geyer's analysis of the interrelation of Russia's domestic and foreign policy during the period 1860 – 1914 has suggested a strong connection between Franco-Russian economic ties during this period and the military alliance at the end of the century.[214] French capital investment in Russian industrial development was crucial during this period. According to Geyer, as a result of French handling of over half of all Russian securities and direct French investment in Russian industrial development, Russia was quickly becoming dependent upon French money markets in the 1890s.[215]

Twentieth century

During the period 1894 – 1914, historians have emphasized, French influence was financial in nature as French capital was particularly important to the Russian economy in the areas of mining and banking.[216] Certain Russian liberals were against a 1906 French loan, fearing that it would strengthen Nicholas II's position against the Duma. As a result of this loan, France would play an important role in influencing Russian foreign policy.[217] Other kinds of interaction between Russia and France were also significant, however, as Russian society approached the turn of the twentieth century. In the 1880s there had been a general enthusiasm among the French public for all things

---

[213] Dominic Lieven, *The End of Tsarist Russia: The March to World War I and Revolution* (New York: Viking, 2015); Sean McMeekin, *The Russian Origins of the First World War* (Cambridge, MA: Harvard University Press, 2011); Ronald Bobroff, *Roads to Glory: Late Imperial Russia and the Turkish Straits* (London: I. B. Tauris, 2006).

[214] Dietrich Geyer, *Russian Imperialism: The Interaction of Domestic and Foreign Policy, 1860 – 1914* (Leamington Spa: Berg, 1987), pp. 169 – 185.

[215] Ibid., p. 173.

[216] Olga Crisp, 'Some Problems of French Investment in Russian Joint-Stock Companies, 1894 – 1914', *The Slavonic and East European Review,* 35 (1956), 223–240.

[217] Olga Crisp, 'The Russian Liberals and the 1906 Anglo-French Loan to Russia', *The Slavonic and East European Review,* 39 (1961), 497–511.

Russian.[218] In particular, Dostoevskii's work was talked about and even emulated by some French writers. Many in France were looking to Russia culturally and even politically, as an ally against the rising threat of Germany. Likewise, tourism increasingly took Russians abroad to France. In her recent dissertation, E.V. Razvozzhaeva studied Russian tourist travel in France in the period 1885 – 1914 and has noted a close relationship between the two countries at the turn of the twentieth century.[219] Her sources from the period include passport and border-patrol documents, travel guides, personal travel diaries, the business records of travel agencies, postcards, and French and Russian periodical publications. Conversely, French people continued to travel to and settled in the Russian empire during the period. Through her study of, among other things, the first All-Russian Census of 1897, Patricia Herlihy observed that the city of Odessa was remarkable for its rapid expansion and cultural diversity.[220] While the French population was relatively small in Odessa at this time (0.3% of the total population), French culture was influential. The Duke de Richelieu, appointed by Alexander I in 1803 as governor of Odessa, had made his mark as had his successors. Herlihy reported numerous French-origin governesses, small industry owners, viticulturists, and transient engineers in Odessa during this period.

In her dissertation on Franco-Russian cultural exchange in the twentieth century, N. O. Shiralieva has shown that active cultural dialogue between the two countries persisted throughout the entire century, despite radical fluctuation in political realities.[221] At the turn of the century, this interchange was particularly connected with one individual, Sergei Diaghilev (1872 – 1929), the renowned fine arts advocate and

---

[218] Salomon M. Teitelbaum, 'Dostoyevski in France of the 1880s', *American Slavic and East European Review*, 5 (1946), 99–108.

[219] E.V. Razvozzhaeva, 'Istochniki po istorii poezdok rossiiskikh poddannykh vo Frantsiiu (1885 – 1914 gg.)' (unpublished doctoral dissertation, St. Petersburg State University, 2009).

[220] Patricia Herlihy, 'The Ethnic Composition of the City of Odessa in the Nineteenth Century', *Harvard Ukrainian Studies*, 1 (1977), 53–78.

[221] N.O. Shiralieva, 'Kul'turnye sviazi Frantsii i Rossii v XX veke' (unpublished doctoral dissertation, Moscow, 2004).

promoter. In Paris, Diaghilev founded the famous *Ballets Russes* in 1909, and it was largely his initiative that established the 'mechanism' for various kinds of cultural exchange between Russia and France during this period. He facilitated the travel of Russian actors, dancers, artists, and composers to Paris. The debut in Paris of the music of Igor Stravinsky, for example, is a well-known episode of this period for music historians. Likewise, Diaghilev brought French painting to Russia and organized a number of joint artistic projects. As this Franco-Russian artistic relationship moved forward, the actual delivery of cultural cooperation would flex with the ever-changing government regulations of Russia's politically turbulent twentieth century. However, according to Shiralieva, 'the foundation laid by Diaghliev made it possible to build a well-constructed system for the cultural interaction of the two countries in the twentieth century, taking into account the changes occurring in the world.'[222]

In the area of literature, Catherine Gouis compared French and Russian decadent literature and art in the late nineteenth and early twentieth century.[223] A number of Russian authors and artists followed the example of French decadents into this new artistic alternative to the rationalist, utilitarian ideology of the radical intelligentsia.

As Russia moved towards revolution and into the Soviet period, free cultural collaboration between France and Russia seems to have become more and more untenable. One study traces the correspondences between Russian playwright Dmitry Merezhkovsky and an associate of the French politician Leon Blum about staging one of Merezhovsky's plays in France. These letters, written between 1905 and 1907, record the breakdown of their relationship, and are a commentary on 'the relationship

---

[222] Ibid., 125.
[223] Catherine Gouis, 'The Woman on the Cross: Ritual and Self-Sacrifice in the Decadent Search for Meaning', *The Russian Review*, 68 (2009), 477–494.

between the Russian and French cultural worlds. They also shed some light on the reasons why this relationship functioned so badly between 1905 and 1917.'[224]

Though the topic is beyond the scope of this study, it bears mentioning that much of the Russia émigré community which had escaped revolutionary Russian had sought refuge in France and many important cultural figures continued to express themselves in exile. Robert Johnston has described Paris as the cultural capital of 'Russia abroad' following the Russian Revolution and subsequent civil war.[225] Johnston's collective biography looks beyond the stereotypes of impoverished Russian aristocrats, Cossack taxi drivers in Paris, and famous exiled politicians like Pavel Miliukov to describe an émigré community in France that included many ordinary Russians. According to Marc Raeff, the Russian émigrés strove to maintain their Russian identity and, to this end, founded cultural organizations abroad, dedicated to producing creative works and fulfilling their 'mission' of preserving Russian values and culture.[226] One example of this phenomenon is a publication entitled *Iakor'* ('The Anchor') which was printed in 1935. It was an anthology of Russian poetry written abroad by the first wave of emigrants. Of the 77 poets whose work is included, 51 were living in France, 46 of those in Paris.[227] According to Shiralieva, Russian intelligentsia exiled in France often expressed their homesickness for Russia in all manners of artistic expression, determining to maintain their Russian cultural identity as a matter of deep principle. Many of them expected Russia's turmoil to be temporary and looked forward to returning home. There are even recorded instances of Russian émigrés refusing to

---

[224] Anna Pondopulo, 'Merezhkovsky, Blum and Petit: An Impossible Relationship', in *Other Voices: Three Centuries of Cultural Dialogue between Russia and Western Europe,* ed. by Graham Roberts (Newcastle upon Tyne: Cambridge Scholars, 2011), pp. 189–202 (p. 189).

[225] Robert H. Johnston, *New Mecca, New Babylon: Paris and the Russian Exiles, 1920 – 1945* (Kingston: McGill-Queen's University Press, 1988).

[226] Marc Raeff, *Russia Abroad: A Cultural History of the Russian Emigration, 1919 – 1939* (New York: Oxford University Press, 1990).

[227] E.N. Dzhusoeva, 'Mnogolikaia nadezhda: poeziia russkoi emigratsii vo Frantsii' in *Frantsuzskii iazyk i kul'tura Frantsii v Rossii XXI veka: Materialy XV mezhdunarodnoi nauchno-prakticheskoi konferentsii Shkoly-seminara im. L.M. Skrelinoi,* ed. by Z.I. Kirnoze and others (Nizhny Novgorod: Nizhegorodskii gosudarstvennyi lingvisticheskii universitet im. N.A. Dobroliubova, 2011), pp. 254–257 (p. 254).

bury their deceased family members on French soil, choosing rather to intern them in metal coffins inside crypts, vowing to repatriate their loved ones to Russia once things got back to normal.[228] Of course this never happened, and the continued presence of these Russian refugees in France was an additional point of contact between the two cultures.

Not long after the tumultuous period of revolution and civil war, Russia's cultural dialogue with France continued, though under the auspices of state supervision rather than private initiative. In the early days of the Soviet Union, Russian ballet continued to be popular in France and French language and literature continued to be popular in the Soviet Union.[229] State censorship and the general instability made Franco-Russian cultural connections precarious and yet a measure of interchange continued. Various art exhibitions and private collections of visual art were nationalized at this time, many of which included French specimens. In 1988, a comparative study of French and Russian/early-Soviet art in the period 1900 – 1930 was sponsored at the Pushkin Art Museum in Moscow.[230] The resultant collection of articles, while more comparative than dealing strictly with direct contact, includes evidence of some ongoing cultural transfer between France and Russia in early Soviet Russia. Cécile Pichon-Bonin has explored the Society of Easel Painters, which existed in the period 1925 – 1932 as part of the New Economic Policy and the interplay of official policy and artistic expression during this period.[231] Picon-Bonin finds that there was clearly definable French reference in Soviet visual art up until 1939, though debates regarding Soviet ideology of artistic expression complicated the interchange.

---

[228] Shiralieva, 'Kul'turnye sviazi Frantsii i Rossii v XX veke', p. 68.

[229] Ibid., p. 126.

[230] *Rossiia. Frantsiia: Problemy kul'tury pervykh desiatiletii XX veka: sbornik statei,* ed. by I. E. Danilova (Moscow: Izdanie gosudarstvennogo muzeia izobrazitel'nykh iskusstv imeni A. S. Pushkina, 1988).

[231] Cecile Pichon-Bonin, 'French References in Soviet Painting of the 1920s and 1930s: The Example of the Creation of Members of "The Society of Easel Painters"', in *Other Voices: Three Centuries of Cultural Dialogue between Russia and Western Europe,* ed. by Graham Roberts (Newcastle upon Tyne: Cambridge Scholars, 2011), pp. 110–137.

Several recent studies have shown that culture and the fine arts were caught up in the ideological battle of the new communist regime and yet the Franco-Russian cultural connection survived through it all. Ludmila Stern explores the tactics of the Soviet government in the interwar period to liaise directly with non-governmental groups and private citizens inside other countries, namely France in the period 1920 – 1940.[232] Soviet organizations like the International Association of Revolutionary Writers (MORP) and the All-Union Society for Cultural Relations with Foreign Countries (VOKS) garnered contact with western intellectuals, especially the French, through wooing, bribery, and coercion to distribute communist ideology abroad. Foreign writers were recruited to write positive articles about the USSR in western publications.

Franco-Russian interface took different forms during this period. One study of the relationship between French leftist parties and the Soviets during the interwar period explores an odd blurring of the line between domestic and international politics.[233] The official Franco-Russian alliance had broken down during World War I and was replaced for a time by the relationship of leftist parties within France directly with Soviet officials. This relationship in turn translated into a certain influence which these groups were able to exert on their own French government.

These exchanges aided the realization of a Franco-Soviet pact of non-aggression in the 1930s. Though a political example, this episode illustrates how interaction between France and Russia persisted relentlessly despite obstacles, taking various forms in light of changing political climates.[234] As with the First World War, more recent English-language histories of World War II—based on archival records made available

---

[232] Ludmila Stern, *Western Intellectuals and the Soviet Union, 1920–40: From Red Square to the Left Bank* (London and New York: Routledge, 2007).

[233] Luther Allen, 'The French Left and Soviet Russia to 1936: Interaction between French Party Alliances and Franco-Soviet Diplomacy' (unpublished doctoral dissertation, University of Chicago, 1955).

[234] This is also explored in Michael David-Fox, *Showcasing the Great Experiment: Cultural Diplomacy and Western Visitors to Soviet Union, 1921–1941* (Oxford: Oxford University Press, 2012).

since 1991—have emphasized the crucial Soviet contribution to defeating the Nazis.[235] The formation of the 'Grand Alliance' of nations against Hitler's Germany once again put France and Russia together in a temporary coalition.[236]

In the World War II period and thereafter, Russia and France were also drawn closer together, culturally. According to Shiralieva, one contributing factor was the fact that France was, at this time, 'the most communist-minded of all the countries of Western Europe.'[237] There was a trend during this period of French intellectuals being drawn to communism. French communism grew for a time following World War II, partly due to the prestige of the Soviet Union immediately after the war, and the role that French communists played in the French resistance movement.[238] In the 1950s the company of the Bolshoi Theatre, Soviet Circus, and other artists travelled on performance tours to France, and French symphonies and opera companies were reciprocally invited to Moscow and Leningrad.[239] Such exchanges were reminiscent of the Diaghilev period, though now under state control, and also included the exchange of motion pictures in both countries. In the 1960s, the French language was studied by Soviet school children as was English and German. Access to French literature, including a massive amount of new translations into Russian, was at an all-time high.

During the Soviet Union's so called 'Era of Stagnation' [*epokha zastoia*], the relationship continued fairly consistently via state-sponsored cultural exchange events, foreign language training in Soviet education programs, the publication of French literature in Russian translation, and a generally permissive atmosphere for the enjoyment of many traditional elements of French culture. French films and French

---

[235] For example, Evan Mawdsley, *Thunder in the East: The Nazi-Soviet War, 1941–1945* (London: Hodder Arnold, 2005); Richard Overy, *Russia's War: A History of the Soviet War Effort, 1941 – 1945* (New York: Penguin, 1997); Antony Beevor, *Stalingrad* (New York: Penguin, 1998).

[236] Michael Howard, 'Grand Alliance', in *The Oxford Companion to World War II*, ed. by Ian Colthurst Blake Dear and Michael R. D. Foot (Oxford: Oxford University Press, 2002), pp. 390 – 395.

[237] Shiralieva, 'Kul'turnye sviazi Frantsii i Rossii v XX veke', p. 127.

[238] Charles A. Micaud, 'French Intellectuals and Communism', *Social Research,* 3 (1954), 286–296.

[239] Shiralieva, 'Kul'turnye sviazi Frantsii i Rossii v XX veke', pp. 71–77.

popular music, unlike American rock-and-roll, was 'officially allowed.'[240] Cultural

relations continued, despite the scandal and embarrassment of Soviet artistic travellers

occasionally defecting to France, beginning in the 1960s. Following the collapse of the

Soviet Union, cultural exchange between France and Russia has continued, once again

with the active participation of private initiative working parallel to those programs

sponsored through official diplomatic channels, such as the aforementioned 'Year of

France in Russia' in 2010. During this diplomatic project, Russian theatres and opera

houses performed French plays and operas, under the direction of visiting French

producers and with the participation of guest soloists from France. Exhibitions of the

newest French artwork, photography, and sculpture were featured in various venues

across Russia, and pieces from the permanent collection of the Musée Picasso in Paris

were borrowed and put on temporary display in Moscow's Pushkin Museum of Fine

Arts. French poets, scientists, ballet companies, and modern dance troupes were

honoured guests at numerous cultural events, and seventeen French authors were invited

to travel from Moscow to Vladivostok on the Trans-Siberian Railway, stopping at seven

large cities along the way to interact with the reading public and participate in literary

forums and book-signings.[241]

The flexibility and resilience of this relationship over the centuries speaks to a

long-standing appeal which transcends official constructs. As Shiralieva concluded, the

diplomatic and political concerns which may have defined the relationship between

Russia and France as nations 'have never been the defining factors in the formation of

[their] properly cultural relations.' Further, the connection between these two cultures

---

[240] Shiralieva, 'Kul'turnye sviazi Frantsii i Rossii v XX veke', p. 127.
[241] '2010: год Франции в России и России во Франции',
<http://web.archive.org/web/20100617045113/http://www.ambafrance-
ru.org/france_russie/spip.php?article7956 > [accessed 19 August 2015]

is an exceptional one. 'Russia is probably not bound so tightly to any other country in the world by cultural dialogue.'[242]

Conclusion

As this survey suggests, historians have long been aware of this special cultural relationship, but western scholarship has been on a long journey towards a systematic study of the relationship or its impact on Russian culture and society. As early as 1948, Nikolai Berdiaev's famous treatise on Russian culture publicized in English his intriguing (if vague) philosophical notion of the 'Russian soul' and its dilemma between East and West. 'It unites two worlds,' wrote Berdiaev, 'and within the Russian soul two principles are always engaged in strife—the Eastern and the Western.'[243] In the 1960s, Hans Rogger wrote about the history of Russia's 'national consciousness', and referred to western influences on the development of Russian customs, language, folklore, and general search for 'a national character.'[244] This work relies heavily on the writings of nineteenth-century Russian historians and focuses largely on the Russian government. In 1983, a study group led by Anthony Cross produced a more focused study on *Russia and the West in the Eighteenth Century* in which authors explored Russian published sources from the period and analyzed them for evidences of English, German, and French influences on Russian culture. Their sources included travel diaries, technical manuals, literary journals, newspapers, and treaty collections, to name a few.[245] Since then, Anthony Cross has written or led extensive research on Anglo-Russian cultural interaction. Much of this, however, has focused on British perceptions of Russian

---

[242] Shiralieva, 'Kul'turnye sviazi Frantsii i Rossii v XX veke', p. 123.

[243] Nikolai Berdiaev, *The Russian Idea* (New York: Macmillan, 1948), p. 2.

[244] Hans Rogger, *National Consciousness in Eighteenth-Century Russia* (Cambridge, Mass.: Harvard University Press, 1969).

[245] Anthony Cross, ed., *Russia and the West in the Eighteenth Century* (Newtonville: Oriental Research Partners, 1983)

culture and society rather than actual influence upon Russian culture.[246] In 2011,

Graham H. Roberts, a British professor of Russian studies teaching in Paris, edited a

collection of essays on 'three centuries of cultural dialogue between Russia and Western

Europe,' most of which explored examples of Western European influence in Russian

literature.[247]

As it relates to French influence specifically, the most relevant recent studies

have been those focusing on Russian uses of the French language in the eighteenth and

nineteenth century and, better still, those few which deal with the issue of French

influence on the Russian language. A 1998 dissertation by American Russianist Kelly

Herold studied the French-language memoirs of Russian nobility during the period 1770

– 1830.[248] Similarly, French historian Marc Fumaroli's anthology of and commentary

on French-language texts written by foreigners from 1714 to 1814—a period Fumaroli

refers to as the 'French century'—included the correspondence of Catherine the Great

with Voltaire and Princess Dashkova's memoirs, which were originally written in

French. This study was originally published in 2001, but translated into English in

2011.[249] Along these same lines was a three-year study project at the University of

Bristol under the leadership of Derek Offord which was completed in 2014.[250] This

project has explored French language acquisition and use in imperial Russia through the

study of documents related to educational institutions such as the Cadet Corps in St.

---

[246] The following books, for example, are all by Anthony Cross: *The 1780s: Russia Under Western Eyes* (Norwich: University of East Anglia, 1981); *Peter the Great Through British Eyes: Perceptions and Representations of the Tsar Since 1698* (Cambridge: Cambridge University Press, 2000); *St Petersburg and the British: The City Through the Eyes of British Visitors and Residents* (London: Frances Lincoln, 2008).

[247] Graham H. Roberts, ed., *Other Voices: Three Centuries of Cultural Dialogue between Russia and Western Europe* (Newcastle upon Tyne: Cambridge Scholars, 2011).

[248] Kelly Herold, 'Russian Autobiographical Literature in French: Recovering a Memoiristic Tradition (1770 – 1830)' (unpublished doctoral dissertation, University of California, Los Angeles, 1998).

[249] Marc Fumaroli, *When the World Spoke French,* trans. by Richard Howard (New York: New York Review Books, 2011).

[250] Derek Offord and others, eds, *French and Russian in Imperial Russia,* 2 vols (Edinburgh: Edinburgh University Press, 2015).

Petersburg, Russian books and other pedagogical materials for learning French, and the private letters of Russian nobility written in French, to name a few of the sources used. The study has looked at the importance of and access to the French language among various groups of Russians in the eighteenth and nineteenth centuries: male versus female, opportunities available to people in varying strata of society, and so forth.[251]

Such inquiry is a step in the right direction towards investigating French influence on Russian culture, but another step is required. These studies reflect Russian interaction with and adoption of French culture, but are less concerned with changes to the Russian culture itself which have resulted from French stimuli. Both Orlando Figes and Hans Rogger, drawing from their study of satirical literature, have referenced the duplicity of eighteenth-century Russian nobility.[252] French customs, clothing, and language were used by upper-class Russians in public gatherings of high society, but were not native to them. Like actors on a stage, they 'played at' being French. Further, even this false French façade applied to only a small segment of the Russian population. More relevant to the present study are more long-lasting influences such as changes to the *Russian* language. May Smith's recent linguistic analysis of Russian literary texts, for example, has identified French phraseological calques in the Russian language.[253] While Smith's study was purely linguistic, such analysis has obvious implications for the historical study of cultural transfer. Likewise, a few of the papers presented during the University of Bristol's recent project relate to such issues in a more historical context. Victor Zhivov presented a paper on French borrowings in Russian romantic language, Iuliia and Sergei Klimenko on French loanwords in Russian architectural

---

[251] <http://www.bristol.ac.uk/arts/research/french-in-russia/> [accessed 2 July 2015]

[252] Rogger, *National Consciousness,* p. 57; Figes, *Natasha's Dance: A Cultural History of Russia* (London: Penguin, 2002), pp. 43 – 45.

[253] May Smith, *The Influence of French on Eighteenth-Century Literary Russian: Semantic and Phraseological Calques* (Oxford: Peter Lang, 2006).

terminology, and Gesine Argent explored eighteenth-century language politics and the debate over French influence between Nikolai Karamzin and Aleksandr Shiskov.[254]

The present dissertation will continue this discussion by comprehensively exploring the presence of all kinds of French loanwords in the Russian language, analyzing them for chronological and thematic patterns, and providing a historical context to the changes to Russian culture suggested by these borrowed words through the study of other period-specific primary sources. By studying the vocabulary of each period—a fundamental aspect of Russian culture, shared broadly by Russians—this thesis will contribute a properly cultural perspective to the myopic view of Russian history which typically focuses on the Russian state or the very narrow elite segment of Russian society about whom much has been written. Further, such analysis connects the present with the past in a way that is not strictly dependent upon traditional periodization—which is also intrinsically statist—to study French impact upon Russian culture as a continuum with peaks and valleys which may or may not coincide chronologically and thematically with traditionally accepted historical mileposts. Finally, this analysis will provide an additional analytical tool—the lexical data—with which to measure the permanent significance of the cultural elements encountered during the subsequent examination of other primary source material in chapters three through five.

---

[254] Victor Zhivov, 'Love à la Mode: Russian Words and French Sources'; Iuliia and Sergei Klimenko, 'The Role of French in the Formation of Architectural Terminology in Eighteenth-Century Russia'; and Gesine Argent, 'The Linguistic Debate Between Karamzin and Shishkov: Evaluating Russian-French Language Contact', in *French and Russian in Imperial Russia*, ed. by Dereck Offord and others, 2 vols (Edinburgh: Edinburgh University Press, 2015), I, pp. 209 – 227, II, pp. 100 – 117, 214 – 241.

CHAPTER TWO

LEXICAL ANALYSIS: FRENCH INFLUENCE IN RUSSIA

The depth of external influences upon Russia across its entire history is attested to by

significant linguistic contributions from abroad. Like counting the rings of a felled tree

or examining the various layers of sediment rock, much can be learned about the

historical development of Russia by studying her language. To this end, the first phase

of primary research examines the presence of French loanwords in Russian dictionaries

from Peter the Great to the present as a means of determining the most significant

period and areas of French cultural influence. A general dictionary of the Russian

language, apart from its other intended functions, can provide the historian with an

indication of the lexicon in existence at the time that the dictionary was published,

making it possible to trace the appearance of different types of French words in the

Russian language. Dictionaries published at different times will include different sets of

borrowed words, overlapping with each other at certain points and differing at others as

new words enter the language or some older words fall out of use. Compared with one

another through critical analysis, these groups of French words in the different Russian

dictionaries reveal patterns of cultural influence.

The selection of dictionaries reflects both chronological progression and faithful

representation of each period's lexicon. Based on a review of secondary literature

related to the history of the Russia language, the following seven periods have been

identified and a dictionary chosen to represent the vocabulary of each: the period up to

and including the reign of Peter the Great; from the death of Peter through Catherine's

reign; the end of Catherine's reign through Pushkin's career; from the death of Pushkin

up to the beginning of Russia's revolutionary period; the revolutionary period; the early

Soviet period up to the mid twentieth century (or, post-World War II generation); and the most recent period, including the remainder of the Soviet era up to 2007. Within this chronological framework, effort has been made to include the most important dictionaries in Russia's lexicographical tradition, especially those considered to be standard or definitive by Russian speakers. Thus, preference has been given to those dictionaries published by the Russian Academy of Sciences, and its pre-Soviet and Soviet manifestations: The Imperial Academy of Sciences and the Academy of Sciences of the USSR. A notable exception would be the dictionary of Vladimir Dal', whose nineteenth-century lexicography is legendary. Finally, first or early editions have been preferred of dictionaries that underwent multiple printings, so as to capture each period's lexicon as perceived and recorded by its contemporaries. Nine dictionaries have been selected for study based upon the above criteria. They are introduced here chronologically, in order of the linguistic period they represent rather than in order of publication date (see figure 2.1).

Figure 2.1: Russian dictionaries selected for lexical study (by period)

Period	Editor	Dictionary	Publication d
Before 1725	N. A. Smirnov	*Zapadnoe vliianie na russkii iazyk v Petrovskuiu epokhu*	1910
1725 – 1794	Russian Academy	*Slovar' akademii rossiiskoi*	1789 – 1794
1794 – 1837	V. V. Vinogradov	*Slovar' iazyka Pushkina: v cheterykh tomakh*	1956 – 1961
1837 – 1882	V. I. Dal'	*Tolkovyi slovar' zhivogo velikorusskogo iazyka*	1880 – 1882 (edn)
	A. Ia. Shaikevich	*Statisticheskii slovar' iazyka Dostoevskogo*	2003
1882 – 1940	D. N. Ushakov	*Tolkovyi slovar' russkogo iazyka*	1935 – 1940
1940 – 1961	S. I. Ozhegov	*Slovar' russkogo iazyka*	1953 (3rd edn)
	A. P. Evgen'eva	*Slovar' russkogo iazyka v cheterekh tomakh*	1957 – 1961
1961 – 2007	S. A. Kuznetsov	*Sovremennyi tolkovyi slovar' russkogo iazyka*	2007

Dictionaries and language development in Russia: Peter the Great to the present

On the eve of Peter the Great's reign, the Russian language already bore marks left by centuries of foreign influence. The earliest of these, Byzantine Greek, gave the Russian language—via Old Church Slavonic—a sophisticated grammatical structure and its very alphabet.[1] Two centuries under Mongol overlords introduced Tatar words to the language, many of which are still in circulation. During the period between Muscovy's liberation from the yoke of the Golden Horde and the ascension of Peter the Great, a number of German and French words entered the Russian language via the intermediary of Polish, a fact sometimes made obvious by the endings of words.[2] Soviet linguist V. V. Vinogradov encapsulated the progress of the Russian language in the second half of the seventeenth century as the decline of Church Slavonic, the growth of external influence on the Russian literary language, and the broadening of the literary functions of Russian speech.[3]

Peter I (r. 1696 – 1725) patronized the translation and publication of secular books in a new 'civil script', a simplified version of the Church Slavonic alphabet which was more conducive to typeset printing. Moreover, it was Peter's intention that works translated from other languages be written in a simpler style that would be understandable to the literate laity for whom they were intended.[4] Furthermore, Peter's modernizing reforms of the Russian state and society resulted in a flood of new words into the Russian language, borrowed directly from English, French, German, and Dutch. The early eighteenth century government administrator and historian, Vasilii

---

[1] W. K. Matthews, 'Russian Language Before 1700', *The Slavonic and East European Review,* 31 (1953), 383.

[2] See discussions of Polish as an intermediary for western linguistic influence during this period in A. P. Vlasto, *A Linguistic History of Russia to the End of the Eighteenth Century* (Oxford: Clarendon, 1988), p. 365 and in N. A. Smirnov, 'Zapadnoe vliianie na russkii iazyk v Petrovskuiu epokhu', in *Sbornik otdeleniia Russkago iazyka i slovesnosti Imperatorskoi akademii nauk,* Volume 88, no. 2, (St. Petersburg: Imperial Academy of Sciences, 1910), p. 12.

[3] V. V. Vinogradov, *Ocherki po istorii russkogo literaturnogo iazyka XVII-XIX vekov* (Moscow: Vysshaia shkola, 1982), p. 55.

[4] James Cracraft, *The Petrine Revolution in Culture* (Cambridge, MA: Belknap, 2004), p. 299.

Tatishchev, referred to the 'needed multiplication of language' taking place as a result of Russia's acquisition of new equipment and technical knowledge from abroad. In Tatishchev's estimation, the influx of European words at the beginning of the eighteenth century was second only to the linguistic influence associated with Byzantine Christian culture.[5] Equally, Lindsey Hughes has suggested that, in Russia's subsequent years, Peter's linguistic borrowing is only matched by that of the modern technology age.[6]

The source chosen for this earliest period of study has been *Zapadnoe vliianie na russkii iazyk v petrovskuiu epokhu* by N. A. Smirnov. Russia's first dictionary of the standard language did not appear until the end of the eighteenth century, but it is important to make distinction between French words entering the Russian language with Peter's activity and those entering later. After the death of Peter the Great in 1725, almost seventy years passed before the first dictionary was published, a period when new French influence was occurring. The empress Catherine II corresponded with Voltaire and entertained philosophes of the Enlightenment at court. Her predecessor, Elizabeth, had introduced French as the court language, replacing German. It only stands to reason that new French words would appear in the Russian language after Peter, but before the publication of the first dictionary. To avoid leaving the lexical contributions of the Petrine and Catherinian eras amalgamated in one list, the work of N. A. Smirnov has been used.[7] In 1910, Smirnov compiled a list of foreign words based on his study of the numerous glossaries, legal codices, and technical manuals produced during Peter's reign. Smirnov's word-list is primarily concerned with word origin. Short definitions are supplied for some terms, but omitted altogether for words that Smirnov considered to be obvious. Though not a dictionary in the strictest sense,

---

[5] Cited in Vinogradov, *Ocherki*, p. 61.
[6] Lindsey Hughes, *Russia in the Age of Peter the Great* (New Haven: Yale University Press, 1998), p. 328.
[7] N. A. Smirnov, *Zapadnoe vliianie na russkii iazyk v Petrovskuiu epokhu* (Saint Peterburg: Tip. Imp. akademii nauk, 1910).

Smirnov's important work is hereafter understood to be included whenever the 'dictionaries' are referred to collectively.

Language development during the remainder of the eighteenth century moved towards a single national language and also featured the rising preeminence of French influence.[8] For representation of the Russian language through the end of Catherine II's reign, the first edition of the *Slovar' akademii rossiiskoi* (published 1789 – 1794) has been chosen.[9] Conceived in the spirit of the Age of Reason, the philosophical underpinnings of 'enlightened despotism' are unmistakable in the opening phrases of the dictionary's introduction: 'To anyone who is well-acquainted with the annals [of history] it is fairly well known that public education [*narodnoe prosveshchenie*] always marches with slow steps unless it is helped along by the wisdom and care of the Sovereign himself.' To this end, Catherine, 'our Great Autocrat', had appointed Princess Ekaterina Vorontsova-Dashkova to head a new Russian Academy (fashioned after the Académie française) which was charged with the ambitious project of producing Russia's first comprehensive dictionary, a major landmark in the development of the language.[10]

In the wake of Peter's reforms and the continued cultural developments of subsequent reigns, a massive amount of new Russian writing and Russian translations of foreign works had produced a 'scattered abundance' of Russian words. The theme of unifying a chaotic word-base is found repeatedly in the new dictionary's preface. 'This very abundance [referring to the rich lexical material to be found], if brought into a single structure, will reveal the needed rules for its establishment, and aid in the perfection of all parts of the verbal sciences; for language is not born of rules, but rules,

---

[8] G. O. Vinokur, *Russkii iazyk: istoricheskii ocherk* (Moscow: URSS, 2010), p. 135.

[9] *Slovar' akademii rossiiskoi*, 6 vols (St. Petersburg: pri Imperatorskoi Akademii Nauk, 1789 – 1794) <http://www.runivers.ru/lib/book3173/> [accessed 31 August 2013]

[10] *Slovar' akademii rossiiskoi*, I (1789), p. v.

rather, flow from the way that language is used.'[11] In other words, the task of the dictionary's creators was to observe existing linguistic practice but also to prescribe norms for future use based on their findings. For example, where compilers found regional differences in spelling, pronunciation, or the accenting of syllables, the usage most commonly occurring in the capital city of St. Petersburg was recorded in the dictionary as correct.[12]

The long collaborative process of compiling words, editing and alphabetizing the list, adding grammatical and etymological notes and finally writing definitions commenced in 1784. Most of the compilation was complete by February 1787 and the first volume was printed in July 1789.[13] Scholars of the newly-formed Russian Academy (not to be confused with the Russian Academy of Sciences) scoured both 'ecclesiastical books and the best secular works: various chronicles, legal codices— ancient and recent—travel diaries and commonly used words from [academic] speeches' in order to create a comprehensive list of words in the Russian language. 'In this manner so great an abundance of words was gathered such as hitherto had never been in one group.' Certain words were eliminated from this massive list: proper nouns, scientific and artistic terminology deemed too technical for inclusion, vulgar words (literally, those 'contrary to decency'), archaic words that had already fallen out of use, speech that was unique to a regional dialect, and any 'unnecessary foreign words.'[14]

While the monumental importance of this six-volume dictionary is undeniable, the predilections of its editors must not be overlooked. First, the list of the dictionary's thirty-eight contributors, in addition to various linguists, scientists, and other scholars, reads like a 'who's who' of Russian society, including a navy admiral, a count, a prince,

---

[11] Ibid., p. vi.
[12] Ibid., p. xiii.
[13] *Slovar' akademii rossiiskoi*, II (1790), pp. iii – v.
[14] Ibid., p. ix.

several clergymen, including two archbishops, and 'His Excellency Ivan Ivanovich

Shuvalov,' an ageing nobleman who was once a favourite of the late empress Elizabeth

Petrovna.[15] This grand convocation of editors speaks, not only to the importance

attached to the project, but also to certain editorial tendencies which can be expected.

To borrow from Mikhail Lomonosov's notion of three 'styles' of eighteenth-century

Russian speech this first dictionary definitely leans towards 'high' Russian.[16] Though

the 'common man' is mentioned, as well as the wealth of linguistic material available in

folk proverbs, only the 'very best of these' was used.[17] In his overview of Russian

lexicography, Morton Benson mentioned this aspect of the dictionary, noting its lack of

colloquial language and extensive use of Church Slavonic forms. In fact the third

edition of this dictionary, published in 1847, would actually be entitled a *Dictionary of

Church Slavonic and Russian.*[18] Editors of the first Soviet dictionary made similar

criticism, insisting that the Academy's Dictionary 'eschews foreign words, avoids

words existing among the lower and middle bourgeoisie, and evaluates words based on

the norms of the higher 'Slavic Language' [*slavenskogo sloga*] of the literature of the

nobility.'[19]

Regarding the dictionary's avoidance of foreign words, an indirect benefit may

be discerned. Princess Dashkova, writing in her memoirs, referred to foreign loanwords

in the Russian language as an impetus to the production of the dictionary. Recalling a

conversation with Catherine, she wrote: 'I expressed my surprise to Her Majesty that…

she should not yet have established a Russian Academy. We needed, I said, rules of

---

[15] *Slovar' akademii rossiiskoi,* II (1790), pp. vii – xiii.

[16] The language is 'high' in the sense of being more influenced by Church Slavonic and less influenced by 'low' colloquial speech. For treatment of Lomonosov's philological theory of the 'three styles' of Russian language, see V. V. Vinogradov, *Ocherki po istorii russkogo literaturnogo iazyka,* pp. 116 – 112, and also A. A. Sokolsky, *A History of the Russian Language* (Madrid: Impr. Taravilla, 1966), pp. 123 – 127.

[17] *Slovar' akademii rossiiskoi,* I (1789), pp. vi – viii, xiv.

[18] Morton Benson, 'A Step Forward in Russian Lexicography', *Slavic and East European Journal,* 39 (1995), 431.

[19] D. N. Ushakov, *Tolkovyi slovar' russkogo iazyka,* 4 vols (Moscow: Gosudarstvennyi Institut Sovetskaia Entsiklopediia, 1935), I, p. 1.

grammar and a good dictionary to do away with the absurdity of using foreign words and terms while having our own which were far more vivid.'[20] The preface admits that foreign words which were not 'necessary' were not included in the dictionary. Conversely, this implies that foreign words which were included had been deemed 'necessary.' That is to say, these are words that had been assimilated into the language as legitimate, albeit borrowed, vocabulary and not frivolous additions due to some superficial mimicking of the West. This seems to be indicated by the fact that a large portion of the French words which are introduced in this dictionary endure to later periods, compared to Smirnov's Petrine glossary and even some early Soviet dictionaries where many French words appear briefly and then disappear just as quickly.

Catherine's death and the turn of the nineteenth century marked the end of an era, which coincided with a new linguistic period for Russia. The next dictionary to be chosen for this study was the *Slovar' iazyka Pushkina.*[21] These four volumes were published between 1956 and 1961, but represent Pushkin's usage of the language in the period from 1813 to 1837, listing every word used by Pushkin in his poetry, prose literature, and even personal letters. The dictionary scrupulously includes full entries even for single-letter connecting words (such as the prepositions *a, v, i,* and *o*) but excludes words found inside inverted commas, indicating Pushkin's use of direct quotation of another author or speaker. This meticulous approach was intended to guarantee that all of Pushkin's and only Pushkin's words be included.[22]

Linguistically, it is difficult to overstate the importance of Aleksandr Pushkin (1799 – 1837) who, in the words of Ivan Turgenev, 'created our poetic, our literary language and all that is left for us and our descendants to do is to walk the path which

---

[20] Kyril Fitzlyon, ed. and trans., *The Memoirs of Princess Dashkova* (Durham and London: Duke University Press, 1995), p. 213.
[21] V. V. Vinogradov and S. I. Bernshtein, eds, *Slovar' iazyka Pushkina: v chetyrekh tomakh* (Moscow: Gosudarsnvennoe izdatel'stvo inostrannykh i natsional'nykh slovarei, 1956 – 1961).
[22] Ibid.

his genius has laid.'[23] Russian school children are still drilled in the basic pronunciation and stylistic flow of the standard Russian language by memorizing and reciting his poems. Over a hundred years after his death, Soviet lexicographers insisted that 'in its structure, the modern Russian language is hardly distinguishable from the language of Pushkin.'[24] Pushkin went against the literary convention of his day by using simple peasant jargon in written form, but also made effective secular use of words and phrases from Church Slavonic. While other authors had attempted mixtures of Church Slavonic and Russian vernacular in their writings—seeking a happy medium between 'high' and 'low' Russian—Pushkin was, in the opinion of one historian of the Russian language, the first to do it well.[25] He also made effective use of French words and constructions, but went beyond the previous generation's straight borrowing of stock phrases for emphasis, a pretension that Pushkin despised.[26] He translated words literally from French into Russian, essentially creating new calques, and used Russian folk words and phrases with French semantics. Inspired by the French language and literature on which he had been reared, Pushkin lifted the Russian language so that it had the same expressive capabilities.[27]

The editors of the *Slovar' iazyka Pushkina,* in addition to recognizing Pushkin's importance to the Russian language in general, were also convinced that analysis of the great author's writing would yield period-specific insights about 'the lexical system of the standard Russian language of the first half of the nineteenth century.'[28] One of the stated purposes of this dictionary is to provide a comparative tool so that 'the historian

---

[23] Vinogradov, *Ocherki,* p. 294.

[24] S. I. Ozhegov, *Slovar' russkogo iazyka* (Moscow: Gosudarsnvennoe Izdatel'stvo Inostrannykh I Natsional'nykh Slovarei, 1953), p. 3.

[25] Vlasto, *Linguistic History of Russia,* p. 393.

[26] Vinokur, *Russkii iazyk,* pp. 156 – 157.

[27] Vinogradov, *Ocherki,* pp. 263 – 269.

[28] Ibid., p. 6.

of the Russian language may confidently… observe the specific historical processes of change in the vocabulary of the Russian language from Pushkin to the modern era.'[29]

After Pushkin, the Russian language continued to develop along a trajectory which made it more accessible to the common man. Vingradov has referred to the 'democratic reform' of language beginning in the 1830s and 1840s whereby uses of Church Slavonic ('high' Russian) were limited, and language of the *narod* came to the fore, including colloquial speech and professional jargon.[30] For Russian vocabulary through 1881, the *Statisticheskii slovar' iazyka Dostoevskogo* was used, representing Dostoevskii's usage during the period 1832 – 1881.[31]

Dostoevskii's importance as a worldwide literary figure extends beyond the realm of Russian studies as his novels are still valued in the twenty-first century for their philosophical commentary on a range of issues that transcend nationality: morality, religion, science, wealth, poverty, and political systems just to name a few.[32] Mikhail Bakhtin has famously argued that his innovations in literary form have influenced the way the world's authors write and the way that humankind thinks.[33] This universal appeal does not, however, diminish his role as a distinctly Russian realist, vividly depicting the struggles of his own time and the culture of his own people.

A recent study by Linda Ivanits highlights the importance of the common Russian people in Dostoevskii's work, not merely as background characters, but as ever-present iconic symbols of his native culture. The simplicity of their faith and the nobility of their charity to one another inspired him, though he explored with equal honesty their wanton drunkenness and the cruelty of which they were sometimes

---

[29] Ibid.

[30] Vinogradov, *Ocherki*, 335.

[31] A. Ia. Shaiikevich and others, eds, *Statisticheskii slovar' iazyka Dostoevskogo* (Moscow: Iazyki slavianskoi kul'tury, 2003).

[32] W. J. Leatherbarrow, 'Introduction', in *The Cambridge Companion to Dostoevskii,* ed. by W. J. Leatherbarrow (Cambridge: Cambridge University Press, 2002), pp. 1 – 20.

[33] Mikhail Bakhtin, *Problems of Dostoevsky's Poetics* (Minneapolis: University of Minnesota Press, 1984).

capable.[34] His connection to the common man can also be seen in his attitudes towards

language. He ridiculed the stilted bureaucratic phraseology of Russia's nineteenth-

century critical literature and lamented the role foreign borrowings had played: 'A

chaos of snippets of feeling, foreign [*chuzhye*] misunderstood thoughts, foreign

conclusions, and foreign habits, but especially words, words, words, and words—the

most European and liberal, of course, but, for us they are still words and only words.'[35]

Therefore, Dostoevskii was less likely to introduce new words to the Russian lexicon.[36]

Rather, the richness and flexibility of his language resulted from his ability to stretch the

connotative range of words already in the language and explore shades of meaning.[37] A

study of Dostoevskii's syntax has concluded that his uniqueness lay in creative

formulation of phrases, figures of speech, and bending the rules of phraseological

convention for expressive effect.[38] Given his propensity to use Russian words already

in circulation, a Dostoevskii wordlist may be taken as fairly representative of mid- to

late-nineteenth-century Russian vocabulary generally.

Compared to the study of Pushkin's vocabulary, scholarly interest in

Dostoevskii as a subject of linguistic analysis is fairly recent.[39] The first full dictionary

of Dostoevskii's language is currently being produced by the Russian Academy of

Sciences and only three volumes have been published, through the letter 'M.'[40] The

Statisticheskii slovar' was published as a prototype of this project and lists all of the

vocabulary employed by Dostoevskii with notes as to frequency of use in various

genres. As it includes no definitions or usage illustrations, this one-volume work

---

[34] Linda Ivanits, *Dostoevsky and the Russian People* (Cambridge: Cambridge University Press, 2008).

[35] Iu. N. Karaulov, ed., *Slovar' iazyka Dostoevskogo: leksicheskii stroi idiolekta* (Moscow: Azbukovnik, 2011), p. xvii.

[36] George Thomas, 'Aspects of the Study of Dostoyevsky's Vocabulary', *The Modern Language Review*, 77 (1982), 673 – 675.

[37] Ibid., pp. ix – xxv.

[38] E. A. Ivanchikova, *Sintaksis khudozhestvennoi prozy Dostoevskogo* (Moscow: Nauka, 1979).

[39] Ibid., 670.

[40] Iu. N. Karaulov, ed., *Slovar' iazyka Dostoevskogo: idioglossarii*, A-V (Moscow: Azbukovnik, 2008.); G-Z, (Moscow: Azbukovnik, 2010.); I-M, (Moscow: Azbukovnik, 2012).

professes a 'humbler aim' than that of the full dictionary, but is perfectly sufficient for the purposes of this dissertation. Drawing from a thirty-volume academic collection of Dostoevskii's works, and including all words used by the writer in his literary works, critical and publicist writings, and even personal letters, it may safely be assumed that this is a thorough representation of Dostoevskii's written vocabulary.[41]

Though reflecting roughly the same period as Dostoevskii, the late nineteenth-century dictionary of Vladimir Dal' could hardly be excluded from this study.[42] As of the 1930s, Dal''s was the most popular Russian dictionary.[43] A 1975 article on Russian linguistics reported that it was 'still the most exhaustive source of Russian vocabulary.'[44] Even in the post-Soviet period, the preface of a 2003 reprinting of the dictionary claimed that 'by wealth of lexical-phraseological material the dictionary of Dal' exceeds all dictionaries in Russia before or since.'[45] Indicative of the work's general acclaim is one scholar's reference to Dal' as the 'immortal Russian lexicographer'.[46]

Of particular importance was Dal''s use of commonly-spoken (ergo 'living') Russian words and phrases. By emphasizing simple, conversational speech, Dal' signalled a clear departure from the tradition of the Academy's dictionary. He insisted that 'if we do not find what we are looking for in books or in high society' then search must be made of 'the living Russian language, as it lives until now in the people. There is but one source: the language of the simple folk [*iazyk prostonarodnyi*].'[47] Though, like the Academy's dictionary, Dal' avoided profanity, he relished down-to-earth

---

[41] *Statisticheskii slovar'*, p. vii.

[42] V. I. Dal', *Tolkovyi slovar' zhivogo velikorusskogo iazyka: v chetyrekh tomakh* (St. Petersburg: M. O. Vol'f, 1880–1882; repr. Moscow: Russkii iazyk media, 2003).

[43] D. N. Ushakov, ed., *Tolkovyi slovar' russkogo iazyka*, 4 vols (Moscow: Gosudarstvennyi institut sovetskaia entsiklopediia, 1935 – 1940), I (1935), p. 2.

[44] Joanna Perelmuter, 'Russian Substandard Usage and the Attitude of Soviet Lexicography', *Canadian Slavonic Papers / Revue Canadienne Des Slavistes,* 16(1974), 437.

[45] Dal', *Tolkovyi slovar'*, I, p. vii.

[46] Boris Brasol, 'V. I. Dahl—Immortal Russian Lexicographer', *The Russian Review,* 23 (1964), 116–130.

[47] As cited by Ushakov, *Tolkovyi slovar'*, I, p. 1.

phraseology, peasant jargon and even regional dialects. In addition to material collected

from books, Dal' spent half a century traveling around Russia, listening to and recording

expressions, folksongs, and stories.[48] To Dal', the lexical material thus collected was

true 'ethnographic riches.'[49]

Considering Dal''s lifelong love for folk culture and the populist strain of his

work, it comes as no surprise that he was generally biased against the import of foreign

words into the Russian language. Scholars have referred to 'Dal''s resolute struggle

with foreign borrowings in the Russian language' and the fact that such borrowings

'deeply disturbed' him.[50] Dal' seems to have coined the distinctly negative-sounding

term *chuzhoslov* to refer to loanwords.[51] While not banning such words from his

dictionary, he did lament their presence in the language. During a speech given in 1860,

he quipped about popular French borrowings, 'if we didn't have the words *koketnichat'*

or *koketka* [in Russian] I would not grieve over them.'[52] He went so far as to invent

new Russian words and include them in the definitions of foreign loanwords as

alternative synonyms.[53] Despite his prejudices, however, Dal' did include foreign

loanwords in his dictionary and provide etymological notation as to their origin.

For the purposes of the present study, the text of the second edition of the

dictionary has been used as it is a fuller representation of the entirety of Dal''s work.

After the release in 1863 – 1866 of the first edition of his dictionary, Dal' spent the rest

of his life making significant revisions and collecting new material for a second edition.

After his death in 1872, the publishing company of M. O. Vol'f completed the editorial

---

[48] Brasol, 120–121.

[49] Dal', *Tolkovyi slovar'*, I, p. v.

[50] Ibid., pp. ix, vi.

[51] Ibid., ix.

[52] Ibid., xxxix – xli.

[53] Ushakov, *Tolkovyi slovar'*, I, p. 2.

work and released the second edition in 1880 – 1882. Also, as a practical matter, print copies of this edition seem to be easier to find.[54]

The turn of the twentieth century in Russia was a time of radical changes to the political, economic, and social order, which in turn brought abrupt changes to the language.[55] The *Tolkovyi slovar' russkogo iazyka,* edited by D. N. Ushakov (1873 – 1942) was the very first Russian dictionary of the Soviet Union and has been chosen as a source for words entering the language during the revolutionary period.[56] The career of Ushakov represents a chronological bridge between the academic worlds of old and new Russia and the struggle for linguistic normalization in early Soviet society. Born in the last decade of Alexander II's reign to an educated family—the son of a doctor and grandson of a priest—he attended gymnasium, graduated from Moscow University in 1895 with a degree in historical linguistics, went on to pursue more advanced degrees while working as a school teacher, and became a full professor at his alma mater in 1921, where he taught from 1907 to 1930. He is known for key linguistic works and textbooks published both in the last days of imperial Russia and the early days of the Soviet Union.[57] He was appointed to the commission which prepared the official diplomatic documents of the agreement ending the Polish-Soviet war in 1921. In the 1930s he ascended the ranks of the Academy of Sciences of the USSR, was lead editor of the first Soviet dictionary (published 1935 – 1940), and, despite his protest, was evacuated to Tashkent at the outbreak of World War II where he died from illness in 1942.[58]

---

[54] In 1935, the Soviet government produced facsimile reprints of the second edition. Dal', *Tolkovyi slovar'*, I, p. xiii.

[55] Bernard Comrie, *Russian Language in the Twentieth Century* (Oxford: Clarendon, 1996), p. 3.

[56] D. N. Ushakov, ed., *Tolkovyi slovar' russkogo iazyka,* 4 vols (Moscow: Gosudarstvennyi Institut Sovetskaia Entsiklopediia, 1935–1940).

[57] 'Ushakov Dmitrii Nikolaevich', in *Letopis' moskovskogo universiteta* < http://letopis.msu.ru/peoples/756> [accessed 16 March 2015]

[58] Archives of the Russian Academy of Sciences (ARAN), f. 502, *Istoricheskaia spravka* <http://isaran.ru/?q=ru/fund&ida=1&guid=CD48523D-674E-259D-3677–99C16D0A0CEA> [accessed 16 March 2015]

Partially inspired by his reading of Dal''s dictionary and also in response to the difficulty facing the Russian language of his day, Lenin had personally requested that Ushakov's dictionary be produced.[59] A large number of new terms had flooded the Russian language due to both industrialization and the new way of life brought on by communism. The appearance of new vocabulary characterizes this dictionary. Writing just ten years after the publication of the dictionary's four volumes, A. P. Vlasto comments that Ushakov's dictionary 'never set out to be all-inclusive, but is particularly informative on neologisms.'[60]

Parallel to the changing Russian vocabulary was a changing Russian readership. A newly literate population was badly in need of grammatical guidance as were the ranks of commoners who were increasingly filling leadership positions. Likewise, the new dictionary would play a pedagogical role for those Soviet subjects for whom the Russian language was not native, a fact alluded to by the dictionary's preface. The editors hint that the notes on spelling, pronunciation, and grammar would be 'useful for Russians and non-Russians.'[61] Unapologetically normative, the dictionary's preface explains that the compilers aimed to produce something exemplary of correct language, at a time when linguistic use was varied. Not unlike the first Academy dictionary over a century earlier, Ushakov's dictionary was charged with unifying a chaotic language and establishing norms. According to Morton Benson, Ushakov's phonological and grammatical notations established precedents that would be followed by all subsequent Soviet lexicographers.[62] Hyperbolically emphasizing the importance of this systematization, Benson goes so far as to claim that 'until the publication of the four-

---

[59] Perelmuter, 'Russian substandard usage', 440.

[60] A. P. Vlasto, 'A Word on Soviet Lexicography, *The Slavonic and East European Review,* 29 (1950), 290.

[61] Ushakov, ed., *Tolkovyi slovar',* I (1935), p. 3.

[62] Morton Benson, 'Soviet Lexicography: A Survey', EuraLEX, 86 (1988), 219 <http://www.euralex.org/elx_proceedings/Euralex1986/031_Morton%20Benson%20%28Pennsylvania%29%20-Soviet%20lexicography_%20A%20survey.pdf> [accessed 2 September, 2012]

volume Ushakov dictionary, there had been no dictionary whatsoever of standard Russian.'[63]

Among the many compilers listed in the second volume of Ushakov's dictionary is a name that would thereafter be prominent in Soviet linguistics.[64] V. V. Vinogradov (1895 – 1969) is remembered as one of the 'outstanding Russian philologists of the twentieth century.'[65] Vinogradov developed systems for the study of Russian grammar and syntax, and made important contributions to the historical analysis of the Russian language, including a famous general history of the Russian language and specialized studies of individual authors.[66] He was, for example, chief editor of the Pushkin dictionary used in the present study and, though the vision of a Dostoevskii dictionary is only now coming to fruition, produced smaller studies on the language of Dostoevskii in the 1920s through 1960s.[67] Vinogradov left behind a veritable dynasty of linguistic scholarship. Among the more notable disciples of the Vinogradov approach [*vinogradovskaia shkola*] are the chief editors of the other two Soviet dictionaries used in this dissertation.[68] Finally, the Russian Language Institute of the Russian Academy of Sciences, founded just two years after Ushakov's death and chaired by Vinogradov in the 1950s and 1960s, bears Vinogradov's name to this day.

During Stalin's 1937 repression, and in the years following, political pressure on lexicography continued to be visible in Russia and a systematic effort was made to

---

[63] Morton Benson, 'A Step Forward in Russian Lexicography', *Slavic and East European Journal,* 39 (1995), 431.

[64] Ushakov, *Tolkovyi slovar',* II (1938), p. i.

[65] Institute of the Russian Language of the Russian Academy of Sciences <http://www.ruslang.ru/agens.php?id=vvv> [accessed 16 March 2015]

[66] Iu. V. Rozhdestvenskii, 'Vinogradovskaia shkola', in V. N. Iartseva, ed., *Lingvisticheskii entsiklopedicheskii slovar'* (Moscow: Sovetskaia entsiklopediia, 1990) <http://tapemark.narod.ru/les/084a.html> [accessed 16 March 2015]

[67] Ivanchikova, *Sintaksis*, pp. 21 – 25.

[68] In an early edition of his one-volume dictionary, S. I. Ozhegov expressed 'particular gratitude to his teacher, Academic V. V. Vinogradov', S. I. Ozhegov, ed., *Slovar' russkogo iazyka* (1953), p. 3.

'purge' the language of foreign influence during this period.[69] The Russian language was considered 'a mighty resource for the communication of the peoples of our socialist fatherland, a powerful weapon in the fight for communism.'[70] Two dictionaries have been selected from the post-World War II generation: a one-volume dictionary, edited by S. I. Ozhegov and a four-volume dictionary released between 1957 and 1961 under the editorial guidance of A. P. Evgen'eva for a more comprehensive treatment of the mid twentieth-century Russian word-base.[71] After obliquely referring to significant linguistic change in the decade prior to its publication, the preface to the first volume (1957) states the dictionary's goal was 'to show the current condition of the vocabulary of the standard Russian language and present with necessary fullness its lexicon.'[72] Unlike Ozhegov, Evgen'eva's dictionary contains etymological notations for words of foreign origin. Ozhegov's dictionary has no such notations and the collection of words is considerably smaller, reflecting more common use.[73] For practical reasons, the third edition of Ozhegov has been used. A first edition of Ozhegov has been more difficult to find in print, whereas the third edition seems to have been more widely distributed and was not so difficult to procure. As a testimony to the increasing circulation of this dictionary, one review states that this third edition was the first one to reach the United States.[74] Published just four years after the 1949 first edition, the third edition may be regarded as basically the same stock of Russian words as the original. The preface states that it was printed 'from stereotype with only a few necessary corrections.'[75]

---

[69] Yvonne Grabowski, 'English Loanwords in Contemporary Russian', *Études Slaves et Est-Européennes / Slavic and East-European Studies,* 17 (1972), 122.

[70] S. I. Ozhegov, ed., *Slovar' russkogo iazyka* (Moscow: Gosudarstvennoe izdatel'stvo inostrannykh i natsional'nykh slovarei, 1953), p. 3.

[71] A. P. Evgen'eva, ed., *Slovar' russkogo iazyka v cheterekh tomakh* (Moscow, Gosudarstvennoe Izdatel'stvo Inostrannykh I Natsional'nykh Slovarei, 1957–1961).

[72] Ibid., I (1957), p. v.

[73] S. I. Ozhegov, ed., *Slovar' russkogo iazyka* (Moscow: Gosudarstvennoe izdatel'stvo inostrannykh i natsional'nykh slovarei, 1953).

[74] Benson, 'A Step Forward in Soviet Lexicography', 431.

[75] Ozhegov, *Slovar' russkogo iazyka*, p. 3.

Up until this point chronologically, multi-volume dictionaries have been selected so as to study something approaching the entire Russian lexicon of each period. Ultimately, however, the aim is to study those French loanwords which are part of the common vocabulary of present-day Russian-speakers, minus obscure terms that the average native speaker may not use or even know. Thus, for the current lexicon, a one-volume dictionary has been chosen. The thorough examination of previous multi-volume dictionaries is primarily a means of tracing trends and determining when those French words currently in common use first entered the language. The past lexicon studied comprehensively, as it were, is being used to shed light on the narrower common lexicon of the present.

Toward this end, however, patterns of lexical ebb and flow across history are also relevant. In so much as it fosters an understanding of the present lexicon and its French imprint, the journey is as relevant as the destination. Along this journey, observing the disappearance of words has often been as insightful as witnessing their appearance. Both phenomena—acquisition and loss of French loanwords—are observed via the discrepancies in chronologically adjacent dictionaries. The inclusion of two dictionaries from the mid-twentieth century—a multi-volume and single-volume—is an extra step designed to help explain discrepancies between the penultimate period considered and current use.

If only a multi-volume dictionary were to be used for the 1950s and then a one-volume dictionary consulted for the present lexicon, a question would remain: do discrepancies between the two dictionaries represent actual lexical change in the past half-century, or merely the difference between a one-volume dictionary and a more thorough four-volume set? To solve this issue, the one-volume Ozhegov has been studied alongside Evgen′eva for mid twentieth-century vocabulary. In many cases, it is the cross-referencing of these two dictionaries that clarifies when a change in vocabulary actually occurred. For example, the word *kartush*, borrowed from French

and referring to a particular item of architectural decoration, appears in the four-volume

Evgen'eva but is absent from the present common lexicon. However, the fact that this

word is also absent from the one-volume Ozhegov (1953) suggests that this is not

necessarily an example of twentieth century linguistic change. Rather, this very

technical term was already too obscure for inclusion in a general one-volume dictionary

as of 1953.[76] On the other hand, the fashion term *tal'ma*, a type of woman's cape,

appears in both Evgen'eva and Ozhegov, but not in the most recent one-volume

dictionary studied. Therefore, it may be surmised that *tal'ma* was a fairly common term

as of the 1950s that has actually fallen out of use in recent years. Without both a multi-

volume and single-volume dictionary for the penultimate period of study, neither of

these examples would be so clear.

It should be noted, however, that Ozhegov's inclusion in this study is more than

an analytical counter-weight to Evgen'eva. Ozhegov's contribution to Soviet

lexicography is significant in its own right. A household name among Russians,

Ozhegov could hardly be passed over in any survey of standard Russian dictionaries.

Still in common use, Ozhegov's dictionary was in its twenty-fifth edition as of 2007. A

testimony to its continuing relevance, publication rights for additional editions of

Ozhegov's work have even been a fiercely contested legal matter in recent years.[77]

Benson called Ozhegov's work a 'direct continuation of Ushakov's tradition.'[78]

Ozhegov himself recalled that 'originally, on the very eve of the Great Patriotic War,

this dictionary was conceived as an abbreviated [version] of the dictionary of Ushakov.'

However, even the first edition (1949) turned out to be far more than just an

---

[76] Though not a common word in general use, *kartush* can in fact be found currently in specialized dictionaries. See for example '*Kartush*' in *Arkhitekturnyi slovar'* available online at <http://mirslovarei.com/content_arh/kartush-89.html> [accessed 3 September 2013]

[77] Margarita Shchits, 'Net slov', *Rossiiskaia Gazeta,* 05 March, 2007 <http://rg.ru/prilog/nauka/03–05–07/1.shtm> [accessed 3 September 2013]

[78] Benson, 'Soviet Lexicography', 219.

abridgement of Ushakov as observed changes in the language since 1930s led the editors to be much more involved than anticipated in actually correcting word definitions and noting stylistic changes in word use.[79] Like Ushakov, Ozhegov and the other editors of this dictionary were normative in their notes on phonology and grammar, suggesting preferred practice where multiple common uses were cited. Benson ascribes this to pressure by the Soviet government to standardize the Russian language.[80] Likewise, political pressure discouraged Ozhegov from using foreign words, perhaps explaining the editorial choice not to make any etymological reference whatsoever to the origin of foreign borrowings.[81] Citing the strides made by the new regime in developing the Russian language, the preface of an early edition makes the claim that 'not much word-borrowing has occurred during the Soviet era',[82] a statement that is obviously inaccurate.[83] The first one-volume Soviet dictionary to be distributed broadly to the masses, Ozhegov's dictionary may be regarded as a further honing of the regime's program to centralize linguistic practice and spread those norms broadly.[84]

Throughout the twentieth century and into the post-Soviet era, the Russian language has continued to borrow foreign vocabulary, though English has been the single greatest source of loanwords since the revolution.[85] The dictionary chosen to represent current use is the *Sovremennyi tolkovyi slovar' russkogo iazyka,* produced under the auspices of the Institute of Linguistic Research of the Russian Academy of

---

[79] Quote take from S. I. Ozhegov, *Slovar' russkogo iazyka,* 25th edn (Moscow: *ONIKS Mir i Obrazovanie,* 2007), p. 3. Quote taken from the preface to the fourth edition, as reprinted in this 2007 edition.

[80] Benson, 'Soviet Lexicography', 219.

[81] Bernard Comrie, *The Russian Language in the Twentieth Century* (Oxford: Clarendon, 1996), p. 209.

[82] Ozhegov, *Slovar russkogo iazyka,* 3rd edn (1953), p. 8.

[83] Even considering only French borrowings, Ushakov's dictionary includes over 750 loanwords which do not occur in any of the pre-revolutionary dictionaries studied. Likewise, the third edition of Ozhegov's own work, from which the above quote is taken, includes over 100 new French borrowings that did not appear in Ushakov. Statements like the one above seem to be made in response to political realities rather than pure linguistic analysis.

[84] Benson 'A Step Forward in Soviet Lexicography', 431.

[85] Comrie, *Russian Language in the Twentieth Century,,* 225.

Science and chiefly edited by S. A. Kuznetsov.[86] Without mentioning previous linguists by name, the dictionary purports to 'continue the tradition of domestic [*otechestvennoi*, literally 'fatherland'] lexicography.'[87] This one-volume dictionary has been selected to represent the current lexicon, in the hope that its brevity will more accurately reflect modern Russian culture by excluding more obscure terms, a goal specifically referenced by the dictionary's editors.[88]

While this one-volume dictionary, like dictionaries before it, aims to represent the standard Russian vocabulary, it is ultimately the frequency with which words are actually used that provides the most conclusive insights regarding the cultural impact of loanwords. As an additional analytical aid, a frequency dictionary of the modern Russian language has also been consulted.[89] Based on the collection of texts in the National Corpus of the Russian Language—a representative word-base of the Russian language from 1950 – 2007—this dictionary analyzes the relative frequency with which various Russian words are used. In this thorough study, word use has been analyzed in thousands of Russian books, magazines, journals, newspapers, advertisements, technical manuals, business communications, television broadcasts, films and recordings of non-public spoken speech. By calculating the number of times per million words of text each Russian vocabulary word occurs, the editors of this frequency dictionary have produced, in addition to an alphabetical listing of words with statistical information, a rank-order listing of words in order of frequency.[90] Such information brings an important perspective to the task of weighing the relative importance of various periods and types of French linguistic import when the dictionaries of each period are so varied in scope and even emphasis. This resource should not be considered a tenth dictionary

---

[86] S. A. Kuznetsov, ed., *Sovremennyi tolkovyi slovar' russkogo iazyka* (Saint-Petersburg: Norint, 2007).
[87] Ibid., p. 3.
[88] Ibid.
[89] O. N. Liashevskaia and S. A. Sharov, eds, *Chastotnyi slovar' sovremennogo russkogo iazyka: na materialakh Natsional'nogo korpusa russkogo iazyka* (Moscow: Azbukovnik, 2009).
[90] Ibid., pp. v – ix.

in the lexical analysis, but rather a final filter to help sort out findings from the other nine and gain a clearer understanding of the strength and nature of each period of French influence upon Russia.

As this survey demonstrates, Russia's lexicographical tradition had been an evolving process with each generation of scholars building upon the work of previous generations though not without the subjective element of prejudices and the agendas of those producing or commissioning the dictionaries. The Academy dictionary of Catherine's day leaned towards the usage of high Russian society, strong in Slavonic heritage though arguably weak in colloquial flavour. Dal', on the other hand, advanced the earthy language of the peasants, veritably thrusting *prostorechie* into the accepted lexicon. The early Soviet dictionaries are rife with political ideology and make little secret of intentionally advancing a cause and centralizing verbal practice for a newly flattened social order. In a word, Russian lexicography has a long tradition of being deliberately normative. The preface to the dictionary edited by Ushakov reveals a measure of self-awareness on this point: 'the history of large dictionaries shows that every one of them is a reflection of the class interests of their era.'[91] Far from disqualifying Russian dictionaries as primary sources, peculiarities such as these provide a running commentary on the society in which the dictionaries were being written and are themselves important factors in the development of the Russian language. Furthermore, as this study moves toward examination of French loanwords, the biases of these dictionaries provide a strange sort of objectivity. Catherine's court, Dal', and the Soviet regime all had reasons to deemphasize and even exclude foreign borrowings. Therefore their inclusion in these dictionaries indirectly argues for the fact of their use in the language of their day. Likewise, the French-origin words to be found

---

[91] Ushakov, *Tolkovyi slovar'*, I (1935), p. 3.

in the Pushkin and Dostoevskii dictionaries are, of course, included based on actual examples of use.

Specific French influences revealed by the lexical analysis

For the present discussion, all of these dictionaries have been thoroughly studied and a categorized master-list of the French loanwords they contain has been compiled. In addition to being marked with a number of word-tags (the topical category and sometimes sub-categories to which each word has been assigned) each word is also marked with chronological notations as to its presence or absence in the various dictionaries. One of the important insights gained by the latter notation is the ability to see when a particular word first entered the Russian language, and whether its usage has endured to the present lexicon. This body of lexical data, arranged both chronologically and by category, has been analyzed for historical implications related to French influence upon Russian culture. A detailed description of the methodology by which this study was completed (including criteria for category assignment and etymological determinations) is included as Appendix A. The wordlist itself is included as Appendix B.

To begin with, this study immediately draws attention to the sheer volume of words in the Russian language that are borrowed from French. 2,983 make up the list of words gleaned from these nine dictionaries. This figure includes all French words entering the language since Peter the Great, many of which have since become antiquated or fallen out of use altogether. Still, the number of words which have endured—1,883 according to the 2007 dictionary—is noteworthy.

When did French loanwords join the Russian lexicon and why? Put differently, what kinds of influence did France exert upon Russia and in what periods? These questions have been answered by categorizing the French loanwords encountered and examining their appearance in the dictionaries of each temporal period. Six broad

categories of borrowed French words are clearly discernible: Cultural words; official

terminology; technology, industry and the sciences; urban and residential design;

philosophy and social thought; and special historical and foreign terms.

Cultural

Words dealing with cultural issues make up the largest group of French loanwords in

Russian, with 743 words—44% of all words categorized—fitting easily into this

category. This underscores the assertion that French influence upon Russia has been

largely cultural. The following chart (figure 2.2) shows the appearance of new cultural

words by sub-category in different periods of Russian history.

Figure 2.2: New Cultural Words Imported from French to Russian (by Period.)

	Before 1725	1725 – 1794	1794 – 1837	1837 – 1881	- 1882	1881 – 1940	1940 – 1957	1957 – 2007	**Total**
Fine arts	6	3	55	51	34	53	10	9	**221**
Fashion	7	9	30	40	47	54	6	11	**204**
Culinary	5	5	12	26	28	47	8	14	**145**
Gaming	1	3	11	10	19	5	2	0	**51**
Polite Society	3	1	13	9	0	1	0	0	**27**
Interpersonal	0	0	3	20	2	1	0	0	**26**
Estrada	0	0	0	2	0	8	1	1	**12**
Other	3	2	10	12	4	21	1	4	**57**
Total	**25**	**23**	**133**	**170**	**134**	**190**	**28**	**39**	**743**

A narrowing of analysis within the broader 'cultural' category suggests specific

ways in which France and French culture have impacted Russian culture. 221 words

related to fine arts (28% of the words in the 'cultural' category) have been borrowed

from French over the centuries. These are terms related to various visual and

performing arts (especially theatre), music and literature. Another large source of

French cultural words is, of course, fashion. 204 fashion words occur in the dictionaries

(27% of the 'cultural' words.) These are articles of clothing, various accessories, and

other elements of fashion including 72 different kinds of fabric! 153 words have to do

with food and food service (21% of the 'cultural' words), including two dozen different

drinks in the Russian language that are of French origin. Finally, Russia has borrowed a

number of cultural words from French that are more abstract and require considerably

more analytical nuance than the mere labelling of particular objects or actions. These

are emotive words, terms dealing with interpersonal relationships, protocols of 'polite

society' and etiquette, of which there are a fair few.

A comparison of French words entering the language in the adjacent periods

represented by the writings of Pushkin and Dostoevskii would seem to indicate a

cultural influence that increasingly deepens. Protocols of etiquette and the outward

trappings of culture make a strong showing in Pushkin's era. In the following

generation, that of Dostoevskii, words appear which are more internal in nature, dealing

with feelings, emotions, and more nuanced description of human interaction. For

example, there are at least 26 French loanwords in Russian that may be categorized as

relating specifically to 'polite society,' roughly half of which enter the language during

Pushkin's lifetime. Russian nobility were attending balls earlier, during the reign of

Catherine II (*bal* is one of the very few words of this category entering prior to

Pushkin), but the real influx of this type of word was in the early nineteenth century. It

was for the first time in Pushkin's era that the Russian language had the vocabulary to

speak of dancing a *val's* or attending a *maskarad*. For the first time in this period, the

word *etiket* enters the language, and the uncouth quality of a person with bad manners

was known as *moveton,* from the French 'mauvais ton', literally 'bad tone.' Though

this last word endures to the present lexicon, the more common (that is, 'Russian') word for the idea would be *nevospitannost'*.[92] These cultural norms relate to human interaction of a primarily external nature. They vary in scope from performing a 'curtsey' [*reverans*] or paying a *kompliment*, all the way to seeking *satisfaktsiia* in a *duel'*, but they are all external, dealing with surface behaviours and norms of protocol. By contrast, in the succeeding period a number of new French words would enter which are more thoughtful and deal with interpersonal relations on a deeper, more nuanced level. During Dostoevskii's writing career, Russians gain (from French) the necessary vocabulary to describe many shades of personal interaction. These facilitate a more sophisticated range of graded communicative options beyond the extremes of curtseying and duelling. Now one might 'impress' [*imponirovat'*], 'convince' [*urezonivat'*], or 'shock' [*shokirovat'*] an interlocutor. If the shock is of a particularly unpleasant nature, then the word would be *frappirovat'*. Continuing in this negative vein, one could simply 'neglect' [*neglizhirovat'*] or 'slight' [*tretirovat'*] an unsavoury person, or perhaps choose to actually *pikirovat'sia* with them and exchange caustic remarks (from the French 'se piquer'.)[93] As tensions escalate, conflicting parties my insult one another with a direct *afront*, which might cause a *skandal* and lead to a strong argument [*kontry*] or even a brawl [*debosh.*] All of these French loan words, imported during Dostoevskii's generation, represent a whole new wealth of gradient expression between previous extremes.

In the area of fashion, analysis of Russian dictionaries in various periods reveals enduring French influence. As fashions change, it is no surprise that each generation has imported a new group of words for clothing, accessories, and types of French fabric. Though the word for fashion itself, *moda*, was first introduced during Pushkin's time, loan words related to clothing, fabric and accessories appear in the Russian language as early as Peter's reign. Seven words related to clothing enter from French during the

---

[92] Ushakov, *Tolkovyi slovar' russkogo iazyka*, II, p. 239.
[93] Ushakov, *Tolkovyi slovar' russkogo iazyka*, III, p. 257.

reign of Peter. It is likely that several of these, such as flannel or twill, originally applied to military uniforms. Nine new words of this category are in the Academy dictionary of Catherine's era. Here the words for 'wig' and 'scarf' appear, as well as the names of a few finer fabrics like dimity and batiste. Thereafter, there is an acceleration of the import of French fashion words. Thirty different words of this category appear in Pushkin's era, 40 in the writing of Dostoevskii and another 47 in Dal''s dictionary. In the twentieth century, there are 71 new fashion words of French origin in the Russian language: 54 appear for the first time in Ushakov, six in Evgen'eva, and eleven in the *Sovremennyi* dictionary.

This statistical pattern suggests that Russian adoption of French fashion styles, concepts, and objects began slowly through the reign of Catherine, increased significantly in the early nineteenth century and remained steady or grew gradually until the Soviet period (see fig. 2.2). This trend of enduring influence seems to be reflected in contemporary Russian attitudes towards French fashion. A recent example will illustrate this. Russian art historian Marina Koleva describes her purchase, from a Parisian antique dealer, of a 1918 unpublished album of watercolour paintings by one Francoise Caron. The album contained Caron's depiction of urban dress from different eras and was accompanied by a few photographs and some personal letters written to a family member in Moscow. In a forward to this collection of early twentieth-century amateur paintings, Russian fashion historian, Aleksandr Vasil'ev, remarks that its publication is evidence of 'the interested and even loving attitude in Russia towards French culture.' Koleva is exemplary of this attitude, referring romantically to the 'forgotten life of the artist Francois Caron' as a 'little flame' [*ogonek*] which has appeared 'at the crossroad of destinies between Paris and Petersburg.' Describing Russia's perpetual appreciation for French fashion, she concludes that 'in the Russian public consciousness, the Frenchwoman is elegance and grace.'[94] As has already been discussed, and as the lexical analysis demonstrates, French fashion influence in Russia has existed to varying degrees and with moments of fluctuation throughout the eighteenth, nineteenth, and twentieth centuries.[95]

Not unlike the area of fashion, culinary words also enter Russian from French fairly consistently across history. A few of these terms appear under Peter and through Catherine, including *limonad, bul'on* and *sous* ('sauce.') No doubt these words trickle into the language as exposure to the West introduces culinary innovations to noble homes. One historian observes that 'In the eighteenth century some major changes took place in Russian diet: upper class diet had long differed from that of the mass of people in terms of quality and quantity, now is also came to differ in style.'[96] Gourmet cooking and the employment of European, especially French, chefs became a status symbol among the nobility. Russian translations of German and French cookbooks appeared at the end of the eighteenth century, even if these innovations only applied to an elite segment of Russia's population.

It was only in the nineteenth century that the masses would experience much change to their diet.[97] Twelve new French-origin words related to food and drink appear for the first time in the writing of Pushkin. Succeeding generations, beginning with that of Dostoevskii, would import an even greater number of French words related to food, drink, and food service. In addition to the names of particular dishes, there is evidence of a budding restaurant culture in Russia in the later nineteenth and early twentieth century, as French words such as *meniu, tabl'dot* (table d'hôte, or multi-course

---

[94] M. Koleva, *Istoriia kostiuma v risunkakh Fransuazy Karon* (Moscow: Avanta, 2011), pp. 5–9.

[95] See the discussion of fashion in the first two chapters of this dissertation, pp. 53 – 58, 119 – 123.

[96] R. E. F. Smith and David Christian, *Bread and Salt: A Social and Economic History of Food and Drink in Russia* (Cambridge : Cambridge University Press, 1984), p. 173.

[97] Kenneth F. Kiple and Kriemhild Conee Ornelas, eds, *The Cambridge World History of Food,* 2 vols (Cambridge: Cambridge University Press, 2000), II, pp. 1242 – 1243.

meal at a fixed price),[98] *kafe, metrdotel'*, and *garson* (a waiter) join the Russian lexicon. The word 'restaurant' itself appears for the first time in Ushakov's dictionary. Drawing from memoirs, Russian literature, Russian cook books, and culinary and cultural histories of Russia, Pavel Romanov's anecdotal history of Russian food culture includes an overview of the development of various levels of public eating establishments during the revolutionary and early Soviet period, ranging from the poshest restaurants to the simplest eateries where clients stood to eat, including cafés, bars, taverns and tea houses.[99] As this pattern illustrates, Russia was delayed in its adoption of the trend sweeping across Europe where events in revolutionary France had contributed to the spread of the modern-day restaurant. In eighteenth-century Europe, according to Romanov, 'meals [*trapeza*] were a domestic affair, among both the common folk as well as aristocrats. However, the French Revolution destroyed this culture and gave birth to a series of restaurants.' Russia, on the other hand, 'preserved its taste for "home-cooking", if only because of its poverty and technical backwardness.'[100] As economic and social conditions of the nineteenth century allowed for the introduction and popularization of finer eating establishments, it is only natural that terminology would be imported to go along with the more complicated aspects of food preparation and presentation which were new to the culture. In the last half of the nineteenth century, a number of high-class restaurants appear in Moscow and foreign waiters and 'maîtres d'hôtel' were often employed to make a more refined impression upon upper-level clientele.[101]

Another small but interesting group of French loanwords first appear in Ushakov's dictionary which speaks to the rise of Estrada culture during the

---

[98] Henry Woolf, ed., *Webster's New Collegiate Dictionary* (Springfield, Mass: G & C Merriam Co., 1979), p. 1176.

[99] P. V. Romanov, *Zastolnaia istoriia gosudarstva rossiiskogo* (Saint Petersburg: Kristall, 2000), pp. 308 – 336.

[100] Romanov, *Zastolnaia istoriia,* p. 518.

[101] Ibid., pp. 308, 313.

revolutionary period. In addition to the word *estrada* itself, *shantan* also appears for the first time in this period, referring to a restaurant with its own variety theatre. There is some rare reference to this type of entertainment earlier—Dostoevskii uses *kafeshantan* just once in all of his Russian writings—but these lower forms of the performing arts become a stable part of the Russian lexicon as of the late nineteenth and early twentieth century.[102] *Kabare* ('cabaret') and *taper* (a restaurant performer who sings and dances) enter the language during the revolutionary period, as does reference to a dance *reviu*. Finally, an interesting word, *etual'* (from the French etoile, 'star'), appeared to describe a 'fashionable actress, performing in light genres: comedies, estrada, etc.'[103] Already notated as 'archaic' by Ushakov, where the word first occurs, this word appears again in Evgen'eva (1957) but does not make it to the 2007 one-volume dictionary, nor is it common enough for inclusion in Ozhegov's 1953 one-volume dictionary. Still, the brief appearance of this 'starlet' in Russia's vocabulary speaks to the introduction during the revolutionary period of forms of performance entertainment other than the classical performing arts.

Richard Stites has described the appearance of new forms of popular entertainment as an urban phenomenon in the last decade of the Old Regime when industrialization brought masses from the middle and lower social classes to the larger cities. 'This pre-revolutionary culture', argued Stites, 'took shape as an amalgam of folk, high, and light urban entertainment genres of old Russia in a context of commercialism, the quickening of technology, relative openness after the revolution of 1905, and increased contact with foreign culture.'[104] Though some of the popular culture that sprang up during these days was later forbidden or strictly controlled by the state after the 1917 revolution, the appearance of a large variety of live performance

---

[102] A. Ia. Shaiikevich and others, *Statisticheskii slovar' iazyka Dostoevskogo*, p. 141.

[103] Ushakov, *Tolkovyi slovar' russkogo iazyka*, IV, p. 1440.

[104] Richard Stites, *Russian Popular Culture: Entertainment and Society Since 1900* (Cambridge: Cambridge University Press, 1992), p. 4

entertainment beyond the 'high culture' of traditional theatre during this time was the base of what would become modern Soviet *Estrada*.[105] If lexical statistics are any guide, the scope of this particular genre of French influence is considerably less than others, but is, rather, a general indicator of the growing diversity in popular entertainment around the turn of the century.

Regarding the fine arts, French influence upon Russia has been noteworthy. There is almost no lexical influence in this area through the reign of Catherine but considerable import thereafter. In each generation beginning with Pushkin and through to 1940, significant French contribution is evident in the number of new words related to music, literature, theatre and visual art. The word *balet* appears in Pushkin's writing, but all other terms related to classical dance are added in later periods, beginning with Dostoevskii. French lexical influence is much less significant throughout the rest of the twentieth century, with the exception of a few new words related to circus performance and avant-garde art.

As this statistical overview of cultural loanwords illustrates, French influence upon the Russian cultural identity has been both massive and intimate. This largest category of lexical import has introduced words dealing with some of the most basic and personal themes imaginable: what and how people eat, how they dress and present themselves, and varying manners of communication, beginning with simple interaction and including vocabulary for all manner of artistic expression. General French-led trends across Europe, initiated by Louis XIV and allowed into Russia beginning with Peter, may be credited to some extent.[106] However, more direct and intense French cultural influence upon Russia in the late eighteenth and early nineteenth century calls for special attention, as the discussion of word frequency still to come will emphasize.

---

[105] Ibid., p. 16

[106] See my discussion of French fashion in chapters one and two, pp. 53 – 58, 119 – 123.

Official Terminology

Terms related to official institutions comprise the second largest category of French

loanwords in the Russian language. Historically, this category represents the earliest

significant area of linguistic import from France to Russia. These make up 23% of all

the French loan words ever imported into Russian and about 15% of the French loan

words in present-day Russian. Altogether, 381 words that fall into this 'Official

Terminology' category have been imported into the Russian language.

Figure 2.3: New Official Terminology Imported from French to Russian

(by Period.)

	Before 1725	1725–1794	1794–1837	1837–1881	- 1881	1881–1940	1940–1961	1961–2007	Total
Military	31	29	33	19	40	21	0	0	**173**
Naval	6	3	2	4	12	7	0	0	**34**
Government	2	1	5	6	3	8	0	0	**25**
Administrative	7	3	7	11	2	19	0	0	**49**
Diplomacy	0	1	1	3	3	3	3	2	**16**
Legal	1	1	0	0	5	4	1	0	**12**
Economic	7	2	11	7	7	21	0	2	**57**
Office	0	1	1	4	1	8	0	0	**15**
Total	**54**	**41**	**60**	**54**	**73**	**91**	**4**	**4**	**381**

These are words related to government structures and procedures, economic

terms, legal language and, of course, the military. Examples of the government-related

words that Russia has borrowed from French include *mer* ('mayor'), *departament, raion*

('district'), and *dekret* ('decree', from the French 'decret'.) There are also a number of

Europeanisms which some of the dictionaries consider to be of French origin: *mandat,*

deputat, prerogativa (as in the 'prerogative' of a monarch), *konstitutsia,* and *parlament,*

to name a few.

The eighteenth century was a time of fundamental change in Russia's government and it is not surprising that terms would have to be borrowed from other languages to describe procedures and institutions foreign to Russia's past experience. L. F. Pisar'kova's study of eighteenth-century government records has traced the complicated process of moving from the old *prikaz* system—where a local government body empowered to rule on a variety of issues answered directly to the Tsar—to a more modern system of administrative colleges, where power was distributed among various institutions, each responsible for the management of a specialized area.[107] Peter's administrative reform of 1708, creation of the Senate in 1711, and further restructuring of government beginning in 1717 were all milestones in this process. He sought to pattern his government and system of laws after those of Sweden, whose legal system was considered to be the best in Europe at the time.[108] This background suggests the need for a somewhat critical response to the etymology assigned certain words by early dictionaries. As many of the official terms related to government administration and jurisprudence which enter the Russian language during Peter's reign and through that of Catherine are Europeanisms, it is difficult to know whether they were necessarily of French origin, though the dictionaries list them as such. Swedish influence is far more likely in Peter's generation. Comparing official terms entering the Russian language from the time of Peter through Catherine with their modern equivalents in French, Swedish, and English, demonstrates this fact (fig. 2.4). Note in particular the Russian words for 'office', 'package', and 'rank', which are similar to their Swedish counterparts, but dissimilar to the French.

The four-volume set of legal codices produced during Peter's reign were largely a theoretical exercise, as the Swedish-inspired collegial (or chancellor) form of

---

[107] L. F. Pisar'kova, *Gosudarstvennoe upravlenie Rossii s kontsa XVII do kontsa XVIII veka: evoliutsiia biurokraticheskoi sistemy* (Moscow: Rossiiskaia Politicheskaia entsiklopediia, 2007), pp. 3–15.
[108] Ibid., 142.

government administration proved problematic to implement across Russia's huge landmass.[109] Though Catherine referred to these Petrine volumes when compiling her own legal codex, the famous *Nakaz*,[110] the latter was more heavily influenced by her reading of French philosopher Montesquieu's *L'Esprit des Lois.* W. Gareth Jones has argued that, whether or not Catherine's actual governance was influenced by Montesquieu's legal philosophy, her literary interaction with his work while compiling the *Nakaz* is significant. [111] It would only be during the reign of Nicholas I that the codification of Russian laws would be fully realized in Mikhail Speranskii's 56-volume *Polnoe sobranie zakonov rossiiskoi imperii.*[112] Still, the reforming efforts of Peter and Catherine marked important early steps in this process of administrative modernization, and contributed to Russia's exposure to European culture.

Fig 2.4 Russian Terms Related to Government, Administration, and Law
(Entering the language from Peter I through Catherine II.)

Russian	French	Swedish	English
Кандидат	Candidat	Kandidat	Candidate
Шеф	Chef	Chief	Chief
Нотариус	Notaire	Notarie	Notary
Манифест	Manifeste	Manifest	Manifesto
Цертификат	Certificats	Certifikat	Certificate
Контрасигнатура	Contreseing	Kontrasignering	Countersignature
Рескрипт	Rescrit	Reskript	Rescript
Министр	Minister	Minister	Minister
Мандат	Mandat	Mandat	Mandate
Гарантировать	Garantir	Garantera	Guarantee
Контора	Fonction	Kontor	Office
Пакет	Forfait	Paket	Package
Ранг	Classer	Rangordna	Rank
Полиция	Police	Polis	Police
Контракт	Contrat	Kontrakt	Contract

[109] Pisar'kova, pp. 532 – 542.

[110] Zamaleev, *Istoriia russkoi kul'tury*, pp. 125–126.

[111] W. Gareth Jones, 'The Spirit of the "Nakaz"': Catherine II's Literary Debt to Montesquieu', *The Slavonic and East European Review*, 76 (1998), 658–671.

[112] Zamaleev, *Istoriia russkoi kul'tury*, p. 126.

Within the broader 'official' category of loanwords across Russian history, the largest sub-group of French words deals with the military and navy. Of the 381 French loan words in the 'official' category, 207 (54%) are either military or naval in nature. From Peter onward, each subsequent generation of Russian-speakers would borrow a new batch of military and naval words. To this day, words of French origin are among the more common Russian military terms, including 'attack', 'retreat', 'manoeuvre', 'campaign', 'trench', 'deserter', and many others.

In the Petrine era, borrowed military terminology was more numerous than any other category of French loanwords, government-related or otherwise. The obviously military words *bastion, serzhant, pistolet* ('pistol'), *ataka* ('to attack' from the French 'attaque'),[113] *desant* (a 'landing'), *patrul,* and *saliut* all entered the Russian language in the age of Peter I. Other words are less obvious. Some terms which have multiple meanings in the present-day Russian language would have been expressly military in Peter's day. For example, the word *pudra* ('powder') can currently be used in Russian to refer to any sort of powdery substance, including very fine confectionary sugar. However, when the word was first borrowed from French in the seventeenth or early eighteenth century, it almost surely referred exclusively to gun powder. Similarly, *pliumazh,* which in more modern times can denote any number of feathery costume decorations, would have referred specifically to part of an officer's uniform in Peter's era. Other examples include *bar'er, bresh'* ('breach'), *eskort, ekipazh* ('crew'), *parol'* ('password'), *transport, barak* ('a temporary structure'), *fas* ('face', as in a military formation), and *priz.* All told, 37 of the French words cited in Smirnov's study of the Petrine vocabulary are unmistakably military or naval in nature, even by modern standards. Another 20 would have been so originally, but today allow other meanings.

---

[113] Ushakov, *Tolkovyi slovar',* I, p. 67.

In light of those Petrine terms which have lost their military connotation, it is worth repeating at this point that only those words have been categorized which very clearly fit into one of the given groups. Words that have multiple meanings or definitions that have changed significantly over time have been classified into the generic 'various' category. As a result, a large quantity of French loanwords remained uncategorized. In this way, the categories themselves are made more potent by the exclusion of vaguely associated words and speak more effectively to the specific spheres of French influence. This does, however, leave numerous words which are too mutable or generic in their denotation to be categorized but are worth considering apart from the broader statistical analysis. Though not contributing to the statistical results, these words often provide relevant narrative insights into French influence as individual lexical case studies. A fair number of these are French terms which entered the Russian language during different periods as military terminology but lost this connotation over time.

When the word *invalid* first appeared in Russian following the 1812 war with France, it referred exclusively to 'retired military who has lost his earning capacity because of injuries or old age.' The publication of a veterans' newspaper entitled *Russkii Invalid* began in 1813 in Petersburg. This journal is referenced in Pushkin's writings, as are the old wounded veterans ('invalids') whose stories young Pushkin remembered listening to with great interest. Pushkin's use of the term *invalid* (from the French 'invalide') carried a tone of respect for those disabled warriors who had defended the Fatherland in a previous generation.[114] Similar deference was attached to the term near the end of the nineteenth century when Dal' defined *invalid* as 'an honoured soldier who has completed his service and is unable to serve because of injury, wounds, or feebleness.' Further, adjectival versions of this word in Dal''s

---

[114] Vinogradov, *Slovar' iazyka Pushkina*, II, p. 228.

definition refer to examples of special *invalidnyi* houses and so forth designed to accommodate these wounded veterans.[115] The word eventually began to be circulated more generically and, by 1935, referred to any person who had lost the ability to work because of injury, illness or old age and use of the term to refer specifically to military veterans was considered 'outdated'. By this time there was even a slang usage of *invalid* to refer to 'an old item which has defects because of long use.'[116] By the 1950s, military usage is not prescribed in any of Evgen'eva's definitions of *invalid*, but illustrations of usage include 'a military *invalid*.'[117] In the 2007 *Sovremennyi* dictionary, the definition of *invalid* is identical to that of Evgen'eva but there is no mention at all of any military connection. Tracing the evolution of this word across time illustrates how a borrowed word can appear in the language due to a very specific sphere of influence (in this case military) but gradually be assimilated into broader usage and eventually lose the original connection altogether.

The Russian word for 'team' [*komanda*], a French loanword, also had a strictly military definition from Catherine's time all the way to the end of the nineteenth century. Only in the first Soviet dictionary was the word also used to refer to 'a group of participants in an athletic competition' and even then this was the seventh in a long line of definitions for the word, the first few more military in nature.[118] When the word first appeared in the Russian language in the Academy's dictionary, it was not defined at all. Rather, the reader was referred to the *chin* family of words—*chin, nachal'nik,* and so forth—all of which refer to governing authority, leadership, and command structure.[119] This connotation remained representative in subsequent dictionaries, becoming more refined and including other examples. In the twentieth century, the uses

---

[115] Dal', *Tolkovyi slovar'*, II, p. 44.

[116] Ushakov, *Tolkovyi slovar'*, I, pp. 1199–1200.

[117] Evgen'eva, *Slovar' russkogo iazyka*, I, p. 917.

[118] Ushakov, *Tolkovyi slovar'*, I, p. 1416.

[119] *Slovar' akademii rossiiskoi*, IV, p. 474.

of the word were even more diverse, including the informal use of the word *komanda* to refer to someone's circle of like-minded compatriots such as 'the president's team.'[120]

Another word, *konduitnyi* (from the French 'conduite') began as a uniquely military term, picked up more general connotation over time, and eventually fell out of use altogether. When the word first appeared in Dal''s dictionary, it referred to a 'list with notes about the behaviour and abilities of a military official.'[121] After the revolutionary period, such a leger might be used to record the 'misconduct' of either students or soldiers.[122] Later in the twentieth century, military reference had disappeared as *konduitnyi* was defined as a 'list, journal with notes about the behaviour and misconduct of students in educational institutions of pre-revolutionary Russia,'[123] though Ozhegov's one-volume dictionary of the same period did make some passing reference to soldiers, apparently copying Ushakov's earlier definition. The 2007 dictionary follows Evgen'eva's example and defines the term historically, as an archaic reference to pre-1917 Russia, making no military connection.[124]

Finally, a very common Russian word, *inzhener* ('engineer' from the French, 'ingenieur') currently refers generically to any 'specialist with higher technical education.'[125] However, when the term was first borrowed from French it was almost exclusively military in nature. In Catherine's time, the word replaced an older Slavic word, *rozmysl,* to indicate 'the one who invents, sketches drawings, [and] produces work related to the sieging of cities or protecting and fortifying of places.'[126] Pushkin's use of the term was in reference to an 'officer, a specialist in military construction, fortification.'[127] By the time of Dal', other definitions were allowed: 'a trained builder,

---

[120] Kuznetsov, *Sovremennyi tolkovyi slovar'*, p. 280.

[121] Dal', *Tolkovyi slovar'*, II, p. 150.

[122] Ushakov, *Tolkovyi slovar'*, I, p. 1435.

[123] Evgen'eva, *Slovar' russkogo iazyka,* II, p. 113.

[124] Kuznetsov, *Sovremennyi tolkovyi slovar'*, p. 284.

[125] Ibid., p. 244. An identical definition for this word given in Ozhegov, *Slovar' russkogo iazyka*, p. 217.

[126] *Slovar' akademii rossiiskoi,* III, pp. 305–306.

[127] Vinogradov, *Slovar' iazyka Pushkina*, II, p. 229.

not of residential houses (that would be an *arkitektor* or *zodchii*) but rather of other types of construction' and military engineers are given as an example.[128] Ushakov is the first to refer to an engineer generically as anyone with a higher technical education, the basic definition which would endure to the present day. *Invalid, komanda, konduitnyi,* and *inzhener* are all words that illustrate both the depth of French military influence in Russian in the eighteenth and early nineteenth century and the extent to which word meanings can change over time.

Other official words that are not military in nature include those dealing with economics, business, legal matters, diplomacy, and administration. Russian economic and business terms of French origin include *bankir, profit,* and *fond.* The words for 'mercantile' and an insurance 'policy' [*polis*] are also of French origin as is the verb *kotirovat'* as in 'to quote' a price. In revolutionary and Soviet times, a person who gained wealth through 'speculation' (another borrowed word) came to be known as *nuvorish. Kurtazh* ('retail') is a French borrowing from the nineteenth century, which came to be used as a descriptor of business practices in capitalistic societies. The term does not appear in the 2007 dictionary. The informal French borrowing *kvit* has been used since Pushkin's time to describe the situation of someone whose debts are all paid up. A number of the terms in the Russian legal vocabulary, such as 'extradition', 'arbitration', 'guarantee' [*garant*], and even 'legalize' [*legalizirovat'*] are all borrowed from French, as are a number of words related to office management, stationery items, and the like: *bloknot* ('notebook'), *biuvar* (a desk pad), *klerk,* and the obvious *reziume.* Several diplomatic terms have entered the Russian language from French over the years, including the word *diplomat, al'ians, attashe* and *duaien* (from the French 'doyen', 'the head of a diplomatic corps.')[129]

---

[128] Dal', *Tolkovyi slovar'*, II, p. 44.
[129] Kuznetsov, *Sovremennyi tolkovyi slovar'*, p. 117.

As Russian society began debating political and social structures in the nineteenth and early twentieth century, French word import suggests that Russians were looking to western examples. Even before the replacement of the monarchy in 1917, historians of the Russian bureaucracy have noted 'rapid expansion of staff and offices' throughout the nineteenth century, and especially changes to local government administration following the abolition of serfdom in 1861.[130] The word *biurokrat*, when it first appeared in the writing of Dostoevskii, seems initially to have been vocabulary for describing a foreign leadership structure. Dal' defines *biuro* primarily as a piece of furniture, but then adds that 'in France [a bureau] is a place [connected with the] government.' As a sub-heading under *biuro*, Dal' defines *biurokratia* as '[a form of] management where a governing official is in charge; gradual subordination' with each official answering to the one above him, and there is a lot of paperwork is involved [*bumazhnoe mnogopisanie.*]'[131] By 1939, the main definition of *biuro* was the 'organ which governs a particular job within an institution' with no mention of France beyond etymology, and bureau as a writing table is demoted to a third sub-definition.[132] A number of new words related to bureaucracy and organizational structure were imported from French to Russian during the early Soviet period. These include the words for 'clerk', 'agency', 'questionnaire' [*anketa*], 'dossier', 'secretariat', 'delegate', 'directive', and a special verb for 'registering a disagreement': *dezavuirovat'* (from the French 'desavouer'.)

For borrowed administrative terms, distinction has been made in the appended wordlist between words specifically related to the government and those denoting organizational structures and policies which might also apply to non-government

---

[130] Don Karl Rowney, 'Structure, Class, and Career: The Problem of Bureaucracy and Society in Russia, 1801 – 1917', *Social Science History*, 6 (1982), 90 – 91. See also the discussion of the Russian bureaucracy and administrative changes across the revolutionary period in Hans Rogger, *Russia in the Age of Modernisation and Revolution: 1881 – 1917* (London: Longman, 1983) pp. 44 – 70.

[131] Dal', *Tolkovyi slovar'*, I, p. 158.

[132] Ushakov, *Tolkovyi slovar'*, I, p. 215.

institutions, such as a large business or the running of an estate. Though there is considerable overlap in use, these words have been divided into two different sub-categories: 'government' and a more generic group of 'administrative' words. In point of fact, all of these words are administrative in nature, but not all of them are necessarily related to the government. For example, an 'authorization' or 'reprimand' might be issued within any organizational structure, but 'ratification' is strictly a government function.

Technology

Three hundred and eleven of the words borrowed from French into Russian—18.4% of those categorized—are words dealing with technology, industry, or the sciences. The table below gives a detailed break-down of these words by time period (fig. 2.5). The borrowing of these words seems to have less to do with the direct influence of French culture and more to do with a general trend towards modernization and industrialization in Russia, especially in the late nineteenth and early twentieth century.[133] As new technologies and studies enter Russia, foreign-named objects enter with them, French or otherwise. Moreover, beginning with Dal', dictionaries seem to take on a more scientific role, serving the function that encyclopedias and other reference books would later take. This can be seen in the 68 French loan words for the names of various plants and animals, the definitions of which often include Latin scientific names. For example, Dal''s definition of 'giraffe', which later Russian dictionaries would consider a French borrowing, has the scientific feel that one might expect from a modern dictionary or encyclopaedia article: '*Zhiraf* or *Giraf:* a split-hooved animal, *Camelo pardalis*, with a low back and incongruously long neck.'[134] Like other scientific and technological terms

---

[133] John P. McKay, *Pioneers for Profit: Foreign Entrepreneurship and Russian Industrialization, 1885–1913* (Chicago: University of Chicago Press, 1970).
[134] Dal', *Tolkovyi slovar'*, I, p. 542.

which enter the language, the import of this French word seems to indicate no particular French influence. Rather, a country that is becoming rapidly modernized is looking beyond its own borders and voraciously importing facts and terms related to any number of scientific disciplines, in this case zoology.

Fig. 2.5: New French loan words related to technology, industry, and the sciences (by period)

	-1725	1725–1794	1794–1837	1837–1881	-1881	1881–1940	1940–1957	1957–2007	To…
Technology									
medical	1	1	2	9	12	15	2	3	4
aviation	0	0	0	1	1	18	2	0	2
transportation	2	0	2	4	1	7	1	0	1
misc.	1	0	3	0	5	24	1	0	3
Industry									
misc.	0	1	3	3	12	33	4	0	5
Science									
animals	1	2	1	3	13	13	1	1	3
plants	0	0	4	5	8	15	1	0	3
chemistry	0	0	0	1	5	4	1	2	1
minerals/geology	0	1	0	0	3	6	2	0	1
measurement	0	0	1	0	3	6	1	0	1
mathematics	1	0	0	1	1	1	1	2	
astronomy	1	0	1	1	2	1	0	0	
biology	0	0	0	1	2	1	0	2	
misc.	0	1	1	1	3	6	2	0	1
TOTAL	7	6	18	30	71	150	19	10	3

French terms related to chemistry, biology, astronomy and medicine appear in the Russian language in the mid to late nineteenth century. Also, the names of various plants, animals, chemicals, and astronomical objects like *planeta* and *meteor* enter the language from French in the nineteenth century. Among medical terms, the word for 'obstetrician' [*akusher*] is borrowed from French as well as the names of certain diseases and pieces of surgical and first-aid equipment like *bandazh, vazelin,* and *bisturi* (a small surgical knife.)

Some of this may be explained by the impact of Alexander II's reforms on the pursuit of scientific research. In particular, the 1863 University Statute gave universities permission to establish scientific societies. Under the statute, these new societies could corporately organize their scholarly activity, seek private funding for research, and publish their findings.[135] The creation and publication of scientific journals in the Russian language was an important development scientifically, linguistically, and even societally. Previously, scientific scholarship had been somewhat of an elite affair. Research was done in foreign languages and published in foreign journals.[136] Going back to the progressive developments of Peter I's programs, Russian science and technology had always been largely dependent upon foreign ideas, materials, and instruction. The Imperial Academy of Sciences, founded in 1725, was an organization in three levels, with upper layers dominated by foreigners, mostly Germans. It would be two decades before any native Russians were elected to the top level of the Academy and over a century before ethnic Russians controlled the Academy.[137] At the time of Alexander II's reforms, the old scientific societies were still limited to those who could read French and German, thereby excluding promising new scholars from the lower nobility or middle class who had not had the benefit of private tutors in those languages.

With the establishment of new organizations and their respective scholarly journals such as The Society of Admirers of Natural Science, Anthropology, and Ethnography (1864), the Russian Chemical Society (1868), and numerous others

---

[135] Alexander Vucinich, *Science in Russian Culture* (Stanford, Calif.: Stanford University Press, 1970), pp. 76–77.
[136] Ibid., p. 17.
[137] Loren Graham, 'Science in Russia: Foreign and Domestic Influences', *Comparative Education Review*, 12 (1968), 235–236.

founded throughout the 1860s and 70s, broader participation in these disciplines was fostered. Regarding the linguistic implications of these developments, Alexander Vucinich has remarked that 'for the first time the pages of a specialized journal were open to chemists who were competent in their science but could not write in French and German.'[138] Membership in these societies grew rapidly, and a wealth of new scholarship was published in the Russian language. Since previous research and writing had always been conducted in French and German, it is only natural that specialized terms in the budding Russian academic literature should be imported from these languages.

Likewise, words related to different kinds of industrial technologies were introduced in the nineteenth and twentieth century. The appearance of foreign terms related to technology and industry is to be expected, as foreign involvement in Russia's industrialization was substantial.[139] One example is the role of foreign capital and imported technology in the building of Russian railways in the last half of the nineteenth century. Despite the availability of metals in the Urals, a large portion of the rails for this construction was imported. Ian Blanchard has ascribed this to a 'technological backwardness' in Russia, which prevented native industry from keeping pace with its own country's needs.[140] Sergei Witte, an important policy maker who oversaw a burst of Russian industrialization in the 1890s, was criticized during his administration for his openness to foreign funds and technology, which he felt was necessary. At this time,

---

[138] Vucinich, *Science in Russian Culture,* p. 82.

[139] For fuller treatment of this topic, see John P. McKay, *Pioneers for Profit: Foreign Entrepreneurship and Russian Industrialization, 1885–1913* (Chicago: University of Chicago Press, 1970). Also, Paul R. Gregory gives a helpful overview of some of the main historical opinions related to Russia's industrial policy of the time as it relates to foreign involvement, including that of McKay, in his article 'Russian Industrialization and Economic Growth: Results and Perspectives of Western Research', *Jahrbücher Für Geschichte Osteuropas,* 25 (1977), 200–218.

[140] Ian Blanchard, 'Russian Railway Construction and the Urals Charcoal Iron and Steel Industry, 1851–1914', *The Economic History Review,* 53 (2000), 107.

there was significant capital investment in Russia from France, Belgium, Germany, England, and Sweden.[141]

Of the 311 French loanwords specifically identified as falling into the broad category of 'technology and sciences', only 62 of them (20%) appear before 1882 when the second edition of Dal''s dictionary was published. 71 words of a scientific or technological nature (23%) appear for the first time in Dal''s dictionary, 150 new French words of this type (48%) appear sixty years later in Ushakov's dictionary and another 29 words (9%) appear throughout the rest of the twentieth century.

Russia would continue to develop technologically throughout the twentieth century. The decrease in technological and scientific French words later in the century is likely due to the increasing Anglicization of these fields. As Russian modernization and industrialization continued its upward trajectory, English borrowings would overshadow French borrowings in Russian as in other European languages. In the study of uniquely French influence on Russian culture, less should be made of the words in this particular category.

Urban and Residential Design

Words in the urban and residential design category, an additional 115 words are those related to city infrastructure and architecture as well as the interior and exterior design of the home. This is 7% of all words classified.

---

[141] Hans Rogger, *Russia in the Age of Modernization and Revolution, 1881–1917* (London: Longman, 1983), p. 103.

Fig. 2.6: New French Loanwords Related to Urban and Residential Design

(by period)

	-1725	1725–1794	1794–1837	1837–1881	-1881	1881–1940	1940–1961	1961–2007	Tot
Architecture	4	3	4	7	13	9	0	0	4(
Interior Décor	0	2	6	13	3	6	3	2	3'
Space Management	3	1	4	7	1	8	0	0	2'
Infrastructure	1	0	5	2	2	1	0	1	1'
Landscaping	0	0	1	1	2	0	0	0	4
Total	**8**	**6**	**20**	**30**	**21**	**24**	**3**	**3**	**11**

Though this category is largely cultural, many of these terms are also technical in nature and are no less important as professional vocabulary than they are for their cultural implications. They may be thought of as representing both the 'science' and 'art' of building cities and homes. Hence a separate category, though they are relatively few. These are architectural terminology of French origin such as *rotunda*, *palisad*, and *rel'ef* (as in a sculptural 'relief' that adorns the outside of a building) as well as less artistic architectural words such as *briket* or *beton* ('concrete.') Words related to city infrastructure also fall into this category, especially the names for types of streets: *aveniu, bul'var, prospect, alleia, shosse* and even the word for 'sidewalk' [*trotuar*]. Inside the home, words for various types of rooms and other terminology related to space management are likewise borrowed from French: *zal* ('hall'), *foie, apartamenty, vestibiul', buduar, koridor, al'kov, avanzal* ('anteroom') and a number of others. The word for 'furniture' [*mebel'*] is borrowed from French as are the names of various types of furniture and other items related to interior design. All of these words speak to the way Russians live: how their cities and homes are built, what they look like, how they are arranged, and the items inside the home with which one surrounds himself. It is only the technical bent of some of these words that prevents the group from being a subset of the cultural category, for their relevance to Russian culture is obvious.

To serve the utopian ideals of the state, Russian architecture consistently looked to France for inspiration beginning with the reign of Peter the Great and through to 1812. During this period, Russian architects studied French theory and French architects were invited to work in Russia.[142] However, as the table in figure 2.6 illustrates, French influence was strongest in Russia in the nineteenth century. One historian of Russian architecture has suggested that 'of all periods of Russian architectural history, the nineteenth century may perhaps most appropriately be termed "the European century."' The reigns of Alexander I and Nicholas I were marked by a return to Catherine II's goal of reproducing French utopian architecture in Russia and the realization of this goal through strict government control of city planning and architecture.[143]

Philosophy and Social Thought

This category is the smallest, containing a mere 66 words (4%), but is a stand-alone grouping because of the importance of the subject matter to Russian society.

Appearing later in the Russian language, these French words describe the ideas which eventually became political movements and the theoretical basis for a new Soviet society. The period representing the writing career of Pushkin (1813 – 1837) saw the introduction of a number of these types of words which were not a part of the Russian lexicon just a generation earlier. The new words *ideal* and *individual'nost'* speak to French influence in a growing philosophical sensitivity. Likewise, the word

---

[142] D. O. Shvidovskii, 'Frantsiia i razvitie russkoi arkhitektury XVIII – nachala XIX v.', in *Frantsiia i Rossiia v nachale XIX stoletiia: Prosveshchenie. Kul'tura. Obshchestvo.*, ed. by T. G. Igumnova (Moscow: Gosudarstvennyi istoricheskii muzei, 2004), pp. 30 – 42.
[143] Dmitry Shvidkovsky, *Russian Architecture and the West* (New Haven: Yale University Press, 2007), p. 309.

Vol'ter'ianets, used to describe an enlightened free-thinker in the tradition of Voltaire, is used for the first time in Pushkin's day. Political terms like *partiia, revoliutsiia, natsiia* ('nation'), and *natsional'nyi* ('national') make their appearance as well. The French Revolution and subsequent reign of terror were events that occurred in the decade immediately prior to Pushkin's birth when the Russian state, nervous about instability in Europe and the possible spread of revolutionary fervour, was closely monitoring events in France.[144] Words alluding to French revolutionary movements past and present, such as *fronda* ('Fronde') and *Iakobinets* ('Jacobin') also enter the Russian vocabulary at this time. It is not at all surprising that Pushkin and his contemporaries would have known these French words and many others like them. The noble class had been exposed to French culture since the reign of Elizabeth and entrenched in it during Catherine's reign. Pushkin and others of the elite minority spoke French and would have conversed on such topics. Pushkin was thirteen years old when Napoleon marched into Moscow. What is significant is that these are all now Russian words, not written with Latin script as they appear in the transliteration above, but in Cyrillic letters as part of the national vocabulary.

French political words continued to trickle into the Russian language after Pushkin's time, as represented in the writing career of Dostoevskii (1844 – 1881).[145] A Russian with an *ideal* could now be referred to as an *idealist. Fraktsiia* (as in a political 'fraction'), *roialist,* and *federatsiia* all become Russian words during this period. Reference to the republican anthem *La Marseillaise* could now be made, using a new Russian noun (*marsel'eza.*) The word *burzhuaziia* also makes its first appearance in the language at this time. A budding interest in French socialism can be seen in the introduction of two new Russian nouns, *sensimonist* and *fur'erist* to denote adherents to

---

[144] James Marcum, 'Catherine II and the French Revolution: a Reappraisal', *Canadian Slavonic Papers,* 16 (1974), 187–201.

[145] These dates refer to Dostoevskii's literary and critical works. If personal letters are included, then the correct dates would be 1832 – 1881. A. Ia. Shaiikevich, *Statisticheskii slovar' iazyka Dostoevskogo*, p. xiv.

the ideas of early French socialist Henri de Saint-Simon and utopian philosopher

Charles Fourier.[146] Near the end of Dostoevskii's life, the word 'communism' enters

the Russian language. Though not of French origin, this new term is somewhat

misplaced in Dal''s dictionary as a sub-definition under the French loan-word

'communication.' *Komunizm* (later spelling would be different) is briefly defined here

as 'a political teaching about equality of status, community of ownership, and

everyone's right to the property of others.'[147] This reductionist definition, along with

the other words cited here, represent the rise of philosophical and political discussions

in mid-nineteenth-century Russian society. Russian thinkers looked to France for

vocabulary, philosophical constructs, and historical examples around which to frame

their developing political ideas, a fact attested to by the steady trickle of loanwords into

the language. Later, during Russia's revolutionary period, this trickle would become a

stream.

The timing of the first Soviet dictionary's publication makes it a helpful primary

source for the study of French influence on Russian social thought. Ushakov's

dictionary (published 1935 – 1940) and the second edition of Dal''s dictionary

(published 1880 – 1882) serve as historical 'bookends' to Russia's revolutionary period.

As such, French words in Ushakov's dictionary that were not present in or before Dal'

may be safely considered new importations that occurred during this turbulent and

crucial period of Russian history. Lexical evidence indicates that French intellectual

influence in this period was significant. Judging from Smirnov's list and the Academy

dictionary, there are few or no French borrowings related to political philosophy from

Peter I through to the end of Catherine's reign. In the writings of Pushkin, Dostoevskii,

---

[146] These French borrowings represent early experiments in Russian social thought. Neither of these new political labels are found in the 2007 *Sovremennyi* dictionary or the one-volume Ozhegov dictionary of 1953. They are, however, both in Ushakov (1935 – 1940) and the Evgen'eva's four-volume dictionary (1957 – 1961.)

[147] Dal', *Tolkovyi slovar'*, II, p. 149.

and Dal''s dictionary combined (representing the period 1813 – 1882), there are fewer than 30 words that would fall into this category, even if historical terms are included which are political in nature (*fronda* and *Iakobinets*, for example.) By contrast, in Ushakov's dictionary alone there are 35 new French loanwords, in addition to those previously borrowed, which overtly relate to political science and social thought, and a number of French historical terms which have political overtones. French-origin terms for the *Avtoritarnyi* ('authoritarian') and *mazhoritarnyi* ('majority rule') forms of government appear in this first Soviet dictionary, as does the short-lived addition, *ministerializm*: 'the opportunistic, compromising policy of the social-democratic parties of the Second International, justifying the practice of socialist participation in bourgeois reactionary governments.'[148] New words for political activity are also imported from France, such as *azhiotazh,* as in the public 'agitation' of political sympathies through propaganda and demonstration. Other words describe actions that the government might take. From the French 'octroyer' ('to grant' or 'bestow') comes the new Russian verb *oktroirovat'*: 'In a monarchist government, to provide certain formal rights or advantages to a particular part of the population or to a certain organization or corporation.'[149] Likewise, verbs for 'demoralizing' a group or individual, taking away or reinstating someone's citizenship rights (*denaturalizovat'* and *renaturalizovat'*) and nullifying (*denonsirovat'*) a diplomatic agreement or contract are all imported from French during this period.

In addition to these clearly French loanwords are other Europeanisms, the specific origin of which is less clear. Though later Russian dictionaries assign French etymology to all of these words, the Ushakov dictionary, where the words first appear,

---

[148] Ushakov, *Tolkovyi slovar'*, II, p. 219. This word does not appear in any of the later Russian dictionaries studied.
[149] Ibid., p. 797.

gives no etymology or suggests Latin or Greek origin. These include words for 'federalism', 'absolutism', 'anti-Semitism' and 'totalitarian', to name a few.

**Fig. 2.7: New French Loan Words
Innately Related to Philosophy and Social Thought (by period)**

Before 1725	1725–1794	1794–1837	1837–1881	-1882	1881–1940	1940–1957	1957–2007	**Total**
3	0	14	10	3	35	1	0	**66**

Fig 2.8: New France-specific Historical Terms (by period)

-1725	1725–1794	1794–1837	1837–1881	-1882	1881–1940	1940–1957	1957–2007	**Total**
7	1	15	13	4	30	3	2	**75**

France-specific Historical Terms

The fact that revolutionary Russia looked to France for inspiration is also evidenced by the appearance of new words related to French history. A table showing the appearance of these France-specific terms (fig. 2.8, above) is shown alongside a similar table for political vocabulary (fig. 2.7) to illustrate that this interest in French history mirrored trends in political thought. Russian transliterations of Girondists, Montagnards and Sans-culottes, all partisan groups in revolutionary France, are included and defined for the first time in Ushakov's dictionary, as are the Jacquerie, a peasant movement in fourteenth-century France. Even the definitions of non-political historical terms related to the old French nobility make veiled allusions to the Marxist idea of class struggle. For example, a *parveniu* was 'in the language of aristocrats, an upstart; a person from the middle class who had achieved access to aristocratic circles or quickly achieved a high position of service.'[150] The frivolity and *dekadans* (another new word) of bourgeois society is highlighted by the inclusion of terms like *metressa* ('mistress') and *demimond*, 'a circle of courtesans who are imitating the life of aristocrats; an upstart.'[151] *Demimond, metressa* and *parveniu* are all notated as being 'archaic' in the definition given by the editors, though they conspicuously appear in this dictionary having never appeared in any previous Russian dictionaries. The inclusion of 'archaic' French words as new vocabulary speaks to a special interest in French history during this period, especially as it related to social classes and political movements. None of these words, nor the names of the revolutionary movements noted earlier, endure to be included in later dictionaries, but represent a very period-specific fascination with the details of French social and political history. Likewise the deliberate inclusion of the word 'bourgeois' in so many definitions of the words related to upper-class French society suggests an effort by revolutionary Russians to identify with the class struggles which led to the French Revolution.

Qualifying the data: applying the test of frequency

The above analysis of French loanwords in the different Russian dictionaries explores the categories of lexical import observable across time, and draws deliberate attention to quantities of words. The goal of these observations is ultimately to draw conclusions as to the most important areas of French influence upon Russia and when they occurred. However, before the statistical information provided by the study of these lexical categories can be effectively applied to various chronological periods, a certain tempering of the data is first necessary. Raw statistical analysis alone without historical context and without 'weighing' the words can obscure the most important patterns, namely giving the impression that later periods of French influence are more significant

---

[150] Ushakov, *Tolkovyi slovar'*, III, p. 44.
[151] Ushakov, *Tolkovyi slovar'*, I, p. 683.

than they really are. Considering the increasing numbers of French loanwords at face

value, it would appear that French influence grew steadily, beginning in earnest with

Catherine II and continuing to the present day. Indeed, the first Soviet dictionary in this

study includes 760 new French loanwords which would seem, at first glance, to

continue an ever-upward trend of French influence. However, such a conclusion would

be deceptive. It is important to consider, for example, the broad scope and function of

Ushakov's 1935 – 1940 dictionary. This large undertaking was an effort to meet the

needs of a new Soviet society which was quickly moving into a changing world. The

public was only recently literate, the new Soviet way of life introduced a score of new

words (stump compounds and the like), and the country was in the midst of rapid

industrialization. There were hordes of new terms of every kind entering the language,

French and otherwise. If Ushakov's dictionary as a whole were to be compared with the

dictionary of Pushkin's language, for example, Ushakov's dictionary has roughly nine

times as many word entries. This disparity alone is liable to skew any linguistic

comparison.

Of the new French loanwords in the 1930s, 148 of them (19%) were technical in

nature, some dealing with various machinery or even aviation. New technology that

Russia was importing from the West would naturally have a foreign name. If some of

the new terms associated with this generic influx of technology happened to be French,

this could hardly be an argument for French cultural influence. Furthermore, 98 of the

new French loanwords in Ushakov's dictionary do not appear just eighteen years later,

or ever thereafter. By the publication of the 2007 dictionary, only about 500 of the 760

new French words introduced by Ushakov's edition (66%) are still included. This large

influx of foreign terms, so many of which were short-lived, is reminiscent of Peter I's

impulsive linguistic borrowings. By contrast, 83% of the new French loanwords in the

late eighteenth-century Academy dictionary are still in circulation, as are 86% the new borrowings use by Pushkin and 78% of those introduced in the writings of Dostoevskii.

The relatively lower turnover rate of French terms emerging in the days of Catherine II,

Pushkin, and Dostoevskii seems to be more indicative of real French impact on the

Russian culture.

Clearly, then, the statistical information must be qualified before it can be

interpreted for cultural implications, especially with the later dictionaries. Simply

counting the number of French borrowings in each generation is only the beginning of

an analytical process if any meaningful implications are to be made. Imported terms

must somehow be 'weighed' as to their importance to Russian society. As the present

study's purpose is ultimately to shed historical light on the origins of those French

influences still palpable in Russia today, a relevant measure of the significance of these

terms is the frequency of their use in recent years. A comprehensive study of this type

has been done by Sergei Sharov and Ol'ga Liashevskaia who have categorized Russian

words by the frequency of their modern usage (during the period 1950 – 2007).[152]

Cross-referencing their work with the French etymological findings from the nine

dictionaries examined reveals an interesting insight. Of the 5,000 most frequently used

words in the Russian language, 278 (5.6%) are of French origin. When the chronology

of their introduction into the Russian language is scrutinized, a pattern appears which

puts the overwhelming quantity of words in later periods into perspective. Figure 2.9

records these findings.

Of the 278 French-origin words that are a part of the most common lexical

material, 39 (14%) were added in the era of Peter I and another 32 (12%) were in the

language by the end of Catherine II's reign. The greatest number of these 278

frequently-used French borrowings, 98 words (35%), made their appearance during the

period of Pushkin's career. Another large (though lesser) influx occurred in the very

---

[152] O. N. Liashevskaia and S. A. Sharov, eds, *Chastotnyi slovar' sovremennogo russkogo iazyka: na materialakh Natsional'nogo korpusa russkogo iazyka* (Moscow: Azbukovnik, 2009).

next generation, with 61 words (22%) entering from French during Dostoevskii's career. Produced near the end of Dostoevskii's lifetime, Dal''s dictionary contains many words in common with Dostoevskii's vocabulary, but there is a small discrepancy. Some of the words that enter in Dal''s second edition that do not appear in Dostoevskii include words related to cutting edge technology like *benzin* ('gasoline') a word that Dostoevskii would have been unlikely to use in his literature, the first combustion engines not really appearing until the last quarter of the nineteenth century.[153] Only about 13 of the 278 (5%) are new to Dal'' and not appearing in Dostoevskii.

Fig. 2.9: Cross-reference of each period's lexicon with Liashevskaia and Sharov's study of frequency.

Dictionary or word-base	Period represented	Number of new French loanwords which are among the 5,000 most frequently-used words as of 2009	Percentage
(work of N. A. Smirnov)	Before 1725	39	14%
Academy Dictionary	1725 – 1794	32	12%
Pushkin's language	1794 – 1837	98	35%
Dostoevskii's language	1837 – 1881	61	22%
Dal' dictionary	- 1882	13	5%
Ushakov dictionary	1881 – 1940	23	8%
Evgen'eva dictionary	1940 – 1957	9	3%
Ozhegov dictionary	(1953, one-volume)	2	1%
Kuznetsov dictionary	1957 – 2007	1	0.4%
TOTAL		**278**	**100%**

In terms of importance being assigned to words that occur more often, note should be made of the sharp decrease in frequently-used words of French origin that are introduced in later years. In Ushakov's dictionary (1935 – 1940), only 23 of the French-origin terms which appear for the first time (and there are over 750 of them) are

---

[153] H. N. Gupta, *Fundamentals of Internal Combustion Engines* (New Delhi: Prentice Hall of India, 2006), pp. 2 – 3.

included among Liashevskaia and Sharov's top 5,000. (That is, 8% the 278 frequently-used French loanwords.) Another 9 (3%) enter the language with Evgen'eva's dictionary, published in 1957, by which time almost all of the 278 frequently found French words were a part of the Russian lexicon. Thus, by focusing on French contribution to Russia's frequently used vocabulary, a distinct pattern is discernible: there is a sharp increase in French import during Pushkin's lifetime, a continued but somewhat decreased rate of import in the very next generation, and a sharp drop-off thereafter (see fig. 2.10).

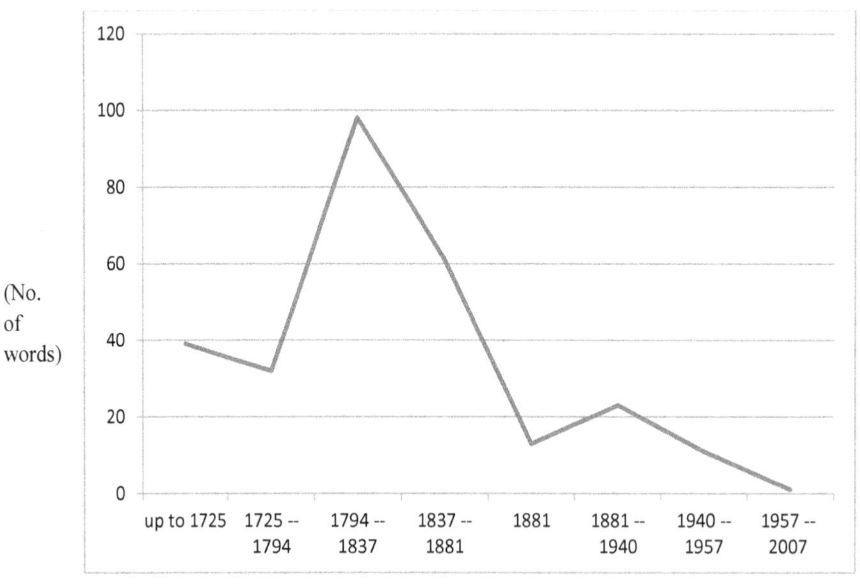

**Fig. 2.10: Introduction of French loanwords
which are still frequently used in the Russian language
(by Period)**

(Period represented by dictionary)

Chronological Overview

Figure 2.11 compares all of the broad categories of French lexical import in each period. Even before applying the criterion of frequency as discussed alongside Liashevaia and

Sharov's work (above), this raw data already suggests the preeminence of French influence which is cultural in nature, with a particular upturn at the very end of the eighteenth century. As this table illustrates, through the end of Catherine II's reign, official terminology stands out as the greatest French lexical contribution. This emphasis changes dramatically in the next two generations as words dealing with culture increase sharply but also become the most numerous in comparison with other word-categories. Cultural language will continue to be the most numerous of French borrowings in subsequent generations, though another significant category of words rivals culture in the early twentieth century: science and technology.[154] Finally, French lexical import of every kind tapers off after the revolutionary period.

Fig. 2.11: New French loanwords by category in each period
(Only words which easily fall within a certain category over long period of use)

	-1725	1725–1794	1794–1837	1837–1881	-1881	1881–1940	1940–1957	1957–2007	Total
Culture	25	23	134	170	134	190	28	39	**743**
Official Terminology	54	41	60	54	73	91	4	4	**381**
Technology, Industry, and Science	7	6	18	30	71	150	19	10	**311**
Urban and Residential Design	8	6	20	30	21	24	3	3	**115**
Philosophy / Social Thought	3	0	14	10	3	35	1	0	**66**
Historical and Foreign Words	7	1	15	13	4	30	3	2	**75**
Total words categorized	**104**	**77**	**261**	**307**	**306**	**520**	**58**	**58**	**1691**

In addition to highlighting the most significant area of influence (cultural influence), lexical analysis also leads to a certain conclusion about the most important period of such influence. Despite Peter's ground-breaking work as a westernizer, the introduction of French cultural elements as a result of Peter's innovations and reforms

---

[154] As already noted, however, this import seems to have more to do with Russia's own technological and industrial boom than any indication of uniquely French influence.

seems to have been minimal. While the initial word-import was explosive during this period, many of the new terms disappeared just as quickly. Of the many French-origin words discovered by Smirnov in the Russian glossaries and codices of Peter's era, nearly half of them do not appear in any subsequent dictionaries. French military words like *defens* and *fortres,* for example, appear in Peter's lists but are never seen again. *Okontrer* (from the French phrase 'au contraire') is identified by Smirnov but never caught on as a Russian negation. Likewise, *mazheste* never found its way into circulation (*velichestvo* would be the monarchial title in Russia), nor did *zhenerozite* (an original Russian word, *velikadushie,* would instead denote noble generosity.) It is not really even accurate to speak of these words 'entering' the Russian language at all. Rather, these words and very many like them were early experiments with linguistic borrowing as a modernizing state was grappling with how to incorporate the mass of new foreign ideas, concepts, and technologies brought on by modernization. Further, many of the French terms that did enter are civic or military in nature, and could just as easily have been imported indirectly through Swedish, German or Polish influence rather than direct contact with France.

By the end of Catherine's reign there were considerably more French words in the language, a great number of them related to government administration. This is unsurprising considering Elizabeth's introduction of the French language at court and Catherine's continuation of this trend, her fascination with the French Enlightenment, correspondence with Voltaire and other philosophes, and desire to make Russia a full-fledged European power. What is surprising, however, was that the type of words being imported were primarily administrative in nature rather than cultural, continuing the Petrine trend. Though Elizabeth did extravagantly indulge in French cuisine and fashions, and Catherine developed a true imperial court after the fashion of Versailles, the import of French words related to culture did not occur with any great significance during this period, an indication of the superficial nature of cultural 'gallomania' in comparison to more substantive cultural import later on.

The influx of French words accelerates in the next generation, with many new cultural terms entering Russian from French during the writing careers of Pushkin and Dostoevskii after him. In fact, statistical analysis of cultural loanwords chronologically and by frequency suggests that it was this period, immediately following the French Revolution and Napoleonic invasion of Russia, which saw the single most significant instance of French cultural influence upon Russia. This speaks to the impact that the French Revolution had on Russian society both directly and indirectly. Indirect influence would come in the form of Catherine's reactionary policy measures, moving away from her former ideas of enlightened despotism and reform, and more towards regulatory strictness designed to shore up her own position and be sure that nothing like 1789 would happen to Russia. This would not explain an influx of French words in the next generation, but does speak to the attention that the events of France were getting inside of Russia.

The direct influences of the French Revolution would come in the form of migration as French emigrants fled to Russia following the revolution in France. The evolution of the word *madam* in Russian is revealing in this regard. Dal''s definition of the word near the end of the nineteenth century gives some clue as to the occupation of certain immigrants. According to Dal', *madam* is defined as a '[female] foreigner, especially a French woman, for children a nanny, governess; keeper of a fashion shop, dressmaker.'[155] As early as Pushkin's time, the word *madam*, in addition to the basic use 'with the family name of a married foreign woman' as in 'Madame Riznich with the Roman nose,' could also be used generically to refer to a foreign governess, or the

---

[155] Dal', *Tolkovyi slovar'*, II, p. 217.

director of a woman's institute.[156] These definitions hint at the fact that it was fairly common for French émigrés in Russia following the French Revolution to find employment in Russia as teachers, nannies, governesses, dressmakers, and proprietors of fashionable shops. French nobility, intellectuals, and others who had fled France sought asylum across Europe, including inside Russia. Russia was a favourite destination for many escapees, because there was still fear of revolutionary fever spreading, and Russia seemed least likely to imitate these events in France.[157] Those who could find a place in Catherine's service or as courtiers joined St. Petersburg high society, but those positions were soon occupied. Many other émigrés worked as tutors, governesses, or shopkeepers, as the aforementioned common usage of 'madame' in Russia illustrates. This large migration of upper-class French refugees, escaping the Reign of Terror, occurred in the twilight of Catherine's life and reign. Thus, Catherine's exit roughly coincided chronologically with a wave of direct French cultural influence into Russia.

Then came 1812 and the Napoleonic invasion of Russia. French soldiers were on Russian territory and Russian soldiers would eventually be in France, bringing French influence back with them after the war.[158] So, when Pushkin began writing in 1813, he did so in a Russia that had known something more substantial than the artificial mimicking of French culture prevalent in the imperial court of the eighteenth century. It is not surprising, then, that the lexical material of Pushkin's collected works contains markedly more French loanwords than were present in the Russian dictionary published near the end of the reign of Catherine II. The Russian Academy's dictionary (published 1789 – 1794) contains 173 words of French origin. By contrast, the written

---

[156] Vinogradov, *Slovar' iazyka Pushkina*, II, p. 530.

[157] Kelly Herold, 'Russian Autobiographical Literature in French: Recovering a Memoiristic Tradition (1770 – 1830)', unpublished PhD thesis, University of California (1998), p. 64.

[158] Raymond McNally, 'The Origins of Russophobia in France: 1812–1830, *American Slavic and East European Review*, 17 (1958), 180.

works of Pushkin contain 493 words that come from French. That is, 91 French loanwords from the previous generation, plus the addition of 402 new French words. 433 of the French-origin words used by Pushkin endure all the way to dictionary published in the twenty-first century, an indication of the permanence of the French lexical and, by implication, cultural impact during this period.

It is also important to consider that the Pushkin dictionary is only a study of the words that Pushkin actually used in his literature and correspondence. 57 of the French words that entered the language in the previous generation and went on to be included in the twenty-first-century dictionary are not used by Pushkin. This is easily explained by the fact that Pushkin's literature was just that: literature and not lexicography. It is not unimaginable that many or all of these 57 words were in circulation during Pushkin's day but did not find their ways into his writings. To demonstrate the feasibility of such a phenomenon, about 20 of these 57 'missing' words also do not appear a generation later in the writings of Dostoevskii, but they do appear in Dal''s dictionary which was compiled and published during Dostoevskii's lifetime. Some of these are technical words related to military equipment, musical instruments or any other number of terms that dictionaries might include though neither Pushkin nor Dostoevskii used them. Taking this into consideration, there were well over 500 French loanwords in the Russian language by the end of Pushkin's lifetime (1837) compared to the mere 173 recorded as of 1793. This significant increase sets this period apart and calls for further study.

The influx of French words would continue in the generation after Pushkin. According to a statistical analysis of Dostoevskii's writing, another 497 new French loanwords enter the lexicon during his career, 387 of which would remain in the language to be included in the 2007 dictionary. The second edition of Dal''s dictionary, published at the end of Dostoevskii's life, would include an additional 472 new French contributions that neither Dostoevskii nor his predecessors used. However, only 271 of these new words are found in the 2007 dictionary. Again, the large discrepancy between Dostoevskii and Dal', though they are not far removed from one another chronologically, is easily explained by the care Dal' would naturally have taken as a lexicographer to be thorough in his inclusion of words, including the latest technical, industrial, scientific, medical, or the military terminology. In a sense, Dostoevskii's literary vocabulary is more reflective of the actual assimilation of French words than is Dal''s dictionary. Of the 497 new French words gleaned from the study of Dostoevskii's writings, only 37 completely fall out of use by 1957. By contrast, of the new French loanwords in Dal''s dictionary, some 100 fall out of use before 1957, over 60 of them disappearing by the 1930s.[159] Still, Dal''s work, studied together with the work of Dostoevskii reveals yet another generation borrowing a large quantity of French words. Of the 1,883 French loanwords in the one-volume *Sovremennyi* dictionary of 2007, 658 of them were new additions in either Dal' or Dostoevskii.

A new wave of influence entered Russia in the late nineteenth and early twentieth century in the form of socialist philosophy that, though important, would mean nothing like the quantity of cultural words borrowed in preceding generations. Furthermore, the fact that so many of these socialist terms look back to the French Revolution as a point of reference speaks indirectly to the importance of that earlier period as well. Finally, technological word import was massive in the late imperial through early Soviet period but this seems to indicate relatively little direct French influence, though many of the new terms happened to be French. Qualifying the significance of these words based on the frequency of their current use magnifies this fact, and brings the primacy of French cultural influence during the early nineteenth century into sharper focus.

---

[159] As per Ushakov's dictionary.

Framed historically, then, after more than a century of moderate, steadily-increasing European influence in Russian culture, beginning with Peter and continuing through Catherine, Russia experienced an explosion of significant and permanent French influence in the generations just after the French Revolution and Napoleonic invasion of Russia, which would be twice that of all other periods of Russian history combined. Lexical analysis of the Russian language's borrowing of French words from Peter to the present leads strongly to the conclusion that the late eighteenth and early nineteenth century is the most important period for historical study where French cultural influence is concerned.

CHAPTER THREE

FRENCH IMMIGRATION TO RUSSIA

In light of the lexical analysis of French loanwords in the previous chapter, reference by the early twentieth-century French historian and slavicist Emile Haumant to an 'apogee of French influences in Russia' during the period 1789 – 1814 seems fitting.[1] Though French influence certainly began earlier than the mid-eighteenth century and continued well into the nineteenth, the peak of enduring French linguistic and, by implication, cultural import during the period between the fall of the Bastille and the decline of Napoleon is unmistakable. This 'apogee of French influences' corresponds chronologically to increased immigration to Russia during this generation. Dimitri Mohrenschildt has noted that, while there was a small French presence at court even before the reign of Elizabeth (r. 1741 – 1762), the greatest French presence was during and just after the reign of Catherine the Great (r. 1762 – 1796).[2] A study of contemporary sources sheds light on some reasons for this immigration and suggests that the type of people moving to Russia corresponds directly to the kinds of influence which the lexical study has already revealed.

Two distinctive waves of French emigration to Russia are discernible in the late eighteenth century. The first of these occurred during the first half of Catherine's reign, apparently in direct response to her policy reforms, and the second took place in the wake of the French Revolution. With the exception of Leonide Ignatieff's study of French émigrés to Russia during this period, little scholarly attention has been given to the cultural distinctions between these two waves, or their implications for Russian culture.[3] Ignatieff's fine study gleans generalized impressions about the two waves of

---

[1] Émile Haumant, *La Culture Française en Russie, 1700 – 1900* (Paris: Libraire Hachette et cie, 1913).

[2] Dimitri Sergius Von Mohrenschildt, *Russia in the Intellectual Life of Eighteenth-Century France* (New York: Octagon Books, 1972).

[3] Leonide Ignatieff, 'French Émigrés in Russia, 1789 – 1825: The Interaction of Cultures in Time of Stress' (unpublished doctoral dissertation, University of Michigan, 1963).

French immigration from Russian literature and then supplements this with a few

anecdotal memoir accounts from the perspective of high-ranking French diplomats. The

present chapter extends this inquiry, exploring the two different periods of French

immigration through a close narrative look at individual Russian-language case studies

of common immigrants and a more systematic study of the broader context in which

they occurred. Rather than relying solely on satirical or literary reference, this chapter

traces lasting cultural impact by cross-referencing lexical data from the previous chapter

with factual information about of the various occupational activities of French

immigrants and their interaction with Russian society.

Immigration before the French Revolution

As the review of secondary literature on the topic has mentioned, some French

immigration to Russia occurred earlier in the eighteenth century, consisting mostly of a

small number of individual specialists and advisors, but it was really during the reign of

Catherine the Great that significant influx began.[4] Upon ascending the throne in 1762,

Catherine issued a manifesto in which she announced that foreigners (other than Jews)

would be allowed to enter and settle in Russia with a great deal of freedom. Likewise, a

measure of amnesty was promised to Russian offenders who had fled abroad during the

rule of her predecessors. Past offences would be forgiven and these Russians could

return to their homeland, provided they live lawfully henceforth.[5] In keeping with the

idea of 'enlightened despotism', this manifesto was billed as the merciful gesture of a

generous potentate in response to the swelling demand among foreigners to enter the

bountiful Russian empire. However, it seems more likely that this move was intended

to advance Russian interests, an attempt at strategic land development in the expanding

---

[4] See my brief overview from secondary sources on French immigration to Russia before and during
Catherine's reign in chapter one, pp. 58 – 65.
[5] *Polnoe sobranie zakonov rossiiskoi imperii (PSZ)*, Tom XVI, 11.720, 4 December 1762
<http://www.runivers.ru/lib/book3130> [accessed 28 June 2014]

empire and cultural enrichment through the intentional recruitment of foreign colonists. Roger Bartlett's study of Russian immigration policy during this period has suggested that the primary goals were to increase the general population in developing areas of the empire and to support agriculture and industry. Bartlett's study focuses much less on the cultural aspects of immigration.[6]

Seven months after the initial manifesto, another legislative act was released, designed to bring order to the subsequent influx and shape its impact. This 1763 pronouncement founded the Office for the Guardianship [*Opekunstva*] of Foreigners to help facilitate the integration of these immigrants and get them settled into appropriate locations within Russia.[7] Officials representing Russia in Europe contracted with private agents who recruited local emigrants to move to Russia. Some of these recruiting agents [*vyzvyvateli*] were paid directly by the Russian state based upon the number of people coming to Russia as a result of their work. Others were given lordship over various amounts of land in Russia commensurate with the number of immigrants they were able to recruit for development of the same. This second type of recruiter paid the expenses of transporting the immigrants, but could receive a loan from the Russian government to cover them.[8] These migrants came from abroad to work Russian land, man Russian factories, and become part of the fabric of society. According to Bartlett, this program drew over 30,000 foreign immigrants to Russia from 1762 to 1775 alone, many of whom were Germans that settled in the lower Volga region.[9]

The influx was not exclusively German, however. Vladislav Rzheutskii's study of French settlement in Russia in the eighteenth and early nineteenth centuries suggests

---

[6] Roger Bartlett, *Human Capital: the settlement of foreigners in Russia 1762 – 1804* (Cambridge: Cambridge University Press, 1979).
[7] *PSZ*, Tom XVI, 11.879, 22 July 1763.
[8] Bartlett, *Human Capital,* pp. 61 – 66.
[9] Ibid., p. 66.

a significant growth of French immigration as a result of these policies by Catherine II.

Less than a year before Catherine's coronation and subsequent manifesto in favour of

immigration, a list of those French people already living in Moscow and the

surrounding areas was compiled by a French diplomat. This list from January 1762

included 156 names. A different list, dated 1777, reports that Moscow's French colony

had grown to more than 650 people by this time. Thus, according to Rzheutskii, 'from

1762 to 1777 in Moscow the number of French grew at least four times over. This

means that the true birth of the French community [*zemliachestvo*] in Moscow comes in

the epoch of Catherine II.'[10] Wealthy Frenchmen living in Russia were allowed to

recruit labourers from their homeland and invite [*vyzvat'*] groups of them by special

contract to come and settle in Russia. For example, via just two of these French

transport groups in 1764 – 65, fifty-one men moved to Russia.[11]

A collection of government records and case files belonging to the Office for the

Guardianship of Foreigners, which oversaw this process of immigration and integration,

has been preserved and provides some information on this first wave of eighteenth-

century French influx.[12] Of particular interest in archival documents of this period are

the narrative glimpses that they give into the life of French immigrants and their new

Russian context. These recruited settlers tend to be of less than aristocratic status,

which makes information about them all the more valuable. The voices of these lower

classes are often inaudible to history, though they vastly outnumber the nobility who

authored most of the extant memoir literature from the period. Their stories introduce a

cultural dimension to the study of this period of immigration, beyond the broader

economic or diplomatic implications more common, for example, in Bartlett's study.

---

[10] V. S. Rzheutskii, 'Istoriia frantsuzskogo zemliachestva v Rossii v XVIII – nachale XIX veka' (unpublished doctoral dissertation, St. Petersburg Institute of History, 2003).

[11] Rzheutskii, 'Istoriia frantsuzskogo zemliachestva v Rossii', p. 117.

[12] Kantseliariia opekunstva inostrannykh pri senate, 1763 – 1782, Rossiiskii gosudarstvennyi arkhiv drevnikh aktov (RGADA), f. 283, op. 2.

One example is a case file related to the 'petition of the French minister Beausset regarding the return to France of the foreign colonist Karl Michel, recruited [*vyzvannyi*] by Baron Beauregard to settle in Russia.'[13] The correspondence preserved in this case file shed light on the sordid ways in which some French immigrants came to be in Russia during this period and tell the compelling story of the plight of one individual. In the summer of 1765, a French boy by the name of Karl Michel, eleven or twelve years of age, was registered among a group of colonists in Amsterdam. He was subsequently conscripted into a transport group to Russia under the pseudonym Jean Pierre Fortune. According to young Michel, his mother sold him into Russian service for twenty-one pieces of gold [*chervonnoi*] against his will and without his knowledge. Having received payment, she led her son to the agreed-upon transport ship and left him there without telling him of her plans. As a result of this deception, Karl arrived in St. Petersburg around December 1765, weary, ill, practically naked, and with frost-bitten feet [*s oznoblennami nogami*]. Upon arrival, someone noticed his condition and escorted him to the home of a French nobleman who took pity on him and received him into his household. Baron Beauregard, who had contracted this transport group, apparently feeling some measure of responsibility for the fate of his young countryman, was apparently motivated by his sense of humanity [*pochelovechestvu*] to give orders concerning Michel's well-being and saw to it that he was set up in the home of another French aristocrat in St. Petersburg. When later it became necessary for Beauregard to move to Moscow, he felt himself no longer able to look after Michel and turned the matter over to the proper authorities. Thus, in February of 1767 the Marquis de Beausset—a French ambassador in St. Petersburg at the time[14]—submitted a petition to

---

[13] Case file on petition to the Russian foreign office, 1767 – 1780, RGADA, f. 283, op. 1, d. 97.

[14] Jean-Henri Castera, *The Life of Catherine II, Empress of Russia*, vol. 2 (London: Longman, 1798), pp. 10, 480. <http://google.books.com> [accessed 24 June 2014]

the Russian government for Michel's repatriation to France, thus preserving this episode in the public record.[15]

It is unclear from this hand-written collection of French letters, Russian translations, and official reports, exactly what became of Karl Michel (also known as Jean Pierre Fortune). The only resolution in this story is that which is found in the final sheet of the file, posted years later to officially close the case. Written retrospectively in 1780, the document repeats the facts of the case and concludes that 'as the Frenchman Fortune was not sent to the settlement colony but remained with the French minister with whom he probably [*chaiatel'no*] departed to his homeland, and as the recruiter [*vyzyvatelia*] is no longer here, this case is to be excluded from among the number of those unresolved' and the relevant documents pertaining to the case forwarded to the appropriate archive.[16]

This story of a young French boy duped into service emphasizes the humble social background of those recruited to populate foreign colonies inside of Russia, the lack of scruples on the part of some functionaries of the system, and the overall inefficiency of the migration program itself. Ultimately, settlers from within Russia would be a cheaper solution to land development and they would assimilate far more easily. Nevertheless, Catherine's program brought many French people to Russia. The wholesale and largely random recruitment of these foreigners—largely from those down on their luck—distinguished this relatively large French influx both from the smaller, more strategic recruitment of individual specialists earlier in the century and from the large influx of revolutionary émigrés later in the century which tended by definition to be from the upper classes.

---

[15] Russian translation of Beausset's memorandum to the Russian foreign ministry, 2 February 1767, RGADA, f. 283, op. 1, d. 97, ll. 2 – 3.
[16] Notation in the journal of the Office for the Guardianship of Foreigners, 9 July 1780, RGADA, f. 283, op. 1, d. 97, l. 12.

The vast majority of the archival documents from this government office pertain to German settlements along the Volga rather than French colonies, which no doubt explains the fact that the Office's headquarters were located in the city of Saratov. Bartlett has summarily rejected, however, the oft-repeated notion that the German face of immigration during this period somehow reflects Catherine's natural affinity for her native land or even a preference for German farming skills. Rather, the activities of Russia's recruiting agents in Europe were hindered in some countries. While France, Spain, and Italy discouraged or even forbade foreign emigration propaganda, the German states were much less regulatory in this regard, resulting in the disproportionate number of German immigrants to Russia beginning in the 1760s.[17] Therefore, French biographical sketches like that of Karl Michel are rare in the Office's files. Nevertheless, these scant traces of narrative detail among the pages of the Office for the Guardianship of Foreigners and the very creation of the office itself speak to a significant period of immigration, including that from France, in which the Russian government had a vested interest. This particular section of government bureaucracy eventually outlived its usefulness and was disbanded. Rather than openly admit how expensive and arguably unprofitable Catherine's settlement schemes had become, the 1782 law which closed the department simply said that 'upon bringing an end to the affairs of the Office of Guardianship of Foreigners, and finding this Office and its representative office [*kontoru*], located in Saratov, unnecessary, we command that it be no more.'[18] This pronouncement, passed in compliance with the 1775 government administration reforms, went on to redistribute its remaining budgetary funds, absorb its remaining workload into other departments, and entrust the stewardship of the associated office buildings in St. Petersburg and Saratov to the state treasury chamber.

---

[17] Bartlett, *Human Capital*, pp. 57 – 59.
[18] *PSZ*, Tom XXI, 15.383, 20 April 1782, p. 491.

Apart from those recruited as a result of Catherine's development program, some French adventurers came to Russia of their own initiative, offering their services as maids, valets, tutors, governesses and the like. Though native Frenchmen, and therefore valued by noble Russians who desired to learn French ways, they were not always top specimens of high culture. Many had been unsuccessful in their native land or were even common criminals who avoided French justice by escaping to Russia where they would be received as bearers of cultural refinement.[19] According to one scholar, the French 'adventurer'(as they were known during this period) may be broadly defined as a 'pariah of the Enlightenment, whose literary ambitions set him apart from the ordinary fortune hunters, charlatans, quacks, or rogue politicians.'[20]

Immigration in the wake of the French Revolution

The second wave of French emigration to Russia, rather than resulting from intentional attraction on the part of the Russian government, was spawned by external events: namely, the French Revolution.[21] K. Miller's study of Russia's French émigrés, gleaned from the anecdotal accounts of French and Russian aristocrats and primarily highlighting the few fortunate Frenchmen who found positions at or near the imperial court, concludes that Russia was a promising destination for French royalists and others escaping the horrors of the Great Terror, and that these émigrés would eventually affect significant and long-lasting influence upon Russia that was both political and cultural.[22] While the future of Western Europe was uncertain in the early 1790s, it was thought unlikely that revolutionary mayhem would spread so far as this remote empire. Further, decades of 'Gallomania' in Russia had convinced members of upper-class French

---

[19] Mosakowski, 'Image of Russia in Eighteenth-Century French Literature', 174.

[20] Olga Tsapina, review of *'Te kto popravliaiut fortunu': avantuiristy Prosveshcheniia* by Aleksandr Stroev, *Eighteenth-Century Studies,* 34 (2001), 318–321 (p. 319).

[21] See my general overview from secondary literature on the cultural impact of the French émigrés in chapter one, pp. 58 – 65.

[22] K. Miller, *Frantsuzskaia emigratsiia i Rossiia v tsarstvovanie Ekateriny II* (Paris: Rodnik, 1931).

society that they could expect a grateful reception and be able to secure a comfortable situation, at least in St. Petersburg, an attractive prospect in these troubled times.

One Russian traveller, Nikolai Karamzin, who would later achieve legendary fame as an author, historian, and literary critic, set out for a journey through Europe in the spring of 1789, reaching Paris by the end of March 1790, where he spent nearly four months. Though he offered little but praise for all that Parisian society had to offer, he remarked that 'Paris now is not what it was… The horrors of the revolution have driven the wealthiest residents away from Paris.'[23] While there, he received a note from a certain French nobleman—unnamed by Karamzin—whose sister, a countess, wished to procure a detailed description of Russia. For, reads the letter, 'The current situation in France is such that each of us must prepare asylum for himself in some other land.' On the reverse of the letter was inscribed a number of very specific questions, with space left in between for a written response. These questions, posed to Nikolai Karamzin in the summer of 1790, reflect the mentality of at least one noble French family who was considering Russia as a refuge: 'Is it possible for a person with fragile health to bear the harshness of your climate?' 'Which times of the year are most pleasant?' 'What amenities does societal life have [to offer]?' 'Do they like foreigners in Russia? Do they receive them well?' 'Are women respected?' A final question, added by the countess's husband who was an avid hunter, enquired whether or not there was much wild game to be had in Russia. To all of these nervous questions, Karamzin gave the most reassuring of answers: warm houses and clothing make the climate quite bearable, diversions of every kind are to be had in Russian society, including hunting, and Russian hospitality is such that foreigners are received with singular grace. As for the chivalrous treatment of women, he assured the countess that women were, in fact, 'enthroned' in Russia. Concluding this episode, Karamzin seeks to convince his

---

[23] Nikolai Karamzin, 'Pis'ma russkogo puteshestvennika' in *Bednaia Liza: povesti,* ed. by G. P. Makogonenko (Moscow: EKSMO, 2005), p. 377.

Russian readers of his efforts to present Russia in the best possible light: 'In a word, if [this] husband and wife do not now come galloping to you all in Moscow, it is not my fault.'[24]

'Come galloping' the French did. As mentioned above, 650 names had been included in a list of French men, women, and children in Moscow and the surrounding area as of 1777. In the wake of the French Revolution, a list of French subjects in Moscow and its outskirts published in 1793 included 934 individuals.[25] This represents a significant increase, though the influx during the period 1762 – 77 (at the height of Catherine's aggressive recruitment program) had been numerically greater. Russia would not have a nationwide census until late in the nineteenth century, and the local population 'revisions' conducted before this were not always complete or consistent in the type of information that they reported.[26] This makes it difficult to get a complete statistical account of French immigration to Russia during this period. Local information from various sources can, however, help to sketch a rough historical picture of the influx and its cultural implications. Dmitrii Rostislavlev's study of archival materials related to the issuing of travel passports and other statistical sources about the French presence in Russia concluded that most of the Frenchmen in Russia as of 1793 had arrived before the revolution, most during the 1770s and 1780s.[27] Rzheutskii's dissertation likewise seems to downplay the role of the French Revolution in bringing French influence to Russia, emphasizing instead the effects of Catherine's policies in the 1760s – 1780s. However, while Rzheutskii and Rostislavlev are correct in their conclusion that the greatest quantity of French immigrants arrived to Russia before the revolution, such analysis does not take into account the importance of the various types

---

^[24] Karamzin, 'Pis'ma russkogo puteshestvennika', pp. 459–460.

[25] This list was published across five separate issues of *Sanktpeterburgskiia vedomosti*, Nos. 47 – 51, 14 – 28 June 1793.

[26] Lee Schwartz, 'A History of Russian and Soviet Censuses', in *Research Guide to the Russian and Soviet Censuses*, ed. by Ralph S. Clem (Ithaca, Cornell University Press, 1986), pp. 48 – 69.

[27] D. A. Rostislavlev, 'Frantsuzy v Rossii v 1793', *Cahiers du Monde russe*, 39 (1998), 297 – 320.

of immigrants arriving before and after the revolution. Immigrants from different social

backgrounds would inevitably affect Russian culture differently.

French courtiers (which came to be known as 'the princes' at Catherine's court)

and other nobles who had fled the Terror saw Catherine as an ally in their hopes to

restore the monarchy in France.[28] French émigrés served at court, acted as advisers,

joined the diplomatic corps, or served in the Russian military. Intermarrying between

Russians and members of the French diplomatic corps was not uncommon during this

period.[29] However, Catherine's court could not absorb all of the French émigrés who

had come to Russia for asylum, particularly those of slightly lower station. Well-bred

French citizens worked in various professions, many in the field of education. Others

opened fashionable shops or worked as tutors and governesses. This new wave of

refugees marked a turning point in the quality and depth of French influence upon

Russian culture, as various case studies and qualitative analyses, below, will

demonstrate.

Paranoia behind the scenes

Karamzin's assurances notwithstanding, the émigrés were not welcomed with entirely

open arms. From 1789 to 1793, references to the French Revolution in Russian

publications tended to be written in muted tones. However, even before Catherine II's

open outrage at the events of 1793, archival evidence indicates that, early on during the

French Revolution, the Russian empress was—behind the scenes—ordering and

receiving surveillance reports about foreigners within her own borders. Her paranoia

about the spread of republican ideals to Russia can be seen in a collection of

communications between Catherine and various high-ranking officials within her

---

[28] Kelly Herold, 'Russian Autobiographical Literature in French: Recovering a Memoiristic Tradition (1770 – 1830)' (unpublished doctoral dissertation, University of California, Los Angeles, 1998), pp. 64–66.

[29] Ibid.

government.[30] As early as October of 1789 (less than four months after the storming of the Bastille), she sent a secret message ordering Moscow's Chief Commander Petr Eropkin to instruct Moscow's police to observe the behaviour and communication of Frenchmen of all ranks, and take revolutionary sympathizers 'into custody and send them here [to St. Petersburg] to the General, Count Grim, to be deported abroad, informing us of such.'[31] One of the replies from Eropkin to his empress includes a list of Poles living in Moscow as well as the anecdotal mention of various Frenchmen living there.[32] Another note, sent by Catherine to Eropkin's successor, Prince Aleksandr Prozorovskii, gives instructions forbidding Freemasonry and ordering the surveillance of one Heinrich Veer. This handwritten order, also marked by the underlined word '*Sekretno*' in the top right corner, makes Catherine's primary concern quite plain. An intercepted letter, addressed to Veer, had been sent from Paris and contained some comments regarding events in France that Catherine found disturbing. Though not referencing the Jacobins directly, the letter in question had made reference to a 'special club' in Paris, which she was sure must have been '…founded in order to try to distribute its corruption everywhere.' Therefore, as with other suspicious characters, Veer was to be observed 'diligently but inconspicuously.' She wanted to know how long he had lived in Russia. 'What are his activities? Who does he live with? With whom is he in contact? What is his behaviour [like]?'[33]

As emigrants continued to flow into Russia, Catherine's suspicion led to increased vigilance by the state. A particularly interesting artifact which speaks to this tendency is the draft of another written order from Catherine II to Prozorovskii in 1792.

---

[30] Snosheniia russkikh gosudarei s raznymi pravitel'stvennymi mestami i dolzhnostnymi litsami, RGADA, f. 168, op. 1, and Dela tainoi ekspeditsii, RGADA f. 7, op. 2.

[31] Rescript from Catherine II to Moscow chief-commander Petr Dmitrivich Eropkin, 25 October 1789, RGADA, f. 168, d. 169, l. 2.

[32] Report by Moscow chief-commander P. D. Eropkin to Catherine II about Poles living in Moscow, 13 December 1789, RGADA, f. 168, op. 1, d. 172, ll. 7 – 7 ob.

[33] Rescript from Catherine to Moscow chief-commander A. A. Prozorovskii, 10 April 1790, RGADA, f. 168, op. 1, d. 179, ll. 1 – 1 ob.

Like previous orders, this one calls for the observation of Frenchmen in Moscow, but is unique in that it prescribes that special attention should be given to the actions of those Frenchmen 'who have arrived recently from there' and about whom little is known. Should any of these so much as 'seem suspicious', they are to be deported.[34]

These glimpses into Catherine II's motivations and the inner workings of her surveillance network, in addition to their valuable contribution of information on the private considerations behind her policies concerning France, are of singular interest to the present study for the light they shed on the French émigré community itself and its influence upon Russian culture. The culture of anti-Jacobin vigilance that was being fostered at this time spawned the surveillance, investigation, and even interrogation of French immigrants in Russia. These police activities have, in turn, left behind documentation which includes information about the lives of individual French subjects living in Russia, not all of whom were not of the noble ranks, (especially those who had arrived before the revolution). Whereas previous scholarship on French cultural influence during this period has had little choice but to rely heavily on memoir literature, most of which was produced by representatives of a small, elite segment of the population, Catherine's paranoia—a gift to the historian—has produced a wealth of biographical information on French expatriates other than court nobility.

Case study: six in a tavern

One example of this phenomenon is the case of Christian Gaag, a teacher of the German language who denounced a group of foreigners that he heard speaking French in a local tavern [*traktir*].[35] In this charged and suspicious climate, it was not uncommon for fellow foreigners to report on each other. One French émigré had even approached

---

[34] Rescript from Catherine to Moscow chief-commander A. A. Prozorovskii, February 14, 1792, RGADA, f. 168, d. 188, ll. 1 – 1 ob.

[35] Case file on the teacher Khristian Gaag's denunciation of Frenchmen who laid down [their] hats in an inn [in a way that looked] like the Tower of Babel, 1795, RGADA f. 7, op. 2, d. 2866.

Russian authorities immediately upon arrival by sea to report his suspicion that another foreigner on the boat with him was a Jacobin.[36] Miller has argued at length that it was the French loyalist émigrés themselves who helped to foster Russia's revolutionary paranoia through their personal contacts at court, their contributions to the Russian press, and in their role as teachers.[37] An example of this was when Gaag reported what he thought to be suspicious behaviour to Mikhail Izmailov, the Chief Commander of Moscow. This triggered an investigation which has left behind a paper trail of correspondences and official reports.

From these documents, the following story can be gleaned: On 1 September 1795, six foreigners were sitting together at a table in a certain Moscow tavern on Miasnitskaia Street, drinking beer and engaging one another in active conversation, speaking in French. One of the six had his hat on the table and another placed his hat on top of the first. A third member of the party protested that this would surely result in the hats being mixed up and one of them lost. Not so, replied the second, placing his finger on his own hat, proving that he could easily tell them apart. Another of the companions then pointed out that these hats, stacked up in such a way looked like the very Tower of Babel. The interchange that ensued digressed into the ramblings of a group of drinking companions: 'You tell lies. It's just like a dentist!' 'Well, if I do lie, then no more than you, and at least I don't smell like tobacco smoke!' From there the conversation moved on to comparing Flemish and Russian beers and, after a time, the band gradually began to disperse.

It is difficult to imagine how this harmless gathering could have inspired any suspicion of political subterfuge, and indeed the matter would eventually be dropped once the facts became clear. Nevertheless, upon overhearing these proceedings in the

---

[36] Report about the Frenchman Lebure's claim that the foreigner Bein is a Jacobin, 4 July 1795, RGADA, f. 7, op. 2, d. 2851, l. 1.

[37] Miller, *Frantsuzskaia emigratsiia i Rossiia.*

tavern, Gaag inferred from this business with the hats some reference to the mythical Tree of Liberty, a revolutionary symbol in France at the time, and reported the matter to the police. All six of the men were subsequently detained and interrogated separately, so that their statements could be compared and thereby refute or corroborate one another. Within a week, the Chief Commander of Moscow sent a letter about the case to Aleksandr Nikolaevich Samoilov, the General-Prosecutor of the Senate in St. Petersburg who in turn sent a complete report on the matter to the empress herself. It was ultimately determined that these men were in no way politically dangerous and any allegations against them were dropped, though they were warned to behave themselves with more decorum in public and refrain from telling rude jokes. The fact that this placid tale was reported up the chain of command all the way to the empress is a testimony to how nervous the government was about France and of the atmosphere of suspicion evident in foreigners denouncing on another so arbitrarily.

As part of their interrogation, in addition to relaying the events described above, each of the six men was asked to give a brief biographical sketch of himself, including his origin, profession, and number of years lived in Russia. With one possible exception, all of these had been living in Russia since well before the outbreak of revolution in France. Judging from their statement of time spent in Russia, they arrived in 1773, 1774, 1780, 1785, 1787, and 1789. Four of the six were originally from France and full names are legible for only a couple of them. Capelina, the dentist in interchange cited above, was originally from Venice and had arrived in Russia six years prior. Ancelin, an engraver who worked with metal as well as wood, had arrived eight years before the incident. He was from the Picardy region of France. Le Gran, a draftsman [*risoval'shchik*] originally from Paris, had been in Russia for twenty-one years. Jean Jacques Dyaumein, born in Spain but living in Russia for the past twenty-two years, was a teacher. Triquet, who had been in Russia for fifteen years, was a sculptor in marble and, as such, claimed to have been in the service of Prince Potemkin for many years. Finally, Nicolas Perrin—the owner of the suspicious hat—was a watchmaker from Plombieres, France, who had been in Russia for ten years.

These professionals and craftsmen who arrived in Russia near the end of the first immigration wave are visible examples of cultural influence outside of the court aristocracy. At the very least, they demonstrate that it was possible, in central Moscow of 1795, to encounter a group of men in a local tavern conversing in French, telling jokes, discussing their professions informally, and comparing local wares to those which might be imported. Whereas the craze for French luxury items and high culture earlier in the eighteenth century belonged exclusively to a narrow elite class, the immigration of middle- or lower-class French professionals and workers during Catherine's reign provided the possibility for cultural interaction with a much broader segment of the Russian population. As the numerical analysis of a list of French immigrants and their occupations later in the chapter will illustrate, their professional activities correlate directly with lasting French influences upon Russian culture.

Case study: a tale of two emigrants

The existence of various categories of French immigrants in Russia, those arriving before the French revolution differing from those that arrive later as émigrés from it, is acutely illustrated by a deportation case of 1795.[38] The matter involved two Frenchmen in Moscow, each representing one of the two aforementioned immigration waves. Desarenne Descarieres, though hailing from a respectable French family, had misspent his youth and a series of irresponsible escapades had carried him across Europe, with a trail of debt behind him. He finally came to Russia, arriving in the late 1770s. The second Frenchman in this story, Morancourt de Selongey, a trained educator, escaped to

---

[38] Case file on the deportation of the Frenchmen De Selongey and Descarieres, suspected of having contact with French revolutionaries, 1795, RGADA, f. 7, op. 2, d. 2870.

Russia during the early days of the French Revolution for the express purpose of seeking employment teaching Russian youth. Through a series of circumstances recorded in the files of the Russian government's Secret Dispatch Office [*tainaia ekspeditsii*], the paths of these two Frenchmen crossed in Moscow in the spring of 1795 and they would both be expelled from Russia soon thereafter because of a scheme involving a forged letter.[39]

Desarenne Descarieres was born to a reputable family in France, subjects of Louis XVI, his father a government advisor. As a young man, he entered the Gardes de la Marine according to the wishes of his father, but soon fell into riotous living [*nekotoryia rasputnosti*], left the service, and began to live on his own, against his father's wishes and initially without his knowledge. He travelled to Italy, Spain, and England seeking adventure and fortune but only incurred debt and constantly had to move on to a new location. From France, his father continued, from time to time, to pay money to his son's creditors, therefore aware of his behaviour. This prodigal son, rather than returning home to his family, sought the assistance of a more distant relative, who was part of a delegation to the French court, whom he met in Hamburg. He told this high-ranking kinsman all about his troubled life and how he dare not return and face his father. Seeing the predicament that Descarieres had created for himself across Europe, his relative advised him to journey to Russia. Descarieres had some education, and a Frenchman could always hope to find gainful employment in this developing empire.

Following this advice, in 1778 or 1779, Descarieres went first to St. Petersburg and then on to Moscow where he worked in various teaching jobs. There he received news from his mother in France that his father had died, and that she was continuing to pay his debts, which had grown by this time to a sum of 130,000 livres. In Russia, he

---

[39] Their biographical details have been gleaned from throughout this archival source, but especially from the Russian translation of statements taken from both men during their interrogation, 24 April 1795, RGADA, f. 7, op. 2, d. 2870, ll. 7 – 15.

changed employment fairly frequently and, as soon as he had built up enough capital to do so, began travelling around country, exploring various cities and looking for opportunities to achieve wealth, returning periodically to Moscow. He visited Orel, Baturin, Glukhov, Voronezh, Khar'kov, Kherson, Kizliar and Astrakhan. He travelled down the Volga to Saratov and Rostov. He explored Perm', Ekaterinburg, and Tobol'sk in search of minerals and precious stones with which to make his entrepreneurial fortune. While in Ekaterinburg, he met an Italian woman, Madame Liuple with whom he fell madly in love. In 1792, they were married in Moscow. Descarieres continued his explorations and eventually found access to precious stones in Siberia and returned to his new wife in Moscow with raw minerals and stones valued at 8000 rubles. In need of cash, Descarieres searched for a buyer and found one in Moscow, Major General Stepan Apraksin. However, there was some disagreement over terms, and it looked as if the deal would fall through. Fearing the loss of this potential capital, Descarieres's wife, Madame Liuple, took matters into her own hands, and, behind her husband's back, presented a bill of sale to one of Apraksin's agents, receiving much less money than Descarier had hoped to gain. Descarier was enraged by this turn of events. After a heated dispute, Madame Liuple departed to Saratov taking the money she had made from the business deal with her, and leaving Descarier bankrupt. At this point, Descarieres came up with a scheme to draw Madame Liuple back to Moscow, but he would need the assistance of an additional player.

Morancourt de Selongey had arrived to Russia in 1790 during the early days of the French Revolution. Though, by his own account, a nobleman, he sought employment as a teacher since there were no positions available to him at the Russian court. Through his acquaintance with General Kutuzov, he obtained a position at the Naval Gentry Cadet Corps [*morskoi shliakhetnoi kadetskoi korpus*], where he taught for two years. In 1792, he married a young lady whom he met in the area. Due to his insufficient salary, he resigned his position at the Cadet Corps to seek other employment and spent the next two years teaching in multiple homes as a tutor. In 1794, his search for gainful employment led him as far afield as a village in the Pskov region where he settled for a time in the home of a Russian nobleman, teaching this nobleman's two sons. However, less than a year later the master of the house died, and the household no longer retained De Selongey's services. He moved into the city of Pskov itself and on to Smolensk in search of work as a teacher and finally to Moscow, where he was allowed to temporarily occupy the apartments of a home belonging to the French church until such time as he could secure a place of employment as a tutor and earn some means with which to support himself and his wife. It was during this period, living on church-owned property and between jobs that he met Desarenne Descarieres.

The 'French church' mentioned in these documents could only refer to the Catholic Church of St. Louis, an important hub of francophone culture in Moscow since the late eighteenth century. A 1786 commercial treaty between Russia and France had guaranteed 'complete freedom of faith' to French subjects on Russian soil, including the freedom to worship in French and 'according to their law' (that is, in a Catholic mass rather than Eastern Orthodox service).[40] In 1789, members of Moscow's growing French community petitioned Moscow's Chief Commander Petr Eropkin to allow them to build their own parish church, a fact recorded in history via an official reply from the Empress. 'Petr Dmitrievich,' wrote Catherine, 'We approve your preliminary response to the request made by the French living in Moscow to be allowed to build themselves a church of the Roman law: but regarding the appointment of a location, it would be better if they were to choose a place in the German quarter.'[41] Construction of a small wooden church commenced shortly thereafter and the completed sanctuary was consecrated on 30 March 1791 in honour of Louis IX, the only canonized king in

---

[40] *PSZ*, Tom XXII, 16.489, St. III, 31 December 1786.
[41] *PSZ*, Tom XXIII, 16.822, 5 December 1789.

French history.[42] In 1832, a more permanent stone structure would be built which remains to the present, on the same plot of land granted by Catherine II in 1790.

It should be noted, however, that the church was not in fact built in the so called 'German quarter'. Rather than sequestering their congregation in the foreign sector of Moscow, as Catherine initially recommended, they obtained permission to build their church near the Kuznetskii bridge, an area inhabited by both French and Russian families. Though distinctly French, the church's location within a prominent area of the city facilitated greater integration with and influence upon the local Russian community through the years. Abbott Adrien Surugue, for example, Prior of the Church from 1807 through 1812, was particularly close with the prominent Rostopchin family, who lived near the church. Through their relationship, the wife of Count Fedor Rostopchin (the statesman who would be Governor-General of Moscow in 1812) actually converted to Catholicism.[43] In addition to personal connections such as these, the church's activities in the community had broader implications for cultural interaction. Though extant sources related to the church give very little detail about its earliest activities, the fact that De Selongey was able to lodge there for a time suggests considerable charitable work in the community. According to information on the church's later activities, an orphanage would be opened there in the 1820s and operated by the church, as well as two educational institutions [*gimnazii*] later in the nineteenth century, one for men and one for women.[44]

The dual dynamic of integrated legitimacy and French distinctiveness characterizes more than just the location of the church. The earliest records in the Moscow City Archives related to the church are dated soon after the construction of the

---

[42] I. I. Osipova, ed., *V teni Lubianki: o sud'bakh nastoiatelei tserkvi Sviatogo Liudovika Frantsuzskogo v Moskve: vospominaniia Leopol'da Brauna i obzor materialov sledstvennykh del* (Moscow: Bratonezh, 2012), p. 6.

[43] Vladimir Ponomarev, 'Tserkov' Sviatogo Liudovika Frantsuzskogo v Moskve: stranitsy istorii 1789 – 1917', *Pokrov: al'manakh rossiiskikh katolikov*, 1 (1999), 15 –19.

[44] Ibid., 18.

new building in the 1830s. It is a routine form, submitted by the church to local officials updating personal details about the French clergy. It reconciled information about the current parish staff with data that had apparently been collected during the seventh population revision, begun in 1816. Since then, three priests had died and more current information for those now serving was provided, including their age and year of ordination. The form is written in a flawless Russian hand, submitted in triplicate, signed by the current French Abbott, dated 1 January 1835 and stamped with the church's seal which reads, in Latin, 'Sigillem Ecclesiz Parochialis Sancii Ludovici Moscuensis.'[45] Having risen steadily and in close cooperation with Russian officials, this unique bastion of French culture was and still is an entrenched institution in the heart of Moscow. Within a few years, the church had purchased adjacent property covering an entire city block.[46] By the time of the Russian Revolution, St. Louis des Français à Moscou would be nestled in the midst of an entire ensemble of related buildings, which 'constituted, in the centre [of Moscow], a small French village.'[47]

It was here, at the infant nucleus of what would become that 'small French village' that the two Frenchmen Descarieres and De Selongey became acquainted in 1795 and told each other of their misfortunes. Descarieres described to De Selongey a plan he had concocted to win back his estranged wife. Though he desperately loved his wife, he knew her to be selfish and greedy, and it was to these baser instincts that he planned to appeal. Descarieres had authored a letter, addressed to himself and supposedly written by his brother-in-law, a high-ranking officer of the French Republic, recently fighting against royalists near Mainz. Descarieres would later tell the Russian officials interrogating him that he did not in fact have any such brother-in-law. He had

---

[45] Register of priests of the Church of St. Louis according to the seventh revision list, 1 January 1835, Tsentral'nyi gosudarstvennyi arkhiv Moskvy (TsGA Moskvy), f. 2193, op. 1, d. 8, l. 2.
[46] P. G. Palamarchuk, *Sorok sorokov*, 4 vols (Moscow: Krom, 1992 – 1995), IV (1995), pp. 431 – 434.
[47] V. G. Cherkasov-Georgievskii, *Moskva: religioznye tsentry i obshchiny* (Moscow: Profizdat, 1992), p. 60.

merely copied campaign locations and a fancy-sounding military rank for this fictitious relative from a newspaper article and from conversations he had overheard. It was all a ruse to make the letter seem more believable to his estranged wife. In the letter, his fabricated brother-in-law wrote of the disgust he felt upon hearing how Descarieres's wife had treated him. However, not to worry, Descarieres had come into some inheritance and if only he would return to France he could expect guaranteed prosperity. Descarieres, of course, intended that his wife should become privy to this letter and come running to his side, motivated by her greed and begging to be taken back. For this to work, however, the letter could not be written in his own hand, which she would certainly recognize. For this, he asked the assistance of his new acquaintance, De Selongey, whose written French was particularly neat, a mark of refinement. De Selongey saw no harm in this small deception, intended as it was to bring a family back together, and agreed to copy the letter.

According to Russian law, however, this was no harmless act. Two years earlier, upon terminating diplomatic relations with France, an imperial act regulated, among other things, correspondences between Russia and France. 'All of our subjects are forbidden to travel to France, or to have communication of any kind with Frenchmen in their homeland [that is, in France], or with those in their army, until such time as order and legal authority are restored in that land...'[48] To make matters worse, Descarieres did not merely send the letter by post to his wife's address, as he had promised De Selongey to do, but showed it to a number of Russians in Moscow. He was so pleased with the finished letter that he boasted of it around town, attempting to somehow make use of society gossip networks to spread the news of his good fortune and thereby further provoke his wife's jealousy. Of course this letter, supposedly received from France, claiming direct contact with the French army, and inviting him to

---

[48] *PSZ*, Tom XXIII, 17.101, 8 February 1793, p. 404.

travel to France, caused nothing but trouble. One of the Russians to whom Descarieres had shown the epistle reported the matter to the authorities who promptly arrested him. Upon interrogating Descarierers, they learned of De Selongey's involvement and arrested him as well. Descarieres's apartment was searched and the original letter in his own handwriting was found, proving that it was all just a scheme. Nevertheless, in May 1795, both men were ordered to leave Russian territory.

The meeting of these two Frenchmen in such a comedy of errors perfectly illustrates key differences in the two waves of French immigration to Russia in the eighteenth century. With his checkered past, instability, dishonesty, and life-long disregard for familial responsibilities, Descarieres verily embodied the Russian stereotypes of Frenchmen most prevalent in satirical literature since the earlier days of 'Gallomania.' He came to Russia in the first place because he had burned proverbial bridges elsewhere and had been assured that the Russian nobility of the 1770s and 1780s were eager to hire native French speakers to teach their children, even if their only qualification was their nationality. Descarieres's personification of the typical Russian notion of an 'immoral Frenchman' is demonstrated in a final postscript which Izmailov adds to his official report on the matter before sending it to St. Petersburg. After searching Descarieres's apartment, he writes, 'P.S. upon consideration of all the papers confiscated from him, nothing else of importance [to the investigation] was found. However, in many of the papers his debauched behaviour and indiscretion is demonstrated.'[49]

De Selongey, on the other hand, is the epitome of a French revolutionary émigré who was beyond the elite circle of the imperial court. Because of an abundance of well-born Frenchmen in Russia by this time, he was forced to take employment lower than his station and even to seek such employment outside of the two capitals. When he did

---

[49] Cover letter from Mikhail Izmailov to Count Aleksandr Samoilov, 1 May 1795, RGADA, f. 7, op. 2, d. 2870, l. 2 ob.

change jobs, it was in response to external circumstances (such as problems with salary or the death of an employer) and not because of personal caprice or the need for adventure. When the scheming, sixty-year old Descarieres came into his life, he was living on church property and looking for a situation in which to earn an honest living. His neat penmanship and graceful use of words bespeak etiquette and refinement. The last piece of evidence in this case is a letter in French, along with its Russian translation, composed in exile by De Selongey on 2 February 1796 and addressed to Mikhail Izmailov. De Selongey wrote from Swedish Finland, where he was residing with his ten-month-old child and young wife, whom he sent to St. Petersburg to deliver the letter as he was forbidden entry. The letter begins 'Forgive me, your Excellency, for being so bold as to write these lines to you. This is done with upmost respect for you and I hope that your Excellency receives it favourably.'[50] The letter goes on to appeal his deportation, once again telling his side of the story, and expressing his desire to return and become a subject of the Russian empire. If allowed to do so, he promised to never leave Russia and would be prepared, if necessary 'to shed the last drop of my blood in service to HER MAJESTY, the EMPRESS of all Russia...'[51] No further action is recorded in the file, and it is unclear whether he even received a reply.

The case of De Selongey and Descarieres suggests certain obvious implications for the prevalence of French immigrants and the nature of their influence upon Russian culture. In addition to illustrating characteristic distinctions between the two seasons of French immigration, this account underscores the widespread employment of Frenchmen as teachers and domestic tutors, the presence of French cultural hubs in larger cities, the interaction of Frenchmen within various circles of Russian society, and in numerous geographical regions of Russia outside of Moscow and St. Petersburg. These cultural catalysts were well-placed and widely-dispersed.

---

[50] Ibid., l.23.

[51] Ibid., l. 25.

Case study: a marked man

This case vividly illustrates that there were clear differences between the two waves of French immigrants. Russian prejudices, however, often failed to make the distinction. Generalization in sarcastic literary reference to Frenchmen, especially tutors, has already been mentioned in the review of secondary literature and is broadly discussed in chapter five.[52] As part of its anti-French propaganda in 1812, the December issue of *Vestnik Evropy* published another anecdotal account of two French teachers, each serving in a separate home in the Russian capital, and a bitter falling-out between them.[53] The premise of the article was that the advantages of learning French from a native speaker did not outweigh the moral detriment to one's children of having a Frenchman in the home. In support of this assertion, a story of two quarrelling French domestic tutors is recounted in the article. At the climax of the tale, one of the two Frenchmen takes his complaint to the master of the house where the other is serving. There, in the Russian nobleman's study, the Frenchman dramatically denounces his countryman as a rogue, and if the Russian employer would only examine the right shoulder of the accused, he would find proof that he had, in fact, been publicly branded in Paris for various kinds of bad behaviour [*za razniya bezdel'nichestva*].[54] Both of the foreigners are ultimately relieved of their positions and forced to seek work in the provinces. The article ends with the humourous punchline that, among the other morals of this story, the Russian landowner learned that it was necessary to include a shoulder-inspection in all future employment interviews whenever hiring a Frenchman.

This last detail, though intended to add a dramatic and humourous flare to the story, actually provides an insightful chronological clue. Though the article is not

---

[52] See this discussion in chapter one, pp. 52 – 53.

[53] 'Anekdot ob uchiteliakh Frantsuzakh', *Vestnik Evropy*, 23 and 24 (1812), 272 – 275.

[54] Ibid., 273.

presented as a work of fiction, it is clearly not an eyewitness account. It is billed as an

'anecdote' and when the author refers to a physical altercation between the main

characters, he adds the qualifier, 'if one is to believe the story [*predanie*].'[55] Further,

the mention of branding suggests that this anecdote—whether or not it is entirely true—

was likely recycled from a much earlier retelling and published in 1812 at the height of

anti-French sentiment. The branding of misdemeanour criminals with a hot iron was a

fairly common punishment for offenders from the lower social classes in mid-

eighteenth-century France, and sometimes coincided with banishment.[56] After the

beginning of the revolution, however, France's National Constituent Assembly banned

the practice in 1791. Branding was partially reinstated by the French Penal Code of

1802 as a punishment for repeat criminal offenders for certain crimes, such as

counterfeiting money or government seals, and broad application of the punishment was

reinstituted by the Napoleonic Criminal Code of 1810. The practice would be finally

abolished in 1832.[57] Therefore, while it is possible that the branded French tutor in this

story was a recent arrival from Napoleonic France who had quickly become established

in a noble home by 1812, it is more probable that he received the mark sometime before

1791 when this was still a common punitive occurrence and came to Russia in search of

a new start, perhaps after being banished from Paris. It seems likely that the Frenchmen

in question—if they were real individuals and not stereotypical amalgamations—

belonged to the earlier wave of immigrants.

---

[55] Ibid.

[56] Richard Mowery Andrews, *Law, Magistry, and Crime in Old Regime Paris, 1735 – 1789* (Cambridge: Cambridge University Press, 1994), pp. 310 – 316, 387 – 388; James Q. Whitman, *Harsh Justice: Criminal Punishment and the Widening Divide between America and Europe* (Oxford: Oxford University Press, 2003), pp. 103 – 121.

[57] Paul Perdrizet, 'La miraculeuse histoire de Pandare et d'Echédore, suivie de recherches sur la marque dans l'Antiquité', in *Archiv für Religionswissenschaft*, ed. by Albrecht Dieterich (Leipzig: B. G. Teubner, 1911), pp. 54 – 129; Jos Monballyu, *Six Centuries of Criminal Law: History of Criminal Law in the Southern Netherlands and Belgium (1400–2000)* (Leiden: Martinus Ninjoff, 2014), pp. 22 – 30.

These narrative examples of French emigrants in Russia, apart from their portrayal of personal drama, also describe examples of how different French people interacted with the Russian host-culture around them. They frequented local establishments, practiced their various trades alongside the Russian community (rather than living as a segregated diaspora), transacted business deals, married local women or other foreigners, started families, taught young people in Russian homes, and were not limited to living in one of the two capital cities. It is not difficult to imagine how this season of broader and deeper French engagement with Russian culture would leave behind a greater cache of loanwords still in frequent use than any other period. Cultural interaction, illustrated above in individual personal stories, can also be seen in a broader study of the arrival of Frenchman to Russia. Just as Catherine's behind-the-scenes correspondences supply information about individual immigrants, her public actions have left behind details regarding the French immigration at large.

The 1793 'census' of French subjects in Russia

As has already been mentioned, Catherine the Great's private concerns about events in France and the possibility of their spread to Russia became quite public all at once. On 8 February 1793, she issued an imperial decree to the Russian senate, severing diplomatic and commercial relations with the French Republic following the execution of Louis XVI.[58] The 1786 Franco-Russian trade agreement was rescinded, any ship flying the French flag was officially forbidden to dock at Russian ports, Russian diplomats were recalled and all Russian subjects residing in France were ordered to leave that country upon receiving news of this proclamation. Henceforth, no private correspondence with France would be allowed, periodical literature published in France could no longer be imported, and all French people currently located in Russia were to

---

[58] *PSZ*, XXIII, 17.101, 8 February 1793.

be deported within three weeks' time unless they agreed to publicly swear an oath of allegiance to the French Crown and renounce the revolution.

This last requirement was no symbolic gesture. The exact text of this oath of allegiance was included with the decree and recorded as law. Oath-swearing ceremonies were to be arranged in larger cities across the empire and all French subjects of both sexes were required to participate or leave Russia. These ceremonies took place primarily in Roman Catholic churches, but could also be conducted in Orthodox or Protestant churches, depending upon the religious affiliation of the one swearing the oath. The local magistrate would officiate at each ceremony and present a certificate to each Frenchman, commemorating his pledge of fidelity. A clergyman was also to stand as a witness, place his signature on each certificate, and in his presence each person completed their vow by kissing the cross. Finally, to be sure of their sincerity and rule out hypocrisy, the names of every French person taking this oath was to be published in Russian and foreign newspapers for all to see.

Catherine was as good as her word and required detailed reports from local governors, including the names of those who had agreed to the oath. According to what was reported, compliance was nearly universal. Of the more than 2000 French living in Russia at the time, only 18 refused to swear the oath and were subsequently expelled from the empire.[59] As reports of these ceremonies and those participating arrived in St. Petersburg, lists of names were in turn forwarded to newspapers for publication. In June 1793, four months after the issuance of the imperial *ukaz*, these lists began to appear in the Russian newspaper *Sanktpeterburgskiia vedomosti*. Because there were too many names to publish conveniently in one edition, the list was released gradually, across twenty-seven issues, the last printed in December 1793. Literate Russians in St. Petersburg and elsewhere in the empire where subscriptions were available, sitting

---

[59] Rostislavev, 'Frantsuzy v Rossii v 1793', 300.

down to read their newspaper throughout the summer and autumn 1793, would see lists of Frenchmen living in St. Petersburg, Moscow, Olenetsk, Revel' (now Tallin), Riga, and the surrounding areas of these important cities, with some personal information about these foreigners included in the articles.

There seems, however, to have been some inconsistency in the exact information collected by the various governors. For example, the two largest lists—those from Moscow and St. Petersburg—both feature an alphabetical register of names, but the additional details are different. The Moscow register publishes a city of origin for each name. The St. Petersburg record does not give this information but, instead, includes information about each Frenchman's profession, a detail absent from the Moscow list. Occupational information is unique to the St. Petersburg record. Lists published for the other cities report the city or region of origin with varying degrees of consistency and only rarely include notations related to occupation.

The record of French subjects living in St. Petersburg as of 1793 is of particular value to the present study because of its nearly universal inclusion of the occupations of those listed.[60] It has already been established that significant influx of French people into Russia occurred only after 1762, with some qualitative difference evident between the pre- and post-revolutionary waves of immigration. It has also been determined, through a lexical analysis of French loanwords appearing in the Russian language, that this period of French influence is of singular importance and that the types of words that entered suggest specific areas of cultural influence. By analyzing the data provided by the list of those French people swearing the oath of allegiance in St. Petersburg, another dimension—various means of influence—is added to this study. Taking St. Petersburg

---

[60] The list of those French subjects swearing the oath of allegiance in St. Petersburg was published across two issues of *Sanktpeterburgskiia vedomosti*, 7 June 1793, 1019 – 1024, and 10 June 1793, 1039 – 1045.

as a case study, the occupations of those Frenchmen present in 1793 may be studied for their correlation to larger patterns of French influence upon Russian culture.

A total of 786 French names are listed as having taking the oath of loyalty in St. Petersburg in 1793. Of these, 153 are described only by their familial relationship, such as 'Abral', Eli, a tailor; Abral', Adelaida, his daughter; Abral', Mari, his wife;'[61] Another 37 names are marked with no description of any kind, and so the only information to be had is their gender. A number of the other names are only 'registered as guests' in the city or have some other generic description. Nevertheless, there is still much information to be gained from this list since 555 of the names are accompanied by a description related to their professional occupation. Unless otherwise noted, proportional comparisons related to occupation will be based on this figure. The most common civilian occupations included teacher, merchant, cook, servant, hairdresser, valet, merchant's agent, goldsmith and governess.

Fig. 3.1: Ten most common civilian occupations among French subjects (Those registered at oath-swearing ceremonies in St. Petersburg, Russia, 1793)

Name of profession	Number registered	Percentage
Teacher	71	13%
Merchant	56	10%
Servant (*sluga, sluzhanka, sluzhitel'*, etc.)	51	9%
Cook	29	5%
Hairdresser	23	4%
Valet	22	4%
Merchant's agent (*prikazchik*)	18	3%
Goldsmith	11	2%
Governess	11	2%
Tailor or Seamstress	13	2%
Total	**305**	**55%**

In terms of assessing cultural influence, it is noteworthy that teaching was the most common profession. Teachers and governesses were in a position of direct influence on the way young Russians thought, spoke, and acted. Likewise, the many cooks, servants,

---

[61] *Sanktpeterburgskiia vedomosti*, 7 June 1793, 1019.

and valets generated the domestic culture of their masters and the rest either clothed

them or provided them luxury goods. In addition to these, 102 of the French in St.

Petersburg (18% of those with occupations listed) were in the military or worked in

some other form of government service. These range in prestige from corporal to major

general in the military, and in other administrative vocations from clerk all the way up

to 'secretary to His Highness.'

Considering these most common careers does not, however, give a full picture of

St. Petersburg's French population at the time, because the other professions listed are

so remarkably specific. For the 786 names included, a total of 157 unique occupations

are listed, one hundred of which occur only once in the entire register. There was only

one 'saddle-maker' [*sedel'nik*], one 'glassworker' [*stekol'shchik*], one 'braider'

[*pozumentshchik*], and just one 'customs warden' [*tsolner*] in the list.[62] However, by

combining narrowly specialized occupations into groups, some clear patterns become

apparent. For example, while only one Frenchman registered himself as a 'floor

polisher' [*poloter*] upon taking the oath, and there is only one instance each of 'steward'

and *mundshenk* (a servant responsible for drinks in a household),[63] these are all

domestic servants. As such, they all play a similar role in Russian society, affecting the

way noble families live and bringing their own native culture into Russian homes. Of

the 555 French names listed by vocation, 128 of them were definitely in some sort of

domestic service. These were cooks, valets, headwaiters, sundry household and kitchen

help and, of course, governesses. This figure does not include the 71 'teachers' listed,

many of whom were probably employed as domestic tutors. Likewise, of the 23 names

---

[62] This last profession, a German loan-word, does not occur in twentieth-century Russian dictionaries. By the late nineteenth century it was already considered to be outdated. See 'tsolner' in V. I. Dal', *Tolkovyi slovar' zhivogo velikorusskogo iazyka: v chetyrekh tomakh* (St. Petersburg: M. O. Vol'f, 1880–1882; repr. Moscow: Russkii iazyk media, 2003), IV, p. 575.

[63] *Slovar' Akademii Rossiiskoi. Chast' IV: ot M. do R.* (St. Petersburg: pri Imperatorskoi Akademii Nauk, 1793), p. 328 <http://www.runivers.ru/lib/book3173/> [accessed 24 June 2014]

described generically as 'a damsel' [*devitsa*], some of these were likely assigned to a noble home, as in '*devitsa vo usluzhenii*', a common phrase for a girl who was 'in service.' All told, 128 – 222 of the French people on the list (23 – 40%) earned their keep in a household: teaching children, preparing and serving meals, cleaning and beautifying homes, and influencing Russian culture at the familial level. A complete list of all the occupations listed in the oath-swearing registers of 1793 is provided in Appendix C.

Another group of occupations are those which provided goods to St. Petersburg's consumers at the end of the eighteenth century. These represent 29% of the French subjects listed by occupation. The city's 56 French merchants have already been mentioned, but if the French shopkeepers and sales agents who assisted them is added, then this number grows to 81 French subjects which may be referred to as a mercantile group. Further, Frenchmen were not only selling goods, but producing them as well. Ten are listed in the register as 'manufacturers' [*fabrikant*]. They produced various forms of cloth, foil, and at least one entrepreneurial lady ran a factory which produced card-stock. Another 71 Frenchmen were craftsmen. Some of these were employed making articles of clothing: hats, shoes, bonnets, garments, or specializing in various types of cloth and fur. Others specialized in handiwork that might beautify interior décor: gold embroidery, various artistic engraving and metal-work, upholstery, and a seemingly well-developed goldsmith profession (St. Petersburg had, in 1793, 12 French goldsmith masters, 5 journeymen, and one apprentice.) As Russians visited fashionable boutique shops, purchased imported goods, and ordered luxury items made by local French masters, the St. Petersburg market-place became yet another platform for French cultural influence.

Seventy-seven people (14%) may be grouped loosely as professionals and tradesmen who provided services rather than goods. In addition to the 23 hairdressers who were already mentioned, these include medical professionals, a few tradesmen in

the printing industry, and members of the artistic community such as actors, musicians,

and theatre workers. The statistical analysis below looks at the presence of French

subjects in St. Petersburg according to the spheres of influence in which they were

employed. That is to say, this grouping of occupations speaks to the various platforms

from which French nationals in the city could exert cultural influence upon their

Russian hosts. Some of them were located in Russian homes. Others interacted with

Russians in some official capacity. The rest impacted Russian society in the

marketplace, providing the goods and services which enriched their lives.

Fig. 3.2: Occupations of Frenchmen in St. Petersburg, 1793 (By spheres of influence.)

Occupation	Number of Frenchmen listed	Percentage
Official posts	**102**	**18%**
Military	80	14%
Government	15	3%
Other administrative	7	1%
Domestic service	**128 – 222**	**22 – 38%**
Consumer goods	**162**	**28%**
Mercantile	81	14%
Manufacturers	10	2%
Craftsmen	71	12%
Services providers	**77**	**13%**
Professional	38	7%
Medical	9	2%
Arts	30	5%
Miscellaneous	**15**	**3%**
TOTAL	**484 – 578**	**84 – 100%**

Examining the professions of these Frenchmen in this way helps to explain some

of the French influences that became apparent in the lexical analysis of loan-word

import. Of the 2,986 borrowed French words discovered in Russian dictionaries across the past three centuries, 501 appear for the first time either in the dictionary commissioned by Catherine the Great (published 1789 – 94) or during the subsequent period represented by the career of Aleksandr Pushkin (1813 – 1837). Out of these, 334 easily fell into categorization groups. The rest (167 words) were words that could have multiple meanings, would change meaning over time, or eventually became so common that the context of their original introduction into the language is lost when considered alongside their subsequent two hundred years of use. Of those categorized, 101 words (30%) relate directly to official institutions, especially the military. 26 words (8%) deal with urban and residential design, including architecture, space management, and interior décor. The greatest influx, 153 words (46%) related to items, activities and concepts that were properly cultural in nature. The correlation between the types of French words entering the Russian language and the types of French people residing in St. Petersburg during this period is unmistakable. New words for military culture and government order appear at a time when Russian officials in the nation's capital were in close proximity to French colleagues. The vocabulary to describe that which makes a home beautiful arrived in Russia during the same period that French manufacturers, craftsmen, and merchants made their wares available and French domestic servants filled noble Russian homes.

However, to fully appreciate the correlation between French immigration and the single largest import of French terms—the 153 cultural words—it is necessary to analyze the occupations of those Frenchman in 1793 St. Petersburg from a different perspective. Having already considered their spheres of influence (domestic versus official, and so forth) it will now be helpful to examine some of those same professions according to the kind of cultural influence to which they pertain, rather than the arena in which they exerted it. For example, hairdressers provided a service in the marketplace, cloth manufacturers produced goods for sale, and shoemakers were considered craftsmen, but these are all professions that relate to fashion.[64] Likewise, words related to food culture comprise an interesting sub-category that is somewhat obscured in the previous classification.[65] When examined in this light, roughly one third of the 555 French people who reported a vocation in 1793 (or 170 names) were engaged in an occupation overtly cultural in nature. Fifty-six of these (33%) were in professions dealing with fashion: hairdressers, makers and sellers of garments, and so called 'fashion masters' [*modnye masteritsy*]. Another 42 people (25%) exerted their cultural influence through the culinary arts as bakers, confectioners, and cooks, to name a few. Forty of the French craftsmen and professionals dealt in items related to home décor. These were upholsterers, engravers, carpenters, and goldsmiths and they comprise 23% of the cultural group. Finally, 32 Frenchmen (19%) contributed to the fine arts as musicians, painters, actors and other theatre personnel. Though not included in the figure above, it is also likely that many of the 81 merchants listed dealt in goods that related to all of these categories.

Fig. 3.3: Occupations of Frenchmen in St. Petersburg, 1793 related to culture

Area of cultural influence	Number of Frenchmen working in this field	Percentage
Fashion	56	33%
Food	42	25%
Home décor	40	24%
Fine arts	32	19%
TOTAL	**170**	**100**

It is reasonable to infer that French settlers such as these contributed to lasting cultural impact upon Russia since these are precisely the areas of cultural influence suggested by French additions to Russia's vocabulary during this period. Forty-seven of the 153 cultural words borrowed from French during this period (31%) were words

---

[64] See my overview of secondary literature related to the popularity of French fashions in Russian during this period in chapter one, pp. 33 – 34, 53 – 58.

[65] See my overview of French cuisine in Russia in chapter two, pp. 123 – 124.

related to the fine arts. Another 39 (or 25%) are terms dealing with fashion. Eighteen new French words (12% of the imported cultural terms) are words associated with food, drink, and food service. The remaining French cultural words which enter the language during this period could also be linked to the presence of French domestic servants, or fraternization with French noblemen who have set up residence in Russia since fleeing the revolution. Fourteen words (9%) for various types of games, especially card games, enter the language, reminiscent of the card-stock manufacturer and her associates who registered at the oath-swearing ceremony. Likewise any of the 14 loanwords related to polite society (another 9% of the imported cultural terms) would be unimaginable without the participation of domestic servants and foreigners with whom to interact socially. Only in this period was there a word for 'lackey' or 'curtsey' in the Russian language. Also during this period, the male partner of a pair of dancers became known as the *kavaler*, and each covering for a formal dinner known as a *kuvert*. The final 14% of French cultural words borrowed during this period were those of a literary nature, abstract words dealing with interpersonal relations, and other miscellaneous items and concepts. These were just as likely to result from Russia's interaction with French literature as they were to necessarily have any connection with immigration. Nevertheless, even this type of influence suggests the contribution of French merchants, educators, and tradesmen in the printing industry who registered in St. Petersburg in 1793.

While words dealing with interior design were categorized in a group apart from cultural words in the lexical analysis, it is worth mentioning here that this period saw the addition of 13 new French words related to home décor and space management. These include the words for 'furniture' [*mebel'*], *tualet* (as a room for dressing) and various fine domestic items that a foreign butler or maid might look after in a noble home, or which may have been introduced to the culture via French merchants or

French nobility selling some of the personal property that they managed to rescue during their escape from France.

The remaining 16% of new French loanwords categorized during this period are those related to philosophy and social thought, technological and scientific words, and properly 'foreign' words dealing specifically with French institutions and French history. Discussion of these areas of influence upon Russian culture is better suited for the more general observations to be made from a review of Russian periodical literature from this period, which will be the focus of chapter five.

Fig. 3.4: New French loanwords in the Russian language (1725 – 1837)

Category	Number of words
Cultural	153
Official (including military)	101
Urban and Residential Design	26
Technological and scientific	24
France-specific terms	16
Philosophy/ social thought	14
Various	167
TOTAL	**501**

Before leaving this comparative analysis of St. Peterburg's late eighteenth-century French population and the lexical import during the same period, one final set of insights can be gleaned from what may be referred to as 'left-over' words. One hundred and sixty-seven of the 501 words borrowed from French during the period of Catherine through Pushkin were not categorized at all during the lexical analysis. A number of words which are now considered to be quite ordinary entered Russian from French during this period, including the words for 'company', 'effect', 'interest', 'manner', 'character', form', and 'address', to name a few. These 'various' words were categorized as such because, at that stage in the research, all periods from Peter I to the present were being considered and it was this broad study of the Russian lexicon which suggested the priority of the late eighteenth and early nineteenth century as it relates to French cultural influence. Because loan words take on new auxiliary meanings over time and become too basic to the receiving language to be catalogued in a specialty group, setting aside these words helped to avoid diluting the other analytical categories. This does not, however, mean that these words are unimportant to the present study of cultural impact. In fact, examined apart from the broader lexical study and within the context of this period and its two waves of French immigration, the circumstances surrounding the introduction of a number of these terms become quite obvious. For example, the word *emigrant* appears for the first time during Pushkin's lifetime and has remained a staple in the Russian vocabulary ever since. Likewise, *madam* as the title for a governess has obvious implications. Ironic reference to a *voiazher*, a bumbling foreign adventurer, enters during the same period but disappeared from the language sometime in the twentieth century. Another new word, *sharlatan*, referred to one who made his living by taking advantage of others or operating under false pretenses. It is not difficult to imagine how both of these last two terms could be used to describe the misadventures of Desarenne Descarieres and others like him who wandered across the border into Russia in the 1770s and 1780s, looking for a better life than the one they had squandered in Europe. Luxury items like jewellery boxes [*shkatulka*], metal thread [*kanitel'*] and *blondy* (a special type of lace) may have been imported earlier, but were prevalent enough during Catherine's lifetime to be included in her first Russian dictionary. Snuff boxes [*tabakerka*] were soon to follow as was the name for a 'clasp' on a handbag [*fermuar*].

Finally, the aforementioned presence of French tradesmen in the publishing industry seems to have contributed a small but interesting group of new loanwords during this period. A short-lived word in the Russian language, *batyrshchik* referred to one who swabbed ink onto the typeset in preparation for printing.[66] Such work was likely included in the duties of the one French typographer as well as the one French compiler [*naborshchik*] who registered at the St. Petersburg oath ceremony. Two bookbinders [*perepletchik*] were also among the Frenchmen on the list. The words 'copy', 'pamphlet', and 'vellum' [*velenevyi*] all came from French to Russian during this period as did the word *tere*, the name of the typed character referred to in English as a 'dash.'

Conclusion

French people living in Russia at the end of the eighteenth century made a significant contribution to multiple aspects of Russian life. Contemporary Russians themselves must have been intuitively aware of this contribution, even without the empirical study above. For proof of this, one has to look no further than the words of Catherine's own proclamation. Even before receiving the detailed reports from her governors, the text of her decree demonstrates the general impression that she already had of French immigrants and their activities. Her command to denounce the revolution was addressed to 'all Frenchmen without exception: merchants and those engaged in craft trades [*meshchanskie promysly imeiushchikh*], artists, craftsmen, those in the service of private people, referring here to teachers [of both genders] and the like...'[67] The outcome of this impromptu census of French residents confirmed these initial impressions, broad though they were, but also expanded and refined them and produced a more complete picture of Russia's French population. They lived, worked and created among the Russians and their impact continues to be relevant, as the enduring lexical legacy illustrates. This lexical legacy and the human influx that accompanied it provide

[66] Dal', *Tolkovyi slovar' zhivogo velikorusskogo iazyka*, Tom 1, p. 54.
[67] *PSZ*, Tom XXIII, 17.101, 8 February 1793, p. 403.

a concrete historical example of significant foreign impact upon a receiving culture, an

area of inquiry that migration studies are increasingly beginning to explore.[68]

---

[68] See my discussion of the present study's relevance to migration studies in the introduction, pp. 17 –
20.

CHAPTER FOUR

THE RUSSIAN ARMY'S FOREIGN CAMPAIGNS OF 1813 – 1815 AND FRENCH CULTURAL INFLUENCE

In the history of French influence upon Russian culture, the year 1814 is of singular importance but it has also been neglected by historians. The events of this year are largely overshadowed by 1812 and Napoleon's fateful invasion of Moscow, an event which marked the beginning of the end for Bonaparte and continues to resound as a defining moment in Russia's sense of national consciousness.[1] Adam Zamoyski's study of the war only briefly mentions the Russian army's subsequent invasion of France as part of his concluding chapter.[2] Armand de Caulaincourt's classic account—which ends with Napoleon's safe arrival in Paris in December 1812—does not deal with this phase of the war at all.[3] Even Dominic Lieven's history, exceptional for its broader coverage of events beyond 1812, devotes less than half of its chapters to Russian military action in Western Europe.[4] As it relates to the present cultural inquiry, however, 1814 cannot be overlooked, for during this year tens of thousands of Russians spent an extended period of time in France, an unprecedented occurrence with profound cultural implications.

Around the time of the sesquicentennial commemoration of 1812, Marc Raeff asserted that the war with Napoleon affected all facets of Russian life, but Soviet studies of the conflict tended to be one-dimensional, focusing broadly on military engagements, and depicting the war as an epic clash of good and evil and the embodiment of class struggle. Such treatment, Raeff argued, ignored the important human element of the

---

[1] See my overview of secondary literature related to the Napoleonic War's impact on Russian cultural and national identity in chapter one, pp. 65 – 69.

[2] Adam Zamoyski, *Moscow 1812: Napoleon's Fatal March* (London: HarperCollins, 2004), pp. 544 – 557.

[3] Armand de Caulaincourt, *With Napoleon in Russia* (Mineola: Dover Publications, 2005).

[4] Dominic Lieven, *Russia Against Napoleon: The Battle for Europe, 1807 to 1814* (London: Allen Lane, 2009).

war and its practical implications for the Russian people.[5] One of these implications, cultural transfer, is the subject of the present chapter.

Following the French army's disastrous invasion of Russia and subsequent retreat therefrom, the Russian army, initially under the command of Mikhail Kutuzov, began an offensive known as the Foreign Campaigns of the Russian Army of 1813 – 1815. By February 1813, the remainder of the French invasion force had been pushed back to the Vistula River in Poland. Later that month, Russia and Prussia signed the Treaty of Kalisz, essentially laying the groundwork for the Sixth Coalition against Napoleon. Over the next months this coalition grew to include Great Britain, Sweden, Austria and some of the German states, became more organized, fought decisive battles in Dresden, Leipzig, and near Berlin, and, by the end of 1813, had driven Napoleon from the German lands.[6] At the beginning of 1814, the ranks of the allies had swelled to 900,000 against Napoleon's 300,000. 453,000 of these allied troops were stationed along the eastern bank of the Rhine River, including 153,000 Russians. In December 1813 – January 1814, they crossed the Rhine and advanced into the heart of France. After a series of battles inside France, Paris was taken in March 1814, Napoleon abdicated later that month, and the Bourbon King Louis XVIII was finally installed on the throne of France by May of the same year.[7]

Over the course of this campaign, Russian regiments, dispersed among the various allied armies, moved westward across northeastern France (see figures 4.1 – 4.3, which show a few examples of the routes taken by the memoirists studied). An estimated 69,000 Russian soldiers were among the 149,000 coalition troops who

---

[5] Marc Raeff, 'The 150th Anniversary of the Campaign of 1812 in Soviet Historical Writing', *Jahrbücher für Geschichte Osteuropas,* 12 (1964), 247–260.

[6] John Kuehn, *The Reasons for the Success of the Sixth Coalition against Napoleon in 1813* (unpublished master's thesis, U. S. Army Command and General Staff College, 1997).

[7] Lievan, *Russia Against Napoleon*; I. I. Rostunov, 'Zagranichnye pokhody russkoi armii 1813 – 14', in *Bol'shaia sovetskaia entsiklopediia* <http://bse.slovaronline.com> [accessed 30 December 2014]

marched all the way to Paris.[8] While in France, these Russians interacted with their surroundings and experienced a foreign culture in addition to fighting a war. Whereas previous exposure to French culture had come through the importation of individual elements into Russia, Russian military personnel were now, themselves, exported into France and experiencing it from within. Though the wartime circumstances certainly made this a much different experience from that of Karamzin, for example, who had travelled as a civilian, the Russian military was still placed in a position to be significantly impacted, culturally speaking. They were experiencing life's most basic activities inside of France: where they slept, what they ate, what they saw around them as they marched through cities and across the countryside, with whom they interacted and how. They were, in many respects, immersed in French culture.

The memoirs and diaries of Russian officers who participated in the campaign attest to this fact and form the source base for this chapter.[9] Soon after the war, excerpts from the recollections of officers were quickly published in Russian literary journals. In this season of awakened patriotism following the victory and yearning for a fully-developed national historiography, there was an insatiable appetite among Russia's reading public for such memoirs. A leading historian of Russia's memoir tradition refers to the earnest appeal made by literary figures of the nineteenth century—including Aleksandr Pushkin—who called upon surviving veterans of the 1812 war and foreign campaigns to record their experiences for posterity.[10] Literary scholars and other enthusiasts, such as General A. I. Mikhailovskii-Danilevskii, laboured to compile and publish them. As early as the 1830s, entire collections of these firsthand accounts

---

[8] M. K. Chiniakov, 'Parizh', in *Zagranichnye pokhody rossiiskoi armii 1813 – 1815 gody: entsiklopediia*, ed. by B. M. Bezotosnyi and others, 2 vols (Moscow: Rosspen, 2011), II, pp. 195 – 205 (pp. 197 – 198).
[9] Original editions of the early nineteenth-century literary journals cited in this study were accessed at the State Public Historical Library of Russia. The nineteenth-century books that are cited—memoir collections and individually published memoirs—are available as digital facsimiles from the Russian State Library's collection of digital books < http://elibrary.rsl.ru/> [accessed 3 January 2015]
[10] A. G. Tartakovskii, *Russkaia memuaristika i istoricheskoe soznanie XIX veka* (Moscow: Arkheograficheskii tsentr, 1997), pp. 259 – 325.

were being published as books and new collections or reprints were released at intervals across the century, especially in conjunction with the major anniversaries of 1812. Even into the late 1800s, historians transcribed oral interviews with elderly veterans, redeeming the last possible opportunities to hear directly from participants in a series of events that had meant so much to Russia's very sense of national identity. [11]

Fig. 4.1: Map of N. N. Murav'ev's recorded route through France

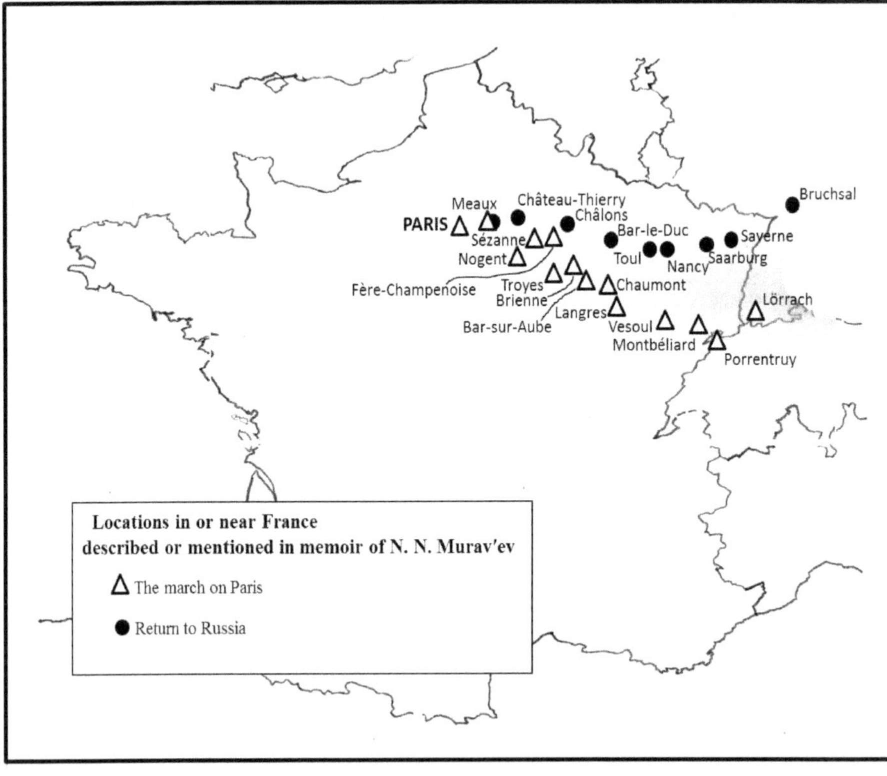

[11] B. P. Totfakushin and B. N. Zemtsov, 'Memuary', in *Zagranichnye pokhody rossiiskoi armii 1813 – 1815 gody: entsiklopediia*, ed. by B. M. Bezotosnyi and others, 2 vols (Moscow: Rosspen, 2011), II, pp. 36 – 46.

Fig. 4.2: Map of I. T. Radozhitskii's recorded route through France

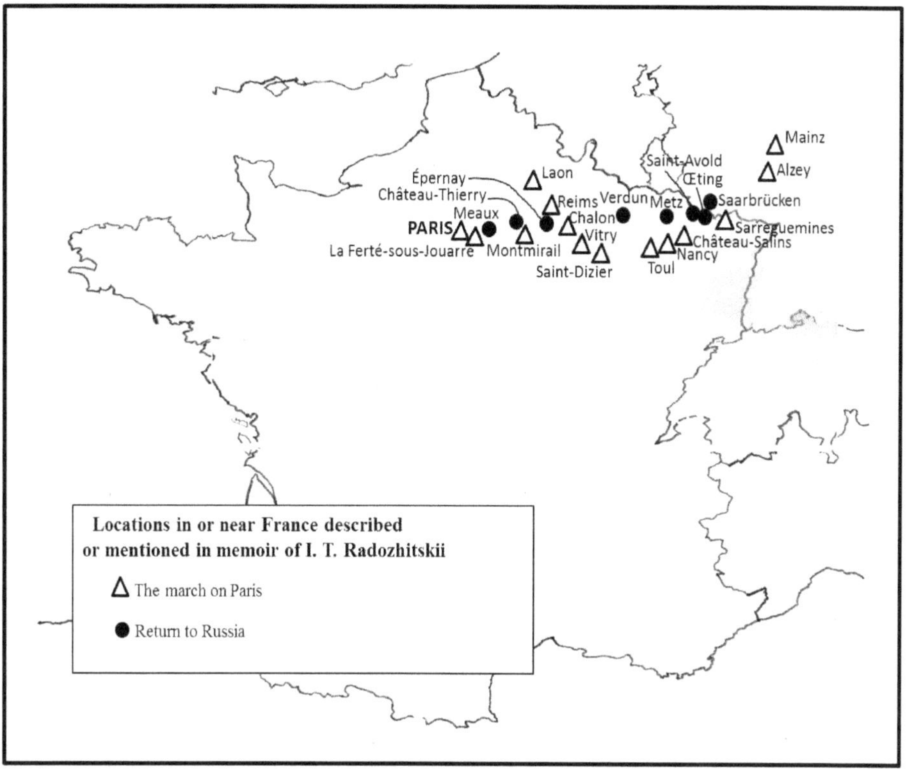

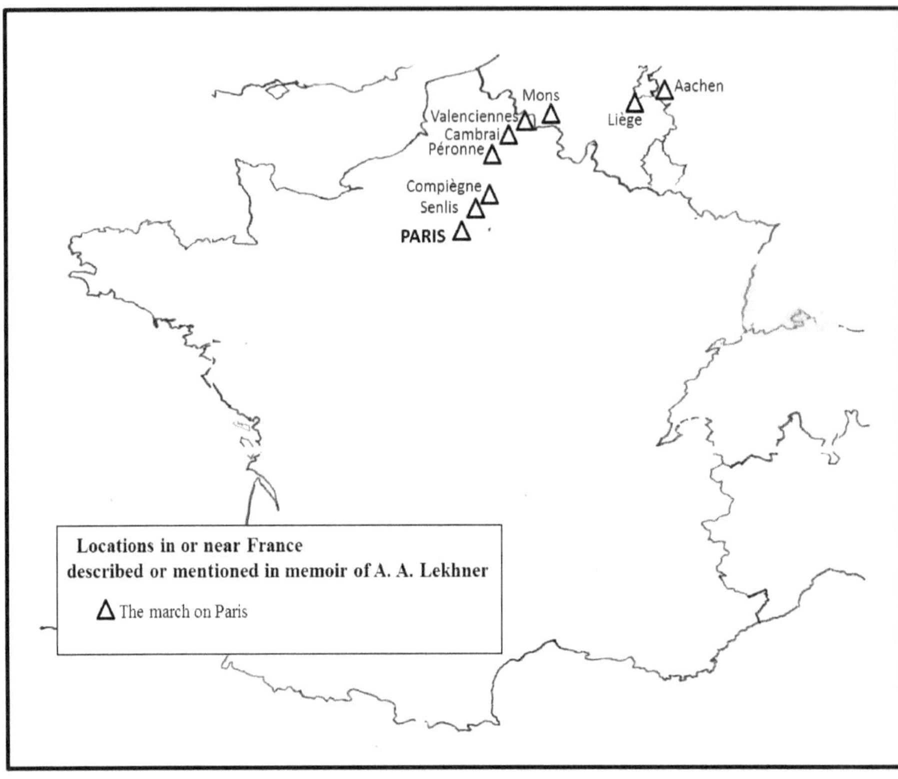

Apart from their obvious worth as sources of military and political history, these

memoirs provide invaluable cultural insights, including snapshots of French cultural

influence upon individual Russian officers and soldiers while they were serving abroad.

With this end in mind, twenty-one different Russian military memoirs have been

studied. While there are many extant memoirs from the 1812 era, only those have been

included which pertain to Russia's 1813 – 1815 foreign campaigns, and the study

focuses specifically on recollections of time spent inside French territory. Because of

their diversity in style and content, the various memoirs contribute to the study in

different ways. Some of those written by staff officers such as Colonel M. F. Orlov—

who had direct access to Alexander I and participated in major negotiations—focus more on key events and notable figures.[12] Memoirs such as these reference French

cultural influences only in the broadest sense, or as it pertained to the upper elite

commanders. Patriotic publicist Sergei Glinka's contribution was equally broad as his

memoir was written in a poetic style and dealt largely in sweeping generalizations.

Others, however, were written by lower-level officers whose recollections are more

prosaic and descriptive of daily life on the march, including their encounters with

cultural elements and observations of the common Russian soldiers with whom they had

direct contact, and the reactions of those soldiers to their French surroundings.

There is also a broad spectrum of detail provided by the memoirs; For example,

those left behind by General A. A. Zakrevskii and Colonel A. A. Lekhner were written

in diary format.[13] Many of their daily entries offer no more than a date and a location.

Memoirs of this type were still helpful, however, as part of a larger comparative

analysis, contributing to the overall picture of routes, landmarks, and events most

commonly cited by Russian officers. On the other hand, several of the memoirists

wrote in eloquent prose and left behind a great deal of engaging anecdotal material.

Finally, the content of some of the memoirs studied was almost exclusively military in

nature, recording troop movements and battles, but offering little insight into cultural

experiences. Nevertheless, studied comparatively, these memoirs complement one

another, and suggest patterns of French cultural impact.

---

[12] When the author of a memoir is first referenced in this chapter, his military rank at the time of the events (if known), initials, and surname are given. For subsequent references, only the author's surname is cited with the exception of Fedor and Sergei Glinka, two brothers who both left behind memoirs relevant to this study. To distinguish them, first names rather than initials are used. In addition to providing more clarity for the reader ('Sergei' and 'Fedor' versus 'S. N.' and 'F. N.'), Sergei and Fedor Glinka both went on to become significant literary figures in their own right. As such, their names appear in the same form as other important historical and literary figures referenced throughout this dissertation.

[13] A. A. Zakrevskii, 'Dnevnik 1815 – 1816 gg., pisannyi rukoi Arseniia Andreevicha Zakrevskago', in *Sbornik starinnykh bumag khraniashchikhsia v muzee P. I. Shchukina, desiataia chast'*, ed. by P. I. Shchukin (Moscow: Tovarishchestvo tipografii A. I. Mamontova, 1902), pp. 92 – 99; A. A. Lekhner, A. A., 'Dnevnik 1813 – 1814 gg', in A. K. Afanas'ev and others, eds, *1812 – 1814: reliatsii. pis'ma. dnevniki* (Moscow: Terra, 1992), pp. 345 – 401

The reflections of Orlov articulate one view as to the overall cultural significance of Russia's foreign campaigns. Russian officers and soldiers, Orlov argued, were uniquely impressionable to French culture. In his memoir, he echoed an opinion often expressed by other memoirists that the French people grew to like the Russians more than they did the other invading allies:

> At that time, and long thereafter, Russians enjoyed much greater favour with the French than did other nations. [Some have] searched for a reason for this in the supposed similarity of our character and tastes. I, on the other hand, attribute this to a combination of special circumstances. We loved the language, literature, civilization, and courage of the French. In all these respects we gave them their fair tribute of astonishment with conviction and enthusiasm. Unlike the English or the Germans, we did not have a literature [of our own] to set up in contrast against [*protivopostavit'*] French literature. Our civilization, [still] being born, could not boast of its own discoveries in the sciences, or successes in the arts. Regarding bravery, both nations are glorious, have met on the battle field multiple times, and have learned mutually to respect one another.[14]

It is precisely these 'tributes of astonishment', elements of French culture deemed by Russian officers to be interesting or surprising enough for inclusion in their wartime memoirs, which form the basis of this chapter.

As with any memoir literature, issues related to the accuracy of an individual author's memory must be considered.[15] This has been dealt with in the present study by reading multiple memoirs comparatively so that the recollections of different officers may corroborate or refute one another. Beyond the issue of accuracy, however, this comparative approach also serves the cultural purposes of this dissertation. By giving greater attention to those events and subjects described in multiple memoirs, this chapter reveals common themes of French cultural influence which were meaningful for the Russian troops.

---

[14] M. F. Orlov, *Kapituliatsiia Parizha. Politicheskie sochineniia. Pis'ma* (Moscow: Izdatel'stvo Akademii Nauk SSSR, 1963), p. 17.

[15] See my general discussion of the issue of memory when using memoirs and other autobiographical literature as primary sources in the introductory chapter, pp. 21 – 23.

It should be noted, however, that many of the impressions recorded apply primarily to the officers who wrote them and others of their class who were able to enjoy similar experiences. The conditions of their quartering, their ability to read, and fluency in French set them apart from common soldiers culturally. The capacity of Russian visitors to be affected by their experiences in France was particularly enhanced by their command of the French language. In addition to simply responding to visual stimuli that they might see along their journey, and sampling French food and drink, those Russians who knew French were able to interact with the culture on a much deeper level. They were able to read local newspapers and journals, buy French books, experience more of Paris by asking passersby for directions, and converse with people in all strata of society in a variety of settings. This aptitude to experience French culture more fully was something that they owed to their parents' and grandparents' generations. Many of the young Russian officers who marched on Paris in 1814 had likely been brought up under the tutelage of French governesses and teachers, many of whom had fled to Russia from the Terror of the 1790s. As the study of immigration in chapter three has suggested, many of these tutors would have been an improvement after the wandering adventurers and other Frenchmen from whom their parents had learned French in the 1760s – 1780s, thanks to the liberal immigration policies of Catherine II. The wellborn officers who wrote these memoirs represented the most francophone generation of Russians thus far, and were therefore uniquely equipped to interact with their surroundings inside France. For broader implications of how Russia's relatively young civilization was being impacted in these same ways, parallel data from the lexical study outlined in chapter two has been included.

French language: transitional areas

As a practical matter, the Russian officers' ability to speak French meant greater freedom of movement and assisted them in carrying out their duties and performing basic tasks, something for which they were all the more grateful, having just travelled through lands where other languages were spoken. Upon arriving in Saint-Avold, General's aide Fedor Glinka mentioned that he was finally able to order food in a tavern.[16] Likewise, when sent on a solo errand to deliver sick and wounded soldiers to a field hospital in Langres, Lieutenant I. M. Kazakov wrote that 'on that trip, a knowledge of the French language helped [*sposobstvovalo*] me.'[17] That the Russians needed to reach France before finding their French language skills useful is a fact that seems almost too obvious to mention, but it is essentially this fact that many of the memoirs emphasize through anecdotal accounts. Lieutenant A. D. Chertkov, General I. V. Kakhovskii, Lieutenant I. T. Radozhitskii, and Fedor Glinka all describe the months-long westward march as a sometimes frustrating process of slowly moving from one linguistic region to another, several citing a gradual border-land between the German- and French-speaking areas. In one case, a 'mixed language' is reported to have been heard near the French border, closer to German than to French.[18] Glinka designated the city of Saint-Avold as a milestone in this regard: 'From the Rhine to this place, French is not yet the common and only language. A large part of the residents speak German. But from Saint-Avold, [French] is already becoming generally dominant.'[19]

This process of gradually entering French-speaking territory was, in its own right, an important part of their journey of cultural discovery. When, at long last, they arrived in France, those Russian officers who had been educated in French were arriving

---

[16] Fedor Glinka, *Pis'ma russkogo ofitsera* (Moscow: Voennoe izdatel'stvo, 1987), p. 226.

[17] I. M. Kazakov, 'Pokhod vo Frantsiiu 1814 g. Po (neizdannym) zapiskam praporshchika leib-gvardii Semenovskago polka Ivana Mikhailovicha Kazakova', in *Rossiiskie memuary epokhi napoleonovskikh voin*, ed. by G. V. Liapishchev (Moscow: Russkii Mir, 2013), p. 522.

[18] I. T. Radozhitskii, *Pokhodnyia zapiski artillerista, c 1812 po 1816 god*, Chast' III (Moscow: Institut Vostochnykh Iazykov, 1835), p. 192.

[19] Fedor Glinka, *Pis'ma russkogo ofitsera*, p. 226.

to something familiar after a long journey through strange lands. Kazakov described the unique sensation of waking up for the first time in the French home where he was quartered in Paris: 'The next day at seven o'clock in the morning, when for the first time since the bivouac I had slept sweetly on clean, soft sheets, I hear the stern order [from the master of the house]: "Levez-vous!" This word was so well familiar to me that I jumped, thinking that I was still at the Page Corps [in Petersburg], where the company commander Rotmaler woke us every day.'[20]

The French language as common

The Russian officers gained new perspective by being immersed in French, the language that, in their own native culture, belonged to society's elite. Of course it would be a step too far to say that they were surprised that the French spoke French, but they did record a sensation akin to awe at finding themselves in a context where their elite language was the common one. Soon after entering French territory, Fedor Glinka entered an inn to have a meal, was led to a separate dining room, and overheard a female voice speaking flawless French in the adjacent room. Because of her correct grammar, clear pronunciation, and the fact that he had grown 'accustomed to always hearing this language in our very best society,' he assumed that this was the voice of a noblewoman. To satisfy his curiosity, he went to glance into the next room from whence he had heard this elegant French diction. The room he peeked into was the kitchen and the voice he heard belonged to the cook. Stunned, he reflected on the status typically bestowed upon French immigrants in Russia: 'Take a stained [*zapachkannaia*] French woman, throw her into Russia somewhere in a field: before a week has passed you will see her in a wealthy home, in luxury and esteem.'[21] I. I. Lazhechnikov, aide to Generals B. V. Poluektov and A. I. Osterman-Tolstoi over the course of the war,

---

[20] Ibid., p. 537.
[21] Fedor Glinka, *Pis'ma russkogo ofitsera*, p. 226.

reported a similar experience in Paris where a well-dressed French woman engaged him in conversation and told him that she had lived in Moscow for several years. She had lived in a prominent area of Moscow, was often received in the best Russian homes, and related to Lazhechnikov the names of several princes and counts who had called upon her while she was there. After she walked away, Lazhechnikov asked a nearby Frenchman who this lady was. '"A laundress living on Rue Saint-Honoré", he replied with a suspicious smile.' After this encounter, Lazhechnikov concluded:

> Here, such ladies are laundresses, but among us they play the role of notable immigrants, and what is most woeful of all is that they are taken in to raise our children. I think that Russians, having been in France, will open the eyes of their relatives and acquaintances concerning these ladies, and gentlemen similar to them, who are, God knows, held in such honour and such respect![22]

Radozhitskii was equally negative in his expression of this discovery. 'It is strange', he wrote, 'to see some ragged man in a blue tunic, or a dirty woman [*zapachkannaia baba*], or a poor boy, speaking clearly in French, the language which is flaunted [in Russia] by all the big-time fashionable people [*modniki bol'shago sveta*]; also, by means of [the French language] they chatter all sort of rubbish: here is the insignificance of our [that is, Russian] fashion.'[23]

As it relates to the cultural influence upon Russian officers during the campaign into France, these accounts and others like them suggest that their linguistic proficiency was a factor with two-pronged significance. On the one hand, their ability to understand and communicate deepened their appreciation of and interaction with the surrounding culture and made it possible for them to be substantially impacted by the experience. On the other, the tone of resentment is unmistakable as these men, brought up to value French language and culture as a mark of privilege and distinction, now encounter it as a common thing. These two dynamics—substantive impressions on clear cultural topics

---

[22] I. I. Lazhechnikov, *Pokhodnyia zapiski ruskago ofitsera* (Moscow: v tipografii N. Stepanova, 1836), pp. 202 – 203.

[23] Radozhitskii, *Pokhodnyia zapiski artillerista*, p. 37.

and disenchantment with their previous romantic elevation of French culture—permeate the recollections of Russian officers in the diaries and memoirs that they left behind. Having grown up with cultural mentors like the French immigrants described in chapter three of this dissertation, their experiences abroad were now bringing them into a new phase of cultural development.

Common Russian soldiers

While the memoirs studied portray cultural influence primarily upon officers, some of their accounts also shed light on how the plebeian soldiers under their command interacted with the French culture. The most obvious examples are those where the noble Russian memoirist is describing the stark contrast between his Russian soldiers and their Parisian surroundings. According to Golitsyn, 'the look of all these Kalmyks and Bashkirs, who roamed the dapper [*Shchegolevashago*] streets of Paris' were, in appearance, 'the exact opposite of the faces and costumes of the Parisians.'[24] When the Russian army entered Paris, Cossack troops set up camp directly on the Champs-Élysées, which was roped-off and became a Russian tent-city in the middle of Paris. Lazhechnikov describes the scene: 'There, where a Parisian dandy [might often] give a bundle of new flowers to his beauty and tremble with excitement, reading her reply in her affectionate glances, a Bashkir stands next to a smoky campfire wearing a greasy hat with long earflaps and roasting his steak at the end of an arrow.' On these famously beautiful lawns 'garlands and flowered coverings were replaced by saddles and shaggy burkas.' The author goes on to describe the spectacle of these two cultures colliding. French onlookers and local gendarmes were not sure what to make of the Cossacks who demonstrated their horse-riding tricks in the park and loudly sang folk songs from the

---

[24] N. B. Golitsyn, *Ofitserskiia zapiski, ili vospominaniia o pokhodakh 1812, 1813 i 1814 godov* (Moscow: v tipografii Avgusta Semena, 1838), p. 92.

Don and Volga.[25] One unnamed author, the commander of an infantry regiment,

likewise confessed that 'I was struck not so much by the French as by our own soldiers

who were roaming among the folks: cuirassiers, infantrymen, dragoons, Cossacks and

the like. How strange they must have seemed to the derisive [*nasmeshlivye*] French.'

According to this officer, the Russian troops stood out as being particularly tall, strong

and handsome as they came from the battlefield directly into French civilian life.[26]

A series of watercolour paintings by artist Emmanuel Opiz (1775 – 1841)

portrays Russian soldiers during their occupation of Paris in 1814, of which Opiz was

an eyewitness. Russian Cossacks are depicted interacting with Parisian pedestrians,

bartering in the local market, visiting museums, distributing leaflets, enjoying the

theatrics of street performers, reading posted announcements, looking into shop

windows, playing cards in salons and gaming houses, playfully engaging local women,

and bathing their horses in the Seine.[27] These eyewitness visual accounts emphasize the

fact that Russian troops other than the noble officers who left behind memoirs were also

experiencing French culture directly.

The memoirs contain a few references to romances between Russian troops and

French women. In addition to the many passing descriptions of French ladies smiling

and nodding as troops passed, throwing white bows to the young officers, or the general

comments of Russians about the appearance and qualities of French ladies, there are a

few more involved anecdotal episodes. Major General N. N. Murav'ev wrote a

humourous account about his old French host trying to match him with a certain French

lady. He found her attractive at first, but became wholly uninterested when he noticed

that she took snuff. After that, no matter how hard she tried to get his attention—

[25] Lazhechnikov, *Pokhodnyia zapiski*, p. 205.

[26] 'Vyderzhki iz voennykh zapisok i vospominanii sluzhivago prezhnikh let. Zaniatie Parizha v 1814 godu', *Atenei*, 1 (1859), 90.

[27] V.M. Bezotosnyi and E.I. Itkina (authors of introductory text), *Russkie kazaki v Parizhe v 1814 godu: akvarel'naia seria G.E. Opitsa iz sobraniia Gosudarstvennogo istoricheskogo muzeia* (Moscow: Gosudarstvennyi istoricheskii muzei, 2012).

singing, playing guitar, casting glances—all he could think of was the snuff, expecting tobacco juice to dribble out of her nose at any moment.[28] Murav'ev also wrote about a fellow officer who fell in love with a Parisian girl with whom he was forced to part when his regiment left Paris. Already in a different city on the homeward march, Murav'ev rendered the tearful tale of his comrade. Drinking away his sorrows in a French tavern, he recalled how the poor girl had fallen down, pleading with him not leave, declaring that she would die without him, and so forth. Overcome by regret, the officer declared that he could not leave his love, and determined to go back to Paris and marry her. His fellow officers persuaded him not to do this as it would amount to deserting his post.[29]

Artillery officer A. M. Baranovich's account of the foreign campaign focuses largely on instances of desertion among common soldiers, whose voices are often inaudible to history. According to this artillery officer, when the time came for their regiment to depart from Epernay after an extended stay, seventeen of his soldiers had deserted. Local farmers had promised them steady employment in their vineyards and had given their daughters to them in marriage.[30]

The attention drawn by common Russian soldiers and their close interaction with the local population is a frequent observation in the memoirs of their officers. Of particular note is their interaction with local vendors and peddlers. According to one Russian memoirist, even before they marched into the capital, French saleswomen came out to meet the Russians on the outskirts of Paris, made their way past the barricades, and mingled amongst the soldiers, offering their wares. Just prior to the triumphal entry, Murav'ev recalls that 'in the morning our camp was filled with Parisians, especially French women, who came to sell vodka… and they earned their living [*i*

---

[28] N. N. Murav'ev, 'Zapiski Nikoaia Nikolaevicha Murav'eva. 1814 god. Chast' piataia', *Russkii arkhiv*, 2 (1886), 116 – 117.

[29] Ibid., 119.

[30] A. M. Baranovich, 'Russkie soldaty vo Frantsii v 1813 – 1814 gg.', *Golos minuvshego*, 5 – 6 (1916), 154.

promyshliali].[31] Another officer described essentially the same scene: local residents coming out to the Russian camp, selling food and other merchandise, and carrying barrels of drink on their neck. 'They all loudly offered their goods: "A shawl, gentlemen, a shawl, who wants a shawl!" shouted one of them. "Fresh eggs, gentlemen!" proclaimed another, and so forth. These sellers, before long were moving around freely among the soldiers in our camp.' The author observed that 'it was funny to see our servicemen trying to be nice [*liubeznichat'*] with vendors, and the agility of the latter, who understood their meaning without understanding their words.'[32]

This sort of interaction continued while they were inside Paris. One officer reported that there were always many locals near the barracks where the Russian soldiers were staying. Among these were 'young tradeswomen with boxes across their shoulders with vodka, snacks, and sweets, crowded near the soldiers on the riverfront next to the barracks.' To avoid misunderstandings during this interaction and to keep an eye on the behaviour of the soldiers, a Russian officer was always stationed nearby. One such officer recalled a humourous incident that he witnessed while on duty near the barracks gate, beyond which non-personnel were not allowed. A Russian grenadier came out, approached a nearby vendor, and said, in Russian, 'well, madam, give me some schnapps' and pointed to one of her bottles.' She poured him a glass, which he quickly drank and asked for another. Apprehensively she complied and, after he disposed of this second dose in the same manner, cried 'Mon Dieu, mon Dieu, il mourra (My God, my God, he will die)!' When the grenadier asked for a third glass, she refused and kept insisting that so much would be harmful to his health. The officer, overhearing the disagreement which was happening in two languages, said to her in French, 'Do not be afraid. Give him another.' The soldier drank the third, paid his bill, and asked the officer to explain to him the meaning of this '*mond'e, mond'e*' that he

---

[31] Murav'ev, 'Zapiski', 102.
[32] 'Vyderzhki iz voennykh zapisok', 85.

kept hearing? When the officer explained that she was afraid he would die from

drinking so much, the grenadier laughed. 'What from three thimbles-full! I could drink

that whole bottle without wincing.' To this the officer replied, 'Well, brother, that is

enough. They do not like drunks here.'[33]

This anecdotal account is an example of a Russian officer, who possesses

language skills and an awareness of French sensitivities, acting as a cultural bridge

between a common Russian soldier and his foreign surroundings. It highlights the

language barrier that Russian soldiers encountered, not having been brought up with the

same education and refinement as the officers who led them. Despite this language

barrier, Captain A. M. Danilevskii described friendly interaction between curious

Parisians and Russian troops who 'listened with pleasure as if they understood the

remarks of passersby regarding their manners and customs; The answers made to the

many suggestions and questions asked of them were either not understood at all or only

partially by their body movements.' He claims, however, that they were at least able to

communicate a 'good nature and sincere harmony' with them via such gesturing.[34]

Various memoirs describe how Russian soldiers would incorporate individual French

words and phrases into their own vocabulary. They invented a new Russian verb to

refer to their looting of local villages as a means of foraging for supplies: *shershit'*, from

the French word chercher, 'to look for.'[35] They also began to refer to their amorous

adventures as *triktrak* (from the name of a French board game) and grew accustomed to

calling red wine *vain*.[36] In contrast to the formal linguistic education that their officers

---

[33] Kazakov, 'Pokhod vo Frantsiiu', in *Rossiiskie memuary,* ed. by Liapishchev p. 540.

[34] This is the same A. I. Mikhailovskii-Danilevskii mentioned earlier in this chapter, who would later become a well-known senator, military historian and compiler of memoirs. Here, he is referred to as A. M. Danilevskii as this is the form of his name given in *Syn otechestva* (1816) and *Ruskoi vestnik* (1819), where his personal recollections of the war first appeared in print. A. M. Danilevskii, 'O prebyvanii ruskikh v Parizhe v 1814m godu', *Ruskoi vestnik*, 9 i 10 (1819), 38.

[35] Kazakov, 'Pokhod vo Frantsiiu', in *Rossiiskie memuary,* ed. by Liapishchev, p. 523.

[36] Murav'ev, 'Zapiski', 102.

had grown up with, these common Russians were experiencing an informal form of language immersion.

Kazakov describes the frustration of some of the troops throughout the course of the foreign campaign as they moved through Poland, the Germanic lands, and finally into France. Just as they were becoming conversant on a rudimentary level in the local language, they passed into another territory with a different language. They expressed displeasure that the German barmaids did not respond to the Polish commands they had recently mastered. Later in their journey, Russian officers were forced to arbitrate new disagreements as a soldier's German-language requests—'*gib brod, gib shnaps*'—failed to illicit the appropriate response from French proprietors at local taverns. Recounting one such episode, Kazakov writes, 'again, it is the same story: there are complaints and explanations: "I asked him civilly, *gib brod.* It is time to eat, but he shook his head as if he does not understand. I see that the bread is lying there… so I broke off a hunk for myself."' The officer then explains to the soldier that the Frenchman simply did not understand him. The soldier asks in bewilderment "'How does he not understand? I did not say it in Russian, but rather *gib brod.*" "He is French and does not understand German." "I am sorry, your honour. I thought that he did not want to feed me."'[37]

These short narratives regarding common Russian soldiers are, of course, written from the perspective of their commanding officers. It cannot be ruled out these Russian officers, proud of their own refinement and ability to communicate fluently with the French, could have exaggerated the provincial blundering of the troops under their command. This would, of course, make them look better in their own story by emphasizing their own cultural refinement by comparison. Nevertheless, the recurrence of such accounts underscores the fact that direct interaction between common Russian soldiers and the French was occurring. They were purchasing local wares, sampling

---

[37] Kazakov 'Pokhod vo Frantsiiu', in *Rossiiskie memuary,* ed. by Liapishchev, pp. 540 – 541.

French food and drink, and even making some effort at communicating in French. Finally, as they passed through the French countryside and into Paris, they were certainly seeing the same architecture, city infrastructure, and gardens that their officers were able to describe in writing, therefore making these memoirs, at least to some extent, representative of what Russian soldiers of lower social strata were also experiencing. One account suggests that there was significant intermingling which even included Russian soldiers helping to work French farms when their regiment was in one place for an extended period of time. As has already been mentioned, some of these soldiers deserted their posts and took French wives.[38] These glimpses into the experiences of common soldiers—who have virtually no historical voice of their own—confirm that they, too, were culturally impacted by their time in France, a fact which extends the cultural importance of this foreign campaign well beyond the noble officers and numerically expands the potential for this campaign to bring French cultural influences back to Russia.

Architecture and city infrastructure

As the Russian troops passed through different French cities, they noticed the architecture, city infrastructure, and landscaping along the way. Architecture proper is a fairly minor theme of the memoirs, but it is present. The small wooden houses of the villages, the taller buildings of the cities, and the Gothic architecture of churches along the way are described by multiple memoirists. The recollections of officers contain many brief references to the height and width of houses, position of windows, where the houses are impressive and where they bespeak poverty. The lexical analysis suggests that architecture was not a particularly intense field of French cultural influence during this period. From the time of Peter to the twentieth century, architectural terms have

---

[38] Baranovich, 'Russkie soldaty vo Frantsii', 153 – 156.

trickled into the Russian language from French. During the period represented by these memoirs, the architectural word import seems to be no more than during other periods. A notable exception would be the very common Russian word *etazh*, referring to the particular 'floor' or 'level' of a building, which entered the language during this period. In Paris, Kazakov wrote that Monsieur Dupuytren, lived on the prestigious *bel'etazh* level of a particular building.[39] *Bel'etazh* is another French loanword that appears in Russian for the first time during this period.

Several officers recorded their impressions of French roads. Fedor Glinka wrote, 'what is good here are the roads: amazing roads!'[40] Praising the industriousness of the French, he described how a particular highway was built into the French countryside. The road had been laid 'in a straight direction, broken through mountains, cut hills, backfilled trenches and gullies, and a smooth path is paved, a *shosse*.'[41] Radozhitskii was likewise impressed with the paved road leading into Saint-Dizier which had been cut out of the slope of a mountain and 'amazes [one] with the boldness and artistry of its work.'[42] Not all of the accounts were so technical. One of the memoirists simply mentions that 'we came to a *shosse*, planted on either side with trees.'[43] Describing the outskirts of Metz, Glinka reported 'a lot of houses, manors, villages, gardens, groves, thickets, roads lined with trees, and people walking, riding, and strolling along them come into sight.'[44] Both Radozhitskii and Chertkov mentioned the particularly wide streets in Nancy.[45] In Paris, on the contrary, Chertkov made note of how narrow the streets were, and complained that most of them 'are very dirty and dark because of the seven- and eight-story buildings located along them,' but admitted

---

[39] Kazakov, 'Pokhod vo Frantsiiu', in *Rossiiskie memuary,* ed. by Liapishchev, p. 535.
[40] Fedor Glinka, *Pis'ma russkogo ofitsera*, p. 223.
[41] Ibid., 224.
[42] Radozhitskii, *Pokhodnyia zapiski artillerista*, p. 47.
[43] 'Vyderzhki iz voennykh zapisok', 80.
[44] Fedor Glinka, *Pis'ma russkogo ofitsera*, p. 227.
[45] See Radozhitskii, *Pokhodnyia zapiski artillerista*, p. 38, and A. D. Chertkov, 'Dnevniki 1813 – 1814 gg', in *1812 – 1814: reliatsii. pis'ma. dnevniki*, ed. by A. K. Afanas'ev and others, p. 444.

that there were some pretty streets, such as the boulevards which had been built during

Napoleon's reign.[46] These descriptions stand out because of their detail, but the

memoirs include many other passing references to roads leading in and out of different

cities and the streets inside the cities.

This seems to be indicative of a general trend of French influence upon Russian

culture at this time. The findings of the lexical analysis reveal that this period of

Russian history introduced more French loanwords related to streets and roads than any

other period. The words *shosse, bul'var, alleia, prospekt,* and the Russian word for

'sidewalk' [*tratuar*] were all imported from French during this period. The

recollections of these officers, filled with new French terms to describe the roads they

travelled on are snapshots of a broader area of French influence upon Russia: city

infrastructure.

In addition to the streets and architecture, attention was given to other aspects of

urban infrastructure and city-planning. The layout of buildings in and around the cities

and towns, whether or not there was a main square and whose statue was featured there,

and the decorative landscaping are all mentioned. The long march allowed the Russians

to examine a wide variety of cities and towns, and they remarked the unique features of

each. Corroborating the praise of other memoirists for Nancy's roads, Kakhovskii

described the city as possessing beautiful streets, squares, and fountains where streets

intersected. He likewise noted the empty pedestal at one of the squares upon which the

statue of Louis XV once stood.[47] Radozhitskii's description of Nancy's wide, tree-lined

streets mentioned a different square which still had a bronze statue of Henry IV and the

nearby storefront with its 'extensive row of glass doors.'[48] Chertkov characterized the

---

[46] Chertkov, 'Dnevniki 1813 – 1814 gg', in *1812 – 1814: reliatsii. pis'ma. dnevniki,* ed. by Afanas'ev and others, p. 437.

[47] I. V. Kakhovskii, 'Zapiski generala Kakhovskago o pokhode vo Frantsiiu v 1814 godu', *Russkaia starina,* 157 (1914), 458.

[48] Radozhitskii, *Pokhodnyia zapiski artillerista,* p. 38.

city of Langres as being 'like a fortress in the mountains,'[49] but Chertkov and Murav'ev both described Troyes as a city that was large but 'poorly built.'[50] Between Meaux and Paris, Danilevskii remarked that 'on both sides of the road there were rich villages, beautiful gardens, and great castles.'[51] As they approached the capital, Fedor Glinka summarized that 'all the towns and villages near Paris are built up well: castles, gardens, chambers [*palaty*], groves, aqueducts, fountains, and the Canal de l'Ourcq [*Urkskii kanal*] dazzles [one] and decorates the outskirts.'[52] Kazakov noticed that there were stone fences around each of the gardens of the homes on the outskirts of Paris.[53]

Though these extant descriptions of French architecture and urban design are from the memoirs of officers, this particular field of cultural influence would not have applied only to the them. As a purely visual influence, these aspects of French cities would have been appreciated on some level by all of the Russian troops, whether or not they understood French or were even literate.

Housing

One of the key venues for cultural immersion was the lodging of soldiers and officers along the way. As their regiments moved through Belgium, Germany, or Switzerland and into French territory on their way to Paris, most of the Russian memoirs make note of where they slept. Sometimes, lodging for just one night [*nochleg*] is recorded if a road march lasted multiple days. In other cases, however, regiments would stay in a single location for much longer. One memoir records staying in Epernay for six weeks in 1813, long enough for lower-level troops to take on temporary work in a

---

[49] Chertkov, 'Dnevniki 1813 – 1814 gg', in *1812 – 1814: reliatsii. pis'ma. dnevniki*, ed. by Afanas'ev and others, p. 427.

[50] Ibid., p. 428, and Murav'ev, 'Zapiski', 79.

[51] A. M. Danilevskii, 'Sluchai, predshestvovavshie vkhodu v Parizh Russiiskikh voisk, v 1814 godu', *Syn otechestva*, 28 (1816), 222.

[52] Fedor Glinka, *Pis'ma russkogo ofitsera*, p. 248.

[53] Kazakov, 'Pokhod vo Frantsiiu', in *Rossiiskie memuary*, ed. by Liapishchev, p. 525.

Frenchman's vineyard for which they were paid in wine.[54] In another example, an

officer's coachman [*kucher*] was instructed to set up shop and work as a blacksmith

during a two-week stint in Chaumont, whereby earning some extra spending money for

his master, whose funds had become depleted along the way.[55]

Whether for extended stays such as these, or the many overnight stops, lodging

is often recorded with detail by the memoirists. Conditions varied but, as a general rule,

lower ranking troops bivouacked in temporary encampments outdoors while officers

were quartered in French houses, often with local families. Whatever housing might be

available, the very best was reserved for commanders and other staff officers, and the

remaining houses were assigned to lower officers, in which young lieutenants often

shared a room. Depending upon the size of the city and whether there had been a

standing French army presence there, it was not always necessary for soldiers to

bivouac. Baranovich described a location near Plombières where 'officers were housed

in apartments and lower ranks [*nizhnie chiny*] in barracks.'[56] The level of comfort in

each location always varied based on one's rank, but, taking a broader view across the

whole of the campaign, Russian military of various ranks experienced a range of

lodging conditions. The housing of lower-level troops ranged from tents to apartments.

Officers were sometimes housed in the finest estates or luxury hotels, but one

Lieutenant records that, on one of his first evenings in Paris, after enjoying a

performance at the opera where Alexander I himself had been present, he returned to his

bivouac outside the city to spend the night.[57]

The quartering of thousands of troops was an important logistical consideration

during the campaign, and memoirs provide some clues as to the systematic approach to

these arrangements. While stationed in a small town between Reims and Soissons,

---

[54] Baranovich, 'Russkie soldaty vo Frantsii', 153.
[55] Murav'ev, 'Zapiski', 85.
[56] Baranovich, 'Russkie soldaty vo Frantsii', 156.
[57] Kazakov, 'Pokhod vo Frantsiiu', in *Rossiiskie memuary,* ed. by Liapishchev, p. 534.

Colonel M. M. Petrov recorded that 'there, my battalion was given thirteen houses. My apartment was on the square of the cathedral... near the church.'[58] In Laon, Staff Officer I. V. Ortenberg mentioned part of the process where a quartermaster calls officers together and tells each of them which village to go to for housing.[59] Multiple memoirs make reference to a billeting system whereby the quartering of allied officers in French homes was regulated by allied military personnel (known as a billeting officer), or even by local French civil servants, enlisted to facilitate this clerical process. At one point in the campaign, Murav'ev served this function in the city of Lörrach, near the French and Swiss border. When housing was no longer available, though many allied officers requested quarter in the city, Murav'ev carried out the order that 'no one in the city was given an apartment with a ticket from me.'[60] In a town outside of Metz, according to Fedor Glinka, it was the mayor of the town who acted as the quartering agent. Glinka recalls that he found this small-town mayor in his municipal office, sewing boots. When the Russian officer entered, he looked up from his handiwork, took out a feather pen and wrote him a quartering ticket.[61] Upon entering a new city, a Russian officer would first report to the person distributing these tickets and then, after receiving one, find the house assigned to him and present his ticket to be quartered in a French home. In his recollection of entering Paris, Kazakov, then a lieutenant, gives a thorough description of the procedure.

> On the evening of 20 March [1814], our regiment was placed in Caserne la Pépiniere from where,[62] after staying for just one day, the regiment was moved to the Caserne Napoleon on the bank of the river Seine across from the Tuileries garden and quartering tickets [*kvartirnye bilety*] were distributed to the officers.

---

[58] M. M. Petrov, 'Rasskazy sluzhivshego v 1-m egerskom polku polkovnika Mikhaila Petrova o voennoi sluzhbe i zhizni svoei i trekh rodnykh brat'ev ego, zachavsheisia v 1789 goda. 1845 g', in *Vospominaniia voinov russkoi armii*, ed. F. A. Petrov and others (Moscow: Mysl', 1991), p. 254.

[59] I. V. Ortenberg, 'Furazhirovka posle srazheniia pod Kraonnov, 23-go fevraliia 1814 goda', *Biblioteka dlia chteniia*, 144 (1857), 20.

[60] Murav'ev, 'Zapiski', 74.

[61] Fedor Glinka, *Pis'ma russkogo ofitsera*, p. 228.

[62] *These were barracks built for the French guard in 1763.* Kazakov, 'Pokhod vo Frantsiiu', in *Rossiiskie memuary*, ed. by Liapishchev, *p.* 551 n. 14.

I was given a ticket on Saint-Honoré Street [where I would stay with] a watchmaker.'[63]

After locating the home of the watchmaker and looking inside, he realized that the accommodations were insufficient and was advised to appeal his assignment at la Mairie de St. Germain l'Auserios. 'Upon arrival, I presented the "billet de logement" that I had been given and explained that there was no room with the watchmaker other than the workshop.' Kazakov was immediately given a new ticket to live with a well-known surgeon, monsieur Dupuytren.[64] Radozhitskii also references this system when recounting his arrival in Chalon where, 'entering by ticket to the appointed apartment... I found myself at a table with several French women and just one sullen Frenchman. The older lady looked at my ticket and then showed me upstairs to a large room.'[65]

The cultural significance of Russian officers staying in French homes is multifaceted. First, the interior design of the house itself was an objective means of cultural influence to which Russians were exposed the moment they entered a home. The layout of rooms, how space was managed, furniture, family portraits, and other decorative items all contributed to the experience of cultural immersion. While all of the Russian officers must have at least been passive recipients of this influence, some of the memoirists explicitly express the impact of these visual stimuli upon them. In the city of Vitry, Radozhitskii was quartered in the home of a member of the city council. Describing his lodging, he writes, 'I got a beautiful apartment, such [an apartment as] I have never had before: two rooms with Chinese wallpaper and rich furniture, a large [obshirnaia] bed under a purple canopy, an ancient bronze clock on the table, a fireplace with a mirror, and large Venetian windows opening directly onto the garden.' At this point, Radozhitskii's contemplation turns inward and he reveals the impression that all of this is making upon him. He continues,

---

[63] Ibid., p. 535.
[64] Ibid.
[65] Radozhitskii, *Pokhodnyia zapiski artillerista*, p. 57.

> Here, for the first time I have felt the pleasure of domestic life and property. If
> only, I thought, I also could at some time have rooms like these, with all that
> goes with them, according to my tastes! If only… Oh, how far I am from this!
> First it would be necessary to learn how to purchase, then be able to take care of
> [it all], and finally to display and enjoy. It is pleasant to sit amongst the
> abundance which surrounds us, where they anticipate our desires, and flatter
> [one's] vanity! Very pleasant! But will it last for long?[66]

Then, returning to reality, he notes that he may soon be trudging through the rain again

as the march continues, and other hosts may not be so gracious nor other homes so

charming. As a general's aide, Lazhechnikov was also in a position to make

observations of the interior of fine homes. On the outskirts of the French capital, in

Belleville, which he describes as 'the harbinger of [Paris'] greatness, panache, and

taste,' Lazhechnikov lists some of the contents of the house that his commander was

occupying:

> A huge mirror, reflecting one object twenty times; elastic *kushety*[67] and
> armchairs… lush sheets which could sooner be called thrones of love and bliss;
> a *tualet*, prepared by the Graces themselves, certainly for one of the sisters,
> surrounded by all the riches of the kingdom of Flora; a small library, including
> all the essence of French letters, with the most beautiful external appearance;
> rugs [with pictures] of nature; Sevres porcelain china; rich lamps [*kenkety*, a
> transliteration from French]; fashionable clasps; secret drawers: in a word,
> everything that you touch or look at is made for the most subtle delight of our
> five senses, for the mind and taste![68]

Russian nobles had been filling their homes with French luxury items for some time, so

these surroundings would not have been totally alien to the Russian authors. On the

contrary, their refined European upbringing made them all the more able to appreciate

them. However, they were now surrounded by these French items in a French context.

These beautiful things were displayed with a sense of French taste and proportion.

While descriptions are not normally as expressive as these accolades by Radozhitskii

---

[66] Radozhitskii, *Pokhodnyia zapiski artillerista*, pp. 51 – 52.

[67] A transliteration of the French 'couchette', referring to a smaller sofa with a headboard, but no back.
The word only ever made its way into the official Russian lexicon in the diminutive, *kushetka*. S. A.
Kuznetsov, ed., *Sovremennyi tolkovyi slovar' russkogo iazyka* (Saint-Petersburg: Norint, 2007), p. 309.

[68] Lazhechnikov, *Pokhodnyia zapiski*, p. 193.

and Lazhechnikov, attention to the interior décor of French homes is frequent in the memoirs. Often these are passing references, such as the aforementioned Kazakov's appreciation for his rooms in the surgeon's home, complete with 'antechamber, corridor, another large room with three windows, and a terrace opposite the Louvre.'[69] Even the interior of much humbler domiciles is mentioned. In Frenelle, Chertkov notes in his diary that 'paper pictures [*kartinki*] in the houses of French peasants are made colourful by various flowers—red ones, blues ones, yellow ones and so forth—and strike those who have come from far away, and especially foreigners, with their fairly funny appearance [*svoim dovol'no zabavnym vidom*].'[70] As Russian officers stayed in French homes during this foreign campaign, the visual stimuli never seem to have gone unnoticed.

A second facet of cultural influence inherent in the quartering of Russian officers was their interaction with the French families who hosted them. The recollections of Russian officers include many examples of interaction that became distinctly personal. Lieutenant G. P. Meshetich recounted being quartered with the director of a local school in one city. He was impressed with how well-mannered the family was and they, in turn, expressed a measure of trust towards him. At one point, Meshetich's host actually asked him to protect his daughter from the Prussians, 'though he was especially afraid of our Cossacks.'[71] As has already been noted, allied troops sometimes had an extended stay in one location, which allowed Russian officers to get to know those with whom they boarded. They slept under the same roof, often ate meals together, conversed, and sometimes even took day trips out with them as if they

---

[69] Kazakov, 'Pokhod vo Frantsiiu', in *Rossiiskie memuary,* ed. by Liapishchev, p. 536.
[70] Chertkov, 'Dnevniki 1813 – 1814 gg', in *1812 – 1814: reliatsii. pis'ma. dnevniki,* ed. by Afanas'ev and others, p. 429.
[71] G. P. Meshetich, 'Istoricheskie zapiski voini rossiian s frantsuzami i dvadtsat'iu plemenami 1812, 1813, 1814 i 1815 godov. 1818 g', in *Vospominaniia voinov russkoi armii,* ed. by F. A. Petrov and others (Moscow: Mysl', 1991), p. 70 n. 1.

were members of the family. Writing about particular families with whom they stayed,

several officers give indication that genuine relationships had developed.

Staying in homes also facilitated their introduction to French social life.

Radozhitskii's memoir informs that influential Frenchmen organized balls and other

social gatherings for the Russian officers in various cities and towns over the course of

the campaign. He recorded that 'in the finest homes here, as in Russia, acquaintances

gather to play cards and talk about politics, without food or drinks being served.'[72]

Such socializing was especially common once the Russian army reached Paris and

armed hostilities had ceased. According to Danilevskii, 'The conduct of our officers in

Paris could not have been more modest and decent; I heard more than once that the

French referred to them as an example of politeness. In a short time they made

acquaintances in the finest homes and with the leading scientists and artists, who found

pleasure in conversing with them.'[73] Kazakov asserted that 'as with us [that is, the

officers] so with the soldiers, life was good in Paris. The thought never came to mind

that we were in an enemy city.'[74] D. V. Dushenkevich, senior aide to Lieutenant

General D. P. Neverovskii, related his stay in the city of Nancy with fondness, recalling

that 'I fell in love with the noble society, and constantly fine order of the unpretentious

life of one royalist family, with whom I was quartered, and where I envied their life

with particular delight and reverence. I spent nearly two months there and became

acquainted with another six similar homes which were enchanting in their family life.'[75]

Murav'ev writes with similar warmth of the three-generation family with whom

he stayed with in Paris, comprised of an elderly man, a middle-aged married couple, and

their three children. He describes how surprised they were to find that he could speak

---

⁷² Radozhitskii, *Pokhodnyia zapiski artillerista*, p. 183.

⁷³ A. M. Danilevskii, 'O prebyvanii ruskikh v Parizhe v 1814m godu', *Ruskoi vestnik*, 9 i 10 (1819), 16.

⁷⁴ Kazakov, 'Pokhod vo Frantsiiu', in *Rossiiskie memuary*, ed. by Liapishchev, p. 540.

⁷⁵ D. V. Dushenkevich, 'Iz moikh vospominanii ot 1812-go goda do (1815-go goda), 1838 g', in *1812 god v vospominaniiakh sovremennikov*, ed. by A. G. Tartakovskii and others (Moscow: Nauk, 1995), pp. 129 – 130.

French so well and how he enjoyed conversing with them and watching the grandfather

play backgammon (tric-trac) with his grandson. Far from simply recording superficial

observations, Murav'ev writes a full paragraph on each member of the household as

well as a brief account of their family history. He ends the episode by affirming his

expectations of long cherishing the happy memories of living among them.[76]

Many of the Russian officers were young and impressionable at the time of these

events—Murav'ev and Dushenkevich were twenty and seventeen years old,

respectively—and these domestic oases were likely to make an impact on them.

Kazakov says as much when relating his experience in the French capital, quartered

with Monsieur Dupuytren. Early in their time together, his host, a prominent French

doctor, took young Kazakov with him to the hospital to show him the syphilis patients

as a warning against visiting brothels while he was in Paris. Reflecting on this,

Kazakov later wrote that 'in this way he won me over to his will, and I came to love and

obey him like a father.'[77] On a separate occasion, Dupuytren asked if he needed any

money. In response to this, Kazakov showed him a large stash of money, sewn into his

waistband, which his father had given him before he left Russia. Dupuytren promptly

confiscated the money and thereafter doled it out to Kazakov as he had need, to prevent

him from spending it all in one place or gambling it away at the card tables of Palais-

Royal. Recalling these experiences, Kazakov wrote in his memoirs,

> I had just turned seventeen years old at the time. I felt that he was behaving
> towards me as a father would, and I regarded his family as if it were my own. It
> was only later that I was fully able to appreciate his love and thank God that I
> happened to end up with him in Paris. Otherwise, in my youth and inexperience
> I could have killed myself physically and morally.[78]

Not all of the memoirists wrote so sentimental about their French hosts, nor was every

lodging experience as positive as those described above. Kakhovskii, for example,

---

[76] Murav'ev, 'Zapiski', 103 – 105.

[77] Ibid., 538.

[78] Ibid., 542.

incessantly complains in his travel log of cold and uncomfortable apartments and surly hosts throughout his march across France.[79] Lieutenant S. G. Khomutov is also consistently negative about his lodging in France.[80] However, the anecdotal accounts cited above highlight the depth of cultural involvement that was possible to Russian soldiers as temporary tenants in France. Family relationships, domestic order, and manners were observed first hand. Likewise, through conversation, these Russians learned about the professions of their hosts, family histories, and in some cases even received guidance in their own moral and intellectual development as young men.

Food and drink

In contrast to the detailed descriptions of interior décor and personal relationships, the memoirists had very little to say about the meals served to them in French homes. Kazakov, Chertkov, Radozhitskii, Kakhovskii, and Infantry Commander I. N. Skobelev all make passing reference to meals, but their descriptions are universally brief. Presumably, they wrote more descriptively about the things that made the greater impression upon them. European fare had already been featured in the homes of the Russian aristocracy for decades. Cooks and other domestic servants had emigrated from France to Russia during the reign of Catherine II and with intensity following the French Revolution. Rather than describing dishes and their presentation in curious detail, upper-class Russians were now experienced enough to simply report that they were served a 'nice lunch.'[81] This suggests, in the lives of these Russian officers before the war, a level of genuine integration with European culture, particularly in the area of fine domestic cuisine. While other French cultural elements were a curiosity, this was not. An important distinction, however, is that they were not particularly amazed by

---

[79] Kakhovskii, 'Zapiski', 444 – 462.
[80] S. G. Khomutov, 'Dnevnik svitskago ofitsera. 1813 god', *Russkii arkhiv*, 1 (1869), 219 – 304.
[81] See my discussion of French influence upon Russian food culture in the dictionary analysis in chapter two, pp. 123 – 124.

domestic cuisine. Their descriptions of restaurants and cafés, on the other hand, were marked by considerable fascination, which will be discussed below.

In addition to that received in homes, the Russian army also encountered French foodstuffs through their foraging for supplies along the march. Beyond the general discussion of food, this issue of foraging illustrates one of the darker aspects of Russian interaction with their French surroundings during the campaign. Ortenberg reported that, upon reaching Chavignon, which the staff officers occupied, orders were given for officers to gather hay, oats, cattle for beef rations, bread, vodka or wine, and with these provisions go establish their positions in Laon. The obedient officers collected these items and forced a local guide to drink some of the wine to prove that it was not poisoned.[82] Though most of the memoirists took pride in the restraint shone by Russian forces as compared to the Austrians and Prussians, Russian troops nonetheless pillaged the fields, homes, and wine-cellars of French villages along their march towards Paris. Though these were considered lawful spoils of war by the standards of the time and a legitimate means of feeding the army, pangs of conscience can be sensed in some recollections, especially when the 'foraging' for food, water, and firewood took place in inhabited areas. Kazakov, after a short treatise on the difference between 'foraging' and plain 'theft', and after affirming the restraint commanded by officers, confessed nonetheless that 'the nearby town next to an army of nearly one hundred thousand, who are sleeping in bivouacs, are robbed and spoiled regardless of any orders.'[83] Continuing his narrative, Kazakov writes that in the Champagne and Epernay region, the foraging yielded barrels of wine rather than water. Also, 'cattle were abandoned in the fields and villages, and so there was sometimes much meat [to be had], and such beautiful cows were butchered as are difficult to describe. And the commanders who gave the strictest

---

[82] Ortenberg, 'Furazhirovka posle srazheniia pod Kraonnov', 18 – 33.
[83] Kazakov, 'Pokhod vo Frantsiiu', in *Rossiiskie memuary*, ed. by Liapishchev, p. 522.

orders not to burn or steal, calmly [*prespokoino*] ate wonderful beef, boiled in good wine.'[84]

Food and drink: Champagne wine

French wine, whether discovered from foraging or as part of the officer's fare while quartered, was praised by multiple authors, especially that of the Champagne region, in which the important battle of Reims was fought. Petrov, Murav'ev, Baranovich, Chertkov, Fedor Glinka, and Colonel N. B. Golitsyn all make specific mention in their memoirs of the wine in this area, in some cases specifically referencing the region's tradition of viticulture and winemaking. Golitsyn, for example, chronicles that 'our advanced guard was the first to set out on the road from Chalon to Reims, and, within a few days, we reached the village of Sillery, famous for its champagne wine, and stopped eight versts from Reims.'[85] Golitsyn and Baranovich both mention that Epernay, which is in the same region, is 'famous for its wine.'[86] Chertkov likewise notes that 'the best champagne is from Reims and Epernay, which is so expensive in Russia.'[87] In some cases, the winemaking renown of the entire Champagne region is cited. In others, the authors simply note the excellence of that which they sampled in a particular city of the region. In Fismes, 'they gave us good wine,'[88] 'I liked the champagne wine here' [in Château-Thierry],[89] and so forth. Fedor Glinka recorded an interesting insight into the comparative discovery afforded him by this experience: 'In a small place in Epernay, we drank the best champagne, and I must confess that, until that moment, I had never drank the real thing.'[90]

---

[84] Ibid., p. 523.

[85] Golitsyn, *Ofitserskiia zapiski,* p. 68.

[86] See Golitsyn, *Ofitserskiia zapiski,* p. 79, and Baranovich, 'Russkie soldaty vo Frantsii', 153.

[87] Chertkov, 'Dnevniki 1813 – 1814 gg', in *1812 – 1814: reliatsii. pis'ma. dnevniki*, ed. by Afanas'ev and others, p. 443.

[88] M. M. Petrov, 'Rasskazy sluzhivshego', in *Vospominaniia voinov*, ed. F. A. Petrov and others, p. 254.

[89] Murav'ev, 'Zapiski', 119.

[90] Fedor Glinka, *Pis'ma russkogo ofitsera,* p. 246.

Lexical analysis suggests the broader significance of this area of influence. The names of six drinks entered the Russian language from French during this period, four of which have remained in the language to the present: *bordo, madera, shampanskoe, and shabli.* Prior to this generation, Russian had only ever borrowed two drink-related words from French, both of which had entered much earlier, during the reign of Peter the Great. From this point forward, however, each subsequent generation all the way through Russia's revolutionary period would see the introduction of a new handful of French beverages to the Russian vocabulary, an indication of enduring influence which began during this period.

Restaurants, taverns, and cafés

Besides the hospitality of French homes or the spoils of foraging, the Russian army also experienced French cuisine during the campaign by paying for it. Many of the memoirs give significant attention to the taverns, cafés, coffee houses, confectionary shops, bakeries, and restaurants that they visited while in France. Though fine Russian homes had been preparing meals inspired by French culture for some time, Russia did not yet have its own restaurant culture. Therefore, it is unsurprising that Russian officers would describe these experiences with greater detail and curiosity than they did the meals served to them as houseguests.

Before arriving in Paris, there are passing references to taverns along the journey. Fedor Glinka specifically mentioned those in Saint-Avold, just inside French territory, and Bondy, where he related his anticipation of soon being in Paris.[91] The closest thing to a French tavern in Russia at that time would have been a *traktir*, an inn that also served food, or the even simpler *kharchevnia*, 'a house in which one may receive something to eat [*kushan'e*] for pay and where food [*s"estnoe*] for sale is

---

[91] Ibid., pp. 226, 247.

prepared.'[92] At least one of the memoirists makes the comparison. Ever displeased,

Kakhovskii wrote the following about one establishment along the road to Lunéville,

not long after crossing into French territory from the Rhineland:

> We stopped for lunch and went into the best *traktir*. It is very similar to one of
> our *kharchevnia*. They gave us a piece of boiled beef with some nasty [*durnoi*]
> Dijon mustard, a piece of duck and an egg each, and for desert an apple each and
> some almonds on a plate. We drank two bottles of Burgundy—the kind they
> have in every house—the very cheapest kind of wine, and the talkative hostess
> [*khozaika*] charged us nine francs.[93]

Chertkov, in the diary he kept each day, expressed disappointment with the French

bread between the river Rhine and Paris. Derisively, he mused,

> Here they are, the Frenchmen who came to us in Russia: despite their supposed
> aversion to the black bread of the Russian peasants, we could not find white
> bread anywhere in France, even in the very largest cities, such as Troyes,
> Langres, etc. Only endless hunger pangs could induce us to take several slices
> of their absolutely sour bread. In Langres, there was only one baker who was
> baking white bread.[94]

Russian officers were, however, considerably more impressed when they finally

reached Paris and experienced the restaurants and other culinary establishments of the

capital. Kazakov hints at the disparity between the culinary culture of smaller towns

and that of the capital. Just after chronicling the allied army's march into Paris, he

writes, 'there were a lot of restaurants, [and], for the first time since entering France, we

had a decent lunch.'[95] While officers were typically fed as part of their boarding

arrangements in Paris, they also visited professional establishments. Furthermore,

according to Chertkov, lower-level officers were given a choice of housing options. A

few days after entry into Paris, 'the cavalry guard and Prussians were sent to Versailles,

but our regiment and the Cossack lifeguard regiment remained at the military school.

---

[92] *Slovar' akademii rossiiskoi*, 6 vols, (St. Petersburg: pri Imperatorskoi Akademii Nauk, 1789–1794), VI
(1794), p. 505 <http://www.runivers.ru/lib/book3173/> [accessed 3 January 2015]
[93] Kakhovskii, 'Zapiski', 456 – 457.
[94] Chertkov, 'Dnevniki 1813 – 1814 gg', in *1812 – 1814: reliatsii. pis'ma. dnevniki*, ed. by Afanas'ev and
others, p. 429.
[95] Kazakov, 'Pokhod vo Frantsiiu', in *Rossiiskie memuary*, ed. by Liapishchev, p. 532.

The officers had apartments in the city… Officers who wanted to remain in the barracks received five francs per day for food, and staff officers received ten francs.'[96] This mention of a per diem allowance suggests the possibility of young Russian officers on leave, strolling around the big city with money in their pockets, a picture that is consistent with how many of the memoirs portray their time spent in Paris.

The memoirs include several detailed descriptions of Parisian restaurants. This is how Fedor Glinka described one of his first experiences dining in Paris:

> I have just been in a Parisian restaurant and I confess that, from the first minute, I was astounded, surprised, and charmed. On the gates, "Beauvilliers" is written in large letters. The entrance by way of stairs did not promise much. I thought that I would find, as in Germany, an extensive, bright, clean tavern and nothing else. I entered and stopped, thinking that I had come into the wrong place. The floor was lacquered, the walls [covered with] mirrors, and the ceiling with chandeliers! Paintings, carving, and [gold] gilding were everywhere. I thought that I had entered some kind of temple of taste and of the arts. Every shiny thing that luxury and fashion have [to offer] was here.

His description of the restaurant's interior continues as does his characterization of the manager [*khozaika*] and her staff who seemed to take their job—and themselves—very seriously. He also notes the complicated menu, creative presentation of dishes, and the unwritten rules of culinary etiquette that he found so challenging to navigate. Apparently, he had made the faux pas of re-ordering a dish for dinner that he had previously enjoyed at lunch:

> Just try and request a lunch dish for dinner and immediately they will basically call you worse than a barbarian, worse than uneducated: they will call ridiculous (ridicule).' This is the worst thing of all: 'A Parisian would sooner agree to being a rogue [*moshennik*] than to be branded as ridiculous! But our friend helped us out of this situation. We ordered our food, paid a lot for it, exchanged compliments with the establishment, and ran away back to our apartment.[97]

Chertkov clearly felt out of place in a foreign food culture. He discovered that 'the French never eat bread with soup that has been seasoned with vegetables or noodles,

[96] Chertkov, 'Dnevniki 1813 – 1814 gg', in *1812 – 1814: reliatsii. pis'ma. dnevniki*, ed. by Afanas'ev and others, pp. 432 – 433.
[97] Fedor Glinka, *Pis'ma russkogo ofitsera,* pp. 250 – 251.

and they always laugh at us [Russians] every time we do eat soup with bread [*pokhlebku s khlebom*], "pain avec le potage."'[98] Though the memoirs give many such indications of the provincial awkwardness sometimes felt by Russian officers in Paris, the pervasive tone of their culinary recollections is more of wonder than resentment. Dining in these establishments was an unfamiliar experience, but a fascinating one. Several Parisian restaurants are mentioned by name. In addition to Glinka's commentary on the restaurant Beauvilliers, Lekhner notes the Café de la Montenpier,[99] and Kazakov recalls enquiring with his quartering host specifically about a famous restaurant on Palais-Royal called 'Very.' In response, the good doctor grabbed his hat, gave his arm to his wife, and the three of them went there together.[100]

Palais-Royal often appears in the various memoirs as a commercial and entertainment hub which included places to eat. Radozhitskii recalled having been impressed by how much could be offered to the consumer in just one building: restaurants and shops with luxury items in the windows.[101] Chertkov wrote about a restaurant in the cellar where, 'you can order a lunch of your choosing in six courses, paying a moderate amount—one franc and fifty centimes.'[102] An anonymous infantry commander made note of the work ethic and effectiveness of the salespeople, mostly ladies, who worked in the coffee houses, confectionaries, and restaurants on Palais-Royal. Like other Russian officers, he described his amazement at the abundance and variety of goods and services available in this one location:

> Having eaten lunch about four o'clock, I went to look at the endless diversity of objects gathered here. Innumerable vendors [*lavki*] with every kind of goods imaginable; inns [*traktiry*], confectioners, even handicraft establishments:

---

[98] Chertkov, 'Dnevniki 1813 – 1814 gg', in *1812 – 1814: reliatsii. pis'ma. dnevniki*, ed. by Afanas'ev and others, p. 437.

[99] A. A. Lekhner, 'Dnevnik 1813 – 1814 gg', in *1812 – 1814: reliatsii. pis'ma. dnevniki*, ed. by A. K. Afanas'ev and others (Moscow: Terra, 1992), pp. 362, 378.

[100] Kazakov, 'Pokhod vo Frantsiiu', in *Rossiiskie memuary*, ed. by Liapishchev, p. 539.

[101] Radozhitskii, *Pokhodnyia zapiski artillerista*, p. 128.

[102] Chertkov, 'Dnevniki 1813 – 1814 gg', in *1812 – 1814: reliatsii. pis'ma. dnevniki*, ed. by Afanas'ev and others, p. 433.

tailors, milliners, in a word, everything is here; Here you can dress yourself from head to foot, have lunch, dinner, and even stay the night [*nochevat'*].'[103]

These examples reflect the impression made upon Russian officers by their dining experiences in Paris. However, it is interesting to note that their descriptions often focus only peripherally on the actual food that was served to them. Their fascination seems to have been more with the culinary establishments themselves as institutions: the layout and decoration of the restaurants, procedures of etiquette related to ordering food, the prices at different establishments, the way in which waiters, hostesses, and shopkeepers approached their work, the visual presentation of food and creative naming of dishes, and the commercial aspect of food service in the context of a larger consumer experience in this fashionable city. The word *restoran*, borrowed from the French language, would not appear in Russian dictionaries until the twentieth century. When found in the memoirs studied, it reflects the later Russian translation of those memoirs which had originally been written by the officers in French. The older *restoratsiia* is, however, used in the Russian-language memoirs. Though not present in the dictionary published by the Russian Academy (1789 – 1794), *restoratsiia* begins to appear in the works of Pushkin, whose early writing career began around the time of these events.[104] This lexical detail supports a more general assertion based on the culinary references of the memoirs studied: while upper-class Russians were not completely unfamiliar with French food and had experienced a rough equivalent to the French tavern in their own homeland, the very concept of a full-fledged restaurant was foreign to Russians in the early nineteenth century. A quarter of a century earlier, Karamzin had roamed the streets of Paris in wonder as an individual traveller.[105] This experience was now multiplied many times over, as thousands of Russian military'

---

[103] 'Vyderzhki iz voennykh zapisok', 89 – 93.

[104] See my discussion of the food-related words encountered in the lexical study in chapter three, pp. 123 – 124.

[105] See my discussions of Nikolai Karamzin's *Pis'ma ruskago puteshestvennika* in chapters three and five, pp. 166 – 167, 306 – 308.

personnel were discovering Paris, including sophisticated food-service outside of the home, something for which Russians were only beginning to even develop thought-categories. It is not surprising that when this culinary culture, which was moving across Europe, finally reached Russia later in the century, the new vocabulary for it would be borrowed largely from French.[106]

The sights of Paris

As the discussion of restaurants has already suggested, the sights of Paris represent a different kind of French cultural influence upon the Russian officers and soldiers. Many of the cultural experiences prior to Paris had been involuntary on the part of the Russians: the homes they stayed in, the food they ate, the architecture that they laid eyes upon, and the various dialects of French language they heard as everyday tasks brought them into contact with local people. As passive recipients of these French stimuli on their five senses, they recorded their impressions of them in their diaries and memoirs. After arriving in Paris, however, the memoirs indicate a flurry of intentional discovery as Russian officers actively sought out cultural experiences.

Thirteen of the memoirs studied give descriptions of particular iconic landmarks in Paris. In these, specific reference to Palais-Royal, the Tuileries, and the Parisian theatres is nearly universal. Champs Élysées is described by seven of the thirteen authors, L'Hôtel des Invalides by nine. Other often-mentioned sights include Notre Dame Cathedral, the river Seine and its bridges, Place de la Concorde (under various names), the Louvre and other galleries, and the botanical gardens. In addition to these major sights, various streets, squares, parks, and cafés, are mentioned by name among the memories collected by Russian officers while strolling through Paris.

---

[106] See my discussion of the food-related words encountered in the lexical study in chapter three, pp. 123 – 124.

Since no one knew that Napoleon was still to return for one final attempt at victory—the famous One Hundred Days—the arrival in Paris and capitulation thereof marked the end of the war for the memoirists, and their recollections take on a distinctly different character at this point. The authors seem to be transformed from invading conquerors into wide-eyed sightseers, seizing the rare opportunity to enjoy this great cultural capital. Several of the memoirists overtly employ the language of a tourist. Golitsyn confessed, 'I visited in that day as much as I could.'[107] Khomutov wrote of his sightseeing experience that it was 'not possible to see everything in one day.'[108] Dushenkevich, knowing that he was only to be stationed in Paris for a short time, prioritized his tourism so as to make the most of the experience. Thereby, he managed to see 'the most important places.'[109] This sense of urgency to soak in the best of Paris permeates those sections of the memoirs and diaries that describe Paris. A prime example of this tendency is found in the writing of Fedor Glinka. While in Châlons-sur-Marne, over a month before arriving in Paris, Glinka and his cohorts actually sat down and made a sightseeing plan. This included where they wanted to stay—the Hotel de Volois, so as to be nearer the Tuileries—as well as a list of the main sights they wanted to be visit. They listed Notre Dame Cathedral, the Pantheon, L'Hôtel des Invalides, a stroll across the Pont Neuf bridge, the legislative assembly chamber, Luxembourg palace, Vandome square, Carousel Square, the Tivoli gardens, and several specific theatres and museums. After recording this list, Glinka wrote, 'I do not know if I will manage to see all of this, for I will not be in Paris for long.'[110]

Chertkov is another example of a memoirist whose account of Paris stands apart, stylistically, from the rest of his narrative. Unlike most of his memoir which reads like

---

[107] Golitsyn, *Ofitserskiia zapiski,* p. 92.

[108] Khomutov, 'Iz dnevnika svitskago ofitsera', 164.

[109] Dushenkevich, 'Iz moikh vospominanii', in *1812 god v vospominaniiakh,* ed. by Tartakovskii and others, pp. 129 – 130.

[110] Fedor Glinka, *Pis'ma russkogo ofitsera,* pp. 245 – 246.

a series of short diary entries, Chertkov's long description of Paris is not even dated. Positioned just after a short paragraph on the battle of Paris (dated 13 March), the section is actually given a title: 'a few notes about Paris,' and the text flows like a chapter from a tourist's guide to the city.[111] Similarly, Lazhechnikov's description of Champs-Élysées is particularly elaborate and poetic in its language, reading more like a short travel guide than a military memoir.[112] These and other authors describe Paris with a style similar to that employed by Sergei Glinka throughout his memoir, including its description of Paris: detached from the menial and focusing less on personal interaction than on key events, great men, and important landmarks. Sergei Glinka's account of Paris is further removed from diary style by its sentimental embellishment, background history, citations from French authors, and flowery platitudes about the exuberant gratitude of the Parisians towards their Liberator, Alexander I.[113] While such generalization and detachment is typical for this one memoir, for most of the other memoirs such prosaic expression was exceptional and set their description of Paris apart from the rest of their recollections. Many of these sketches could easily have been written after the fact or without even visiting Paris by simply reading a history of the city or literature about Parisian landmarks. In fact, Fedor Glinka actually referenced such a book, entitled *Ukazatel' Parizha*, which was instrumental in helping him to compose his sightseeing plan prior to entering the city.[114]

This is not to say that Russian officers were not writing from their own experiences, but rather that the observations of their personal Parisian experiences were supplemented by an interest in and familiarity with the city that they had acquired over the course of their earlier education. In addition to their personal impressions and

---

[111] Chertkov, 'Dnevniki 1813 – 1814 gg', in *1812 – 1814: reliatsii. pis'ma. dnevniki*, ed. by Afanas'ev and others, pp. 433 – 437.

[112] Lazhechnikov, *Pokhodnyia zapiski*, pp. 199 – 200.

[113] S. N. Glinka, *Zapiski o Moskve i o zagranichnykh proisshestviiakh ot iskhoda 1812 do poloviny 1815 goda* (St. Petersburg: v tipografii imperatorskoi rossiiskoi akademii, 1837), pp. 159 – 172.

[114] Fedor Glinka, *Pis'ma russkogo ofitsera*, p. 252.

anecdotal accounts of their stay in Paris, several of the officers included what could be described as very short descriptive essays, occasionally including background history and often focusing on the same landmarks and events. This is indicative of the fact that upper-class Russians had already studied Paris from afar and approached the city in anticipation of what they would experience there. Considered apart from its military context, the trip to Paris was a pilgrimage to the focal point of the culture they had long been emulating.

Theatre

Judging from the frequency of its mention in the memoirs, one of the single greatest sources of French cultural influence upon Russian military personnel while they were in France was the theatre. Fourteen of the memoirs and diaries studied include stories of Russian officers and soldiers visiting operatic, dramatic, and show theatres during their time in France. An iconic example of this cultural exposure was Tsar Alexander I's visit to the Paris Opera shortly after allied armies marched into Paris on 19 (31) March 1814. Eight of the aforementioned memoirs give a detailed account of this one event.

After the brief battle of Paris, it did not take long for cultural institutions to reopen their doors and receive allied troops as patrons and audience members. According to Danilevskii, 'from the second day of the taking of Paris, there were performances in the theatres, the post began to operate as before, [and] the city gates were open...'[115] A special gala in honour of the triumphal entry of the allied monarchs seems to have been one of the very first of these performances, as Khomutov's description of the event is dated just one day after the surrender of Paris.[116] In all eight accounts, there is nearly universal mention of the fact that a performance of *Le Triomphe de Trajan* had been scheduled, but a programming change was made at the

---

[115] Danilevskii, 'O prebyvanii ruskikh v Parizhe', 11.
[116] Khomutov, 'Iz dnevnika svitskago ofitsera', 161 – 174 (p. 164).

last moment. Most of the memoirs ascribe this to Alexander's modesty, who requested that something less military be performed as this opera was clearly chosen as a nod to the recent victory of the conquering allies. An anonymous infantry commander, however, suggests that one of the key performers had become ill and, for this reason, the change was made.[117] The unhappy audience, determined that Alexander and the Prussian king should be honoured, cried out in protest, 'Trajan! Trajan!'[118] In preparation for their arrival, the large emblem of an eagle above the stage, a representation of Napoleon's reign, had been covered with white cloth.[119] According to Golitsyn, the crowd actually came in later and broke this eagle.[120] The arrival of Alexander, the Prussian King, and other allied commanders to the theatre on that evening was a momentous occasion. In Dushenkevich's description of the main sites of Paris from his perspective, he includes 'the two main theatres, where the delight of the Parisians at seeing the Emperor Alexander approached delirium.'[121] Sergei Glinka, whose chronicling of the events of the foreign campaign related mostly to the very upper elite command structure, recorded that members of the Parisian audience shouted out 'Vive Alexandre!' when the Russian emperor entered the theatre on the evening.[122] He was given a special box [*lozha*], from which to enjoy the performance. Multiple memoirists mention one of the actors coming out onto the stage before the beginning of the performance with a piece of paper in hand, from which he recited a poem which had recently been penned in honour of Alexander I.

On this same evening, Kazakov described the cries of 'L'officier de la garde! L'officier de la garde!' which he heard as he and his fellow officers made their way to

---

[117] 'Vyderzhki iz voennykh zapisok', 94.
[118] Khomutov, 'Iz dnevnika svitskago ofitsera', 165.
[119] Danilevskii, 'O prebyvanii ruskikh v Parizhe', 20.
[120] Golitsyn, *Ofitserskiia zapiski,* p. 92.
[121] Dushenkevich, 'Iz moikh vospominanii', in *1812 god v vospominaniiakh,* ed. by Tartakovskii and others, p. 130.
[122] S. N. Glinka, *Zapiski o Moskve,* p. 164.

their assigned seats on the lower level of the theatre.[123] From the balconies and boxes

of the opera house, French ladies tossed white bows to the Russian officers below, a

symbol of their support for the deposed Bourbon dynasty, identical in symbolism to the

white cloth which by this time enshrouded the Napoleonic eagle above the stage. In

solidarity with them, the latter took up these bows and attached them to their uniforms

'that very minute.'[124]

In addition to the excitement around the emperor's presence on that evening, the

memoirs also include some detail about the theatre itself. Lazhechnikov records his

impressions of the performance, the scenery on stage, and the architecture of the opera

building, including the regal balconies inside the great hall.[125] Writing with anticipation

before the event, another officer referenced rumours he had heard that Alexander would

be present at this performance of *Le Triomphe de Trajan*, which was to be complete

with a live horse on stage.[126] After the fact, he described his entire experience at the

theatre, including paying too much for his ticket, which he bought from a private seller

outside the theatre. He recalled having to fight through the crowds to get in, his

difficulty finding a seat, and finally his impressions of the actual performance.[127] It is

significant that this anonymous infantry commander gave so much attention to this one

event, considering that his memoir records only a single day in Paris. The importance

of the event can be explained by the presence of the Tsar, the symbolism of the evening

as a shared peace-time experience to emphasize the end of hostilities, but also the

impression made upon Russians by French theatre itself.

The theatre is written about often in the memoirs apart from this memorable

account of Alexander's appearance in Paris. In fact, Russian troops were exposed to the

---

[123] Kazakov, 'Pokhod vo Frantsiiu', in *Rossiiskie memuary,* ed. by Liapishchev, p. 532.
[124] Danilevskii, 'O prebyvanii ruskikh v Parizhe', 20.
[125] Lazhechnikov, *Pokhodnyia zapiski,* pp. 210 – 216.
[126] 'Vyderzhki iz voennykh zapisok', 89.
[127] Ibid., 93 – 98.

French musical and theatrical arts long before even arriving in Paris. Though the allied armies were moving across France as invaders and battles were being fought along the way, they were also able to enjoy cultural events during the quieter moments of the campaign, especially in the larger cities. In Toul, Radozhitskii was quartered in the home of some local actresses. When asked how many officers would be in their city, he answered that there would be a total of around 4,000 troops stationed there. 'Well then,' one of them replied, 'our directress will put on an opera for you!'[128] This response is indicative of a repeated practice that is recorded in multiple accounts. Whenever a large number of troops were present in a city, the local theatre would often arrange a performance for them, exposing the advancing Russians to yet another cultural experience. This was the case during the march on Paris as well as on the homeward journey back through France. Memoir literature from the campaign specifically references French theatrical performances in Nancy, Toul, Chalon, and Bar-de-Luc. Chertkov asserts that there were theatres 'in all of the cities that we passed through.' In Nancy, performances at the local theatre were given every day while the Russian army was there.[129] Radozhitskii remarked that the Nancy theatre was large [*velik*], but poor in both music and wardrobe.[130] Meshetich was slightly more complimentary of the Nancy theatre, referring to 'a stone theatre, in which, during the passage of Russian troops, plays were performed, and not sad ones.'[131] In Chalon, Golitsyn recalled attending a presentation of the comedy *Le sourd ou l'auberge pleine*, the performance of which was 'not bad.'[132]

Like the fine homes in which officers stayed, the odd phenomenon of wartime theatre punctuated the monotony and drudgery of the long march with pleasantness just

---

[128] Radozhitskii, *Pokhodnyia zapiski artillerista*, pp. 57 – 58.
[129] Chertkov, 'Dnevniki 1813 – 1814 gg', in *1812 – 1814: reliatsii. pis'ma. dnevniki*, ed. by Afanas'ev and others, p. 444.
[130] Radozhitskii, *Pokhodnyia zapiski artillerista*, p. 40.
[131] Meshetich, 'Istoricheskie zapiski', in *Vospominaniia voinov*, ed. by F. A. Petrov and others, p. 67.
[132] Golitsyn, *Ofitserskiia zapiski,* p. 68.

as the battles were punctuating it with suffering. In Golitsyn's words, 'In time of war it is not always possible to attend the theatre. How could one not take advantage of this opportunity to forget, at least for the time of the performance, that we ourselves are formidable actors with a sword in our hands, and that France is our theatre?'[133] These moments of artistic expression, against the backdrop of prolonged war, left lasting impressions upon those who put their thoughts into writing. They were moments of humanity. Radozhitskii recalled his interaction with some young French boys while sitting in the theatre in Nancy before the start of the performance. The performance was, as usual, organized specially for the allied troops and these children were among the very few locals present in the theatre. Among other things, the boys asked whether the Russians would burn Paris when they reached it: 'Please do not burn Paris. You will be ashamed if you do.' Radozhitskii was struck by this serendipitous political conversation and concluded the anecdote with a statement about how quickly these children were being forced to grow up.[134]

Upon reaching Paris, attending the theatre seems to have been among the favourite pastimes of Russian officers during their stay in the capital. Murav'ev made it a point to visit the theatre, though he did not experience many of the other forms of entertainment enjoyed by his comrades.[135] Kazakov wrote that, of all the attractions available in Paris, he 'went to the opera most often of all.'[136] Lekhner's daily diary entries for the month of April 1814 reveal that he attended the theatre almost every evening.[137] His brief entries include references to specific plays and even the names of actors who made an impression. François-Joseph Talma, Marguerite Georges, and Catherine-Joséphine Duchesnois, three of the most famous stage performers in France

---

[133] Ibid.

[134] Radozhitskii, *Pokhodnyia zapiski artillerista*, p. 41

[135] Murav'ev, 'Zapiski', 110.

[136] Kazakov, 'Pokhod vo Frantsiiu', in *Rossiiskie memuary*, ed. by Liapishchev, p. 539.

[137] Lekhner, 'Dnevnik', in *1812 – 1814: reliatsii. pis'ma. dnevniki*, ed. by Afanas'ev and others, pp. 379 – 382.

during the reign of Napoleon,[138] are all mentioned by name in Lekhner's diary. In

Hamlet, Talma 'performs excellently.'[139] Talma is also mentioned in the role of Nero in

Britannicus, and as Arsasa in *Semiramis*, where he played opposite Mademoiselle

Georges, who was in the title role. A few days after this latter performance, Lekhner

saw Mademoiselle Duchesnois in the role of Phaedra.[140] Similarly, Petrov recorded

attending the Paris Opera with his brother, Grenadier Colonel I. M. Petrov, where they

saw a performance of a biblical tragedy in which an actor named Lais played the role of

David.[141]

There was ample opportunity for Russian officers to indulge in such diversion as

there were, according to Chertkov, performances every day in eight different Parisian

theatres: le Théâtre Français; le Grand Opéra; l'Odéon, ou cidevant Théâtre de

l'Impératrice; le Vaudeville; les Variétés; l'Opéra Comique ou Théâtre Faydeau; le

Théâtre Gaïeté; and, finally l'Ambigu Comique. As a commentary on their popularity,

Chertkov wrote:

> These eight theatres are so full each evening, that if you are half an hour late,
> you might not find a seat—so great is the passion of the Parisians for the theatre.
> Before the theatre box office is open, a huge crowd of people is already gathered
> and waiting in the vestibule of the theatre. Sometimes it is even worse if a new
> play, or a play on the topic of the day is being performed, or, finally, if the
> theatre is honoured with a visit by the king or some other august person—then it
> is necessary to arrive three or four hours before the curtain is raised.[142]

Fedor Glinka's description of the Paris Opera reveals that he was particularly impressed

by the visual aspect of the experience. His account features more details about the

backdrops and props of the theatrical set than of the actual performance. He also

included notes on the history of the opera house, which had been built in 1793, and a

---

[138] See Fredrick Hawkins, *The French Stage in the Eighteenth Century*, 2 vols (London: Chapman and Hall, 1888), II, pp. 344 – 374, and F. B. Goodrich, *The Court of Napoleon* (New York: Derby and Jackson, 1857), pp. 383 – 404, both available online at <https://archive.org> [accessed 13 December 2014]

[139] Lekhner, 'Dnevnik', in *1812 – 1814: reliatsii. pis'ma. dnevniki*, ed. by Afanas'ev and others, p. 382.

[140] Ibid., p. 378.

[141] M. M. Petrov, 'Rasskazy sluzhivshego', in *Vospominaniia voinov*, ed. F. A. Petrov and others, p. 271.

[142] Chertkov, 'Dnevniki 1813 – 1814 gg', in *1812 – 1814: reliatsii. pis'ma. dnevniki*, ed. by Afanas'ev and others, p. 434.

description of the various paintings and other interior design elements.[143] Petrov, in his account of the evening spent with his brother at the opera, gives a great deal of attention to what other audience members were wearing and the generally impressive atmosphere.[144]

As alluded to in the lexical analysis, a significant number of French words dealing with music and theatre became permanent additions to the Russian vocabulary during this period. During Aleksandr Pushkin's writing career (1814 – 1837), he uses fifteen borrowed French theatrical terms which were not included in the Academy's dictionary, published 1789 – 1794. All of these are still in use today. Of all the periods studied in the lexical analysis, this represents the greatest single period of theatrical word-import from French to Russian. These include *benuar, lozha,* and *parter*, all referring to physical structures inside a theatre, concert hall, or opera house which facilitate multi-level seating. These words, previously absent in the Russian language, were indispensable in describing the precise location of Alexander I when he received shouts of grateful praise at the Paris Opera, or the place from which French ladies tossed down symbolic tokens to the young Russian officers below. The Russian words in use today for 'actor,' 'actress', 'spectacle', 'play', 'role', 'skit', performance 'advertisement' [*afisha*], and even the verb 'to applaud' were all borrowed from the French language during this very period. By attending French performances, these Russian officers and others visitors like them were soaking in an experience that would be a permanent fixture in Russian culture, valued to the present day: the experience of going to the theatre. This is not to say that Russia had no theatrical culture previously. The study of Russian periodical literature from the late eighteenth century has given evidence of Russian emulation of French literature, arts, and performance culture much

---

[143] Fedor Glinka, *Pis'ma russkogo ofitsera,* pp. 253 – 254.
[144] M. M. Petrov, 'Rasskazy sluzhivshego', in *Vospominaniia voinov,* ed. F. A. Petrov and others, pp. 271 – 272.

earlier. Karamzin had essentially begun copying the Parisian concept of critical performance-review two decades earlier.[145] However, never before had so many Russian spectators at one time been exposed to the original. The significance of the foreign campaign of 1813 – 1815 for Russia's concert-going culture is evident both in the memoir accounts and the permanent imprint upon the Russian vocabulary.

Museums

After the theatre, accounts of the various museums and galleries are among the more vivid descriptions of Parisian cultural attractions. Danilevskii recalled strolling 'around the Tuileries palace, as the Sovereign was arriving there.' Subsequently, Danilevskii had the opportunity to accompany Alexander I to the Musée Napoléon, a museum referred to by several of the memoirists. According to Danilevskii, Alexander noticed some empty pedestals while he was admiring the collection of statues and enquired about them. His guides explained to him that these were particularly famous sculptures and had been moved to Orleans for safekeeping before the allies arrived. To this, Alexander replied, 'I assure you that no one would have touched them; but now, if Cossacks take them along the road it will be a lawful prize.'[146] Radozhitskii likewise made note of the auspiciously empty frames and pedestals in this particular museum, evidence that the most treasured artwork had been hidden. Nevertheless, there was still plenty to see and the author gave special attention to one painting, a portrayal of Christ being lowered from the cross. 'This is the first time,' wrote Radozhitskii, 'that I have seen nature so faithfully depicted on canvas.' The entire experience was described, including the honest boys outside on the street who had agreed to hold his horse while he was inside.[147]

---

[145] See chapter five of this dissertation on Russian periodical literature.

[146] Danilevskii, 'O prebyvanii russkikh v Parizhe', 14 – 15.

[147] Radozhitskii, *Pokhodnyia zapiski artillerista*, pp. 131 – 132.

Art galleries and museums were among the favourite attractions of Russian officers. Petrov reported that 'we were in the museum of painting and sculpture more than ten times.'[148] Apparently not an art aficionado himself, Murav'ev took the opportunity to visit several galleries and museums. In one picture gallery, he seemed as impressed with the building as he was with the art. He measured the hall with his steps and recorded that the interior of the gallery was 'three hundred steps long.' He confessed that he was 'unable to judge the beauty of the paintings and statues, but in an involuntary manner stopped before the best ones and admired them.' This rare experience included the chance to see items of antiquity and other historical artifacts. 'I saw the famous Apollo Belvedere, Venus, and many ancient statues brought from Rome. With particular respect, I paid attention to the artistry which had created such beauty. I also visited the Musée d'Artillerie in which all kinds of weapons are collected. In expansive halls the weapons of the most illustrious French knights are arranged.'[149] Other passing references to cultural institutions were more generic. For example, it is only an editorial footnote in the published edition of Lekhner's diary that informs the reader that 'the museum' that he visited was probably the Louvre.[150] These accounts imply that it was common for Russian officers to visit Parisian museums and art galleries during their stay.

Prior to the events of the French Revolution and subsequent Napoleonic Wars, hardly any French words dealing with visual art had been borrowed. According to the dictionaries studied, the only three possible exceptions would be the words *skul'pturnyi* and *p'edestal* during the reign of Peter the Great and *graver* [engraver] by the end of Catherine II's reign. However, during the period in which these events occur (1794 – 1837), nine new visual art terms are imported from French in a single generation. These

<hr>

[148] M. M. Petrov, 'Rasskazy sluzhivshego', in *Vospominaniia voinov*, ed. F. A. Petrov and others, p. 269.
[149] Murav'ev, 'Zapiski', 111.
[150] Lekhner, 'Dnevnik', in *1812 – 1814: reliatsii. pis'ma. dnevniki*, ed. by Afanas'ev and others, p. 378.

include the current Russian words for 'statue', 'bust', 'torso', 'album', 'caricature', 'portrait', 'palette', and the 'background' [*fon*] of a painting. During the subsequent period (1838 – 1881), another batch of visual art words entered Russian from French, including the current Russian words for 'landscape' [*peizazh*], 'watercolour' [*akvarel'*], 'gouache' (a type of paint), 'sketch' [*eskiz*], 'foreshortening' [*rakurs*], the verb 'to pose', and others. Thereafter, a steady influx of French terms related to visual arts technique is visible in each period.

Public transportation

The Russian officers who were able to visit Paris also made mention of the means of public transportation that they used while they were there. This is a relatively minor point in multiple memoirs, but is interesting as a commentary on the general notion of loanwords acting as clues about intercultural exchange. Employing French words to designate three distinct types of carriages—*fiakr, kabriolet,* and *dilizhans*—Russian officers described paid public transportation as something of a novelty. Fedor Glinka wrote about the larger stagecoaches on which perfect strangers could ride together from one city to another: 'A *dilizhans* is an enormous, most effective carriage in which anyone can hire a place for a fair price. Here you sit, as if in a room, in the company of fifteen or sixteen people of varying rank, quality, and often different nationalities.'[151] For transportation within the city, smaller carriages could be hired as taxis. In Paris, according to Chertkov, 'police rules dictate that one must pay one and a half francs for a ride in a *fiakr*, and one franc if in a *kabriolet.* Usually, we paid for the *fiakr.* Hired for the entire day, [it cost] twenty five to thirty francs. For a *kabriolet* [the price is] approximately the same amount, but the latter carriage is undoubtedly preferable, as better horses are always harnessed to it, and consequently you ride considerably

---

[151] Fedor Glinka, *Pis'ma russkogo ofitsera*, p. 246.

faster.'[152] While this text is taken from the Russian translation, Chertkov originally

wrote his memoir in French, using the words 'fiacre' and 'cabriolet' for these

carriages.[153] Khomutov, who also wrote his diary in French, used these words as

well.[154] Those who wrote their recollections in Russian, including Golitsyn, Fedor

Glinka, Radozhitskii, Lazhechnikov, Kazakov and the anonymous infantry officer all

used Russian transliterations of these same words, long before they were common in the

Russian lexicon. Of the three terms, only *dilizhans* appears at all in the works of

Pushkin. Dostoevskii (1821 – 1881) employs the three terms only two times each in the

course of his entire published career.[155] From the late nineteenth century forward,

however, they all appear in standard Russian dictionaries. The Russian term for a

carriage or wagon, *kareta* (which Dostoevskii used 237 times),[156] was too generic to

convey the distinction between various forms of public transportation that the officers

found interesting in France. They inserted the foreign terms, along with an explanation

where necessary, because their own language lacked the words to precisely designate

the objects about which they wanted to write. This is just one example of the process by

which foreign loanwords creep into a language and how the study thereof can give clues

about areas of interaction and influence, in this case dealing with public transportation.

Clothing and fashion

The prominence of French influence in the areas of clothing and fashion has already

been established by the lexical analysis, archival documents related to immigration, and

periodical literature from the period, and this is an obvious theme to look for in the

recollections of those Russian officers who invaded France in 1813 and 1814.

---

[152] Chertkov, 'Dnevniki 1813 – 1814 gg', in *1812 – 1814: reliatsii. pis'ma. dnevniki*, ed. by Afanas'ev and others, p. 437.

[153] Ibid., p. 424.

[154] Khomutov, 'Iz dnevnika svitskago ofitsera', 164.

[155] A. Ia. Shaiikevich and others, eds, *Statisticheskii slovar' iazyka Dostoevskogo* (Moscow: Iazyki slavianskoi kul'tury, 2003), pp. 84, 135, 432.

[156] Ibid., p. 139.

Surprisingly, however, mention of French fashion is considerably less prominent in the memoirs than are other aspects of French culture. Further, Russian officers seemed to write with more fascination about the clothes of the French peasants along the way than they did the high fashion of Parisian society. 'French peasants', wrote Chertkov, 'wear hoodies [*balakhony*] or shirts of white or blue canvas, which were put on over their clothes. Inside a room, they always wear their hats (mostly triangular ones), even during meals; residents of the cities use powder, but most of the peasants tie their hair back in long braids.'[157]

The memoirists wrote with a sense of surprise at encountering poverty in France. Radozhitskii reported that local peasants were all impoverished and poorly dressed in tunics, caps, and wooden shoes. He concluded that the common Frenchman was worse dressed than a common Russian man [*russkii muzhik*].[158] Meshetich made similar observations: 'In the villages in many places poverty was visible. Villagers live untidily, in general the men wear their blue shirts over their camisoles, women wear wooden shoes and, in general, their way of life was far behind that of the Germanic peoples in terms of its pleasantness.'[159] Radozhitskii and Meshetich's mention of the wooden shoes of the French peasants is echoed in several memoirs. In Chavignon, Ortenberg makes passing reference to them in his description of the few elderly men, women, and children encountered in this city, which had been occupied by the allied staff officers. 'They came out with wooden shoes, [carrying] lanterns, cursing Napoleon, and having to act as guides to the Russian cavalry.'[160] In a moment of cultural self-analysis, these wooden shoes become the object of Fedor Glinka's sardonic reflection on Russian emulation of French fashion. He remarked that, because of the

---

[157] Chertkov, 'Dnevniki 1813 – 1814 gg', in *1812 – 1814: reliatsii. pis'ma. dnevniki*, ed. by Afanas'ev and others, p. 428.
[158] Radozhitskii, *Pokhodnyia zapiski artillerista*, pp. 38 – 39.
[159] Meshetich, 'Istoricheskie zapiski voini', in *Vospominaniia voinov*, ed. by F. A. Petrov and others, p. 67.
[160] Ortenberg, 'Furazhirovka posle srazheniia pod Kraonnov', 20.

wide variety of clothing that he witnessed, 'As far as I have travelled, I do not know how French women dress. Villagers wrap their heads with some sort of cloth and call this a "bonnêt"', and they wear wooden shoes. 'Russian shoes are a lot nicer and more comfortable, but carry these wooden shoes to Russia and they will become the honoured fashion!'[161]

The observations were not all negative, however. In Paris, Radozhitskii recorded his admiration of the simple French women that he saw walking along the streets. 'Many of them are pretty [*khoroshen'kie*]. They all dress simply, handsomely, neatly, and all the same [*odinakovo*].' Then, after a few remarks on the shape of their faces, hair-colour, and eyes, he continued, 'they have thin shawls... short dresses... and hide their hands in their pockets; they wear their hair gathered under a net or cap.'[162] An anonymous infantry officer did not find French women so beautiful. The best of them were only 'not bad,' but he did admit that they were impressive in their 'manners, clothing, and especially shoes.'[163] Fedor Glinka was equally begrudging in his praise of the ladies he saw in villages and towns near Paris. Young girls verily danced or jumped as they strolled through the streets, carrying baskets. 'They are not so much beautiful as they are comely [*milovidny*]. Their outfit is made up of a slim blouse [*koftochka*], apron and a straw hat or pretty bonnet.'[164]

After arriving in Paris, only a few of the officers recorded their impressions of the fashionable shops. On Palais-Royal, Radozhitskii noted the life-like waxen busts in the shop windows which had wigs on them, as well as the clothes and other fashion accessories in these establishments.[165] Chertkov went into considerable detail about the Salon de la Paix, a shop at Palais-Royal where shoes are cleaned. His focus, however,

---

[161] Fedor Glinka, *Pis'ma russkogo ofitsera*, p. 229.
[162] Radozhitskii, *Pokhodnyia zapiski artillerista*, p. 134.
[163] 'Vyderzhki iz voennykh zapisok', 91.
[164] Fedor Glinka, *Pis'ma russkogo ofitsera*, p. 248.
[165] Radozhitskii, *Pokhodnyia zapiski artillerista*, p. 128.

is more on the commercial aspect of this small business than the fashion. After learning

that the proprietor paid 3,000 francs per year for the facility where his shop was located,

he calculated that the shoe-shiner would have to clean 60,000 shoes to cover his rent,

not counting wages for five or six shoe-cleaning masters, subscriptions to three

newspapers for the customers to read and the waxes and other supplies used.[166] As with

the aforementioned cafés and restaurants of Paris, examination of the Parisian fashion

industry further exposed Russian officers to a developed consumer culture.

While fewer sartorial observations were recorded than might be expected given

the enduring influence of French fashion suggested by the lexical analysis, the Russian

memoirists do record a significant means of interacting with this aspect of culture that

goes beyond mere observation. Russian military personnel actually participated in the

culture by wearing French clothes while they were in Paris. This applied mostly to

officers who had the means to purchase clothing, but Baranovich even recorded a

situation in which common Russian soldiers were decked out in the garb of Frenchmen.

According to this artillery officer, he was responsible for a group of Russian soldiers,

former prisoners of war who had recently been released following the conclusion of

peace. They arrived to Versailles wearing the ragged remains of their uniforms and

were greeted by generous locals who helped them to improve their situation. 'Right

away, they brought them stockings, shoes, trousers, sweaters [*kofty*], hats, shirts [*bluzy*],

and dressed our soldiers and officers so funny, that you could not tell who they were,

Frenchmen or Russians!'[167] Apart from such serendipitous occurrences, the wearing of

French clothing actually became a matter of command policy. Kazakov recorded that

'it had been ordered in Paris that, when off duty [*vne sluzhby*], we were to wear civilian

clothes [*partikuliarnoe plat'e*].' The French doctor with whom he was staying helped

---

[166] Chertkov, 'Dnevniki 1813 – 1814 gg', in *1812 – 1814: reliatsii. pis'ma. dnevniki*, ed. by Afanas'ev and others, p. 436.
[167] Baranovich, 'Russkie soldaty vo Frantsii', 155.

him to choose something appropriate and would not let him out of the house in tails during the day.[168] According to Danilevskii, this practice of wearing civilian clothes facilitated a better relationship with the local population than other allied soldiers enjoyed.

> At this time, we were allowed to wear tailcoats [*fraki*] by means of which we were already in society, not as conquerors, but as civilians. The Prussians and Austrians continued to wear their uniforms. The latter have the habit of wearing several green leaves on their shakos and hats, which offended the French as they took this as a representation of laurels… But the Parisians very much liked that we wore white bands on our left arms, and added white rims to our bows.'[169]

This last addition of white accessories was a symbol of their support for the Bourbons who were returning to rule France, and this token, in addition to their civilian dress, endeared the Russians to the local population who also wore white cockades on their hats in support of the dynasty.[170] Fedor Glinka recalled making every effort upon arriving in Paris to find some civilian clothes to wear while off duty. Even though a lot of the stores were closed in this post-war city, one of their comrades ran to Palais-Royal and brought back a local vendor with ready-made clothing. 'We bought frock-coats [*siurtuki*], round hats, stockings [*chulki*], shoes [*bashmaki*], thin canes, and in a moment we were dressed up as Parisian civilians. All of ours [that is, the Russians] do the same; for a Russian officer in uniform meets everywhere with sidelong glances and a thousand troubles [*tysiacha nepriiatnostei*].'[171] Regarding the canes that these officers purchased, Petrov likewise noticed Frenchmen carrying walking sticks while he was at the opera and remarked that they were 'in fashion in Paris at the time.'[172]

This effort to blend in, while partially a political decision on the part of Russian commanders aimed at fostering better public relations, also facilitated a deeper level of

---

[168] Kazakov, 'Pokhod vo Frantsiiu', in *Rossiiskie memuary,* ed. by Liapishchev, p. 539.
[169] Danilevskii, 'O prebyvanii ruskikh v Parizhe', 34 – 35.
[170] Ibid.
[171] Fedor Glinka, *Pis'ma russkogo ofitsera,* p. 250.
[172] M. M. Petrov, 'Rasskazy sluzhivshego', in *Vospominaniia voinov,* ed. F. A. Petrov and others, p. 271.

cultural interaction for the Russian officers. The timing of this interaction coincides with the broader cultural tendency made evident by the lexical study. Very few French loanwords related to clothing and fashion appeared in the Dictionary published by the Russian Academy in 1789 – 1794 apart from various kinds of fabric. However, between 1814 and 1837, the writing of Aleksandr Pushkin featured thirty new fashion terms which were borrowed from the French language, twenty-three of which are still in use today. These included many articles of clothing, accessories, the 'style' of something [*fason*], and even the word for 'fashion' itself [*moda*]. Several of these new terms are employed by the memoirists. Among the new terms related to clothing were the *fraki* that Russian officers wore while off-duty in Paris, and the shawl [*shal'*] of the French girl who caught Radozhitskii's eye. While the French loanword for a shirt or blouse [*bluza*] does not appear in the broader lexicon until later in the nineteenth century, Baranovich already employed the term in his recollections. The Russian words for 'lorgnette', 'bracelet', 'vest', 'costume', 'skirt', 'corset', and 'beret' also entered the language from French during this period. For Russia, this was to be the first of many generations to import a significant number of French words related to fashion.

Decadent Morality

In addition to merely recording events and experiences, some of the writers of memoirs became more reflective and even philosophical in their observations of French culture. Reminiscent of the anti-gallomania chastisement in Russian periodical literature of the 1790s, memoirists of the foreign campaign often include a negative moral assessment of French society. In Paris, several of the officers portrayed the Palais-Royal as a place buzzing with questionable commercial activity and decadent entertainment. Their descriptions of the overwhelming sensory experience of visiting this sector are a mixture of fascination and disapproval. Gambling halls, brothels, scheming charlatans, and the brawling or even duelling that accompany over-indulgence in strong drink were among the vices that shocked the young Russian officers who explored Palais-Royal. Petrov characterized 'this hundred-year-old marketplace of feelings, raging from one end to the other' as a veritable 'arena of human passions.'[173] One anonymous infantry officer was perusing a book store in the area when the proprietor asked him, 'perhaps you are looking for number thirteen?' Not understanding this code, the curious Russian inquired further and was shown to a less-public collection of literature which included vulgar pictures.[174] Chertkov discovered building number 113 at Palais-Royal and was astonished to find so much moral depravity under one roof. The third floor was a 'gathering of public girls' (a brothel), a roulette game was taking place on the second floor, a loan office was in the attic, and a gun shop was on the first floor. 'This house is a detailed and true picture of that to which rampant passions will lead us.'[175] Fedor Glinka called Palais-Royal a 'centre of temptations,'[176] and the good doctor Dupuytren warned of Palais-Royal specifically in his fatherly exhortations to seventeen-year-old Kazakov.[177]

Writing more broadly, Radozhitskii summarized that all the values in Paris seemed to be superficial and Petersburg was to be preferred. Having read so much about France and its capital, Radozhitskii found himself disappointed when seeing it with his own eyes. This repeated theme of disappointment, including this assessment of the moral climate, is pervasive in his memoir. He expressed disapproval, for example, of the immodest costumes of actresses in one of the local theatres which they visited along the march.[178] He indicted French émigré women for bringing bad morals to Russia, and was, at one point, incensed when asked by a French person whether

---

[173] M. M. Petrov, 'Rasskazy sluzhivshego', in *Vospominaniia voinov*, ed. F. A. Petrov and others, p. 270.

[174] 'Vyderzhki iz voennykh zapisok', 93.

[175] Chertkov, 'Dnevniki 1813 – 1814 gg', in *1812 – 1814: reliatsii. pis'ma. dnevniki*, ed. by Afanas'ev and others, p. 433.

[176] Fedor Glinka, *Pis'ma russkogo ofitsera*, p. 252.

[177] Kazakov, 'Pokhod vo Frantsiiu', in *Rossiiskie memuary*, ed. by Liapishchev, pp. 538 – 542.

[178] Radozhitskii, *Pokhodnyia zapiski artillerista*, p. 188.

polygamy were practiced in Russia and how many wives a Russian man typically had. In response, he declared that 'women [in our country] are in greater respect than here. We in no way observe [such] Asiatic customs; but if there is some deterioration of morals among the Russian nobility, it is because of tutors and madams who, leaving France during the revolution, along with the French language brought many vices to Russia.'[179] Seemingly writing from a sense of wounded pride, Radozhitskii often noted the surprise of the French who expected the Russian invaders to be Barbarians. Apart from being a military memoir, his recollections are a defence of Russia as a civilized nation and an exercise in cultural introspection, evaluating previous French influence upon Russian society in light of his new eyewitness perspective on French culture. Though expressed more explicitly by Radozhitskii than others, asserting the moral superiority of Russian culture is a repeated theme in the Franco-Russian comparative analyses of the memoirists. Radozhitskii concludes that 'to tell the truth, the condition France was in, as we saw it, disappointed our high opinion of her.'[180]

Religion

The Christian faith of the Russians informed some of their observations and is another repeated theme in the memoirs. Throughout the campaign, references are made to their own religious thoughts and also to their interaction with French Christianity. In one section of his memoir, Chertkov made note of which regions were more predominately Catholic and which were primarily Protestant as he passed through them.[181] The memoirists made notes about the architecture of churches in Reims, Vitry, Laon, and other cities through which they travelled, sometimes asking for tours, and even attending worship services, though their own confession was Russian Orthodoxy.

---

[179] Ibid., p. 173.
[180] Ibid., pp. 191 – 192.
[181] Chertkov, 'Dnevniki 1813 – 1814 gg', in *1812 – 1814: reliatsii. pis'ma. dnevniki*, ed. by Afanas'ev and others, p. 425.

Russian officers were largely unimpressed with French piety. On the whole, they found the French to be frivolous, immoral, and lacking in depth of feeling, including religious sensitivities. Radozhitskii recorded his experience worshipping with local parishioners in one of the towns along the road between Verdun and Chalon. In addition to his detailed description of the Catholic liturgy, he noted that people were nodding off during the sermon, the well-dressed ladies in the pews seemed primarily interested in socializing, and congregants even conversed and laughed during the service.[182] Several of the memoir authors specifically blamed the godless French Revolution for marring the moral and spiritual fabric of French society. Golitsyn, who accompanied the Russian Emperor to Paris before being called away on other official duties, expressed such a sentiment when recalling his first brief visit to the city. 'I was only able to glance at Paris,' wrote Golitsyn, 'but at least I gained an understanding of the appearance of this huge capital, the old God-forsaken sinner [*staraia greshnitsa*] who, for fifty years, has enjoyed the entirely unenviable privilege of endowing Europe with war and unrest.'[183] Fedor Glinka reminisced about a better time in French society, and lamented the spiritual damage inflicted by the revolution which, from his perspective, was a direct result of the Age of Reason: 'Back then, minds were sharp, hearts were happy, and souls were pious. France prayed, sang, and loved its sovereigns. But when was this? Long ago! Other times came and brought with them different morals. Half of an education has eclipsed a sound mind.'[184] Chertkov, reflecting on the desecration of churches in the wake of the French Revolution, described a scene that eerily foreshadows Soviet actions after his own country's revolution a century later.

> The place where the Franconi Circus is located was, before the revolution, the site of a Capuchin monastery. Twenty years ago monks lived at this place. But by the will of chance, in place of a church, stables are now located. Different times, different morals! And, having broken the dome of the old church on Rue

---

[182] Radozhitskii, *Pokhodnyia zapiski artillerista,* pp. 161 – 163.
[183] Golitsyn, *Ofitserskiia zapiski,* p. 93.
[184] Fedor Glinka, *Pis'ma russkogo ofitsera,* p. 224.

des Grands-Augustins, they have turned it into a market where they sell meat, birds, and so forth.[185]

Kakhovskii mentioned similar impressions after observing the damage done to one of the churches in Nancy after the revolution.[186]

Contrasting the impious French with the God-fearing Russians is a repeated theme in the memoirs. Danilevskii wrote that 'the Parisians, famous for their writing about unbelief, having turned from religion at the beginning of the revolution, were surprised that [Alexander I] and the officers of his entourage went to church every day. We did this because we were in Paris on Passion Week.'[187] Khomutov likewise recorded going to confession and witnessing the Grand Dukes and the Emperor himself asking forgiveness of Russian soldiers after one of the Passion Week services.[188] Even Captain M. P. Romanov, whose memoir is almost entirely military in nature and otherwise contributes very little cultural information to the present study, specifically mentioned celebrating Easter near Paris.[189] Radozhitskii's journal entry for 29 March 1814 begins simply: 'Christ is Risen!' He describes how the Russian troops, following the example of the Tsar himself, fasted in the days before Easter, after the Eastern Orthodox tradition.[190] Those, like Radozhitskii, who were stationed outside of Paris celebrated Easter in local churches, while those chosen to be in the capital took part in a special ceremony.

The Easter service held in Paris on the Place de la Concorde just days after the triumphal entry of the allied monarchs in March 1814 is one of the events described most often in the various memoirs. On the morning of 29 March 1814, Troops were

---

[185] Chertkov, 'Dnevniki 1813 – 1814 gg', in *1812 – 1814: reliatsii. pis'ma. dnevniki*, ed. by Afanas'ev and others, p. 435.

[186] Kakhovskii, 'Zapiski', 458.

[187] Danilevskii, 'O prebyvanii russkikh v Parizhe',15.

[188] Khomutov, 'Iz dnevnika svitskago ofitsera', 166.

[189] M. P. Romanov, 'Zapiski otstavnogo podpolkovnika Mikhaila Petrovicha Romanova voennym deistviiam v Rossii i za granitsei s 1812 i po 1817 god, v kotorykh on uchastvoval. 1838 g', in *Vospominaniia voinov russkoi armii*, ed. by F. A. Petrov and others (Moscow: Mysl', 1991), p. 407.

[190] Radozhitskii, *Pokhodnyia zapiski artillerista*, pp. 145 – 146.

standing in formation in parade dress on the square or stationed in other locations along

nearby streets. 'A boundless multitude of people covered the streets, the square and the

adjoining alleys of the Tuileries garden and Champs-Élysée. The beautiful spring

weather added even more lustre to our celebration.'[191] Military leaders and other

dignitaries from various countries were present, all of whom had gathered 'to worship

the Risen Christ.'[192] A platform [*amvon*] three fathoms [about eighteen feet] high had

been constructed and set up on the very spot where the French king Louis XVI had been

executed.[193] Clergymen ascended the scarlet-covered steps up the platform carrying

icons and waited to begin the service. As Alexander I, King Frederick William III of

Prussia, and several French marshals rode out to inspect the troops and take their places

on the square, the singing of Russian clergymen could be heard. The command was

given for the banners of each regiment to be brought out and placed around the

platform.[194] Alexander 'and all those around him, including [those with the] rank of

marshal, bowed their knees where the blood of a virtuous monarch had been spilt

twenty years prior.'[195] All troops removed their shakos for prayer.[196] From the

temporary pulpit, a prayer of thanksgiving was said 'for the final victory, for the taking

of Paris, and the return of the Bourbons to the throne.'[197] Upon conclusion of the

prayer, the hushed reverence was suddenly broken by the sound of gunfire as one

hundred and one Russian cannons fired a salute.[198] Danilevskii vividly describes this

moment:

> But with what feelings did it fill us when we celebrated victory in the midst of
> the conquered city, the revered capital of the universe? We were so intoxicated
> with the exultation of the past days, that it became necessary for our hearts to be

---

[191] Danilevskii, 'O prebyvanii ruskikh v Parizhe', 38.

[192] Khomutov, 'Iz dnevnika svitskago ofitsera', 168.

[193] Kazakov, 'Pokhod vo Frantsiiu', in *Rossiiskie memuary,* ed. by Liapishchev, p. 539.

[194] Ibid.

[195] Danilevskii, 'O prebyvanii ruskikh v Parizhe', 39.

[196] Kazakov, 'Pokhod vo Frantsiiu', in *Rossiiskie memuary,* ed. by Liapishchev, p. 539.

[197] Khomutov, 'Iz dnevnika svitskago ofitsera', 168.

[198] Ibid.

humbled before the Creator. When the prayer was finished, the rumble [*gul*] of Russian cannons rang out across Paris; The thundering of weapons, taking the place of the silence during the service, shook the depth of our souls.[199]

According to Khomutov, 'everyone had tears in their eyes' on this momentous occasion.[200] This was clearly a meaningful event for the Russians, both for its spiritual significance and, symbolically, to mark the end of a long war.

In descriptions of this event and other prayer meetings, the memoirists depict the Russian troops as having been deeply religious people long before arriving in France. While they observed and interacted with French Christianity while abroad, they do not seem to have been deeply impacted by it. It is not surprising, therefore, that very few French religious terms were borrowed into the Russian language during this or any other historical period. The only two exceptions during this particular period are the word for a religious 'sect' [*sekta*] and the word for 'missionary'. Most of the French religious terms which enter the language later are proper nouns which might simply be necessary for historical discourse, such as 'Huguenot', 'Jesuit', 'Calvinism', or the names of certain Catholic priestly garments or orders that are foreign to Russia. While the memoirs include a number of anecdotes which suggest Russian curiosity about French spirituality, they appear to have come away largely uninfluenced in this area.

Books and other printed literature

In addition to their interaction with French people and their tangible surroundings, access to the printed word was another source of cultural influence upon the Francophone members of Russia's invading armies. One venue for access to French books was the personal and institutional libraries that they encountered along the march. Radozhitskii recorded that the home in which he was quartered at Saint-Menoux

---

[199] Danilevskii, 'O prebyvanii ruskikh v Parizhe', 39 – 40.
[200] Khomutov, 'Iz dnevnika svitskago ofitsera', 168.

belonged to a naturalist and there were many books in the house.[201] In a village near

Villars-Sexelles, wrote Chertkov, 'the mayor of the village has a library and we used it

because we did not have anything to read.'[202] Along the road between Meaux and Paris,

Danilevskii examined the abandoned castles and recalled that 'everywhere, I found

libraries and picture galleries.'[203] Lazhechnikov's description of the fine home where

he stayed in Belleville, just outside Paris, included the fact that there was 'a small

library, including all the essence of French letters, with the most beautiful external

appearance.'[204] In Paris, Petrov mentioned his visit to a library which boasted of

400,000 books and 150,000 manuscripts.[205] Lekhner, whose brief diary entries often

comprised no more than a date and a location, specifically referenced several

opportunities to visit libraries while in Paris in April 1814. He examined topographical

maps of Switzerland, France, and the Netherlands, and, at the library of the French

Academy, looked at a large globe.[206]

Particularly relevant to the general issue of books was an episode at the Château

Brienne recorded by Murav'ev, who recalled two separate visits to this great palace

around the time of the battle of Brienne. Murav'ev described a glorious library and

office of natural history during his first visit. When he returned some time later, he

found the Château ransacked. Walking around the library to investigate, he noticed

books, artifacts, and broken glass under his feet, and lamented the 'pitiful condition' to

which this famous library had been reduced. This high-ranking Russian officer went

from room to room, rescuing as many interesting novels a he could find and stuffed

them into his pockets to read later by the campfire. 'I examined all of the books', he

---

[201] Radozhitskii, *Pokhodnyia zapiski artillerista,* pp. 160 – 161.

[202] Chertkov, 'Dnevniki 1813 – 1814 gg', in *1812 – 1814: reliatsii. pis'ma. dnevniki*, ed. by Afanas'ev and others, p. 425.

[203] Danilevskii, 'Sluchai, predshestvovavshie vkhodu v Parizh', 222.

[204] Lazhechnikov, *Pokhodnyia zapiski,* p. 193.

[205] M. M. Petrov, 'Rasskazy sluzhivshego, in *Vospominaniia voinov*, ed. F. A. Petrov and others, p. 269.

[206] Lekhner, 'Dnevnik', in *1812 – 1814: reliatsii. pis'ma. dnevniki*, ed. by Afanas'ev and others, pp. 378 – 380.

wrote, 'and regretted that I was not able to take them all with me.' Murav'ev read these novels to pass the time at the bivouac each evening and then, to lighten his load, added the books to the fire as he finished them. According to Murav'ev, Prince P. M. Volkonskii discovered the library and asked the Tsar's permission to transport the books back to the main headquarters in Petersburg. Permission was granted, but this large cache of books transported only as far as Chaumont. The French army had cut off their access to Reims and they were forced by a sudden change of route to abandon the books.[207]

Memoirists also reported the occasional opportunity to purchase reading material along the way. Chertkov complained that Vesoul was 'a fairly pitiful city,' but had the redeeming quality of possessing two books shops [*knizhnye lavki*].[208] In Paris, he found a bookseller on the riverfront 'where you can cheaply buy good quality books.' Here, he bought a three-volume dictionary of physics for ten francs. Chertkov also made note of the various political newspapers—including the well-known *Le Moniteur*—to which one could subscribe in Paris.[209] The various memoirs contain several passing references to newspapers. Soon after entering Paris, one infantry officer recorded eating lunch at a restaurant and buying some French newspapers to read.[210] Lekhner was on the homeward march towards Belgium when he read confirmation in a Parisian newspaper that Bonaparte had been granted a pension and was departing with his family for the island of Elba.'[211] Radozhitskii was also on his way home when he read in a French newspaper that Louis XVIII had entered Paris three days earlier to a cheering crowd.[212]

---

[207] Murav'ev, 'Zapiski', 78, 86 – 89.

[208] Chertkov, 'Dnevniki 1813 – 1814 gg', in *1812 – 1814: reliatsii. pis'ma. dnevniki*, ed. by Afanas'ev and others, p. 425.

[209] Ibid., p. 437.

[210] 'Vyderzhki iz voennykh zapisok', 88.

[211] Lekhner, 'Dnevnik', in *1812 – 1814: reliatsii. pis'ma. dnevniki*, ed. by Afanas'ev and others, p. 377.

[212] Radozhitskii, *Pokhodnyia zapiski artillerista*, p. 175.

In addition to books and newspapers, literate Russians were exposed to other popular forms of literature, some of which described the presence of Russians in Paris. Danilevskii and Fedor Glinka both relate the French perceptions of Russians to be found in the various pamphlets, short-story collections, and journals that they picked up in Paris. According to Danilevskii, French journalists had nothing but praise for the noble, pious Russians who entered Paris as liberators and 'told of their feats from the Moscow River to the Seine.'[213] During these first days in Paris, locals were peddling images of Alexander I and poems about him, recently created by French artists and poets.[214] Danilevskii included his translation of an entire article from one of the French publications purchased in Paris. The article begins, 'what a pleasant and majestic sight are these monarchs who have come to us with weapons in their hands in order to provide for our peace and prosperity!' The article continues with flattery for the tall, strong Russian soldiers and the suggestion of a historical parallel between Peter the Great's visit to Paris and the arrival of Alexander.[215] According to Danilevskii, the Russian Emperor had brought much joy to Paris, announcing that he was 'returning 200,000 captured Frenchmen which were located in Russia. Immediately, news of this was printed in the newspapers, nailed to the walls of houses, and distributed everywhere.'[216]

Fedor Glinka bought a short booklet entitled *The Russians' Farewell to the Parisians* from one of a group of French boys who were competing with one another to sell it to him. This short work, written in French, purports to express the Russian perspective on what has made Paris so charming to them. According to the booklet, Russians love the streets, museums, theatres, cuisine, and tailors of Paris. Glinka includes his translation of an excerpt from this short work. Judging from the portions

---

[213] Danilevskii, 'O prebyvanii ruskikh v Parizhe', 15 – 17.
[214] Ibid., 21.
[215] Ibid., 23 – 27.
[216] Ibid., 12 – 13.

he chooses to translate and his commentary thereon, Glinka is clearly incensed. The piece ends as follows: 'So, we [that is, the Russians who are saying farewell] will make every effort so that the society of both our capitals might come alive, and be adorned with the French mind and spirit.' To this, Glinka replies 'So speaks a Frenchman on behalf of the Russians, but true Russians will in fact be repeating in their morning and evening prayers, "deliver us, Lord, from pestilence, flood, fire, and from the French spirit!"'[217]

Glinka's expression of irritation with French boasting and Danilevskii's self-aggrandizing selection of flattering passages to translate both represent thoughtful interaction with French prose and a measure of self-analysis regarding Russia's cultural relationship with France. Russians had already been reading French books and periodical publications, but the availability of so broad a selection of French literature to so many Russian officers occurred at a significant moment in the history of Russia's linguistic and literary development. Chronologically, this moment may roughly be viewed as the boundary between the eighteenth century—characterized by the struggle for a normalized Russian language, largely exercised via translation and emulation of French literature—and the nineteenth century, widely regarded as the Golden Age of Russian literature, featuring Pushkin and his immediate followers.[218]

While an in-depth analysis of Russia's literary history is beyond the scope of the present study, it is worth noting the number of new French loanwords related to literature that enter the Russian language during this period. Previously, virtually no terms explicitly related to the study of literature had entered the Russian language from French. During this period, however, twelve literary terms were borrowed from French,

---

[217] Fedor Glinka, *Pis'ma russkogo ofitsera*, pp. 261 – 263.

[218] V. V. Zhivov, *Iazyk i kul'tura v rossii XVIII veka* (Moscow: Shkola Iazyk Russkoi Kul'tury, 1996), pp. 441 – 455; V. V. Vinogradov, *Ocherki po Istorii russkogo literaturnogo iazyka XVII-XIX Vekov* (Moscow: Vysshaia Shkola, 1982), pp. 164 – 294; G. O. Vinokur, *Russkii iazyk: Istoricheskii ocherk* (Moscow: URSS, 2010), pp. 135 – 158.

more than any previous or subsequent period. These included the names of genres,
literary devices, and other technical terms: *ballada, kuplet, roman* ['novel'], *madrigal,*
and *triolet*, to name a few. This period also witnessed the introduction from French of
the words 'journalism' and 'pamphlet' into the Russian language. Finally, a significant
number of philosophical terms related to social and political thought were imported
during this period, though virtually none had been borrowed earlier. These include the
Russian words for 'nation', 'national', 'party', 'revolution', and 'counterrevolution' as
well as less overtly political terms like 'ideal', 'idealism' and 'materialism.' This last
group of words is not primarily significant for a large number, but for a tendency of
which these words signal a beginning.[219] Russia's social and political vocabulary would
continue to grow—partially by borrowing from French—and would verily explode in
the twentieth century, but this tendency to seriously explore democratic political
philosophy really began in the wake of the French revolution and Russia's foreign
campaign into France.

The enduring cultural significance of the foreign campaigns

In 1860, a story was published by the Decembrist author Nikolai Bestuzhev entitled
Russkii v Parizhe 1814 goda.[220] This novelette of historical fiction about 'a Russian in
Paris' is just one example of the lasting impression left by these events upon Russia's
cultural memory. The main character of Bestuzhev's tale, a fictional young lieutenant,
Vadim Glinskii, is remarkably similar to the many real-life participants described in the
memoirs examined in this study. In this story, Glinskii is quartered in the home of a
French marquis while stationed in Paris in 1814. The central plot is his blossoming

---

[219] See my overview of secondary literature linking the Decembrist uprising to the French influences
encountered by the young Russian officers during this foreign campaign in chapter one, pp. 69 – 74, and
in my conclusion, pp. 327 – 330.
[220] Nikolai Bestuzhev, 'Russkii v Parizhe 1814 goda', in *Russkaia istoricheskaia povest' pervoi poloviny XIX
veka,* ed. by B. T. Bashkirovoi and others (Moscow: Izdatel'stvo "Pravda", 1986), pp. 531 – 714.

romance with Emily, the marquis' young daughter who is already a widow. The streets, buildings, and landmarks of the city, the restoration of the French monarchy, post-war Parisian cultural life, and the bustle of the allied occupation all serve as the backdrop of this fictional love-story, which is complete with a duel. The ticketing system by which officers were housed with families, the moral peril which young men navigated in the shady districts of Paris, disappointments with French morals, and the general surprise of the French people at the civilized Russian soldiers are all portrayed. Glinskii dines in the home of the marquis and in local restaurants, visits museums and art galleries with Emily, and his thoughts on French food, clothing, and culture are provided by the omniscient narrator. The fatherly affection of the marquis for Glinskii echoes the recollections of the real-life Kazakov about his gracious host, Dupuytren. Glinskii's heart-broken goodbye with Emily corresponds with that of Murav'ev's fellow officer in the tavern. Like several of the memoir authors, the fictional Glinksii makes note of the fact that the Emperor Alexander attended church for every holiday while in Paris. Finally, the noble, well-mannered sophistication which makes Glinskii perfectly equal to the French nobles, culturally, and a head taller, morally, is indistinguishable from how most of the memoirists portray themselves. In a word, Glinskii is like a romanticized conglomeration of the experiences of numerous Russian officers in the real 1814, a testimony to the cultural ingredients which seasoned this last phase of the Napoleonic Wars for its Russian participants.

The types of French influence upon Russian soldiers and officers of the foreign campaigns of 1813 – 1815 were not conceptually new to Russian culture. The topical patterns apparent in the memoirs and diaries from this period mirror the areas of Russian culture impacted by French immigrants in the late eighteenth century. Food and drink, clothing and fashion, theatre, visual art, urban infrastructure, architecture, interior design, and the customs associated with refined social interaction; these same categories of French stimulus are suggested by Russian archival documents and periodical publications well before 1812 and its aftermath.[221] Not only the categories but, reductively speaking, the means of cultural influence were also the same: people, things, and books. However, the way they were experienced by Russians in 1814 was much different than the way they were experienced in the 1790s. First, Russians were now experiencing these components from within the culture of origin, rather than as imported novelties. By being immersed in the French culture, even those Russians who were already familiar with its individual elements were now interacting with them in a new context: French furniture and décor as displayed in a French home, French language spoken commonly in society rather than serving as the dividing-line between castes, the simpler styles of clothing worn by French people who were not of the upper elite, French cuisine in the context of Parisian restaurant culture, and so forth. Russian officers were familiar enough with French culture to appreciate their surroundings and were now given a more informed perspective.

In addition to the new depth of this cultural experience, 1814 is also significant because of its breadth. It is estimated that there were just over 2,000 French people living in Russia in 1793, and it has already been established that these émigrés made significant contributions to Russian culture.[222] By contrast, in the first days of 1814, over 100,000 Russians were marching into France and would spend months of immersion in this culture. Those Russians who made it to Paris were literally surrounded by curious French citizens, who would have outnumbered them more than eight to one.[223]

---

[221] See chapter three and five on immigration and Russian periodical literature respectively.
[222] See chapter three on immigration.
[223] According to M. K. Chiniakov, 69,000 Russian troops marched on Paris. According to Chertkov's memoir, the population of Paris at the time was around 600,000. See Chiniakov, 'Parizh', pp. 197 – 198, and Chertkov, 'Dnevniki 1813 – 1814 gg', in *1812 – 1814: reliatsii. pis'ma. dnevniki*, ed. by Afanas'ev and others, p. 437.

The majority of those being exposed to French culture at this time were common soldiers, most of whom were almost certainly illiterate, had not been raised by French governesses, and would have been given far fewer opportunities for cultural enrichment in their home country. In short, never before had so many Russians from such varied backgrounds been in direct contact with so many Frenchmen. Their return to Russia was, potentially, a cultural wave that numerically dwarfed the previous French wave of immigration.

Moreover, the popularity of 1812-era memoir literature ensured that the experiences of Russians in France would be shared with Russia's reading public for generations to come. Well into the twentieth century, memoir collections were republished at each major anniversary of 1812, in addition to previously unpublished recollections that were found in museums, archives, and family collections.

Finally, the officers who wrote in their memoirs about their time in France were prompted by the experience to think and write about Russian culture and how it had been influenced by the French. Orlov, Danilevskii, Radozhitskii, and Fedor Glinka are especially explicit in their self-conscious reflection on the strides made by their own civilization, and their memoirs share a strain of disenchantment with the Gallomania of the past and a desire for Russian cultural independence, while, at the same time, admitting the undeniable magnitude of French investment in Russia's cultural development. By propelling the memoir genre forward in Russia, the events of 1812 – 1815 not only facilitated deep French cultural impact, they also fostered a literary forum for ongoing analysis of the same.

CHAPTER FIVE

RUSSIAN PERIODICAL LITERATURE AND FRENCH INFLUENCE: 1788 – 1825

The analysis of loanwords in chapter two has identified the late eighteenth and early nineteenth century as the key period for permanent cultural transfer from France to Russia. As the goal of this dissertation on Russian culture has been to move beyond a singular focus on the Russian state and its iconic leaders, the two subsequent chapters closely examined the most prominent events within this period which facilitated widespread Franco-Russian interaction at the personal level. These events were, namely, immigration from France to Russia which occurred in two qualitatively distinct waves during the reign of Catherine II and the Russian army's unique experience of marching through France in 1814. The present chapter is chronologically and thematically broader, and puts both of these events in the context of French influences upon Russian society across the entire period beginning just before the outbreak of revolution in France and up to and including the entire reign of Alexander I.

To this end, periodical literature published between 1788 and 1825 has been studied. Two different types of periodical sources—a Russian newspaper and numerous literary journals—have been sampled for this period so as to glean two different kinds of insights: objective French influences upon daily life within Russia, and the broader influences apparent in Russian cultural expression. French stimuli in the daily lives of Russians included the employment of foreigners as tutors and domestic servants, the availability of French goods and services, and the regular importation of French books and luxury items. Broader influences include Russian perceptions of French influence upon their culture, public awareness of political circumstances beyond and approaching Russia's borders, and the evident French influence upon the development of Russian periodical literature itself and upon the Russian literary and historiographical professions, illustrated particularly in the life and work of Nikolai Karamzin. As this survey will show, the key events—French immigration and the war with Napoleon— were uniquely important cultural phenomena which burst on the scene and left the greatest permanent mark, but they occurred during a time of steady French literary influence over a longer period of time which seems to have transcended political circumstances.

The Russian publishing industry under Catherine II, Paul I, and Alexander I

This period witnessed great developmental strides in the printing, publishing, and journalism industries of Russia but also seasons of significant government repression of the same. As her indulgence of satirical literature in the 1760s and 1770s illustrates, Catherine II began her reign fairly liberally where censorship was concerned, and two imperial decrees in 1771 and 1776 gave special permission to certain German-born printers to operate private presses within clear boundaries.[1] The first of these allowed Johann Hartung, considered Russia's first private publisher, to produce books in foreign languages only.[2] The second decree allowed the booksellers Johann Weitbrecht and Johann Schnoor to operate their own printing press and publish books, not only in foreign languages, but in Russian as well.[3] Then, in 1783, in a move that Russian censorship historian P. S. Reifman has referred to as 'the height of her liberalism',[4] Catherine issued a general decree permitting anyone in any city of her empire to operate their own independent press [*vol'naia tipografiia*].[5] Printing entrepreneurs were no longer required to apply for special permission before opening their publishing houses, but simply inform local authorities of their activities. Of course, any publication was

---

[1] Gary Marker, *Publishing, Printing, and the Origins of the Intellectual Life in Russia, 1700 – 1800* (Princeton: Princeton University Press, 1985), pp. 103 – 134.

[2] *PSZ*, Tom XIX, 13.572, 1 March 1771.

[3] *PSZ*, Tom XX, 14.495, 22 August 1776.

[4] P. S. Reifman, *Tsenzura v dorevoliutsionnoi, sovetskoi i postsovetskoi Rossii*, 2 vols (Moscow: Probel-2000, 2015), I, p. 38.

[5] *PSZ*, Tom XXI, 15.634, 15 January 1783.

subject to censure by the police, and should be careful not to print anything that was 'contrary to God's laws or civil [laws].'[6] In practice, however, this initial period of journalistic freedom was characterized by relaxed oversight and the police censured very few publications, though they technically could have.[7] As a result of these new freedoms, and the subsequent activity of private printing in the two capitals and the provinces, many new literary journals and other publications appeared during this period. Of the 11,000 books published in Russia throughout the 1700s, close to 6,500 of them were released in the last quarter of the century, and annual statistics peak in 1789 when 439 titles were released.[8]

B. I. Esin, who has written on the history of Russian publishing and journalism for decades, has emphasized the importance of these new private journals for influencing opinions in Russian society and informing the reading public about events in the world since the two Russian newspapers were still little more than announcement tools of the state.[9] Journals provided a public platform for discussing various social issues where the editors and contributing authors of various journals could express views in disagreement with one another. Gary Marker's study of Russian publishing during this period essentially argues that this is the key contribution of the publishing industry to Russian culture: creating a division between intellectual and political life, and providing this non-governmental platform for educated writers to express themselves.[10] Subsequently, Esin has identified opposing philosophical strains that manifested themselves in the journals of this period, which tended towards one of two persuasions: those that were more conservative, strongly in support of the monarchy

---

[6] Ibid.

[7] Reifman, *Tsenzura*, p. 38.

[8] Anthony Cross, *N. M. Karamzin: A Study of His Literary Career, 1783 – 1803* (Carbondale: Southern Illinois University Press, 1971), p. xv.

[9] B. I. Esin, *Istoriia russkoi zhurnalistiki, 1703 – 1917* (Moscow: Nauka, 2009), pp. 9 – 17.

[10] Marker, *Publishing*.

and the institution of serfdom, and those that were more democratic in their sympathies, opposed serfdom and tended to be less monarchial.[11]

As an 'enlightened despot', seeking to demonstrate her forward-thinking affinity to the French Enlightenment, Catherine II made some allowance for such exchange of ideas even before she opened the floodgates of private printers and authors. In 1769, for example, Catherine personally oversaw the publication of the journal *Vsiakaia vsiachina* which engaged in open polemical debate with the satirical journals of Nikolai Novikov over the nature of appropriate satire, various moral issues among the Russian nobility, and even more controversial issues such as bribery and the institution of serfdom.[12] Both *Vsiakaia vsiachina* and the satirical journals of Novikov and his circle were printed on the same press, that of the Academy of Sciences.[13]

In reaction to the French Revolution, Catherine's increased control over domestic publishing gradually brought an end to this season of relative freedom of expression. Because censorship practices were reactionary and Catherine failed to establish a specific institution for the administration of censorship, Gary Marker has argued that the result was inconsistent, sporadic censorship, though regulation was generally stricter in the 1780s and 1790s.[14] Reifman argued, however, that Catherine's increased control over publishing was not only in response to events in France, but had begun as early as 1786 with the repression of the publishing activities of Masonic presses like the one established by Novikov following the 1783 decree. Catherine feared extra-governmental secret societies like the Masons because of the influence they could potentially wield in Russia.[15] In the late 1780s and early 1790s, Catherine's tightened grip caused more books to be banned, booksellers were raided and portions of

---

[11] Ibid., pp. 15 – 16.
[12] A. G. Dement'eva and others, eds, *Russkaia periodicheskaia pechat', 1702 – 1894* (Moscow: Gosudarstvennoe izdatel'stvo politicheskoi literatury, 1959), pp. 33 – 39.
[13] I. P. Kondakov and others, eds, *Svodnyi katalog russkoi knigi grazhdanskoi pechati XVIII veka, 1725 – 1800*, 6 vols (St. Petersburg: Al'faret, 2007), IV, pp. 123 – 124, 133 – 134, 201.
[14] Marker, *Publishing*, pp. 212 – 232.
[15] Reifman, *Tsenzura*, pp. 40 – 41.

their stock confiscated and burned, and literary figures with supposed 'republican'

tendencies such as Novikov and Aleksandr Radishchev were imprisoned or exiled. The

window of publishing freedom which had been flung open in 1783 began to close and

was slammed shut in 1796 when one of Catherine's final decrees banned private

printing presses altogether,[16] placed stricter controls on the importation of foreign

books, and established local censorship commissions which amounted to greater

bureaucratic complications for authors, editors, and publishers, essentially rescinding

the decree of 1783.[17]

The numerous decrees related to printing during Paul I's short reign (1796 –

1801), going so far as to ban the importation of all foreign-language books,[18] continued

the prohibitive tendency of Catherine's later years, which was aimed at protecting

Russia and its monarchy from the dangerous ideas of revolutionary Europe, especially

France.[19] Soon after ascending the throne, however, Alexander I lifted the ban on

foreign books and reestablished the freedom of private printing, returning Russia to

something like the liberal publication policies of 1783.[20] One of Alexander's early

decrees created the Ministry of Public Education [*Ministerstvo narodnogo

prosveshcheniia*].[21] Responsibility for censorship would lie ultimately with this

ministry rather than the police and would be facilitated by officials at the universities.

In 1804, an imperial manifesto on censorship provided the objective criteria by which

these specialists were to provide censorial oversight, rather than leaving the matter to

reactionary whims.[22]

The new system and its regulation of printing and publishing were considered

liberal by contemporaries and during Alexander's reign the number of books and

---

[16] *PSZ*, Tom XXIII, 17.508, 16 September 1796.
[17] Reifman, *Tsenzura*, pp. 42 – 54.
[18] *PSZ*, Tom XXVI, 19.387, 18 April 1800.
[19] Reifman, *Tsenzura*, pp. 56 – 57.
[20] Ibid., pp. 61 – 70.
[21] *PSZ*, Tom XXVII, 20.406, 8 September 1802.
[22] *PSZ*, Tom XXVIII, 21.388, 9 July 1804.

periodicals that were published in Russia increased sharply.[23] According to Reifman, however, publishing freedom under Alexander I is best characterized as belonging to two distinctive periods: before and after 1812. The former period (1801 – 1812) featured moderate oversight, development of more modern administrative structures (such as well-ordered universities and schools, each with its own approved charter, including guidelines for censorship), and an overall atmosphere that was representative of the democratic sympathies of the Tsar and his free-thinking Francophone upbringing. Napoleon's invasion of Russia put Alexander on the defensive and this affected, among other things, censorship policy. The second period (1812 – 1825), not unlike Catherine's approach to censorship after 1789, was more reactionary and less conducive to literary freedoms. One example of this is the renewed participation of the police in censorial oversight after the Ministry of the Police was combined with the Ministry of Internal Affairs in 1819.[24] Across these early decades of the nineteenth century, Esin has identified two opposing streams of journalistic thought very similar to those suggested by Marker during Catherine's reign: conservative, pro-monarchial versus liberal, democratic, anti-serfdom.

This brief overview of Russian printing and censorship during the late eighteenth and early nineteenth century, in addition to providing the historical background for the review of periodical literature that is to follow, demonstrates that the very development of Russia's periodical press ebbed and flowed partially in response to France. Philosophical inclinations learned from French letters encouraged progress and a measure of literary freedom in the early reigns of both Catherine and Alexander. Defensive reaction to large political movements out of France stifled the press during their latter reigns of both sovereigns and the entirety of Paul's.

---

[23] V. N. Zaitsev and others, eds, *Svodnyi katalog serial'nykh izdanii Rossii, 1801 – 1825*, 3 vols (St. Petersburg: Izdatel'stvo rossiiskoi natsional'noi biblioteki, 1997 – 2006), I (1997), p. iii.
[24] Reifman, *Tsenzura*, pp. 61 – 88.

The newspaper *Sanktpeterburgskiia vedomosti*

Information about French influences in the daily lives of Russians can be observed in

the newspaper *Sanktpeterburgskiia vedomosti.* While Russia's individual literary

journals tended to be short-lived at this time, requiring the study of multiple journals in

order to cover the whole period, the newspaper *Sanktpeterburgskiia vedomosti* was

more stable, making it possible to study just one publication across the entire period of

1788 – 1825.[25] The successor of *vedomosti,* Russia's first published newspaper which

had been established by Peter the Great in 1702, *Sanktpeterburgskiia vedomosti* (as the

paper was known from 1728 onward) was published by the Academy of Sciences and

on their press and was Russia's only newspaper until 1756 when the printing press of

the newly-established Moscow University began producing a second newspaper,

Moskovskiia vedomosti. At least until the end of the eighteenth century, however, the

St. Petersburg newspaper was considered the main newspaper of Russia.[26]

Determining the reach of this newspaper—and thereby the breadth of its

influence upon Russian culture—has been complicated by the difficulty in acquiring

circulation and distribution statistics for any periodical publications during this period.

Unlike current Russian newspapers and journals, each copy of which is tagged with an

---

[25] Regarding research methodology, one issue of *Sanktpeterburgskiia vedomosti* per year was sampled across the thirty-eight-year period between 1788 and 1825, except for the years 1796 – 1800, during which one edition every other year was sampled. All eighteenth-century editions of the newspaper are kept in a special wing of the State Public Historical Library of Russia—the Department of Rare Books— which was closed unexpectedly and indefinitely for remodeling before the sampling for this study could be completed. As most issues of *Sanktpeterburgskiia vedomosti* from the eighteenth and nineteenth century have not yet been digitized, accessing them involved the retrieval of oversized hardcopy volumes which are stored behind glass in an antique bookcase, double-shelfed with other publications (often stacked horizontally) and arranged in only roughly chronological order. Once retrieved—a process that involved opening to the title pages as markings on the spine were not always legible—a volume may be read in the reading room affiliated with that collection during the same visit, making it time-consuming and impractical to return to the same bound volume on multiple occasions for the purposes of sampling. Nevertheless, reading one edition per year was sufficient to gain a general sense of the French influences evidenced by the publication, as the type of information provided was fairly consistent across the period.

[26] According to the Library of the Russian Academy of Sciences. <http://ved.infotec.ru/?r=2> [accessed 20 July 2015]

indication of the number of copies printed, known as the *tirazh*—a French loanword that did not enter the Russian language until the twentieth century—eighteenth- and nineteenth-century publications contain no such marker. Writing in 1981, Esin lamented the lack of available information, concluding that 'to follow the circulation trends [*dinamika*] of a single newspaper across the entire period of its existence would be a historian's dream.'[27] More recent scholarship, however, has provided many details that were previously unavailable. Previously uncatalogued library collections, archival documents of Russian printing presses and even private letters of editors and publishers have been studied and continue to yield additional details.[28] Though still incomplete, the circulation statistics currently available for *Sanktpeterburgskiia vedomosti* are among the most thorough compared to other publications, another reason for the paper's inclusion in the present study. For example, between the years 1788 and 1800 Russian bibliographers have determined that the number of copies printed for each issue fluctuated between 1,160 and 2,858 copies.[29] No such information is available for *Moskovskiia vedomosti* during the same period.[30]

Though the layout changed somewhat through the years, the basic format of the paper endured throughout the period. Domestic news, mostly consisting of the publication of government decrees and personnel changes for official posts, is typically the first information given in each edition. Next, foreign news, often dealing with battles and troop movements abroad, is reported. This section of the paper speaks to an important platform for French influence, namely the attention given to international politics. All eyes were on Europe and particularly the French army, especially in the 1790s and through to 1815. After reporting on foreign events, which typically consisted of translated articles from French and other European publications, *Sanktpeterburgskiia*

---

[27] B. I. Esin, *Russkaia gazeta i gazetnoe delo v Rossii* (Moscow: Izdatel'stvo MGU, 1981), p. 21.
[28] A. Iu. Samarin, 'Kak naiti tirazh?', *Pro knigi*, 4 (2008), 85 – 90.
[29] Kondakov and others, eds, *Svodnyi katalog*, IV, pp. 103 – 113.
[30] Ibid., pp. 14 – 50.

vedomosti published the latest so called 'book news.' Among other things, this section included the arrival to local booksellers of books in the French language or recently translated books from French to Russian.

The next section, one of the more useful features of the paper for the present study, is that referred to as 'personal news.' This section, similar to the classified advertisements in a modern newspaper, included various announcements of a personal or private commercial nature. The loss or discovery of personal items, notices regarding runaway servants and pets, personal items posted for sale, the sale or rent of houses and apartments, and advertisements by those requesting or offering various goods and services in the city of St. Petersburg were among the announcements printed in this section of the paper. This feature is particularly interesting because these 'personal news' reveal a continued French presence and influence in St. Petersburg across the period. French luxury goods are valued, including candy, produce, spirits, porcelain tea-sets, and carriages. French craftsmen offer their services: feather-workers, hairdressers, engravers, and chefs, to name a few. Teachers of the French language were especially sought or seeking employment, with varying degrees of intensity across the period. The same can be said of French nannies, butlers, maids, and lackeys. While not dominant, French residents themselves were also among those posting announcements. This was particularly true in the late eighteenth and early nineteenth century, but increasingly less so as the nineteenth century progressed toward the middle to end of Alexander I's reign.

Employment opportunities for Frenchmen
Upon examination of this newspaper, the first obvious indication of French influence upon the daily lives of Russians is the newspaper's reference to their employment of foreigners. The classified advertisements of *Sanktpeterburgskiia vedomosti* provide

some useful insights as to the types of jobs that French emigrants sought or were sought

for. A common phrase found in the announcements of those looking for domestic

employment stated that the individual in question 'wishes to join a respectable home'

[*zhelaet vstupit' v gospodskii dom*], often offering their services teaching the French

language to children. Such advertisements were especially prominent in the 1790s as a

wave of literate French emigrants arrived in Russia, looking for secure employment and

lodging. The following examples are typical for the period: 'An elderly Frenchman

seeks a position [*zhelaet opredelit'sia*] in the home of an aristocrat, looking after

cleanliness and order in the home, among the staff, and the looking after the carriage

[*ekipazh*].[31] If anyone is in need of such a person, he may enquire about him at the

inn…';[32] 'The Frenchman Nikolas Gatvist seeks employment in a respectable home…

looking after small children; He lives in the inn…';[33] 'A Frenchman who knows how to

read and write in French looks for employment teaching children in a home. He is

staying at…'[34] Though many of these were likely recent arrivals, others seeking such

employment in the 1790s seem to have been in Russia for some time, or were Russians

who had already benefited from a generation of readily-available instruction in the

French language: 'A certain damsel of good behaviour who is able to read and write in

French and Russian desires to join a respectable home, to teach children or to look after

the domestic economy…'[35]

Supply and demand both seem to have been strong in this job market.

Alongside the announcements by those looking for work were those submitted by

---

[31] This French loan-word, spelled differently here than in modern usage: екипаж rather than экипаж, did not appear in the Academy's dictionary (published 1789 – 94), nor was it used in Pushkin's writing. It appeared much later, in the writings of Dostoevskii and Dal''s dictionary. However, the word was present in the list of foreign words imported by Peter the Great in the early eighteenth century. This is an example of a foreign word floating around in the language for a long time before achieving literary status as part of the Russian lexicon.

[32] *Sanktpeterburgskiia vedomosti,* 6 January 1794, p. 31.

[33] Ibid., 3 January 1791, p. 9.

[34] Ibid., 3 January 1800, p. 24.

[35] Ibid., 1 January 1790, p. 9.

domestic employers who were looking for help. 'A certain nobleman [*gospodin*], who lives in his own village 350 versts from St. Petersburg [about 230 miles], wishes to have a teacher for the education of his three young children in the French and German languages and rudimentary mathematics.' The advertisement continues that enquiry about an employment contract could be made with a certain sergeant at the admiralty.[36] Another advertisement reads, 'Required in the home: a French lady [*frantsuzhenka*] to look after children; those wishing to be employed may find out about conditions near the Fontanka, across from the home of Count Sheremetev, in house number four, on the middle floor.'[37]

As early as 1800, however, occasional clues suggest that enthusiasm about hiring foreigners was not unanimous. 'One landlord… desires to have a (female) teacher [*uchitel'nitsa*] for his children, or an elderly (male) teacher [*uchitel'*]. Knowledge of the German and French language is required.' The employer will be 'satisfied with a foreigner, but a native Russian [*prirodnyi rossiianin*] would be preferable.'[38] Such advertisements hint at the reticence felt by some Russians at entrusting their children to French tutors, though the French language was a necessary part of their children's education. This could be explained by Russian suspicion as it related to the morality of Frenchmen and also by the fact that quality French instruction was more readily available in Russia by this time, and domestic employers could afford to be more discriminating. One 1810 posting stands out for its very specific standards: 'A nanny is sought for a four-year-old child.' Applicants should include those who have come from 'a convent or some other institution, who are able to speak French and [know some sort of] handiwork.'[39]

---

[36] *Sanktpeterburgskiia vedomosti*, 1 July 1796, p. 1254.
[37] Ibid., 3 January 1802, pp. 12 –13.
[38] Ibid., 3 January 1800, p. 25.
[39] Ibid., 4 January 1810, p. 19.

After the French invasion of 1812 and the tide of Russian nationalism which

followed, potential employers and employees continued to make such postings, but

those seeking positions often excluded their nationality. For example, none of those

announcing their search for employment in the first issue of 1814 included any

information about their nationality. In fact, though proficiency in French had always

been a credit to one's resume, even mention of the language seems to have been

specifically avoided. One applicant who is looking for a position doing clerical work

simply informs potential employers that he knows Russian 'and other languages.'[40]

Later, when it did became common once again to include nationality in such

announcements, additional information was included about the applicant. 'A French

subject who has good certificates seeks a position in a respectable home as a teacher or

tutor for children [*uchitelem ili guvernerom pri detiakh*].'[41] The implication is that

being a native speaker was no longer sufficient, in itself, to qualify one as a teacher.

This trend would continue and, by 1818, it was quite uncommon to see the

advertisements from employers looking for Frenchmen to teach children.

French teachers could also seek employment in official education institutions

and other non-domestic venues. The case study regarding Morancourt de Selongey, one

of the deportees featured in chapter three, included his employment at the Naval Gentry

Cadet Corps [*morskoi shliakhetnoi kadetskoi korpus*] as a teacher during the period

1790 – 1792. It seems that this very position, or one like it, was advertised in

Sanktpeterburgskiia vedomosti: 'At the Naval Gentry Cadet Corps, a teacher is wanted

for training cadets in the French language, history, and geography.'[42] Announcements

can also be found from across the period by French teachers who offer their services on

an hourly basis, something much different than being a live-in tutor or governess.

---

[40] Ibid., 2 Januay 1814, p. 6.

[41] Ibid., 4 January 1816, vtoroe pribavlenie, p. vii.

[42] *Sanktpeterburgskiia vedomosti*, 1 January 1790, p. 7.

Though, in the later years of Alexander I's reign, *Sanktpeterburgskiia vedomosti* contains fewer advertisements for French nannies and domestic tutors, it seems that native speakers were still highly valued at the academic level at this time. In 1816 the need for three very specific educators was published: a Russian, a Frenchman, and a German who could each teach their own native language and divide teaching duties among themselves for geography, physics, natural history, and arithmetic. Those interested in applying were instructed to enquire at the bookseller of the Academy of Sciences.[43]

Beyond the field of education, foreigners, including the French, were valued for their skills in various other professions as well. In 1794, for example, an inn in St. Petersburg announced the following vacancy: 'Wanted from among the Frenchmen or Germans: a master chef [*iskusnoi povar*].'[44] Extensive study has already been made of the various professions in which French citizens living in St. Petersburg were engaged as of 1793, as reported in the list of those participating in the obligatory oath-swearing ceremony. Beyond those professional or service-oriented jobs discussed in the previous chapter, a number of classified ads in *Sanktpeterburgskiia vedomosti* show some examples of miscellaneous work and odd jobs available to foreigners. In 1806 a maid and personal servant who spoke German and French were sought to accompany someone preparing for a trip to Berlin.[45] Conversely, in 1810, a foreigner who was able to speak, read, and write Russian, German, and French sought employment as a domestic steward [*domopravitelem*] or for trips abroad as a valet [*kammerdinerom*].[46] This does not seem to have been entirely uncommon. For his famous journey into Europe, Nikolai Karamzin reports that he likewise procured the services of 'a Frenchman, a hired lackey, who accompanied me' [*naemnoi lakei, provozhavshii*

---

[43] Ibid., 4 January 1816, vtoroe pribavlenie, p. viii.

[44] Ibid., 6 January 1794, p. 33.

[45] Ibid., 2 January 1806, p. 10.

[46] Ibid., 4 January 1810, p. 19.

meniia].[47] Another foreigner, proficient in French, German, and Russian, was simply looking for a position as a conversation partner [*sobesednikom*].[48]

Daily life: French goods, services, and books

The advertisements of various French merchants, craftsmen, and other professionals show another form of cultural influence, the introduction of various goods and services to the Russian public. Though the very presence of French labour and French items in the open marketplace suggests at least some measure of cultural exposure to the general populous, these goods and services still seem to have been primarily available to upper-class Russians, though no longer exclusively those at court. In 1790, long before Russia had anything resembling an indigenous restaurant culture of its own, the following announcement appeared in the paper: 'The Frenchman Reno hereby notifies that he offers lunch [*daet obedennoi stol*] at a very fair price,' also offering dishes that may be taken home. From Reno, one could 'always receive and special-order various types of pies and patés, both hot and cold for the road. He lives on Nevskii Prospekt in the home of *gospodin* Gubkina, number 66 on the first floor.'[49] Russian merchants often advertised imported French goods in the newspaper, following the Franco-Russian trade agreement of 1786, including *ranety* (a type of apple), vodka, and white wine. French craftsmen and entrepreneurs advertised their private businesses, marketing specialized skills related to luxury items. In 1794, a French craftsman specializing in feathers [*pliumazhnago mastera*] practiced his trade in a very prominent district of the capital. This specialist, one 'Natiera, who lives on Bol'shaia Milionnaia [Street] across from His Excellency Count Ivan Andreevich Osterman' offers 'various types of feathers for hats, for ladies' and theatre attire [*damskikh i teatral'nykh uborov*] and for the decoration of

---

[47] Nikolai Karamzin, 'Pis'ma russkago puteshestvennika', *Moskovskoi zhurnal,* 1 (1791), p. 174.
[48] *Sanktpeterburgskiia vedomosti,* 2 January 1812, p. 9.
[49] *Sanktpeterburgskiia vedomosti,* 1 January 1790, p. 11.

carriages [*ekipazhei*], beds and the like.' In addition to selling new feathers, Natiera

was also able to 'wash [feathers] like new and dye [them] any colour.'[50] The same

edition of the paper carried an advertisement for another Frenchman, an engraver named

Gripo, who lived in the same building. Gripo offered his services 'engraving emblems

[*pechati*] and name monograms on precious stones and all types of metal.'[51] Obviously,

announcements of such services were primarily of interest to those Russians who could

afford them, an indication of the newspaper's intended audience. Sometimes, even the

language of the announcements themselves referenced their exclusive nature. In 1798,

the following notice appeared as a classified advertisement in the paper: 'A French

dressmaker, arrived here from London, offers her services to the respectable public

[*pochtennoi publike*].' Like the previous businessmen, her residence was on Bol'shaia

Milionnaia Street.[52] The elite nature of other advertisements was even more

pronounced, as they were published only in French. Though the newspaper was

published almost entirely in Russian, the occasional paragraph in French was not

uncommon. This is true, for example, of a French-language posting from 1810 in which

a tobacco merchant gives the address, also on Bol'shaia Milionnaia, where people can

purchase snuff and smoking tobacco.[53]

Another form of cultural influence evident in *Sanktpeterburgskiia vedomosti*

during this period was the availability of French books, the demand for which had been

growing significantly in Russia since the time of Peter the Great according to recent

scholarship. During Peter's reign dozens of young noblemen began studying French,

and the emperor encouraged the practice of importing foreign books with various

---

[50] Ibid., 3 January 1794, p. 15.
[51] Ibid.
[52] Ibid., 1 January 1798, p. 15.
[53] Ibid., 4 January 1810, p. 16.

incentives such as discounted customs tariffs on printed materials from abroad.[54] His

reforms also led to the printing of secular books inside Russian, many of them in foreign

languages.[55] During the reigns of Anna and Elizabeth (1730 – 1761) the study of

French became one of the so called 'gentry sciences' and this priority was reflected in

the curriculums of the Cadet Corps, Moscow University, private schools and in the

hiring of foreign governesses. From the 1730s to 1750s Russian book publishers and

sellers could not keep up with the Russian demand for French books, even though

multiple copies of over 3,000 different French books passed through the hands of the

Academy during that period.[56] By the 1740s, the Petersburg Academy of Sciences

contained about 4,000 French books. In the 1730s French books had ranked third in

popularity in Russia among foreign books after Latin and German. Just two decades

later, in 1752, French literature accounted for 59% of the entire book trade in Russia.[57]

Beginning in the 1750s, at least 2,000 – 3,000 Russian people each year were studying

French, especially young noblewomen whose home-based education included the study

of foreign languages, particularly French.[58] Among the important factors related to the

circulation of all books, including those published in French, were the growing library

of the Petersburg Academy of Sciences for which books were procured, the expanse of

printing presses in Russia, the initiation of book exchange programs, increased public

access brought on by the advent of Moscow's book *lavki* [small booksellers, literally

'benches'], and the general growth of Russia's book-selling industry. Parallel to this

generic trend towards increased access to published materials is the spread of

---

[54] N.A. Kopanev, 'Frantsuzskaia kniga i russkaia kul'tura v seredine XVIII veka' (unpublished doctoral dissertation, Leningrad State University, 1990).

[55] Ibid.

[56] N.A. Kopanev, 'Frantsuzskaia kniga i russkaia kul'tura v seredine XVIII veka' (unpublished doctoral dissertation, Leningrad State University, 1990), p. 11.

[57] L.A. Letaeva, 'Frantsuzskaia kniga v kul'turnom prostranstve Rossii serediny vtoroi poloviny XVIII veka', in *Frantsiia – Rossiia: problema kul'turnykh diffuzii*, ed. by L.I. Lipskaia (Tiumen': Tipografiia 'Pechatnik', 2008), pp. 28–35.

[58] Natal'ia Pushkareva, 'Russian Noblewoman's Education in the Home as Revealed in Late Eighteenth- and Early Nineteenth-Century Memoirs', in *Women and Gender in Eighteenth-Century Russia*, ed. Wendy Rosslyn (Burlington, VT: Ashgate, 2003), pp. 111–128.

specifically French-language reading, both geographically and across social classes. In the middle of the eighteenth century it was mostly titled nobility who read French books, but during the last half of the century lower nobility, merchants, and other non-nobles did so as well,[59] and French-language book collections from the eighteenth century have recently been found as far away as the Vologda Oblast'.[60]

As elsewhere in the world, there was a great demand for French books in Russia, not only due to a love for French literature, but also because the great literary works from all over Europe were being translated into French, the *lingua franca* of the eighteenth-century literate world. The works of Thomas Hobbes, John Locke, and Gottfried Leibniz were primarily circulated throughout Europe in the eighteenth century, not in the original English and German, but in their French translations.[61] As Russia joined the other nations of the western world as a formidable trade and naval power, Russians began to desire French books to give them a broader view of the world they were joining. French influence can even be seen in the decorative designs printed on the title pages of Russian books published in the eighteenth century. These ornamental designs, known as vignettes, were likely obtained by Russian printers through German intermediaries, but the borrowed Rococo style betrays their French origin.[62] The book culture being fostered in the young Russian empire was quite literally embossed with French inspiration.

As this brief overview of recent scholarship on Russia's eighteenth-century book trade illustrates, this particular area of cultural import was well established by the beginning of the period which is of interest to the present study. French literature,

---

[59] Letaeva, 'Frantsuzskaia kniga', pp. 32–33.

[60] M.G. Il'iushina, *Frantsuzskaia kul'tura v russkoi provintsii (vologodskii krai): materialy chtenii* (Vologda: Vologodskaia oblastnaia universal'naia nauchnaia biblioteka im. I.V. Babushkina, 2000).

[61] Marc Fumaroli, *When the World Spoke French,* trans. by Richard Howard (New York: New York Review Books, 2001), p. 241.

[62] E.V. Borshch, 'K voprosu o frantsuzskom proiskhozhdenii russkikh knizhnykh vin'etok XVIII v.', in *Frantsiia – Rossiia: problem kul'turnykh diffuzii,* ed. by L.I. Lipskaia (Tiumen': Tipografiia 'Pechatnik', 2008), pp. 36–40.

recent translations of academic works from French, Russian-French dictionaries, and the like were advertised regularly in *Sanktpeterburgskiia vedomosti* across the entire period. The prominent advertisement space just after domestic and foreign news headlines was regularly allotted to the book shop of the Academy of Sciences. This section, entitled 'book news' nearly always included books from, about, or related to France, French culture, the French language, or the findings of French scholars. Likewise, advertisements posted in the classified ads by private book *lavki* regularly featured French offerings. A typical example from 1806 advertises 'Christmas gifts for children, various pocket-sized books [*karmannyia knizhki*] for 1806, the newest French and German books, many new musical works, [sheet music for] piano, flute, violin, and so forth. For a reasonable price' these items may be purchased at 'F. Dinemann and Company, on Nevskaia Perspektiva in the Veberov house, ascending one flight of stairs.'[63]

Though other forms of overt cultural influence—employment adverts related to French emigrants, specific reference to French merchants, and even coverage of foreign news from France—seemed to wane after 1815, the availability of French books remains constant across the entire period studied. Even during the turbulent atmosphere of the French Revolution and later Napoleonic Wars, this tendency never seems to diminish. There were, however, instances where political sentiments are expressed along with the announcement of these resources. For example, a book review of a collection of anecdotal narrative accounts from 1789 France was published in 1804. The passion with which the book is recommended by the newspaper's editors leaves little doubt as to the official position towards events in France. 'People with a gentle spirit, with a sensitive heart, will find much... that they will like in this book.' The review promises a captivating read, because here are depicted 'some events that

---

[63] *Sanktpeterburgskiia vedomosti*, 2 January 1806, pp. 9 – 10.

happened in France at the beginning of the revolution, incidents which arouse the deepest compassion for the unhappy victims of the onset of national blindness [*narodnogo oslepleniia*].'[64] Later, despite the so called 'patriotic' rhetoric which disparaged the acceptance of French elements for a short time, it does not seem that political realities themselves ever actually diminished Russia's connection with French culture. In fact, after 1812, *Sanktpeterburgskiia vedomosti* announced the establishment of a sanctioned French-language newspaper, *Conservateur Impartial*, published in St. Petersburg. Like *Sanktpeterburgskiia vedomosti*, it was printed twice weekly and subscriptions could be made by post from any city in the Russian empire. Subscribers outside of the capital had only to pay an additional delivery fee.[65] Though marketed as a regular newspaper, *Conservateur Impartial* was actually a propaganda project of the Russian Ministry of Foreign Affairs, and, as such, which was allotted an annual operating budget of 13,000 rubles by special imperial decree.[66] This French-language paper ran from 1812 to 1825, a mark of the continued relevance of the French language and the diplomatic importance of Francophone readership to the Russian state.[67]

Russian literary journals

While these newspaper excerpts reflect influences that French culture exerted on the daily lives of Russians through immigration, books, and commerce, Russian literary journals contain evidence of a different kind of influence which is much broader. Russians with a professional interest in shaping their own nation's culture—writers, publishers, educators, and patrons of the arts—were reaching abroad to France and

---

[64] Ibid., 1 January 1804, p. 16.

[65] Ibid., 2 Januay 1814, vtoroe pribavlenie, p. iii.

[66] *PSZ*, Tom XXXII, 25.374, 22 April 1813.

[67] T. N. Zhukovskaia, 'Izdaniia epokhi Aleksandra I v N'iu-Iorkskoi publichnoi biblioteke', *Rossika v SShA. Materialy k istorii russkoi politicheskoi emigratsii*, 7 (2001), 205 – 226; F. A. Brokgauz and I. A. Efron, eds, *Entsiklopedicheskii slovar'*, 82 vols (St. Petersburg: Tipo-litografia I. A. Efrona, 1890 – 1904), XIV (1892), p. 805.

emulating French culture at its source. Even before considering their content, it is worth noting that Russia's literary journals were, themselves, established in emulation of their French counterparts. In other words, whereas French immigrants had brought cultural influence to the everyday lives of individual Russians, there was a Russian-led process of widespread cultural development which featured the formation of indigenous cultural institutions, in this case the literary journal, fashioned after French examples. This process, a much older form of influence reminiscent of Peter the Great's foundation of his Academy of Sciences after the French model, was certainly enhanced by Catherine's initiation of foreign immigration, but was rooted in Russian interaction with French culture through the written word and travels abroad.

One of the journals included in the present study, *S: Peterburgskii Merkurii*, obviously borrowed its title from a popular French journal, *Mercure de France*. The editors make their emulation quite clear in the foreword to the journal's first issue:

> 'The goal of our publication is two-fold: both a desire to satisfy and be useful to our readers. There are a multitude of periodical publications; many good ones; But there are barely two journals in our language which are similar to the foreign journals... why not tell the public about new works of Russian literature? Why not announce about the theatre, what new [plays] are performed there and how [well] they were performed? This is an allowed right [*sie pravo pozvolennoe*], and we want to take advantage of it.'[68]

This jealous question, 'why do we not have such?' is a recurrently expressed motivation. For example, Russian writers had been inspired by foreign authors in their use of short anecdotes as a narrative genre. In an early issue of *Merkurii*, the editors present a collection of distinctly 'Russian anecdotes' [*rossiiskiia anekdoty*] written for Russians, by Russians, and (as a matter of principle) about Russians. There had already been many 'volumes of French, English, and German anecdotes' published. The editor asks, rhetorically, 'have Russians really done less, both good and evil, than others?'[69]

---

[68] *S: Peterburgskii merkurii*, 1 (1793), pp. iii – iv.
[69] *S: Peterburgskii merkurii*, 1 (1793), p. 82.

Russia had its own story to tell. A similar justification is given for the creation of an almanac of Russian poetry:

> 'In almost every European language a collection is published each year of new short poems [*melkikh stikhotvorenii*], known as a calendar of the Muses (*almanac des Muses*); I wanted to produce something similar in Russian as well, for lovers of poetry: Here is the first attempt by the name of *Aonidy*.'

An asterisk after the word *Aonidy* refers the reader to a footnote explaining that this is simply 'another name for the Muses.'[70] This periodical was obviously created in the image of the French poetry journal *L'Almanach des Muses*. Having interacted with French literary journals, Russian literary scholars were now seeing the need to create their own version of them in which to feature the works of Russian authors. Both of the French journals mentioned above were often cited and borrowed from by various Russian journals. For example, a number of the theatre reviews published in 1791 – 1792 were translations of articles from *Mercure de France*. Likewise, the editors of a Russian journal in 1799 specifically reference the 1797 edition of *Almanach des Muses* for their centennial tribute to the French fabulist Jean de La Fontaine.[71]

Russia's literary tradition developed, in large measure, due to its emulation of that of France. Russian authors and editors showed remarkable self-awareness of this fact and were simultaneously pushing forward in search of cultural independence. In rhymed verse addressed to the Muses, a Russian poet in 1799 made optimistic declaration that Russian culture was finding its own voice in a literary tradition that was less and less dependent upon foreign importation:

> You do not spoil the Russian language
> With the mixture of many foreign [*chuzhye*] words
> But, knowing how great the beauty in it
> For clear prose and verse
> And how strong the Russian word is
> Rich, full, and abundant

---

[70] *Aonidy, ili sobranie raznykh, novykh stikhotvorenii*, 1 (1796), p. iii.
[71] *Ippokrena*, 2 (1799), p. 54.

> You do not seek French words
> And into clear syllable you do not lead them
> But you find many Russian words,
> In which are more beauty.[72]

Of course this sentiment is not entirely accurate. On the contrary, French word import was increasing at this time and was yet to reach its peak. Russian authors were still very much influenced by the French books that they read. What this poem represents, however, is the growing desire for independence and self-identity and the forms of Russian expression that interaction with French culture was inspiring.

All of this underscores particular relevance of Russian literary journals as a source of insight into nature of French cultural influence during this crucial period. Unlike the one long-running newspaper examined in this chapter, however, eighteenth-century Russian journals were typically published for a relatively short time, some lasting only a few issues. As such, it was necessary to study a number of different journals in order to gain a sense of the French influences discernible across the entire period, using the chronological card catalogue of periodical literature at the State Public Historical Library of Russia in Moscow to explore the body of available material from this period.[73] Preference was given to those journals which ran for at least a year, in order to trace patterns within the relative stability of a single publication. In addition to this criterion of simple longevity, priority was placed on those publications which most included original Russian expression. Much of what was published in these journals, particularly the earlier ones, included little more than translated foreign literature,

---

[72] 'Oda v chest' moemu drugu', *Ippokrena*, 4 (1799), pp. 21 – 22.

[73] The sampling methodology for the short-lived eighteenth-century journals was different than that used with the newspaper as the style, structure, and content of each publication varied, making it less predictable which sections of a given journal would contain information relevant to the present study. Tables of contents, where available, were consulted for every issue and relevant articles read. Otherwise, the twentieth page of every edition was sampled in search of passing references to French cultural influence and the use of French loanwords. For the one journal with a long publication run, *Vestnik Evropy*, which was published more often and contained many more pages per issue than the other journals, a method of sampling similar to that used with the newspaper was employed.

particularly that of France. To be sure, a Russian journal's choice of materials to be published and the way in which they were translated yield its own set of insights. Of greater interest to the present study, however, are those thoughts recorded by the Russians themselves and how those original Russian thoughts bear the marks of French influence. Finally, though much of the material available in the journals is literary—poems, short-stories and songs—priority has been given to those journals which include cultural expression beyond these literary genres. That is to say, commentary on contemporary Russian culture, opinions, and descriptions of Russian practices were preferred to artistic collections of literary expression, much of which was initially emulative of France's literary tradition and could be quite detached from what was actually happening inside of Russia. Ultimately, however, in order to cover the entire period 1786 – 1825, extant Russian journals had to be chosen which met the above criteria with varying degrees of consistency.

Lekarstvo ot skuki i zabot was a weekly journal which ran for about one year (1786 – 87) and published translations of foreign short-stories, Russian poetry, riddles, and moralistic parables, and commentary on foreign political events. Though printed on the aforementioned independent press of Johann Schnoor and therefore a private publication not speaking on behalf of the state, it is unlikely that the editorial sympathies behind this journal were in any way anti-monarchial. The editor, F. O. Tumanskii, was in state service for much of his later career and eventually became one of the stricter censorship officials in Riga during the reign of Paul I. As a censor, he was notorious for long, slow review processes and the detention of many books at the border. One prominent bookseller made a special trip from Riga to St. Petersburg to file a complaint against Tumanskii. The reply that he received from a Russian senator was that 'it would be better for hundreds of good books to be burned than for one to slip by in which may be found even a single expression containing the slightest revolutionary hint.'[74] Another account suggests that it was Tumanskii who, in 1800, denounced a certain pastor for having French books in his library with revolutionary overtones, for which the pastor was sentenced to receive twenty lashes with a whip.[75] These anecdotal accounts demonstrate both the charged climate of paranoia to come and the sympathies for which Tumanskii would later come to be known. *Lekarstvo ot skuki i zabot,* however, was published during a window of relative freedom on one of the many independent presses that sprang up across Russia following Catherine's 1783 decree. The journal included interesting information about foreign cultures and occasional fashion 'news' from Paris. French influence is visible in these references to French fashion, satirical reference to immigrant teachers and servants from France, and some mention of French history and politics, though in no dominant sense as such information for other European countries and the Ottoman Empire was included just as often.

Published weekly over a six-month period in 1788, *Utrennie chasy* was a literary journal that featured a great deal of philosophical discourse and moral instruction. The titles of some of the short literary pieces in this journal included 'on good deeds', 'justice', 'human life and death', 'charity', 'on the greatness of God', and 'on man and the insignificance of earthly things.' The moralistic nature of this journal makes it an insightful source on Russian values at the time, including occasional commentary on western influence inside of Russia. The journal was published on the presses of I. G. Rakhmaninov, another one of the many private publishers who sprang up in Russia following Catherine's 1783 decree. Though original work by Russian authors was included, much of the journal consisted of translations from French literary journals. Rakhmaninov himself was a prolific translator of Voltaire and later went on to publish a

---

[74] P. S. Reifman, *Tsenzura*, p. 58.
[75] Ibid., p. 59.

collection of all Voltaire's works available in Russian at the time.[76] Ironically, Rakhmaninov's affinity for Voltaire—an intellectual hero of Catherine's—made him a target during the revolutionary paranoia of the 1790s when a portion of his published materials were confiscated as potentially subversive in a police raid.[77] This particular journal, published by those with an interest in French literature, but in a journalistic tradition which critically observed Russia's cultural connection with the West, was released just before Catherine's reactionary measures. The few extant details about the printing and circulation of *Utrennie chasy* reveal that the journal's reach, though limited, extended beyond the capital cities. This was one of several journals published during this period that sent over half of its subscriptions to Russian provinces.[78] According to the journal's published list of subscribers, one hundred and five copies were distributed, though several hundred copies of each volume of the journal were found among the books confiscated from Rakhmaninov's publishing house in 1794.[79] Rakhmaninov's short-lived press operated in St. Petersburg during the stint of this journal's publication, but was transferred to the village of Kazinka—some three hundred miles south of Moscow—in 1791, where its operations continued until 1794.[80]

Another publication, *Satiricheskii vestnik* (1790 – 1791), was obviously intended to be a spoof version of a newspaper like *Moskovskie* or *Sanktpeterburgskiia vedomosti*. The sections of the journal are fashioned after newspaper headings: 'items for sale', 'arrivals and departures', and 'news' [*izvestie*]. Clearly, however, this journalistic structure is entirely satirical. None of the articles or announcements is intended to be taken seriously, a fact made clear by the dates. For example, one of the news stories of

---

[76] A. G. Dement'eva and others, eds, *Russkaia periodicheskaia pechat', 1702 – 1894* (Moscow: Gosudarstvennoe izdatel'stvo politicheskoi literatury, 1959), p. 77.

[77] I. P. Kondakov and others, eds, *Svodnyi katalog russkoi knigi grazhdanskoi pechati XVIII veka, 1725 – 1800*, 6 vols (St. Petersburg: Al'faret, 2007), IV, p. 205; Reifman, *Tsenzura*, p. 53.

[78] Gary Marker, 'The Creation of Journals and the Profession of Letters in the Eighteenth Century', in *Literary Journals in Imperial Russia*, ed. by Deborah A. Martinsen (Cambridge: Cambridge University Press, 1997), p. 25.

[79] Kondakov and others, eds, *Svodnyi katalog*, IV, p. 205.

[80] Ibid., p. 283, n. 1, p. 289, n. 8.

this journal is reported to have occurred 'on the 325th day of an unknown month.'[81]

Another is dated 'the year 897167.'[82] The journal was published in nine parts and while

specific circulation statistics are unavailable, the fact that all nine parts were released

speaks to the journal's popularity. A second printing of the first three parts was done

shortly thereafter, and the first seven parts were reprinted in 1795.[83] The journal was

printed on the printing press of Moscow University during a short period in which the

press was leased by V. I. Okorokova. Previously, from 1779 to 1789, Nikolai Novikov

had leased this same press.[84] The editor and primary author of *Satiricheskii vestnik*, N.

I. Strakhov, had previously been in Novikov's literary and publishing circle and this

journal continues in his satirical tradition.[85] According to one Soviet historian, this

journal was one of a very few that actually did so during this period.[86] After the

'intense but short-lived' period of satirical journalism led by Novikov in 1769 – 1774, a

number of journals from 1780 onward purported to be satirical, but should be more

precisely categorized as 'humourous' journals, sharing the entertaining style of

Novikov's work but carefully avoiding controversy, thereby falling short of actual

satire. Strakhov's journal, however, does not shy away from issues such as serfdom and

the morals of the nobility. Through the use of humour and false narrative, the author

pokes fun at his own Russian culture, including the quirks of modern society and modes

of fashion. As for French influence, what these authors satirize tells a lot about the

types of French influence observed at the end of the eighteenth century and

stereotypical opinion of them within society. The bumbling of French teachers,

prevalence of imported fashions, popularity of local French shops, and the wild

clamouring of Russians for all things French are treated with biting humour. Also

---

[81] *Satiricheskii vestnik,* 3 (1790), p. 68.

[82] Ibid., 9 (1792), p. 62.

[83] Kondakov and others, eds, *Svodnyi katalog*, IV, pp. 187 – 188.

[84] Kondakov and others, eds, *Svodnyi katalog*, IV, pp. 187 – 188, 286, 287

[85] A. V. Zapadov, *Russkaia zhurnalistika XVIII veka* (Moscow: Nauka, 1964), pp. 204 – 206.

[86] P. N. Berkov, *Istoriia russkoi zhurnalistiki XVIII veka* (Moscow: Izdatel'stvo akademii nauk, 1952), p. 435.

satirized is the superficial nature of the Russian nobility as it relates to the French

language. Russians are depicted using individual French words and phrases as a

prestigious token of their supposed refinement. Depicted in numerous articles, the

Russian *petimetr* [a dandy or fop after the French fashion] embodies the pretentious

vanity associated with one who puts on airs through by mimicking French cultural

elements.

This journal essentially maintains a tone of contempt for Gallomania that began

earlier in Russia.[87] One historian refers to this period of journalistic and dramatic satire

as a 'fight against gallomania' in which Aleksandr Sumarokov, Nikolai Novikov, Denis

Fonvizin and other authors were not merely poking fun, but genuinely felt threatened

and sought to protect Russian society from what they felt to be harmful French

influences. Fonvizin, for example, is said to have feared the 'danger' of following the

cultural path that France had taken in the 1770s.[88] The French clothing, language, and

manners adopted by wealthy Russians were seen as something artificial and foreign.

Publicly, these Russians acted out life in fashionable European style as if on a stage,

while their domestic manner was drastically different; simpler and more Russian.

Further, French cultural behaviour became associated with a frivolous, trite attitude

towards life, moral lapse, and the atheism of the French enlightenment. Satirical

journals often made the 'connection between the young fop's infatuation with all things

French and his inhuman treatment of his peasants, his carefree attitude towards family

ties and his obligations as a citizen.'[89] Vladimir Lukin, another prominent eighteenth-

century writer in this vein, exemplified this inclination to associate French influence

with immorality, seeming to believe that 'anyone afflicted with Gallomania' must be

---

[87] See my discussion of critical literary reaction to Gallomania in eighteenth-century Russia in chapter
one, pp. 52 – 53 and chapter five, pp. 295 – 296.
[88] I. Z. Serman, 'Rossiia i Zapad', in *Russia and the West in the Eighteenth Century,* ed. by A.G. Cross
(Newtonville: Oriental Research Partners, 1983), pp. 59–63.
[89] Rogger, *National Consciousness in Eighteenth-Century Russia,* p. 57.

'incapable of the virtue which the theatre ought to instil in audiences.'[90] *Satiricheskii vestnik*, published not long after 1789, is obviously reminiscent of this earlier attitude.

Moskovskoi zhurnal, which ran for two years (1791 – 1792), was the creation of one man, Nikolai Karamzin. It presented news about the release of foreign books, recent translations into Russian, the repertoire of Parisian and Moscow theatres, and original Russian writing. Like *Satiricheskii vestnik,* it was printed on the presses of Moscow University. According to subscription lists, 258 complete sets of the issues printed in 1791 were distributed and 274 sets of those published in 1792.[91] The entire collection was republished in a second edition in 1803, a mark of the journal's popularity and the rising fame of Karamzin.[92] In addition to its importance for Karamzin's early career, according to Anthony Cross, *Moskovskoi zhurnal* was important to the broader development of Russian literature.[93] Marking a departure from earlier Russian journals which had been moralistic or satirical, Karamzin looked to western examples to produce a true literary journal. One feature, novel for this period, is the journal's inclusion of original Russian short stories, a practice that would be emulated by future Russian journals. Previously, almost all of the short stories published in Russian journals were translations of foreign works. Of particular interest in this journal is the original release of Karamzin's famous *Pis'ma russkago puteshestvennika* in serial instalments. Also, this was the first Russian journal to contain a regular section dedicated to theatrical and literary criticism.[94] The journal included book reviews, poems, anecdotes, and a section entitled *smes'*, a gossip column of sorts, about European events. French influence is evident in Karamzin's obvious fascination with French culture. In addition to the latest repertoire of French theatres,

---

[90] D. J. Welsh, 'Satirical Themes in Eighteenth-Century Russian Comedies', *The Slavonic and East European Review,* 42 (1964), 413.

[91] Kondakov and others, eds, *Svodnyi katalog*, IV, pp. 149 – 151.

[92] Dement'eva and others, eds, *Russkaia periodicheskaia pechat'*, pp. 85 – 86.

[93] Anthony Cross, 'Karamzin's "Moskovskii Zhurnal": Voice of a Writer, Broadsheet of a Movement', *Cahiers du Monde russe et soviétique,* 28 (1987), 121 – 126.

[94] Dement'eva and others, eds, *Russkaia periodicheskaia pechat'*, pp. 85 – 86.

the publication included translated articles from French journals, many of the foreign

books reviewed were French, and many of the 'new' Russian books reviewed were

translations from French. Finally, a number of the anecdotes recounted were those

relating to the French nobility.

S: Peterburgskii merkurii, a literary journal, edited by Ivan Krylov and

Aleksandr Klushin and published during 1793, contains Russian poetry, verses, odes,

short-stories, book reviews, anecdotes, and a few theatrical reviews. Though he is

remembered primarily as a fabulist, Krylov's lesser-known journalist career is also

significant, particularly his contribution to the development of the satire genre in the

1780s and 1790s. Rather than targeting individuals, Krylov was more nuanced in his

approach and, through his use of language, parodied an entire style of writing: the

language of Russia's official newspapers.[95] Krylov printed the first issues of this

journal himself. I. Krylov and Associates, operating from 1792 to 1794, was one of the

last independent presses in existence during this period of rapidly narrowing freedom of

the press.[96] Due to increased censorship activity, circulation of several issues was

delayed, and the complications of dealing with this bureaucracy became overwhelming

for Krylov. Subsequently, he made a deal with the Academy of Sciences which

transferred publication of the journal to their presses, where 580 copies of all issues

were printed.[97] *S: Peterburgskii merkurii* is the last journal included in the present

study to have been published on a privately-owned printing press. As these printing

details demonstrate, the aforementioned revolutionary paranoia of the state and

subsequent suppression of publishing was in full force by this time. At the time this

journal was released, the earlier satirist Novikov was already languishing in the

Shlissel'burg fortress near St. Petersburg for his supposedly subversive publishing

---

[95] Berkov, *Istoriia russkoi zhurnalistiki,* pp. 478 – 496.

[96] Kondakov and others, eds, *Svodnyi katalog*, IV, pp. 186 – 187, 282, n. 2.

[97] Ibid., pp. 186 – 187.

activities.[98] Like Strakhov's *Satiricheskii vestnik,* Krylov's journal continued in the

tradition of Novikov's genre, but was more careful, usually avoiding direct reference to

controversial socio-political issues.[99]

The only overt French influence in this journal seems to be the idea for the

publication itself. The title of the journal is obviously borrowed from a French

publication of the same name: *Mercure de France.* Likewise, the editor's justification

for the publication's existence is that there are so few Russian periodicals that

accomplish what the foreign journals accomplish: showcasing new creations by native

writers.[100] Though theatrical reviews are promised in the introduction to this journal

(something reminiscent of Parisian cultural life) there is very little of this in the actual

issues. The names of literary genres, such as *romans,* and other occasional French

loanwords (such as *koketka*) are among the few overtly French borrowings.

Another literary journal, *Priiatnoe i poleznoe preprovozhdenie vremeni* (1794) is

filled with poetry, short-stories, satire, songs, and articles. This and all later eighteenth-

century journals featured in the present chapter were printed on the press of Moscow

University, which was leased during the entire period 1794 – 1800 to the booksellers

Kh. Ridiger and Kh. A. Klaudii.[101] Though statistics for this journal related to the

number of copies printed and distributed have not yet come to light, the context of its

distribution is clear. This journal was included as an optional insert to *Moskovskiia*

vedomosti, Russia's second most important newspaper during the period, and

subscribers could receive it for an additional fee.[102] While not providing hard

circulation facts, this connection with *Moskovskiia vedomosti* suggests at least the

potential for a broad reach. Some of the published works were translations from

---

[98] Reifman, *Tsenzura,* pp. 41 – 46.

[99] Dement'eva and others, eds, *Russkaia periodicheskaia pechat',* pp. 91 – 92.

[100] *S: Peterburgskii merkurii,* 1 (1793), pp. iii – iv.

[101] Kondakov and others, eds, *Svodnyi katalog,* IV, pp. 173 – 174, 287.

[102] Ibid., pp. 173 – 174.

European languages (mostly French and German) and others were written by Russian authors. This journal also featured a genre which may be called wisdom literature, such as parables, a hypothetical conversation between a father and son which bestows counsel for life, and so forth. French influence can be seen in the form of published translations from French.

Aglaia is another literary journal by Karamzin, published in the period 1794 – 1795 and featuring only the work of Russian authors. After leaving *Moskovskoi zhurnal,* Karamzin followed the French precedent of publishing an annual almanac of recent poetry and began producing this collection of Russian verse. According to William Mills Todd III, publication of this 'elegant pocket-sized volume' of Russian poetry was marketed to a reading public 'with pretenses to refinement.'[103] Distinguished by its categorical exclusion of translated material, this and other almanacs (*Aonidy*, for example) was an important vehicle for the spread of original Russian poetry and literature. The reach and influence of these almanacs extended well beyond the geographical and chronological context of their publication. The nineteenth century historian Vasilii Kliuchevskii (1841 – 1911) recalled that, as a young boy growing up in a Russian province, *Agalaia* was one of the first books read to him at a time and in a region 'where a non-church book was a great rarity.'[104] In addition to Russian poetry, this journal also includes the continuation of Karamzin's *Pis'ma russkago puteshestvennika.*

A subsequent project of Karamzin, *Aonidy*, was released in 1796 – 1799. Like *Aglaia,* this is was Karamzin's attempt at a Russian version of European almanacs which featured the contemporary verse of their popular poets from the past year.

---

[103] William Mills Todd III, 'Periodicals in Literary Life of the Early Nineteenth Century', in *Literary Journals in Imperial Russia*, ed. by Deborah A. Martinsen book (Cambridge: Cambridge University Press, 1997), p. 46.

[104] As cited in Anthony Cross, *N. M. Karamzin: A Study of his Literary Career, 1783 – 1803* (Carbondale: Southern Illinois University Press, 1971), p. 219.

Produced during the reign of Paul I, characterized by strict control over print media, *Aonidy* proved to be a frustrating project for Karamzin. In a personal letter to fellow author Ivan Dmitriev, Karamzin complained that specific works had been edited out of *Aonidy* by official censors. His *poslanie k zhenshchinam* ('an epistle to women') was deemed inappropriate, and other works were censured for referencing foreign authors who were now considered 'republicans', though they had long been read in official circles. Melodramatically, Karamzin concluded in his letter that it would be better to quit altogether rather than submit to such a 'vile operation' and that such smothering regulations would cause him to 'disappear' as an author.[105] Obviously, Karamzin did not quit, nor did he disappear, but this episode illustrates the restrictive conditions under which creative thinkers were working at the very end of the eighteenth century.

While most of the works published in *Aglaia* had been written by Karamzin himself, Karamzin recruited a broader circle of authors for this almanac. Lamenting the lack of native works, Karamzin did include some foreign translations in *Aonidy*, especially the works of Voltaire and Jean de La Fontaine.[106] French influence seems to be more literary than otherwise. The introduction to the second volume ends with a lengthy quote in French from the writings of Voltaire. Two different compositions entitled 'Imitation of Fontaine' (a seventeenth-century French fabulist) are found in volume three.[107] There is also passing reference to Rousseau throughout the almanac. Interestingly, the title page of the third volume contains two lines of French text that, though not credited, are taken from a philosophical treatise by Nicolas Charmant, a moderate Jacobin.[108] Other than literary references, which look mostly to the past (particularly the Encyclopedists of the French Englightenment), there is no great

---

[105] Kondakov and others, eds, *Svodnyi katalog*, IV, pp. 118 – 119.

[106] Dement'eva and others, eds, *Russkaia periodicheskaia pechat'*, p. 94.

[107] *Aonidy*, 3 (1798 – 1799), 79 – 80, 215.

[108] Ibid., i. The inscription on the title page is taken from an essay entitled 'L'homme de Lettres, discourse philosophique en vers.' See *Oeuvres Completes de Chamfort, Tome Premier* (Paris: Chez Chaumerot Jeune, Libraire, 1824), p. 412.

evidence of direct French influence in this journal. A sampling of the journal has even revealed relatively little use of French loanwords other than the names of literary genres and devices. Various odes to Russian royalty and military victories, poems and songs on general subjects (such as spring, friendship, truth, love, and human life) are reminiscent of previous French journals, but the subjects are distinctly Russian.

Another publication studied was *Ippokrena, ili utekhi liubosloviia* (1799 – 1801) which was offered as an optional insert to *Moskovskiia vedomosti*, replacing the previous insert, *Priiatnoe i poleznoe preprovozhdenie vremeni* which had one of the same editors.[109] Like other eighteenth-century literary journals, this one included short-stories, novel excerpts, and anecdotes translated from French, German, and English. However, this journal featured mostly original Russian poetry. As opposed to some of Karamzin's earlier journals, which included a great deal of material from a single author, this publication included the work of about one hundred different Russian authors.[110] French influence is only slight in this journal, via the occasional borrowed word, especially for the names of literary genres.

Finally, a very influential journal at the beginning of the nineteenth century, *Vestnik Evropy* endured for a much longer publication run than previous journals (1802 – 1830). A particularly important journal for forming Russian social thought, *Vestnik Evropy* published international political news, poetry, translated excerpts from books and articles about modern history and society, academic news, and translations of the military memoirs of foreign officers.

The first in a long line of so-called 'thick' journals in nineteenth-century Russia, *Vestnik Evropy* was the first to engage in open critical discussion of political ideas. According to Anthony Cross, this influential journal shows the evolution of Karamzin's

---

[109] Dement'eva and others, eds, *Russkaia periodicheskaia pechat'*, p. 98

[110] Kondakov and others, eds, *Svodnyi katalog*, IV, pp. 140 – 141.

thought when compared to his earlier work.[111] In *Moskovskoi zhurnal,* Karamzin was a poet, author of literary prose, and sentimentally democratic idealist. In *Vestnik Evropy,* he is a historian and political publicist whose democratic ideals have been tempered by disenchantment with events in revolutionary France, and his tone is comparatively more conservative. In *Vestnik Evropy,* Karamzin still criticized the gentry, wanted to see advancements in public education, and more humane treatment of serfs (echoes of his younger self), but he had now taken on a patriotic and even nationalist tone and wanted to see the fundamental structure of society—including the institutions of serfdom and the rights of landed gentry—remain intact. He wanted Russia to learn from the West, but remain distinctly Russian and avoid the mistakes of the West, namely revolutionary regime-change.

It is important to note, however, that perfect continuity cannot be expected across the entire lifespan of *Vestnik Evropy.* In many ways, the journal reflected its editors at any given time. The journal was edited by Karamzin for only the first year of its existence. Though, for a time, the journal would continue along the course set by its founder, *Vestnik Evropy* eventually adopted an even more conservative tone. M. T. Kachenovskii, who served several stints as editor after Karamzin, initially continued in the tradition of the journal's founder. Over time, however, Kachenovskii, who was, in the estimation of one scholar, a 'scrupulous historian' but not much of a literati, led the journal to become less dynamic, avoided controversy and settled in to become a stable, conservative publication.[112] Following Karamzin's tenure as editor, the journal gradually became less political and was mostly literary. As a result, authors loyal to Karamzin did not submit as much writing and the journal became less popular. In its later years, typical sentiment has been that the journal became dryer, more boring, and

---

[111] Anthony Cross, 'N. M. Karamzin's "Messenger of Europe" (Vestnik Evropy), 1802 – 1803', *Forum for Modern Language Studies,* 5 (1969), 1 – 25.
[112] I. A. Aussem, 'Ot Karamzina do Kachenovskogo', *Russkaia rech',* 1 (2002), 77 – 84.

eventually 'died a natural death.'[113] From another point of view, however,

Kachenovskii's career gave stability to the journal and established the legitimacy of the

historian's profession in Russia.[114] As a scholar who was loyal to the crown, and

therefore less impeded by official censorship, Kachenovskii was able to advance the

study of history, protected by the state from 'unenlightened elements' of society. Even

in post-1812 Russia, a period when scholarship and publication was once again more

strictly regulated, Kachenovksii was able to 'carve out' space for a measure of academic

freedom and move Russia's historical profession forward, a fact attested to by the

unusually long publication stint of *Vestnik Evropy.*

In 1809, the journal began to be organized in five sections: poetry and prose

literature; arts and sciences, including travel writing; literary criticism; news; and a

miscellaneous section. This format endured throughout the rest of the journal's

publication history and became the example that later journals would follow. Embodied

in this journal is Russia's effort to come to an understanding of its own place in the

world by making sense of international events. This was truly an important publication

for historico-political thought in Russia. During the Napoleonic Wars, Russian eyes

were on France, as this journal demonstrates, and understanding this war was an

important factor in the development of Russia's national consciousness, especially after

1812. After Napoleon's decline, the apparent decline in singular focus on France and

all things French can likewise be discerned in this journal. During the life-span of this

publication's unique mixture of artistic expression and real-time commentary on world

events, tendencies can be traced which mark the peak and decline of French cultural

influence in Russia. Even after the popularity of the journal waned, its reach was

---

[113] V. N. Zaitsev and others, eds, *Svodnyi katalog serial'nykh izdanii Rossii, 1801 – 1825*, 3 vols (St. Petersburg: Izdatel'stvo rossiiskoi natsional'noi biblioteki, 1997 – 2006), I (1997), p. 192.

[114] Allison Y. Katsev, 'In the Forge of Criticism: M. T. Kachenovskii and Professional Autonomy in Pre-Reform Russia', in *Historiography of Imperial Russia: The Profession and Writing of History in a Multinational State*, ed. by Thomas Sanders (London: Routledge, 1999), pp. 45 – 68.

unusually broad. Publication documents and personal letters have revealed patches of information that help to describe the journal's sphere of influence. In January 1801, ahead of its original release, 580 people had subscribed to receive the journal. This number quickly grew to 1,200. According to Karamzin, *Vestnik Evropy* was being read as far away as Siberia and Georgia within two to three months of the first issue's publication.[115] In1822, the number of subscribers was still as high as 1,000 but had dropped to 755 by 1824.[116] These figures alone set the journal apart from previous journals as the only one whose circulation actually rivals that of the state newspaper *Sanktpeterburgskiia vedomosti.* Issues of this journal have been studied from 1802 to 1825.

Nikolai Karamzin

The career of Nikolai Karamzin (1766 – 1826), who founded four of the ten journals examined in the present study, is an important case study which illustrates the process of evolution in Russia's literary and cultural emulation of France. In terms of his overall importance, Karamzin is one of the few Russian authors who bear the distinction of having an entire literary period associated with his name. Anthony Cross, in his study of Karamzin's literary career in the period 1791 – 1803, emphasized that the season of sentimentalist literature—a developmental bridge between the classicism of writers like Mikhail Lomonosov and the age of literary romanticism led by Aleksandr Pushkin—may be fairly considered the 'Karamzinian period' of Russian literature.[117]

Karamzin's literary activity began in the 1780s as a student in Moscow, where he was affiliated with the literary and publishing circle of Nikolai Novikov, under whom he worked, translating foreign essays into Russian during a very productive

---

[115] Zaitsev and others, eds, *Svodnyi katalog*, I, p. 189.
[116] Ibid., p. 191.
[117] Cross, *N. M. Karamzin*, p. 231.

period of Novikov's career during which he was in charge of the Moscow university press, was chief editor of the *Moskovskiia vedomosti* newspaper, and prolifically published Russian books and literary journals. Following these formative educational years, Karamzin set out on a tour of Europe where he copiously documented his cultural experiences and introspective observations about his own native culture, notes that would later appear in his literary writings and work as a historian. After returning from Europe, Karamzin founded a series of literary journals which, along with his famous history, contributed to the development of Russian literature and socio-political thought and also document Karamzin's own developmental journey which he began as an 'enthusiastic cosmopolitan' and ended as a 'conservative nationalist'.[118]

Henry Nebel's literary analysis of Karamzin's sentimentalism suggested that its lasting influence was not only literary—introducing an expressive use of emotional language—but also cultural, advancing enlightened thought in Russian.[119] Stylistically, Karamzin broke with earlier literary classicism and its lofty odes and grand themes of battles and coronations and moved Russian literature toward more humanistic, democratic thought. He wrote about his daily life and described Russian peasants as human individuals with feelings and values, but without calling for institutional change. His descriptions evoked sympathy rather than guilt.

J. L. Black has studied the last third of Karamzin's literary career and the development of his political ideas, interpretations of Russian history, and their impact upon Russian society.[120] After leaving *Vestnik Evropy* in 1803, Karamzin was appointed official historian to the imperial court and spent the next two decades corresponding with fellow writers and highly-placed political figures about Russian history, culture, and political philosophy, and also working on his famous history of the

---

[118] Ibid.

[119] Henry M. Nebel, Jr., *N. M. Karamzin: A Russian Sentimentalist* (The Hague: Mouton and Co., 1967).

[120] J. L. Black, *Nicholas Karamzin and Russian Society in the Nineteenth Century: A Study in Russian Political and Historical Thought* (Toronto: University of Toronto Press, 1975).

Russian state. According to Black, his multi-volume *Istoriia gosudarstva rossiiskogo* (published 1818 – 1829) fundamentally influenced Russian leaders and citizens in the nineteenth century and beyond, both in their approach to historiography—a mixture of modern historical method and romanticized nationalism—and in their sense of national identity as Russians.[121] Karamzin's brand of conservatism was unique in its ability to 'make a viable synthesis of native and foreign traditions.'[122]

French influence upon Karamzin's developmental journey may be traced in the journals examined in the present study. It is a process which begins with achieving the fluent ability to interact with the foreign culture—speaking French, reading French books and periodicals, and listening to French music and plays. The next phase involves translating these foreign cultural elements into Russian, so that those who are not so fluent can enjoy these masterpieces. Then, indigenous creations appear within the literary genres of those French works which inspired Russian authors. Initially, these appear in mixed collections: Russian poems, for example, in a journal that is otherwise filled with translations of French fiction, or translations of the work of foreign scholars on Russian history, which include corrective footnotes written by Russian editors and the like. Finally, something like a clean break is made and an independent Russian literary tradition has begun, the French inspiration for which is hardly visible along the surface.

In *Pis'ma ruskago puteshestvennika,* Karamzin chronicled his eighteen-month journey through Europe via St. Petersburg and Riga, through the Germanic lands, France, England and back again. Four months of this journey were spent just in Paris. A particular impression was made upon him by the arts in Paris, theatre, Parisian society at various gatherings in hotels and salons, architecture, and the scholarly world to which he was exposed at the Académie des Sciences. As already mentioned, the timing of his

---

[121] Ibid., pp. 187 – 189.
[122] Ibid., p. 189.

journey (1789 – 1790) provides a unique Russian perspective on revolutionary France, from which the French aristocracy was in the process of fleeing. Nearer the end of his journey, Karamzin shares with the reader a moment of nationalistic introspection while he is in England. He marks the love and pride that Englishmen have for their own language, though many of them knew French quite well. By contrast, in Karamzin's analysis, refined Russians tended to disparage their own native language in favour of French, whether or not they actually knew the French language well. This adventure by young Karamzin was one of wonder—at the opportunity to be immersed in the culture he had so passionately studied from afar—and one of self-discovery, as romantic nostalgia for his homeland inspired him to give voice to Russia's own cultural identity.

The very idea of a travel memoir was borrowed from earlier European examples, a noteworthy instance of foreign influence even before specific cultural experiences along Karamzin's journey are considered. One historian referred to the seventeenth and eighteenth century as a 'silver age of travel and travel literature' during which merchants, explorers, ambassadors, scientists, missionaries, and wealthy leisure travellers on their 'grand tours' left behind a wealth of memoirs.[123] Reuel Wilson's study of Russian travel literature has argued that Denis Fonvizin, Aleksandr Radishchev, and Karamzin all emulated earlier authors in their own travelogues.[124] In particular, they were influenced by the English author Laurence Sterne's *Sentimental Journey through France and Italy* as well as the French memoirs of Jean-Baptiste Dupaty and Xavier De Maistre. Sara Dickinson has added the French travelogues of François Fénelon, Jean-Baptiste Tavernier, and Louis-Antoine Bougainville to this list of inspirations and suggested that Russia's three classic travel memoirists were actually preceded by pre-literary emulations of the genre by Aleksandr Kurakin and Ekaterina

---

[123] Percy Adams, 'Travel Literature of the Seventeenth and Eighteenth Centuries: A Review of Recent Approaches', *Texas Studies in Literature and Language*, 20 (1978).
[124] Reuel K. Wilson, *The Literary Travelogue: A Comparative Study with Special Relevance to Russian Literature from Fonvizin to Pushkin* (The Hague: Martinus Nijhoff, 1973).

Dashkova.[125] The flexibility of this simple narrative genre provided Russian authors an opportunity to hone their skills of description, narrative, moralizing (while comparing their own society to that seen on their journey, for example) and was an important intermediary genre in Russian literature's development towards the novel.[126]

Karamzin's account was originally released as a serial travel memoir, part of which was published in *Moskovskoi zhurnal* (1791 – 1792) and continued in *Aglaia*.[127] While in Paris, Karamzin had the opportunity to visit French theatres and simultaneously read the critical reviews of those performances in journals like *Mercure de France*. This experience was clearly transferred to his work as editor of *Moskovskoi zhurnal*, which featured articles on the repertoires of both Parisian and Muscovite theatres, in addition to reviews of French books and their Russian translations, and instalments of his travel memoir. Karamzin's next major editorial project, *Aglaia* (published 1794 – 1795), represents a new phase of cultural development. In his introduction, Karamzin makes a point of declaring the distinction of this journal as containing 'only Russian works [*sochineniia*]; there are no translations.'[128] His next literary journal, *Aonidy* (published 1796 – 1799), continues this trend and includes only the poetry of Russian authors, as already mentioned, above.

As with literary criticism, theatrical reviews, and poetry, a similar process can be seen in Karamzin's development as a historian. While in France, Karamzin had the opportunity to meet Pierre-Charles Levesque, a scholar who had written a history of Russia. Though admitting that Levesque's history was well-written, Karamzin complained that the work, while logical and factually accurate, lacked the vivid expression that he would desire to see in a history of Russia. Such was to be expected,

---

[125] Sara Dickinson, *Breaking Ground: Travel and National Culture in Russia from Peter I to the Era of Pushkin* (New York: Rudopi, 2006), pp. 27 – 45.

[126] Wilson, *Literary Travelogue*, pp. ix – xii; see also Dereck Offord, *Journeys to a Graveyard: Perceptions of Europe in Classical Russian Travel Writing* (Dordrecht: Springer, 2005).

[127] Iurii Lotman, 'Kommentarii', in *Bednaia Liza: povesti,* ed. by G. P. Makogonenko (Moscow: EKSMO, 2005), p. 592.

[128] *Aglaia*, 1 (1794), p. 144.

Karamzin reflected. 'To him, Russia is not Mother. It is not our blood that flows in his veins. Can he speak of Russia with the same feeling that a Russian could?'[129] It would be almost two decades before Karazmin's own famous Russian history would be published.

As noted earlier, in 1802 he founded another literary journal, *Vestnik Evropy* which would be published beyond Karamzin's own lifetime and achieve great success as a formative publication for the development of historical, social, and political thought in Russian society. In this publication, a number of the earlier historical offerings were translations from French, but editorial comments added in footnotes provided an outlet for historical discourse.

French influence upon Russian historiography can be traced throughout the publication history of *Vestnik Evropy*. Initially, this is seen in the form of translated articles or chapters from foreign books about historical events that would be of interest to Russian readers. The very first issue of *Vestnik Evropy* includes a historical article, translated from French into Russian, on the horrors of the French Revolution and Reign of Terror.[130] Russian authors themselves gradually wade in to this scholarly genre by adding their own commentary to the original author's thoughts in footnotes. For example, one article about the Enlightenment in Europe included a translated excerpt from the work of Voltaire, which argued that 'Great minds are the true heroes of history' and went on to praise the eighteenth-century Prussian king, Frederick the Great (1712 – 1786), who 'founded his own glory by victories, but established it with wise laws.' Immediately following Voltaire's claim that 'not since the [Roman] emperor Julian had Fate raised such a Genius to the throne', the Russian editor could not resist

---

[129] Nikolai Karamzin, 'Pis'ma russkogo puteshestvennika', in *Bednaia Liza: povesti,* ed. by G. P. Makogonenko (Moscow: EKSMO, 2005), p. 412.

[130] 'Istoriia frantsuzskoi revoliutsii, izbrannaia iz latinskikh pisatelei', *Vestnik Evropy,* 1 (January 1802), 20 – 37.

inserting an asterisk with the following comment: 'What about Peter the Great?'[131]

Translated articles appear in the journal related to older European history, the historical implications of Europe's recent revolutions, and, very soon after Napoleon's decline, conjecture about the form his image would take as a historical figure.[132] With the help of foreign historical literature, this Russian journal presented its readers with a broader view of the world and, by implication, Russia's place in it.

Likewise, Russia's own historiographical tradition seems to have been propelled forward at this time by a fascination with the writing of foreign authors about Russia. As already alluded to, the first volumes of Karamzin's famous *Istoriia gosudarstva rossiiskago* would not be released until 1816 and this monumental work was, at least partially, inspired by his reading of foreign authors on Russia's history. This sort of stimulus is discernible in numerous historical articles in *Vestnik Evropy*. For example, an 1806 article about the advances in pre-Petrine Russian begins with a lengthy review of foreign literature which explores the topic.[133]

In 1807, the Russian translation of a French article about the period immediately prior to and including the reign of Peter the Great was published in *Vestnik Evropy*.[134] This article is a prime example of western historians serving as a catalyst for historical inquiry in Russia. The Russian footnotes to this French article take on a life of their own, some of which are quite lengthy. The commentary in these footnotes is so participatory, and occurs so often throughout the article, that there is sometimes ambiguity as to whose thoughts are more prominent, the author's or the editor's. It reads more like two articles flowing parallel to one another than a single article with occasional footnotes. For example, during a section on Aleksei Mikhailovich, the

---

[131] 'o prosveshchenii', *Vestnik Evropy,* 1 (January 1802), 44 n1.

[132] For example, 'Cherty dlia budushchago izobrazheniia Napoleona', 2 (January 1815), 135 – 143.

[133] 'Chto sdelano v Rossii dlia prosveshcheniia naroda i dlia slavy otechestva ot vremen Riurika do Petra Velikago', *Vestnik Evropy,* 1 (January 1806), pp. 3 – 20.

[134] 'Mysli o Rossii, ili nekotoriya zamechaniia o tsarstvovaniia Petra Velikago', *Vestnik Evropy,* 1 (January 1807), pp. 3 – 29.

French author discusses the Moscow Council which advised the Tsar and how notions of honour and keeping one's word figured in to their decision-making process. At this point in the article, the Russian editor inserts a commentarial footnote which goes on for over a page. In this particular footnote, the seeds of Russia's romantic historiography can be discerned: 'This simplicity of our ancestors, to be ashamed of not keeping one's word, is already unfashionable in the enlightened countries of the current scientific age. Russians, not yet so enlightened as foreigners were, held to the old [ways], with the exception of a few who had learned the new wisdom of the French, who set them free from bashfulness.'[135] Hereafter, the footnote spins out of control and becomes a miniature treatise on the innate purity and decency of traditionally Russian society, which has been and is being corrupted by western elements. These include gambling, materialism, and dishonesty. The editor reminisces about his own youth, and how western greed and depravity have influenced society since then. Eventually, the footnote returns to the historical period in question, for which this long digression was an illustration: 'immediately the difference is revealed between the ethics of the *enlightened* people of the current age and the ethics of those Russians [of that time], whom these clever gentlemen call Barbarians!'[136] This excerpt is an example of how Russian reaction to a French account of Russian history can become a historical inquiry in its own right.

Another translated article was published in *Vestnik Evropy* about the general tendency in eighteenth-century Europe to emulate French culture and fashions. Written about Europe broadly, this French essay only deals with Russia in passing.[137] However, when the Slavic world is first mentioned, the editors insert the following footnote:

> 'Finally, it is our turn! [*doshla ochered i do nas!*] Specifically for the following lines was this entire excerpt translated… Just let our French chatterboxes and

---

[135] Ibid., 19 – 20.
[136] Ibid., 21.
[137] 'O podrazhanii vsemu frantsuzskomu', *Vestnik Evropy*, 2 (January 1816), pp. 95 – 104.

authors [*frantsuzskie govoruny i avtory,* those Russians who speak and write in French] learn the impartial opinion of intelligent people about their harmful and ridiculous affection for a foreign language. In this case, Madame Stal', as a French woman and as one who speaks in spite of the benefits to her own national pride, has the right to be trusted.'[138]

Reactions such as these demonstrate a growing self-awareness among Russian authors, no longer satisfied with merely mimicking Europe, but endeavouring to find Russia's place in it. The reaction of French periodicals to Russia's role in the Napoleonic Wars was published in the journal.[139] Likewise, the chapter of a German linguistic book was included which summarized the history of the Russian language.[140] Though sometimes objecting to what they read, Russian scholars and budding historians were helped along in their journey of self-discovery by their consideration of what others had written about Russia. The pages of *Vestnik Evropy* served as a laboratory of historical reflection as translations of foreign selections were published and the Russian editors transparently interacted with them.

Translation as a factor in cultural influence

An obvious aspect of cultural interaction in all of the journals studied is the process of translation itself when foreign materials were re-published. Reference has already been made to Karamzin's work as a translator during his early literary career, and one recent study—citing various experts in linguistic theory and social historiography—has suggested that translation played a major role in the modernizing and westernizing of Russia throughout the eighteenth century.[141] Prior to Karamzin, some of Russia's most important scholars from this century worked as translators, including Trediakovskii,

---

[138] Ibid., pp. 100 – 101.

[139] 'Zagranichnyia izvestiia', *Vestnik Evropy,* 2 (January 1813), pp. 159 – 167.

[140] 'O proiskhozhdenii russkago iazyka i o byvshikh s nim peremenakh', *Vestnik Evropy,* 2 (January 1823), pp. 113 – 128.

[141] Sergey Tyulenev, 'The Role of Translation in the Westernization of Russia in the Eighteenth Century' (unpublished doctoral thesis, University of Ottawa, 2009).

Kantemir, Lomonosov, and Sumarokov. [142] Recent linguistic analyses of eighteenth-century French-to-Russian translations have suggested that the translation process itself (not just the information transmitted) was formative for the Russian language and culture.[143] Certain linguistic nuances related to word usage, spelling and grammar all indicate the influence of the French original on the Russian language of the translation.[144] Beyond linguistic mechanics, translation was a social phenomenon that pushed back boundaries, opened Russian society to new ideas and advanced Russian thought and society forward.[145]

Only occasionally were translators actually credited for the various foreign stories and news articles used in the journals studied in this chapter. When they were mentioned, it was rarely a full citation. For example, a Russian translation of an essay by Jean-Jacques Rousseau appeared in a 1794 journal with the following footnote: 'for this translation we are obliged to one lady. I.'[146] Though often done in anonymity, this work was of singular importance to the development of the Russian language and to Russian incorporation of French cultural elements. One 1786 article about French fashions provides an interesting perspective on how the translation process can facilitate the importation of new words. The article is apparently translated or paraphrased from a French fashion journal and describes various accessories, fabrics, and colours, some of which do not have a direct equivalent in the Russian language. For these, the author uses italics to indicate his best translation of such words and includes the original French in parentheses, in Latin script.[147] Another article in *Moskovskoi zhurnal* is a

---

[142] Ibid., p. 112.

[143] I. E. Barenbaum, *Frantsuzskaia perevodnaia kniga v Rossii v XVIII veke* (Moscow: Nauka, 2006).

[144] V.M. Kruglov, *Russkii iazyk v nachale XVIII veka: uzus petrovskikh perevodchikov* (St. Petersburg: Nauka, 2004).

[145] Sergey Tyulenev, 'The Role of Translation in the Westernization of Russia in the Eighteenth Century' (unpublished doctoral thesis, University of Ottawa, 2009).

[146] 'O samoubiistve. Iz sochinenii Zh. Zh. Russo', *Priiatnoe i poleznoe preprovozhdenie vremeni,* 2 (1794), p. 117.

[147] *Lekarstvo ot skuki i zabot,* 1 (1786), pp. 19 – 21.

theatrical review in which the author mentions the Russian translation of a particular

play. The critic writes,

> The translation is worthy of praise, but it is too bad that *gospodin perevodchik*
> ('Mr. Translator') uses the words *sie* and *onoe*, which are always unpleasant to
> the ear in the theatre. Do we use these words in conversation? If not, then in
> comedy, which is the representation of everyday life [*obshchezhiniia*], they
> should not be used. The simpler and more natural the language of theatrical
> plays, the better.[148]

Sie and *onoe,* Church Slavonic for 'this' and 'that' sounded, to the critic's ear, too high

for comedy, but apparently felt quite natural to the one doing the translating. These are

simple examples, but illustrate how Russian authors and editors, operating in two

languages, had to make linguistic decisions when communicating French thoughts in

Russian. In the former case, the translator essentially invented new Russian words to

communicate what he had read in French. In the latter, the Russian translator and his

critic disagree on how formal or informal the language must be in a particular artistic

setting. Though glimpses such as these into the actual translation process are quite rare

in the journals of this period, they are a reminder that this tension is always present just

beneath the surface, a significant, though often invisible factor in Franco-Russian

cultural interaction.

Direct literary reaction to French influences

In addition to these implicitly French influences—the rationale for creating the

publications, the genres and topics of which they were comprised, and even the process

of translating non-original works for publication—the journals also contain explicit

reference to French influences upon Russian culture and society. As the overview of

newspaper articles has already highlighted, the arrival of French immigrants and the

goods and services that they brought with them had a profound impact on the daily lives

---

[148] 'O moskovskom teatre', *Moskovskoi zhurnal*, 1 (1791), p. 357.

of Russians, a fact also referenced by the literary journals of the period. For example, a journal from 1800 includes a short story about a provincial Russian girl, Filon', who learned to play the piano and speak French while working as a domestic servant in a noble Russian home where a French nanny looked after the children.[149] In addition to incidental references such as this one, contemporary Russian authors have also left behind an indication of how they felt about the French influences that they recognized in their daily lives. Contempt for the frivolity of French culture and especially for those noblemen who mimicked it was a recurring theme, especially in satirical literature. The pejorative term *shchegol'* was used repeatedly to refer to a Russian dandy or fop. A cursory glance at the contents of one 1788 journal reveals a dichotomy between the wholesome Russian traditions and imported foreign vanity. Honourable article titles like 'on the greatness of God, on the insignificance of earthly things and of man' and 'advice from a father to a son' stand out in contrast to 'the dressing table of the fashionable *shchegolikh*.'[150] The adjective 'fashionable' (*modnyi*—an adaptation of the French noun, *mode*) was often employed with a hint of sarcasm and resentment for the pretentiousness of those who dressed themselves in the French style or seasoned their conversation with French words.

The words of one Russian author in 1786 provide interesting insights on some stereotypes that existed in Russia regarding different nationalities including the French.[151] These stereotypes follow the reductionist principle that 'different peoples [*narody*] have different customs.' Italians, for example, are distinguished by their cunning or guile [*khitrost'*]. Englishmen are primarily known for their aversion to imitating the French, and the Germans represent an even balance in most things [*derzhat'sia srediny*]. As for the French, the Russian author categorizes them as being

---

[149] 'Lina', *Ippokrena, ili utekhi liubosloviia*, 5 (1800), pp. 279 – 286.

[150] *Utrennie chasy*, 2 (1788), p. 209.

[151] *Lekarstov ot skuki i zabot*, 2 (8 July 1786), pp. 32 – 35.

flighty or trivial. Not to be taken seriously, the French are characterized by frivolity, *legkomyslie,* a compound word more literally translated as 'lightness of thought.' These sweeping generalizations about 'the frivolity of the French and the guile of the Italians' are suggestive of the attitudes of the period. This sentiment about French *legkomyslie,* and indeed the word itself, is repeated many times in journals across the period.

Satirical literature of the period includes anecdotes about Russians who speak French badly, but are terribly proud of how chic it makes them appear, wear French clothes, and employ incompetent French domestic servants. The journal *Satiricheskii vestnik* (published 1790 – 91) is filled with biting sarcasm for Gallomania. The role of French goods and services brought to Russia through immigration is referenced in the following exaggerated list of recent arrivals:

> 'From the 102nd day of Monkey month to the 180th day of Imitation month, [the following] arrived: 6796 French ladies who sell bonnets, 10100 hairdressers, 3000 perfume sellers, 900 dancing instructors… 8600 men's and women's tailors and shoemakers, 630 merchants with lorgnettes, 10000 merchants of haberdashery. Departed from this region: 50 hairdressers, each of which had amassed fifteen thousand rubles; 200 French ladies, who had converted their bonnets into a great sum of money, tailors, merchants' and the like.[152]

These barbs were often hurled with more humour than venom, poking fun at the silly little Frenchman with his frills and airs and the funny Russian noblemen who tried to copy him. At other times, the distinction between Russian seriousness and French lightness took less jovial tone, signifying an actual moral judgment. A letter to the editor of a 1794 journal was written in protest of their recent article comparing men and women.[153] The author of the letter, a lady educated in a Russian monastery, objects to the article's assertion that every 'woman is always a coquette.' Her complaint goes on to state her suspicion that this 'parallel between men and women' was nothing more than a translation of a French article, a fact which the editors confirm in a footnote. The article that had been translated and published, and to which the author of this letter

---

[152] *Satiricheskii vestnik,* 1 (1790), pp. 111 – 112.
[153] 'Pis'mo k izdateliam', *Priiatnoe i poleznoe preprovozhdenie vremeni,* 1 (1794), pp. 296 – 298.

objected, was written by a Frenchman. At this point, she pens the following judgment, which is indicative of a common understanding of the dichotomy between Russian and French character: 'For him this is excusable; but it is not excusable for the Russian translator, who should know his countrywomen. [He] should know that with us, women are incomparably more pious and steady than [those] coquettes.'[154] The inference is clear: Russian women are morally superior to French women.

This notion of Russian culture being of a higher moral quality than that of France is a fairly common theme. An earlier journal expressed a similar thought in a fictional travel story in which the Russian narrator describes his journey to Paris, accompanied by a Siamese travel companion. The story begins, 'There is nothing more pleasant and useful [*poleznee*] than to travel the world; from this, one can obtain the best fruits of the knowledge of morals and varying human propensities.'[155] This hypothetical journey presents the notion of Russian culture as a balance of East and West. The wise Russian narrator seems to represent a happy medium between the decadence of the West and the provincial ignorance of the East. The Russian traveller reports the surprise of his Siamese friend at the hustle and bustle of Paris. There were so many people, always in a hurry, never stopping for a moment, constantly busy in their clamouring for luxury. Regarding fashion, he enlightens this 'wild Siamese man' [*dikoi siamets*] who, from a distance, mistakes the colourful hats of Parisian ladies walking in the Tuileries for a flock of exotic birds. Finally, they observe the different games of chance to be found in Parisian salons. With some regret, the Russian narrator conveys how familiar all of this seems to his heathen friend, who compares French gambling to his own native idol-worship. This idea of Russian culture being morally

---

[154] Ibid., p. 296.

[155] 'Zabavnyi puteshestvennik. Puteshestvie pervoe: stolichnyi gorod', *Utrennie chasy* (20 July 1788), p. 12.

superior to Europe (and, in this case, Eastern culture) is a notion that has been repeated

by multiple authors in multiple publications.

As it relates to French influence, one common implication of this notion is that

Russians are learning more than language and fashion from the French: they are

learning immorality. The following spoof classified advertisement illustrates this

concern, albeit with humour:

> 'a certain *shchegol'* is in need of a person to, 1. teach him to pronounce Russian
> words in the manner of the French; 2. With the help of stupid words, teach him
> perfect eloquence, and 3. Teach him to swear to an untruth without the
> condemnation of fashionable honour; and swear about that which is impossible,
> in no way breaking the fashionable conscience. Those desiring employment
> teaching these three skills [*naukam*] may find the aforementioned *shchegol'* at
> Affection-for-foreign-stupidity Street, on the first block of Destroyed
> Conscience, number 32.'[156]

Another satirical article explains how local fashionable young men have learned to

justify any behaviour with one simple French phrase: *pour passer le tems* ('for passing

the time.') Defrauding young ladies, not paying one's debts, and breaking promises are

all done *pour passer le tems*, while simple decency, honesty, hard work, and common

sense are considered 'pedantic' and 'simple' by the fashionably urbane.[157] The late

eighteenth-century literary journals studied testify to a universal contempt for the

superfluous fashions and light morals for which French influence was culpable. While

the eighteenth-century version of this criticism was mostly light-hearted and humourous

and only occasionally morally judgmental, 1812-era patriotism would later return to

these sentiments, reprising them with a venomous zeal.

Europe political news as a source of cultural influence

---

[156] *Satiricheskii vestnik,* 7 (1791), pp. 85 – 86.
[157] *Satiricheskii vestnik,* 6 (1790), pp. 64 – 66.

As with *Sanktpeterburgskiia vedomosti* and, to a lesser degree, some of the other literary journals studied, *Vestnik Evropy* published news articles and commentary related to events abroad. This window on the world allowed Russians to read about political situations in the international community that Russia was becoming a part of. All eyes were on France in the early nineteenth century. Early issues of the journal begin optimistically where France was concerned, reflecting a period of relative calm in Europe and the moderate policies of Alexander I who had ascended the Russian throne less than a year prior. A translated article from a French fashion magazine described Paris as having been restored to something like her former calm, thanks to Bonaparte.[158] The Terror had passed, regular commerce had resumed, street markets were vibrant, and the reactionary excesses of the revolution had subsided. Though France was now a republic and not a monarchy, the title 'citizen' was only used in formal settings. Those selling in the market addressed their well-dressed clients as 'monsieur' as in the old days. Likewise, many of the street names in Paris reflected its royalist past. Such was the picture of Paris and the French nation as depicted by this Russian journal in 1802. Attitudes towards France would ebb and flow over the next decade as diplomatic and political realities fluctuated. 1803 and 1804 were reported as a continuation of this period of relative peace.

By the beginning of 1806, however, the political landscape had changed. Along with Austria, Russia had joined the coalition against France and it was suggested that perhaps 1806 would be a year of war [*voennyi god*] as conflict was spreading across Europe. Discrepancies in French journalism were now exposed such as their diminishing of military failures and inflation of successes. 'Everyone knows that the French fight well, but they write even better.'[159] Taken from foreign newspapers and even French army bulletins, updates on troop movements and engagements were printed

---

[158] 'Nechto o nyneshnem Parizhe', *Vestnik Evropy*, 1 (January 1802), p. 63 – 65.
[159] 'Izvestiia i zamechaniia', *Vestnik Evropy*, 1 (January 1806), p. 77.

regularly. The war with Napoleon dominated the news and the rhetoric continued to escalate. By 1807, the following humourless judgment was made: 'in all these actions of the Enemy of the human race [that is, the Devil] the telltale signs of madness in the mind are seen.'[160] Then, after a tumultuous period of 'horrible strife between two nations [*narody*]; battles on the seas... the appearance of new kingdoms; the sudden upheaval of several thrones,' Alexander and Napoleon met on a raft in the Nieman river and the Treaty of Tilsit was reached.[161] Alexander had achieved a measure of peace and stability for Russia. During the next few years, the journal continues to report on military engagements and political manoeuvres in Europe, but as more of an outsider, observing a large conflict between England and France from afar. For the next few years, the journal maintained a neutral or even positive tone in relation to France. Carefully-weighted words of affirmation for Napoleon's supposed efforts at achieving peace in Europe were printed during the interim period of Franco-Russian détente (1807 – 1812.)

Attitudes towards France do not seem to have turned fiercely negative prior to 1812. Events occurred so relatively quickly that much of what was printed in *Vestnik Evropy* maintains a conciliatory tone as late as 1811. Less than two years before Napoleon marched into Moscow, the journal referred to him as 'His Highness the Emperor,'[162] and published affirmations of mutual cultural appreciation, such as an article about French veneration of St. Nicholas, a particularly beloved saint among Russian Orthodox believers.[163] During 1811 and early 1812 the journal continued to publish translated dispatches and news articles about events in Europe with an air of neutrality. This would of course change abruptly when news finally reached the editors that Napoleon had invaded Russia.

---

[160] 'Izvestiia i zamechaniia', *Vestnik Evropy,* 1 (January 1807), p. 72.
[161] 'Obozrenie proshedshago goda', *Vestnik Evropy,* 1 (January 1808), pp. 83 – 84.
[162] 'Obozrenie zagranichnykh proizshestvii', *Vestnik Evropy,* 1 (January 1811), p. 77.
[163] 'O pochitanii Sv. Nikolaia vo Frantsii', *Vestnik Evropy,* 1 (January 1811), pp. 53 – 57.

Though Napoleon's invasion of Russian began 11 – 12 (23 – 24) June 1812 when he crossed the river Nieman,[164] it is unclear exactly when the editors of *Vestnik Evropy* became aware of this fact. The journal was printed twice monthly. The first edition of July 1812 included reference to Alexander's pronouncement from Vilnius (13 June 1812) that France had 'treacherously violated the peace.'[165] The same issue included reviews of Moscow's theatrical repertoire up to 25 June.[166] However, the latest foreign political news was a dispatch from Berlin, dated 18 June.[167] The second edition of July does not mention the invasion, nor does the first edition of August. These two issues included a two-part article about key figures in French history, a number of translated pieces of literature, and the next set of foreign dispatches read like the continuation of news reported in due course. The second edition of August warns that 'the Oppressor of western Europe [that is, Napoleon] is already standing at our borders',[168] though, of course, he had long since crossed Russia's border and was well on his way to Moscow by this time. From September 1812 forward, however, the full reality of the situation had reached Moscow—Napoleon's army entered the evacuated city 2 (14) September—and the tone of the journal changed drastically and overnight.[169]

Vestnik Evropy quickly became a dispenser of patriotic propaganda and anti-French rhetoric. A section of the journal known as *Moskovskiia zapiski* gave vivid reports of French soldiers looting and pillaging Moscow, stealing jewellery, clothing, and shoes from the unarmed civilians remaining in the city. By contrast, noble Russian peasants had shown kindness to many a French soldier, according to these reports. According to the authors, such theft and want of decency was typical French behaviour. To prove this point, one article refers to the prevalent theft committed by French troops

---

[164] Janet Hartley, *Alexander I* (London: Longman, 1994), p. 111.

[165] 'Chustvovanie russkago po prochtenii vysochaishago reskripta, dannago v Vil'ne 13 iiunia o verolomnom narushenii mira frantsuzami', *Vestnik Evropy,* 13 (July 1812), pp. 55 – 57.

[166] 'Teatr', *Vestnik Evropy,* 13 (July 1812), pp. 59 – 66.

[167] 'Obozrenie zagranichnykh proizshestvii', *Vestnik Evropy,* 13 (July 1812), p. 77.

[168] 'K zhiteliam Ostzeiskikh provintsii Rossii', *Vestnik Evropy,* 16 (August 1812), p. 306.

[169] Janet Hartley, *Alexander I*, p. 115.

in Vienna in 1805, and suggested a parallel to the behaviour of the French crusaders long ago who sacked Constantinople in the thirteenth century.[170] The feelings that such rhetoric is meant to conjure are obvious. A greedy enemy from West was once again raiding the homeland of Orthodox Christians. Good riddance is bid to the French actors and shopkeepers who were being expelled. At any rate, Russian merchants were to be preferred.[171] This same edition recounted narratives which ridicule the French army, impoverished, incompetent, and ill-equipped to deal with Russia's climate. One darkly humourous anecdote tells of French soldiers slaughtering one of their own horses so that they might use its hide as a garment. One of the soldiers, vain and impractical to the end, is said to have written a letter home, explaining that his new horse-skin coat was intended primarily for warmth and not fashion.[172]

Throughout 1812, news articles, anecdotes, and poetry were published to inspire the patriotic courage of the Russian population. Among these were tales of valour in which Russian serfs are depicted rescuing noble ladies from French invaders, often risking their own life in the process. By contrast, Napoleon's troops showed no respect for the life or property of their victims. Their greed and lack of honour was so great that they even committed the sacrilege of robbing churches, stealing altar candles for common use.[173] Eyewitness narrative of Napoleon's invasion of Moscow appears in 1813, apparently intended to inspire courage, love for the fatherland, and contempt for the godless invader.

Although nationalistic and anti-French rhetoric characterize much of the journal's content during this period, *Vestnik Evropy* never gives evidence of a real break with French culture. Throughout the war with Napoleon, even during the peak of conflict, when French troops were in Moscow itself, literary works translated from

---

[170] 'Moskovskiia zapiski', *Vestnik Evropy,* 17 (September 1812), pp. 63 – 68.
[171] Ibid.
[172] 'Izvestiia i zamechaniia', *Vestnik Evropy,* 17 (September 1812), pp. 79 – 80.
[173] 'Primery chestnosti i userdiia slug russkikh', *Vestnik Evropy,* 19 – 20 (October 1812), pp. 272 – 290.

French, and news dispatches from French publications continued to be included. In a single edition from September 1812—when Napoleon's troops were in or very near Moscow—two translated articles from the French historian and journalist Jean Charles Dominique de Lacretelle (1766 – 1855) were included: a short historical essay on the Prussian king Fredrick the Great and a moralistic article about having the importance of having 'a kind heart.'[174] The same issue included another moralistic article, a 'portrait of an egotistical person', whose author is not credited but which was taken 'from a French journal.'[175] Anti-French patriotism was a temporary phenomenon in the journal, but Franco-Russian cultural ties survived it. During 1814 and 1815, the rhetoric mellowed as Alexander I and his armies were hailed as victors. The French people were not the enemy but the oppressed, and Alexander had liberated them from their tyrant leader.

After 1815 and through the end of 1825, political news from abroad would continue to be printed in *Vestnik Evropy*. At first, the aftermath of the war with Napoleon was a prominent feature, including humourous anecdotes about Napoleon's disappointments, heroic tales of the Russian army in Europe, various victorious pronouncements, news of the criminal trials of Napoleon's remaining supporters, and the early work of historians who were already seeking to explain the war's significance. As early as January 1815 (less than a year after Bonaparte's first abdication) the Russian translation of a German article on the 'features of Napoleon's future image' was published.[176] However, as this decade gave way to the 1820s, the foreign news articles of this journal were increasingly less dominated by France. Soon after the war, the political section of the journal was organized by regional headings. The various sub-headings in this section of foreign news included 'Spain', 'England', 'Turkey', 'Italy',

---

[174] 'Fridrikh II, korol' prusskii. Iz sochinenii Lakretellia'; 'Dobroe serdtse', *Vestnik Evropy,* 18 (September 1812), 81 – 83, 83 – 89.

[175] 'Portret egoista', *Vestnik Evropy,* 18 (September 1812), 89 – 92.

[176] 'Cherty dlia budushchago izobrazheniia Napoleona', *Vestnik Evropy,* 2 (January 1815), 135 – 143.

and 'France' was now just one among several. Chronologically, Russia's end of

hostilities with France coincides with the beginning of a general decline in overt French

cultural influence. It never disappears totally, but becomes much less pronounced.

The era's end reflected in the language

To illustrate this decline, a selective word-study has been done of *Vestnik Evropy* during

the period 1802 – 1825, based upon the larger lexical study of this dissertation. Of all

the French loanwords in the Russian language related to the military, polite society,

urban and residential design, and philosophy or social thought, those entering the

language during the period 1725 – 1833 have been cross-referenced with their

occurrence in any issue of *Vestnik Evropy* during the period studied.[177] In other words,

some of the words appearing initially in the first Russian Academy dictionary

(published 1789 – 1794) or appearing for the first time during Pushkin's writing career

(1813 – 1833) have been searched for in all issues of *Vestnik Evropy* up until 1825.

This makes it possible, on a small scale, to trace patterns of word import within this

narrower period. For example, words used in the journal in 1802 and thereafter were

either already in the language prior to 1802 or are new words as of 1802. By contrast,

words not used in any of the issues of the period 1802 – 1807, for example, but

appearing in 1808 and thereafter are words that the authors of *Vestnik Evropy* began to

use only in 1808. The results of this exercise indicate that the import of new French

words to the Russian language as reflected in the journal virtually ceases during the

Napoleonic Wars. Each year from 1802 to 1808, authors of *Vestnik Evropy* begin using

new French words related to the military, with the exception of 1806. After 1808,

---

[177] The journal *Vestnik Evropy* has been digitized but is only accessible via the on-site computers of the State Public Historical Library in Moscow. The 'search' feature of the library's electronic collection recognizes and displays all occurrences of a given word anywhere in the journal in all declensions and conjugations so long as the desired word is entered in the nominative case for nouns or adjectives or in the infinitive for verbs. This electronic resource was invaluable in cross-referencing words in the journal with the words from the lexical study done for chapter two.

virtually no new military words are borrowed, but words which were already in circulation continue to be used. Exactly the same can be said of new French terms related to polite society which also enter usage only up until 1808. Similarly, a number of French words related to urban and residential design trickle into the journal until 1811, but none thereafter. Finally, the last year in which *Vestnik Evropy* introduces new French loanwords pertaining to philosophy or social thought, including political terminology, is 1816. As the table in Fig. 5.1 demonstrates, no new French loanwords from any of these four categories were used by the journal's authors from 1817 – 1825.

Fig. 5.1: New French loanwords (by category) used each year in *Vestnik Evropy*

YEAR	Military	Urban/Res.	Phil./Social	Polite society	**TOTAL**
1802	11	7	6	6	**30**
1803	5	2	0	2	**9**
1804	6	3	1	1	**11**
1805	3	0	0	0	**3**
1806	0	0	1	0	**1**
1807	1	0	0	0	**1**
1808	5	1	0	1	**7**
1809	0	0	0	0	**0**
1810	0	2	0	0	**2**
1811	0	1	0	0	**1**
1812	0	0	1	0	**1**
1813	0	0	0	0	**0**
1814	0	0	1	0	**1**
1815	0	0	0	0	**0**
1816	0	0	2	0	**2**
1817 – 1825	0	0	0	0	**0**

This pattern suggests the beginning of a new phase in Russia's cultural development, during which wholesale emulation of France fades away. The war with Napoleon had brought Russia and France closer together, as Napoleon's army invaded Russia and Alexander's army later marched across Europe into Paris. At the same time, Russia's culture had developed a greater sense of its own sense of identity.

By 1821, Karamzin's history of Russia was already available in French as well as Russian. In this year, one of the literary reviews in *Vestnik Evropy* was of a French article about Karamzin's history.[178] It was a review of a review. Less than two decades after Russia's upcoming historians were editorializing French authors from afar, looking for any small mention of Russia to which they might append a passionate footnote, a Parisian journal had now devoted an entire review to a significant Russian historical accomplishment and *Vestnik Evropy* was publishing a reply. The literary awareness of Moscow and Paris was becoming mutual. After a great wave of deeply significant French influence upon Russia, the tide had shifted and the balance was equalizing. At this very point in the history of Franco-Russian cultural relations, as of the 1820s, the age of unilateral emulation had passed and an age of bilateral interaction was dawning.

---

[178]'O bespristrastii istorika i o tom, v chem imenno sostoit zanimatel'nost' russkoi istorii dlia inozemnykh chitatelei', *Vestnik Evropy* 1 (January 1821), pp. 35 – 44.

CONCLUSION

The officers who marched onto St. Petersburg's Senate Square on 14 December 1825 to

protest the ascension of Nicholas I and call for reform were, in a sense, a product of

French influences. They were born around the time of the second and—culturally

speaking—more potent of two waves of French immigration. These immigrants were

their governesses, tutors and academy instructors, as well as the vendors, craftsmen, and

domestic servants who enriched their childhood. Then, having been raised in French

ways by quality French experts, their launch into early adulthood was marked by the

life-altering experience of chasing Napoleon deep into the birthplace of those French

ways, at the head of tens of thousands of their plebeian countrymen.

Historians of the Decembrist movement invariably cite this time abroad as a

defining event in their ideological journey towards revolt.[1] Having seen the relative

dignity with which Western European peasants lived, they returned to their homeland

dissatisfied with the plight of the Russian serf. Further, having come into closer contact

with a nation governed by a constitution, they desired the same for Russia, that she

might take her place among the civilized countries of the world. When questioned after

the revolt by the Investigating Commission about the origins of their liberal ideas,

various Decembrists cited their experiences during the foreign campaign, lectures they

had attended in Paris, and their reading of French philosophical and political literature

before and after the war.[2] Their notions of government according to a constitution and

the innate equality of all men were inspired by French examples. These young Russian

minds had been intellectually conditioned, however, to receive such an example much

earlier when they read works of seventeenth-century classical French literature at the

instruction of their émigré tutors, and the works of eighteenth-century enlightened

---

[1] See, for example, M. V. Nechkina, *Dekabristy* (Moscow: Nauka, 1983), pp. 18 – 20; and Patrick
O'Meara, *The Decembrist Pavel Pestel* (New York: Palgrave Macmillan, 2003), pp. 18 – 19;
[2] G. R. V. Barratt, *Voices in Exile: The Decembrist Memoirs* (Montreal: McGill-Queen's University Press,
1974), pp. 142 – 150.

thinkers such as Rousseau, Diderot, and Montesquieu in their fathers' libraries.[3]

Building upon this theoretical base, the events of the French Revolution and Napoleonic

wars provided them with a practical template by which to envision real change in

Russia. They returned home with an appetite for further study and political action.[4]

When these young idealists began to gather in secret societies, beginning in

1816, they discussed the social and political ideas of French authors of the eighteenth

and nineteenth century, and some societies even conducted their business in French.[5]

Though there were philosophical disagreements among the Decembrists themselves—

N. I. Murav'ev, for example, envisioned a constitutional monarchy for Russia while P. I.

Pestel' favoured regicide and the establishment of something like a Jacobin provisional

government, a ruling body to immediately replace the monarchy until a new republican

order could be established—all of the ideas were largely inspired by the French. A

recent study of the written works of key Decembrists identifies clear connections with

specific French literature. Pavel Pestel''s *Russkaia pravda* seems to have been inspired

by the Jacobin dictatorship, Murav'ev's constitution shows interaction with the works of

Benjamin Constant and Madame de Staël, M. F. Orlov seems to emulate the writings of

Joseph de Maistre, M. S. Lunin that of François-René de Chateaubriand, and so forth.[6]

Though they did not succeed in overthrowing the government in December 1825, the

writings left behind by the Decembrists and those sympathetic to them and the

mythologizing of their memory across the rest of the century would figure greatly in

Russian socio-political thought and action.[7] In addition to the importance of the

Decembrist legend as an inspiration for Russia's emerging revolutionary movement in

---

[3] V. S. Parsamov, *Dekabristy i Frantsiia* (Moscow: *Rossiiskii gosudarstvennyi gumanitarnyi universitet*, 2010), p. 12.

[4] S. N. Chernov, *Pavel Pestel': Izbrannye stat'i po istorii dekabrizma* (St. Petersburg: Liki Rossii, 2004), pp. 89 – 114.

[5] O'Meara, *The Decembrist Pavel Pestel*, pp. 37 – 48.

[6] Parsamov, *Dekabristy i Frantsiia*.

[7] Ludmilla A. Trigos, *The Decembrist Myth in Russian Culture* (New York: Palgrave Macmillan, 2009); Anatole G. Mazour, *The First Russian Revolution, 1825: The Decembrist Movement, Its Origins, Development, and Significance* (Stanford: Stanford University Press, 1964).

the nineteenth century, Anatole Mazour has argued that their influence is seen much

earlier in Nicholas I's codification of Russian laws.[8]

While the Decembrist uprising is often remembered as the premonitory

rumblings before the gathering of Russia's revolutionary storm clouds, for the present

study this event marks an end rather than a beginning. It was the last flourish of this,

the most significant age of direct French influence upon Russian culture. The age had

begun during the reign of Catherine II, even if it was by no means the first or last period

of French influence. As the extant secondary literature on the topic reviewed in chapter

one suggests, Russia's contact with western nations, including France, began even

before the reign of Peter the Great and the means of cultural influence—people,

imported items, and books—have been flowing into Russia from France since the time

of Peter's reforms. Furthermore, French stimulus persisted throughout Russia's

imperial, revolutionary, soviet, and post-soviet history.

This study has argued that it would be wrong, however, to imagine the French

contribution to Russia's cultural fabric as one continual, steady progression, part of the

gradual progress some romantics have seen in the sloped base of St. Petersburg's

Bronze Horseman statue: ever upward, ever westward.[9] For a more realistic framing of

when and how Russian culture was most deeply affected by French stimuli, chapter two

explored that true and dynamic indicator of culture: language. Borrowed French words

in the Russian vocabulary testify to varying levels of French cultural influence across

history. Statistical data from Russian dictionaries over the last three centuries indicates

that the greatest influx of French loanwords still in frequent circulation today occurred

in the late eighteenth and early nineteenth century. Further, clear categories of

borrowed words suggest specific areas of French influence. The presence of French-

---

[8] Mazour, *The First Russian Revolution,* pp. 261 – 272.
[9] Sergey Tyulenev, 'The Role of Translation in the Westernization of Russia in the Eighteenth Century' (unpublished PhD thesis, University of Ottawa, 2009), pp. 49 – 62.

origin words related to culture proper (fashion, cuisine, and the arts, to name a few), official language, technology, industry and the sciences, urban and residential design, philosophy and social thought suggests that Franco-Russian interaction in these areas was significant to Russia's cultural development. The results of this lexical study have directed the remainder of the dissertation and sharpened its focus throughout. Within the chronological parameters suggested by this lexical analysis and in light of other scholarly discussion of Franco-Russian cultural interaction, the most obviously relevant events are the French Revolution and Russia's war with Napoleon.

France's revolution brought scores of French émigrés to Russia and the war with Napoleon took thousands of Russian soldiers into France. Both events made permanent contributions to Russian culture. French immigration to Russia may not have begun with the storming of the Bastille or even the regicide in 1793; as legal codices and archival records referenced in chapter three indicate, Catherine II's proactive policies to invite foreign settlers began bringing large numbers of Frenchmen to Russia as early as 1762. However, biographical information gleaned from police records, anecdotal accounts from various archival and literary sources, and lists of immigrants registered in oath-swearing ceremonies suggest two waves of French immigration to Russia. Generally, the first of these was characterized by immigrants of lower social status, some of whom with a colourful and even criminal past. By contrast, those French people most likely to flee to Russia during the revolution—the second wave of immigrants—were those of the privileged class who had the independent means to travel and were, presumably, the most in danger of Jacobin Terror. These immigrants were better equipped to make higher-quality contribution to Russian culture through their work as teachers and through social interaction. Primary source material reveals not only the differences between these two classes of immigrants, but the broad dispersal of well-born French émigrés working in many different locations in Russia as tutors, governors, and shopkeepers once the Russian court and other official posts became saturated. Unlike previous generations or groups of foreigners in Russia, French immigrants were interwoven in Russian society, rather than living apart in isolation, a fact which enhanced their cultural influence upon their Russian hosts. Their most common occupations were those which brought them into close contact with Russians, suggesting maximum potential for cultural interaction. They were teachers, government employees, merchants, luxury artisans, cooks, hairdressers, performers, artists, and domestic servants for the Russian nobility. Categories of lexical import during this period parallel the types of professions in which these resident foreigners were engaged, confirming the impression these foreigners made upon contemporary Russians and generations of Russians to follow.

The second great event in Franco-Russian relations during the period determined by the lexical analysis was, of course, Napoleon's invasion of Russia and the subsequent foreign campaigns of the Russian army. The cultural experience of Russian officers, and to some extent lower-ranking soldiers, was, in a sense, a magnified and inverted version of the French cultural influence previously experienced by the Russian population as a result of immigration. The number of soldiers that marched into France was greater than the number of French immigrants who had been in Russia, these Russians were now immersed in French culture rather than importing individual elements, and they were experiencing various cultural elements—some of the quite familiar to them by now—at their source. The memoirs of Russian authors studied in chapter four provide vivid narrative details of their cultural experiences in between battle scenes, especially after arriving in Paris following the cessation of hostilities. They attended French theatre, dined in French restaurants, stayed in French homes (with their impressive interior décor) and recorded an array of impressions on various aspects of the culture which also correlate to the introduction of specific loanwords, suggesting the effect of these experiences on the development of Russian theatre, interior décor, restaurant culture, and other cultural aspects after the troops returned home to Russia.

Finally, in chapter five, a sampling of Russian periodical literature during the period 1788 – 1825 has provided insights into contemporary Russian perceptions of French influences. The first of these is satirical reference to Russia's French residents and the propensity of fashionable Russians to emulate them. This stereotype, rooted in earlier days of Gallomania when the former wave of adventurers and other French immigrants made its mark, endures without much noticeable awareness of the new level of quality influence represented by the émigrés after 1789. The second is the steady arc of French influence across the period, rising in the late eighteenth century and waning in the 1820s. Despite temporary flashes of strong opinion towards France: political concern in 1789, outrage in 1793, and the propaganda of righteous indignation in 1812, significant French influence never stopped. Employment adverts for French subjects, French goods for sale, French books recently imported, translations of French stories and plays, and coverage of French political events were all mainstays across the period, suggesting a deep cultural connection at the human level which transcended politics.

By contrast, from the 1820s forward, French lexical import went back to what it had always been, a steady reality: each generation borrowed a new set of words related to fashion, and new technological terms entered as new items were being invented and imported, some of them happening to have French names, but there was never another period of French cultural influence like that beginning late in the reign of Catherine II and through the reign of her grandson, Alexander I. A second but drastically smaller peak in French loanwords is seen during Russia's revolutionary period, but even this indirectly suggests the importance of the French Revolution to which political philosophers of the late nineteenth century and participants in the 1917 revolution once again looked for inspiration and the vocabulary with which to articulate a vision for their own country.[10]

The historical significance of this conclusion is not so much its novelty as the empirical basis it provides. Russians intuitively know that there is a long-standing Franco-Russian cultural connection. The introduction of lexical analysis, archival data, and contemporary memoir and periodical literature grounds these assumptions in fact and provides a context that is rooted in the lives of real people other than iconic sovereigns and generals (and their myths), or artistic interpretations like eighteenth-century satirical literature or Tolstoi's *War and Peace.*

Histories of Russian culture have typically dealt with the issue of French influence in a cursory manner by taking one of two courses. Orlando Figes and Hans Rogger have both cited Russian literary references such as fictional examples of Francophile Russians in the works of Pushkin and Tolstoi or the mocking of such Francophile tendencies in the plays of Denis Fonvizin or eighteenth-century literary journals.[11] A second approach has been to focus largely on the imperial court and other Russian elites for anecdotal examples of French influence at this level of society: Elizabeth Petrovna's fondness for French luxury items, Catherine II's correspondences with philosophes and written attitudes towards the French enlightenment, specific works of art commissioned by the Russian state, and so forth. The work of James Billington

---

[10] See discussions of this historical parallel in Dmitry Shlapentokh, *The French Revolution in Russian Intellectual Life: 1865 – 1905* (Westport, CT: Praeger, 1996), *The French Revolution and the Russian Anti-Democratic Tradition: a Case of False Consciousness* (New Brunswick: Transaction, 1997), and *The Counter-Revolution in Revolution: Images of Thermidor and Napoleon at the Time of Russian Revolution and Civil War* (New York: St. Martin's Press, 1999); John Keep, 'The Russian Army's Response to the French Revolution', *Jahrbücher für Geschichte Osteuropas,* 28 (1980), 500–523, and '1917: The Tyranny of Paris over Petrograd', *Soviet Studies,* 20 (1968), 22 – 35; George Jackson, 'The Influence of the French Revolution on Lenin's Conception of the Russian Revolution' in *The French Revolution of 1789 and Its Impact,* ed. by Gail M. Schwab and John R. Jeanneney (Westport: Greenwood Press, 1995), pp. 273 – 284; G. V. Plekhanov, *History of Russian Social Thought,* trans. by Boris M. Bekkar and others (New York: Fertig, 1967).

[11] Orlando Figes, *Natasha's Dance: a Cultural History of Russia* (London: Penguin, 2002), pp. 36 – 68, 94 – 118.; Hans Rogger, *National Consciousness in Eighteenth-Century Russia* (Cambridge, Mass.: Harvard University Press, 1969), pp. 45 – 84.

and W. Bruce Lincoln are notable examples of this approach.[12] Both of these methods, while valid, only provide general observations about French cultural influence.[13] The reader is held at a distance from actual Russian culture—provided mostly with fictional accounts or evidence from only the most elite segment of the population. The present study has provided a closer historical look at Russian culture and its French influences. The lives of ordinary people are explored factually, and the ruling class, when featured, is considered primarily as a means of understanding the broader cultural issues involved, such as policies affecting immigration or command decisions that put Russian troops on French soil.

In recent years, a few studies have appeared which explore Franco-Russian cultural contact within a particular period, or in a specialized area such as the book trade, literature, or immigration, but very little attention is given to the broader issue of cultural transfer, especially that which is still palpable in Russia.[14] More broadly speaking, the very concept of culture has been defined in various ways, and scholarly inquiry into the impact of immigration on receiving cultures is still in its infancy. Despite these issues, examination of Russian primary source material related to French

---

[12] James H. Billington, *The Icon and the Axe: An Interpretive History of Russian Culture* (New York: Knopf, 1970), pp. 210 – 268; W. Bruce Lincoln, *Between Heaven and Hell: The Story of a Thousand Years of Artistic Life in Russia* (New York: Viking, 1998), pp. 69 – 125.

[13] A notable exception to this tendency is a particular study of French émigrés in Russia, which provided an invaluable starting-point for finding archival material for chapter three of this dissertation: Leonide Ignatieff, 'French Émigrés in Russia, 1789 – 1825: The Interaction of Cultures in Time of Stress' (unpublished PhD dissertation, University of Michigan, 1963).

[14] See, for example, I. V. Ivanskaia, 'Frantsuzskaia kul'tura v Rossii epokhi Petra I' (unpublished doctoral dissertation, Saint Petersburg State University, 2007); Inna Gorbatov, *Catherine the Great and the French Philosophers of the Enlightenment: Montesquieu, Voltaire, Rousseau, Diderot and Grimm* (Bethesda: Academica Press, 2006); L. A. Letaeva, 'Frantsuzskaia kniga v kul'turnom prostranstve Rossii serediny vtoroi poloviny XVIII veka',and A.P. Iarkov, 'Liudi i obrazy Frantsii v zapadnoi sibiri v XVIII – XIX vv.', in *Frantsiia – Rossiia: problem kul'turnykh diffuzii*, ed. by L.I. Lipskaia (Tiumen': Tipografiia Pechatnik, 2008), pp. 28 – 35, 45 – 49 ; Ulrike Lentz, 'The Representation of Western European Governesses and Tutors on the Russian Country Estate in Historical Documents and Literary Texts' (unpublished PhD thesis, University of Surrey, 2008); and N. O. Shiralieva, 'Kul'turnye sviazi Frantsii i Rossii v XX veke' (unpublished doctoral dissertation, Moscow, 2004).

immigration and the Russian military campaign in France alongside vocabulary data as a measurable rubric permits clear conclusions. Beyond intuition, it can be affirmed that Russian culture *has* been influenced by France and the French. Further, it has been possible to determine roughly *when* that influence occurred, *what kind* of influence, and to provide narrative examples. The results of the present dissertation, apart from indicating and exploring the key period of enduring French influence, introduce a new method of historical inquiry to this area of study: wide-ranging lexical analysis using dictionaries as primary sources, an approach relevant to the study of cultural transfer generally. Beyond examination of Franco-Russian cultural transfer specifically, the implications for such analysis extend to any national culture whose language has a developed lexicographical tradition. Further, by combining and cross-referencing a selection of different types of primary sources for the resultant target period—unpublished archival records, memoirs, legal codices, and periodical publications—this study moves beyond a mere linguistic exercise and provides historical context for observed (rather than assumed or inferred) instances of cultural transfer.

If history is anything, it is the study of past human interaction. No individual, group, or nation exists in a vacuum. As people, we are forever influencing, learning from, trading with, depending upon, and, all too often, mistreating one another. All of these experiences are necessary components in an understanding of any nation or ethno-linguistic group of people, and Russians are no exception, though most cultural histories of Russia have made only general reference to the lasting impression made by Russia's interaction with various foreign cultures. The present study's narrower focus on specific means of measurable influence in a particular bi-lateral cultural relationship is a logical next step in the trajectory of previous scholarship aimed at understanding Russian culture. The inter-disciplinary research of leading historical linguist V. M. Zhivov (1945 – 2013), for example, seems to have been moving in this direction. An early adopter of the semiotic approach to cultural history founded by Iurii Lotman (known as the *Moskovsko-tartuskaia semioticheskaia shkola*), Zhivov used his technical background in linguistics and philology to study Russian cultural history parallel to the development of the Russian language.[15] Later in his career, he chaired a department of the Russian Academy of Science's Institute of the Russian Language, taking his place as one of the heirs of Vinogradov's linguistic dynasty.[16] During the last year of his life, he took part in the University of Bristol's research on the history of the French language in Russia, the first large-scale study to focus on this particular area of inquiry. Of the dozens of articles, chapters, and papers produced by this ground-breaking collabouration, however, Zhivov's presentation on French loanwords in the Russian language was one of only a very few dedicated to French influence upon the Russian language rather than the Russian nobility's use of French as a popular foreign language.[17] At the end of a long career examining the parallel development of Russia's language and culture, his perspective highlighted French influence *upon* the Russian culture itself, rather than merely French culture *in* Russia.

Another example of this trajectory was G. S. Pomerants (1918 – 2013) who analyzed Russian society as a philosopher and cultural theorist, though he is better remembered for his activism as a Soviet *samizdat* dissident writer.[18] Near the end of a seven-decade period of studying the literary thought of Dostoevskii, the history of world

---

[15] Information on Zhivov's career taken from a collection of memorial articles in *Novoe literaturnoe obozrenie*, 125 (2014) <http://www.nlobooks.ru/node/4494>; and from an obituary for Zhivov by the University of California at Berkely <http://senate.universityofcalifornia.edu/news/ViktorMarkovichZhivov.html> [both accessed 29 May 2015]

[16] Zhivov obituary from the Russian Language Institute of the Russian Academy of Sciences <http://www.ruslang.ru/doc/zhivov.pdf> [accessed 29 May 2015]

[17] V. M. Zhivov, 'Liubov' à la mode: russkie slova i frantsuzskie istochniki', French in Russia conference booklet, pp. 62 – 63 < http://www.bristol.ac.uk/arts/research/french-in-russia/conference/> [accessed 29 May 2015]

[18] 'O roli lichnosti: v Moskve na 95-m godu zhizni umer Grigorii Pomerants', *Gazeta.ru,* 18 February 2013 <http://www.gazeta.ru/culture/2013/02/18/a_4971933.shtml>; 'In Memory of Grigory Pomerants', *Prava cheloveka v Rossii*, 18 February 2013 <http://hro.rightsinrussia.info/archive/human-rights-defenders/pomerants/obituary> [both accessed 29 May 2015]

religions and political systems, Pomerants developed his notion that Russia's very

identity exists at the crossroads of the other cultures with which it has interacted.[19] This

theme is especially recurrent in his lectures and articles in the early twenty-first

century.[20] One of his last works, which metaphorically refers to Russian culture as a

unique carpet made of various European threads, signalled a departure from his

characteristically broad philosophical generalizations about Russia's simultaneous

identification with 'the East' and 'the West' by giving more focused attention

specifically to the French cultural strain that is still discernible in Russia and giving

specific examples.[21] The present study has taken up the challenge of Zhivov, Pomerants

and other students of Russia's cultural history by looking beyond generalizations to

specific cultural markers in the Russian language and tracing them back to their

historical origins.

Further inquiry into Russian cultural history should explore instances of

interaction with other nations, and, more importantly, the imprint which these events

have left behind upon Russian patterns of behaviour, shared values and understandings

of meaning, imprints which can be discerned in the Russian language. A historical

understanding of Russian cultural development as the ongoing interaction with foreign

influences best views these influences as overlapping continuums rather than a series of

consecutive periods. The present study, rather than simplistically affirming French

influence generally in the late eighteenth and early nineteenth century, has provided a

sketch of the lexical landscape across time and highlighted the period during which

French influence was at its height.

---

[19] See, for example, his article from the 1970s, Grigorii Pomerants, 'Rossiia na perekrestke kul'tur', in *Vykhod iz transa* (Moscow: Rosspen, 2010), pp. 216 – 224.

[20] Grigorii Pomerants and Zinaida Mirkina, *Spor tsivilizatsii i dialog kul'tur: lektsii i stat'i nulevykh godov* (St. Petersburg: Tsentr gumanitarnykh initsiativ, 2014).

[21] G. S. Pomerants, 'Frantsuzskii sled v russkoi kul'ture', *Obrazy mira* <http://www.niworld.ru/Statei/pomerants/Franz_sled.htm> [accessed 20 February 2015]

Though the French lexical strain is the single greatest, there are other bi-lateral landscapes in Russia's cultural history. Similar analysis could be made, for example, of Greek, German, Dutch, or English loanwords and the aspects of Russian culture highlighted by those patterns and correlating events. By separating these layers and observing the development, peak, and decline of individual strains of influence across a longer span of time rather than attempting to sort out all of the cultural events within an isolated chronological period, clarity is added to a realm of scholarship that is otherwise quite diffuse. Each strain studied will further enhance history's understanding of the Russian culture, past and present.

APPENDIX A

Methodology of the Lexical Study

The first stage of this study—compilation of the categorized wordlist—involved seven steps: dictionary selection; a first read-through of all dictionaries for French words; a second read-through to cross-reference the dictionaries for etymological discrepancies; combining of wordlists; category assignment; quality control of categorization; and ongoing adjustments to categories. The historical justification for selection of the specific dictionaries used in this study is dealt with in the text of chapter two.

During a first read-through of all these dictionaries, a list of words of French origin was compiled for each dictionary, relying on the etymological information provided within word-definitions by the editors. This step was somewhat complicated by the fact that the dictionaries of Pushkin's and Dostoevskii's language and Ozhegov's dictionary were published without any etymological notations. This difficulty has been overcome by first studying the other dictionaries and then checking the Pushkin, Dostoevskii and Ozhegov dictionaries against those which do carry information about word origin. Since the dictionaries studied are roughly a generation apart chronologically, the assumption is that French words will not appear for the first time in one of the non-etymological dictionaries and then drop out of use in the same generation. The French words in each of these three dictionaries should be present either in their predecessor, successor, or both. Of course the odd French word which appears only in one of these dictionaries cannot be definitively ruled out, but this is not of grave concern to the present study. A chief concern is tracing the emergence of French-origin words which still occur in the Russian language, achieved with the non-etymological dictionaries when they are cross-referenced with the 2007 *Sovremennyi* dictionary. At the end of this initial read-through, the result was a separate list of French-origin words for each of the dictionaries.

In a second reading of all the dictionaries, every dictionary was cross-referenced with every other dictionary to detect any etymological discrepancies. The dictionaries were published by different editors at different times, and there can be disagreement on the origin of certain words, which can create deceptive incongruities between wordlists. A word assigned an alternative etymology by a given edition (or assigned no etymology at all because it was considered by the editors to be a fully naturalized Russian word) looks as if it were absent in that dictionary if that dictionary's French wordlist, as produced in the first read-through, is taken at face value. For example, the 2007 dictionary regards the culinary word *gastronom* as being of French origin, while Ushakov considers the word to be Greek. Meanwhile, Dal′ assigned a Latin origin to the same word. Theoretically, all three could be correct. Without cross-referencing, it looks as if *gastronom* is a relatively new French word in the Russian language, appearing only in the 2007 dictionary, when in fact the word dates back to the time of Pushkin. For the sake of consistency, all words considered to be of French origin by any of the dictionaries have been included in the listings. Hence, this second pass through each dictionary was crucial, adding words to each dictionary's French-list which were not recorded the first time through but are considered to be of French origin by other dictionaries. This step was also a helpful safeguard if French words were simply overlooked during the first pass. The result of this step was a more accurate set of French words from each dictionary.

The next step was to combine the separate lists into one, making note of which dictionaries contain each word. Due to various orthographic reforms and other factors, there have been some (usually minor) spelling changes for these words over time. For the sake of consistency and ease of computer-assisted analysis later on, the spelling of each word has been conformed to the latest version of that word. The result of this step comes close to a single master-list of French-origin words in the Russian language, with each word chronologically notated as to its appearance or absence in each of the dictionaries.

Category assignment was next. In what might be called a partial third read-through of all the dictionaries, word definitions were now looked at more closely and at least one category (or word-tag) was assigned to each word. This process began with a number of potential categories already in mind. Based on secondary reading about the history of the Russian language and general Russian history related to culture and foreign influence, there are certain types of French words that one would expect to find at the outset. This provided some preliminary structure to the process and helped to avoid labeling words with arbitrarily unique categories, which would have resulted in something virtually impossible to statistically analyze later on. At the same time, it has been important to keep an 'open mind' when studying word definitions for categories that may not have been anticipated and give an honest characterization of each word. In addition to the light shed by secondary source reading, the work of the dictionary editors themselves often contributed to the process. Apart from etymological information, words were sometimes identified in the definition as a 'technical', 'medical', 'military', 'theatrical', or 'musical' term, and so forth. Such notations have been helpful in tagging words. Finally, in order to get a clear picture of themes around which words really group, it has been important to categorize only those words that fit into their prospective groups quite obviously. For example the Russian words for 'balance', 'control', and 'intensity' are borrowed from French, but are so general that none of them recognizably identify with words of any thematic group. Forcing a word into a category that does not really suite it would only dilute the category itself and impair its critical effectiveness. Hence, it has been important to freely allow a large number of borrowed French words to be tagged generically in a miscellaneous category. This category has been named 'various.' A study of words that did more naturally fit into groups suggested six broad classifications of Russian terms imported from French: cultural terms,[1] words related to urban and residential design, official terminology (military, legal, government, etc.), vocabulary for technology, industry and the sciences, words associated with philosophy and social thought, and special historical and foreign terms.

After this, 'quality-control' of the categories was necessary. When working through two or three thousand words alphabetically, certain category assignments seem obvious at first, but upon further reflection are not optimal. Furthermore, patterns become more discernible as numerous words of similar type are encountered in the categorization read-through. Consequently, words categorized earlier in the alphabet, before a given pattern has become a matter of intuition, will not have been tagged as consistently as those cataloged later in the process. This inconsistency is dealt with in the 'quality control' step. This is accomplished by arranging the master-list according to categories (versus alphabetically, which is how they were first encountered), and reading through the wordlist again, consulting the dictionaries where necessary and studying words of each category as a group. Some characterizations which seemed logical when working through the list alphabetically are easily recognizable as anomalies when the given word is seen side by side with the other words of its supposed category. As a result of this step, a number of words were re-assigned to different categories, or moved to the generic category when it was clear that they did not reflect the thematic character of the group. *Afront*, for example was initially categorized as an 'emotive' word, a category which ultimately proved too sparsely represented to really benefit the overall analysis. However, as words that are similar in character to *afront* were encountered in the alphabetical progression—*bespardonnyi* (unforgiveable), *blezir*

---

[1] All of these categories are broadly relevant to Russian culture as defined in the introduction of this thesis. Here, however, the word 'cultural' is understood to refer to 'high culture' or 'culture proper': fashion, cuisine, literary and performing arts, and etiquette rules of high society.

(a joking manner), *visavi,* and so forth—it became gradually clear that these words represented a wave of French-origin terms related to nuanced interaction among interlocutors. Most of these words, later categorized as 'interpersonal' words, came into the Russian language in Dostoevskii's generation. They form a clear sub-group within the cultural category which was not immediately obvious. Another example of redacted classification is for the word *vikont* (from the French 'Vicomte'.) Upon initial consideration, this word, occurring very early in the alphabet, was categorized as 'administrative' in nature, as it described someone in a high-ranking position. However, when later compared with the borrowed words for 'certificate', 'regulation', 'district', 'organization', 'rescript' and other such words which really were administrative or governmental in nature, *vikont* was easily recognizable as being out of place. A pattern of France-specific historical terms became apparent later in the alphabet by words such as *baron, vitseroi, graf, diushes, markis, printessa,* and other such titles of nobility which were imported at a similar time. In retrospect, *vikont* clearly belonged to this group and was reassigned. Similarly, *grot* (a 'grotto' or 'cave') was initially categorized as a geological term, though it was later evident that this term really belongs to architecture alongside *arkada, fasad, rel'ef* and the like. Though the words that needed to be reclassified were relatively few, this step was necessary to maximize the consistency with which categories were applied and words sorted.

Finally, several more passes have been made to tweak the categories. These ongoing adjustments have been smaller changes that facilitate increasing clarity and bring the picture of cultural influence over time into sharper focus. Smaller groups of words have been combined into new, larger categories, given a title in line with a larger discipline. There were, for example, only a very few words each in the 'biology', 'mathematics', 'physics', and 'geometry' categories. These words were pulled together as 'science' words, with their original category serving as a sub-heading. Conversely, within some larger categories, significant sub-themes appear, the historical implications of which should be considered. For example, the many French loanwords tagged as 'economic terms' may speak to different developments at different times. Some of these words are more related to business and retail while others apply to macroeconomic trends and the banking industry. Adding sub-categories was a helpful means of exploring this. These are just a few examples, but this is a process that has been ongoing and open-ended. As new insights from further reading direct attention to certain time periods and certain areas of culture impact, small changes to classification have yielded new levels of insight as to the ways in which French culture has impacted Russia.

With the above steps followed, the result comes close to a master-list of French loanwords, which is included as Appendix B. The list is both arranged by category and notated as to which dictionaries contain each word. One of the important insights gained by the later notation is the ability to see when a particular word first entered the Russian language, and whether its usage endured to the present lexicon. The master-list is an instrument that may be empirically analyzed according to various criteria. Two statistical paradigms are now available that, leveraged against one another, have the potential for applying significant analytical rigor. These paradigms are, namely, subject area and time. The inclusion (especially for the first time) of a certain type of French word in the various dictionaries may be interpreted as representing a pattern of that particular flavor of cultural influence across time. When was Russian theatre, for example, more influenced by France and when was it less so? Which areas of French influence date back to the age of Peter the Great and which developments are only seen later? Are there any spheres of French import which are consistent in every generation? These are the types of questions that can be approached by studying the master-list chronologically. Conversely, individual time periods may be examined thematically so as to determine the weight of imported French vocabulary of a particular type. Does any individual category of French loanwords stand out during the reign of Catherine II? Did the Russian language receive a noticeably large number of French philosophical and/or political terms in the generation immediately preceding the Russian Revolution? These are just a few of the questions that may be explored, and with a measure of statistical objectivity, merely by examining, from different perspectives, the data yielded by this lexical cataloging.

www.ingramcontent.com/pod-product-compliance
Lightning Source LLC
LaVergne TN
LVHW051254200726
843510LV00010B/1114